Revolutionary Cuba

UNIVERSITY PRESS OF FLORIDA

Florida A&M University, Tallahassee
Florida Atlantic University, Boca Raton
Florida Gulf Coast University, Ft. Myers
Florida International University, Miami
Florida State University, Tallahassee
New College of Florida, Sarasota
University of Central Florida, Orlando
University of Florida, Gainesville
University of North Florida, Jacksonville
University of South Florida, Tampa
University of West Florida, Pensacola

Revolutionary Cuba

A

HISTORY

LUIS MARTÍNEZ-FERNÁNDEZ

University Press of Florida
Gainesville · Tallahassee · Tampa · Boca Raton
Pensacola · Orlando · Miami · Jacksonville · Ft. Myers · Sarasota

This book may be available in an electronic edition.

19 18 17 16 15 14   6 5 4 3 2 1

Library of Congress Control Number: 2014937647
ISBN 978-0-8130-4995-3

The University Press of Florida is the scholarly publishing agency for the State
University System of Florida, comprising Florida A&M University, Florida Atlantic
University, Florida Gulf Coast University, Florida International University, Florida
State University, New College of Florida, University of Central Florida, University of
Florida, University of North Florida, University of South Florida, and University of
West Florida.

University Press of Florida
15 Northwest 15th Street
Gainesville, FL 32611-2079
http://www.upf.com

Para mi papá
Celestino Martínez Lindín (1933–2005)
y para mi abuelo
Luis Fernández Martínez (1917–),
con amor y agradecimiento

A printing press is an army.

José Martí

Contents

Illustrations

Figures

Tables

Acknowledgments

This book was eight years in the making, and over that period, I have benefited from the encouragement, advice, and collegial support of numerous individuals. I should start by thanking historian Louis A. Pérez Jr., who, back in 2004—in Las Vegas, of all places—suggested that I write a general history of the Cuban Revolution. As the publication of this book makes patent, I followed his recommendation, and I am grateful for his friendship, support, and thorough critical reading of an early draft of this book.

Over the years, I have also benefited from intellectual exchanges about this project with several colleagues and friends. At the risk of unintentionally leaving some of them out, I wish to acknowledge José "Pepín" Álvarez, Diana Arteaga, Pablo J. Davis, Antonio de la Cova, Cristóbal Díaz Ayala, Jorge Duany, Carlos Eire, Danilo Figueredo, Guadalupe García, Humberto García Muñiz, María Dolores González-Ripoll, Carole Grimshaw, Elaine Maisner, Myriam Márquez, Consuelo Naranjo Orovio, Luis Plazas, Eddy Ponce de León, Armando Portela, Cecilia Rodríguez-Milanés, Orlando Rivero, John Settle, Paolo Spadoni, Antonio Santamaría, Vladimir Solonari, Dania Suárez, Juan Valdés, José Francisco Vales Bermudes, José Vázquez, Markus Wiener, Paul Wolf, Antonio Zamora, and the late Colonel Ramón Barquín and Carlos Franqui. Stimulating class discussions with students at the University of Central Florida who took my Cuban History course in the fall of 2013 helped me rethink aspects of the manuscript I was wrapping up at the time.

I also extend my gratitude to those institutions and individuals that granted permission to reproduce some of the illustrations that grace the pages of this book. A large number of them appear courtesy of Associated Press; one courtesy of Reuters. Others have been reproduced from Cuban publications such as the weekly magazine *Bohemia* and *Granma*, Cuba's official newspaper. My friend Gustavo Arvelo allowed me to use a photograph from his collection of Carlos Núñez photographs, and film-maker Eduardo Lamora and ALBALENA Films gave permission to use a still image from the extraordinary documentary *Cuba: el arte de espera*. Three of the book's photographs, including the one that illustrates the epilogue, were taken by my late father, Celestino Martínez Lindín.

I am also grateful for the support of the staff of several libraries and depositories in which I conducted research including those of my own institution, the University of Central Florida, and the Cuban Heritage Collection of the Otto Richter Library of the University of Miami, the Latin American Collection of the University of Florida, and the Florida International University Library. I also wish to express my gratitude to the University of Central Florida for awarding me a competitive sabbatical leave in 2010–11, which allowed me to make considerable progress toward finishing this book.

I am also indebted to Sian Hunter and Amy Gorelick, senior acquisitions editors for the University Press of Florida, who warmly embraced my project and worked diligently to move it forward and in the process—a long and challenging one—proved that it was possible for an academic press to publish a balanced and honest scholarly book on the contentious and polarizing subject of the Cuban Revolution. Project editor Nevil Parker gracefully shepherded the manuscript through the process of becoming a book; Kate Babbitt took special care copyediting the manuscript, and Robert Swanson did a superb job preparing the index.

My wife, Margie, and my two sons, Luis Alberto and Andrés, have always been supportive of my scholarly projects, and this book was no exception. I thank them for their love, patience, and encouragement. I extend this gratitude to the rest of my family, particularly my late father, Celestino Martínez Lindín; my mother, Luisa Martínez; my aunt, Mercedes Fernández; and my grandfather, Luis Fernández Martínez.

Abbreviations

ALBA	Alianza Bolivariana para los Pueblos de Nuestra América (Bolivarian Alliance for the Peoples of Our America)
ANC	African National Congress
ANDHAC	Asociación Nacional de Hacendados de Cuba (National Association of Sugar Mill Owners of Cuba)
ASCE	Association for the Study of the Cuban Economy
CANF	Cuban American National Foundation
CCPDH	Comité Cubano Pro Derechos Humanos (Cuban Committee for Human Rights)
CCDHRN	Comisión Cubana de Derechos Humanos y Reconciliación Nacional (Cuban Commission on Human Rights and National Reconciliation)
CDRs	Comités de Defensa de la Revolución (Committees for the Defense of the Revolution)
CENESEX	Centro Nacional de Educación Sexual (National Sex Education Center)
CMEA	Council for Mutual Economic Assistance (also known as COMECON)
CORU	Coordinadora de Organizaciones Revolucionarias Unidas (Coordinator of United Revolutionary Organizations)
CRC	Concilio Revolucionario Cubano
CRI	Cuban Research Institute, Florida International University
CTC	Confederación de Trabajadores de Cuba (Confederation of Cuban Workers), later renamed Central de Trabajadores de Cuba (Central Union of Cuban Workers)

DR	Directorio Revolucionario (Revolutionary Directorate); also known as DRE
EU	European Union
FAO	Food and Agricultural Organization
FAR	Fuerzas Armadas Revolucionarias (Revolutionary Armed Forces)
FEU	Federación Estudiantil Universitaria (Federation of University Students)
FIU	Florida International University, Miami
FMC	Federación de Mujeres Cubanas (Federation of Cuban Women)
FNLA	Frente Nacional para a Libertação de Angola (National Front for the Liberation of Angola)
ICAIC	Instituto Cubano del Arte e Industria Cinematográficos (Cuban Institute of Cinematographic Arts and Industry)
ICCAS	Institute of Cuban and Cuban American Studies, University of Miami
INRA	Instituto Nacional de Reforma Agraria (National Agrarian Reform Institute)
M-26-7	Movimiento Veintiséis de Julio (26 of July Movement)
MCL	Movimiento Cristiano de Liberación (Christian Liberation Movement)
MININT	Ministerio del Interior (Ministry of the Interior)
MNR	Movimiento Nacional Revolucionario (National Revolutionary Movement)
MPLA	Movimiento Popular da Libertação de Angola (People's Movement for the Liberation of Angola)
MSR	Movimiento Socialista Revolucionario (Socialist Revolutionary Movement)
NAM	Non-Aligned Movement
OA	Organización Auténtica (Authentic Organization)
OAS	Organization of American States
ONE	Oficina Nacional de Estadísticas (National Office of Statistics)

ORI   Organizaciones Revolucionarias Integradas (Integrated Revolutionary Organizations)

OSPAAAL   Organización de Solidaridad de los Pueblos de África, Asia y América Latina (Organization of Solidarity with the Peoples of Africa, Asia and Latin America)

PCC   Partido Comunista de Cuba (Cuban Communist Party)

PSP   Partido Socialista Popular (People's Socialist Party)

PURS   Partido Unido de la Revolución Socialista de Cuba (United Party of the Cuban Socialist Revolution)

SDPE   Sistema de Dirección y Planificación de la Economía (System of Direction and Planning of the Economy)

UIR   Unión Insurreccional Revolucionaria (Insurrectional Revolutionary Union)

UMAPs   Unidades Militares de Ayuda a la Producción (Military Units to Aid Production)

UNEAC   Unión Nacional de Artistas y Escritores de Cuba (National Union of Cuban Artists and Writers)

UNITA   União Nacional para a Independência Total de Angola (National Union for the Total Liberation of Angola)

Introduction

In the production of sugar it is a question of power; sugar is conservative, if not reactionary.

Fernando Ortiz, *Cuban Counterpoint*

On July 26, 1953, Fidel Castro and around 160 rebels launched a nearly suicidal attack on Santiago's Moncada army garrison, Cuba's second most important military installation. While the attack failed and about a third of the rebels were killed by soldiers and policemen, the episode marked the beginning of a widespread rebellion to oust caudillo Fulgencio Batista.

Not only were the rebels successful in battlefields and city streets, but shortly upon reaching power they launched a radical, socialist revolution—as Castro put it, "under the very nose of the United States."[1] Defying all odds, all prognostications, and even common sense, the Castro brothers are still alive and Raúl, the youngest, remains at the helm of the revolution they launched fifty-five years earlier. They have survived multiple assassination attempts; a U.S.-backed armed invasion in 1961; an unremitting U.S. trade embargo; the sudden collapse of their superpower benefactor, the Soviet Union; a full-blown economic depression; and the current prolonged state of precarious economic survival.

The revolution dramatically transformed Cuba and its relations with the rest of the world. Former allies became enemies as new alliances were forged. From the onset, the revolution had profound international reverberations. For many in the Third World, Cuba became a source of inspiration and a model for anti-imperialist struggle and alternative economic development. The rebel island exported revolution and personnel and material support to all four corners of the world: Algeria, the Congo, Bolivia, Vietnam, and eventually Angola and Nicaragua. In short, Cuba was changed forever, and in the process, it helped change the world.

The revolution most certainly changed my world. I was supposed to be born in 1959, the year of the triumph of the revolution, but as Providence had it, my delivery was delayed until January of the following year. I was one among tens of thousands of children born during the 1959–62 baby boom, the so-called Fidel Generation.

My birthplace was in the outskirts of Havana, four blocks from the Atlantic Ocean and half way between Camp Columbia and the Comodoro Hotel. The military camp and the luxury hotel that flanked my neighborhood were symbols of pre-revolutionary Cuba, representative on the one hand of the strong-fisted military rule of Batista, and on the other of the island's close economic and cultural bonds with the United States. Both soon became symbols of a radically different emerging Cuba. On January 8, 1959, a youthful Fidel Castro gave his first Havana victory speech to a jubilant crowd gathered inside Camp Columbia. Eight months later, in a symbolic swords-to-plowshares action, the revolution turned the military camp into an education complex, renaming it Ciudad Libertad. The following year, the government nationalized the previously exclusive American-owned Comodoro Hotel, where Errol Flynn, Ava Gardner, and many other Hollywood stars had routinely frolicked obliviously, and opened its doors to Cubans of all races and social backgrounds.

In 1959, Cuba was actually two Cubas, one in the past, the other in the future. Socially, it was also two Cubas, hence the need for profound transformations to forge a single, integrated, more just society. The old, more affluent Cuba, however, refused to accept defeat and rejected the establishment of yet another dictatorship, this time under the guise of anti-imperialism and social justice and eventually of socialism. A few fought against the emerging regime but many detractors left, believing that Castro's government would collapse within a few months. There was no way, many believed, that the superpower to the north, then at the peak of its hemispheric and global hegemony, would let Cuba go astray. Not only did Cuba slip away from U.S. dominance, it became a nemesis and even the unthinkable, a Soviet ally just ninety miles from its territory.

This book is my attempt to make sense of the historic, social, and political forces that led to the triumph of Castro's rebels in 1959 and allowed the revolution to consolidate in the early 1960s, become semi-institutionalized during the 1970s, survive the catastrophic Special Period crisis of the 1990s, outlive Fidel Castro's tenure as president, and, against all odds, continue well into the second decade of the twenty-first century. For me, seeking explanations to these phenomena is not just a matter of intellectual curiosity or an opportunity to make a political statement about one of the hemisphere's most important and dramatic historical twists. It is a quest to understand and explain the unfolding drama of the past sixty years of history of my beloved homeland and its people, both on the island and dispersed throughout the world.

This book is a comprehensive, interdisciplinary synthesis of the Cuban Revolution. It serves several purposes and is intended to be read in different ways: as an introduction to the subject, as a primary reference on the topic, and as an interpretative analysis. It provides an unbroken interpretive narrative of the entire sweep of the Cuban Revolution, beginning with Batista's March 10, 1952, coup, which immediately sparked the rebellion that culminated with the 1959 rebel victory, and ends with coverage of the very last developments of 2013.

While this book is interdisciplinary, it is a history book and as such is informed and guided by the disciplinary principles, perspectives, and methods of the historian's craft: recourse to primary documentation; attention to change over time; the recognition of the interrelatedness of human phenomena that urges historians to view economic, political, social, and cultural changes and continuities as interconnected rather than in isolation; and a balanced combination of narrative, description, and analysis. It rests on the study of a voluminous body of works on various topics of the Cuban Revolution and numerous primary materials, from traditional ones such as letters and government reports to cyber-age sources such as videos of speeches from YouTube and classified correspondence from U.S. diplomats stationed in Havana that have been made public through WikiLeaks since 2006.

This work is also informed by my two and a half decades of research, reflection, and writing on early colonial and nineteenth-century history and my deeply held conviction that in order to understand the past 50-odd years of Cuban history, it is important to be informed about the island's earlier history, particularly the nineteenth century, a time when the island's sugar system reached maturity, generating a host of socioeconomic misfortunes that continue to plague Cuba today. The nineteenth century was also a time when many aspects of Cuban culture, including nationalism, race relations, and modes of social and political resistance took shape.

Also valuable for the preparation of this book were my nine trips to Cuba between 1994 and 2004, which allowed me to see firsthand, without the distorting lenses of Cuban government tours to a sanitized list of destinations, the everyday realities endured by my fellow Cubans during the devastating Special Period, when, beginning in 1990, the island's economy plunged into a profound and prolonged depression. During those visits, I interacted with Cubans from all walks of life; I rode among them in crowded buses; stood in long winding queues; went shopping at their ration *bodegas* and pharmacies; ate their food—*picadillo* from ground plantain rinds and all; and even visited, free of charge, my neighborhood clinic, where a kind and highly competent physician examined me for a persistent cough.

But I was also able to witness and enjoy a Cuba beyond the grasp and means of most Cubans: I rode in private taxis—legal and illegal—and in late-model Mercedes Benz tourist buses; shopped for items that were forbidden to regular Cubans, such as milk, beef, and seafood; and drank Coca-Colas and mojitos at foreigners-only beachfront hotels; and had my cough not subsided, I would have paid for world-class, bargain-price medical services at a dollar-charging, state-of-the-art hospital. My Cuba had once again become two Cubas, one for the impoverished masses, the other for the military and party brass, pleasure-seeking tourists, and a host of political tourists hailing from the four corners of the world.

This history of the revolution resorts to multiple windows to the past, some rather unorthodox: sources of information and voices that provide insights that go beyond the conventional sources used by most students of the revolution. These include the analysis of the revolution's guiding slogans, emblematic official names given to each year since 1959, and billboard messages. Each chapter's title is the period's guiding slogan followed by an explanatory subtitle. While these windows shed light on the revolution as dictated from above, other windows point to the people's responses, sometimes supportive, other times acquiescent or outright oppositional: everyday forms of adaptation and resistance, *choteo* (Cuba's quintessential irreverent, mocking humor), even baby-naming trends. While introducing and alluding to the revolution's protagonists, I also interject the experiences and words of common individuals throughout the book, be it a child who was sent to exile alone to the United States or a guerrillero or a dissident jailed during the Black Spring of 2003 or the young widow of a *balsero* who perished at sea.

This work also resorts to cultural manifestations both official and unofficial—artistic creations as windows to the revolution and its diaspora. These range from song lyrics and films to photographs and ballet productions. In a nation where reality and fiction are often blurred (the 1960s and 1970s literary wave known as magical realism was actually born in Cuba) works of literature often capture the essence of a particular moment more intimately and perhaps more accurately than narrowly focused monographs or bundles of official documents. Throughout this book, I use excerpts from poems, novels, and other literary genres as windows into the material and emotional realities of the revolution.

Capitalizing on the extraordinary photogeneity of Cuba and its people, this book includes thirty-two photographs and stills. Among these illustrations are classic images of the revolution such as an iconic image of Fidel Castro's victory speech in Havana, but many of them are relatively unknown photographs which I have interwoven into the text to provide graphic support for an intentionally visual prose.

This is also a very Cuban book; I have deliberately written it as such. While I was partially professionally trained in the United States, my intellectual development is rooted in the Latin American and Caribbean tradition. I have purposely retained a Cuban voice and painted this book with the bright colors of the Cuban literary palette: passion; a playfulness with words and ideas; the use of irony, metaphor, and humor—even hidden *choteo*; orality manifested through storytelling and dialogue; a sense of rhythm in both prose and structure; recourse to the sensorial: sounds, sights, and sensations; and an almost pathological commitment to honesty.

Seven Threads in the Labyrinth

Attempting to understand the complex phenomenon of the Cuban Revolution is no easy task; it is akin to entering a labyrinth and then seeking to find one's way out. While researching and writing this book I recurred to seven threads that helped me find a sense of direction and build a framework for an overarching analysis. I have named these threads—tropes, if you will—"many Cubas," "an island on horseback," "the longest ninety miles," "the pendular revolution," "the art of triangulation," "the revolution's third man," and "the persistent plantation."

Many Cubas

I have already alluded to this thread: a Cuba of the past and a Cuba of the future, one prosperous, the other impoverished; then two other Cubas, one insular and one that floated away into exile, two Cubas that like cells eventually split into two more Cubas, two on the island and two others in exile.

Four centuries ago, Spanish authorities divided the elongated island into two jurisdictions, East and West. The long distance between the eastern and western ends—777 miles—and other geographic factors, including wind and water currents, helped forge two separate Cubas, each with its own distinct economy, racial patterns, and culture: a wealthier, western, Havana-dominated, sugar-centered, slave-based Cuba and a poorer, eastern, subsistence agriculture–based, more racially mixed Cuba. Tensions between both Cubas manifested themselves throughout history, most dramatically perhaps, during the nineteenth-century wars of independence, which pitted one Cuba against the other. The wars of independence, the rebellion of the 1950s, and the consolidation of the revolution in 1959–61 can be seen, largely, as conflicts between a liberal and revolutionarily inclined Oriente and a conservative-leaning Occidente.

The prevalence of social and geographic cleavages and racial and class divisions produced conditions favorable to regional tensions in pre-1959 Cuba, between West and East, between poorer and richer Cubans, and among racial groups, all of which fueled the civil war of the 1950s, the counterrevolutionary efforts of 1959–62, and over five decades of bitter antagonism between socialist Cuba and capitalist Cuban Miami.

In general, works on the topic of the revolution have paid only tangential attention to the Cuban diaspora and its ongoing interactions with the country its members left behind. Worse yet, when mentioned, Cuban exiles are generally maligned, stereotyped, and caricaturized as greedy, violence-bent fanatics. This book seeks to remedy that by providing a respectful, nuanced, and compassionate depiction of the "Cuba outside of Cuba" by systematically integrating it into the narrative of the revolution. For over half a century, exiles have been an integral part of the larger story, as an exodus that early on deprived the island of the talents and resources of its bourgeoisie and professional and managerial sectors; mounted a trenchant, offshore opposition to the regime; and paradoxically, over the past two and a half decades, has become one of Cuba's primary sources of income through generous remittances that hovered at around $1 billion per year during the 1990s and early 2000s and have surpassed $2 billion since 2011.[2] Since the enactment of small-scale but significant economic reforms in 2011, Cubans living abroad, many of them recent emigrants, have contributed substantially to the surge in small private business activities on the island by remitting start-up funds, equipment, and materials.

Nonetheless, this book is strongly critical of the extremist, intransigent and sometime violent strategies the most radical exiles pursued.

An Island on Horseback

The second thread is Cuba as "an island on horseback," to borrow Belkis Cuza Malé's poetic metaphor; the prevalence of militarism, political violence, and caudilloism throughout Cuba's troubled history. Such has been the case since the 1500s, when Cuba, Havana in particular, became a fortified Spanish defensive bastion. The recourse to bullets rather than ballots and the veneration of military prowess are ingrained in Cuba's cultural DNA and help explain a proclivity to military solutions such as the wars of independence, Batista's coup of 1952, and the ensuing armed insurrection seeking to restore democracy. Such cultural traits have been pervasive throughout the revolution as manifested by the Castros' authoritarian rule and the supremacy of military officers over civilian leadership and by some exiled leaders holding hard-line, belligerent anti-communist stances. That said, culture changes—sometimes slowly—and there are numerous examples of nations that have shed authoritarian traditions in favor of democracy and vice versa. Cuba is certainly not condemned to eternal militarism and authoritarian rule.

It would be misleading, moreover, to overemphasize the role of men on horseback at the expense of ignoring the many men and women who on foot and wielding pens or typewriters rather than machetes or machine guns have for centuries fought for freedom, national sovereignty, and social justice: a Father Félix Varela from the pulpit of exile; a José Martí from his desks and podiums on three different continents; an Eduardo Chibás through the airwaves of CMQ Radio; and a Yoani Sánchez from her keyboard and cell phone. When his honor was challenged by some contemporary men on horseback, Martí headed to the battlefields of *la manigua* in 1895. Only five weeks after arrival on May 19—his first day on a battlefield—he received three deadly gunshots. As he rode on his white horse toward a Spanish army hailstorm of bullets, he died with a small-caliber pistol on his right hand and a manuscript in his pocket, along with his ever-present fountain pen.

The Longest Ninety Miles

This is yet another useful thread: the recognition that in spite of close geographic proximity, a history of intimate ties, and many shared aspects of material culture, Cuba and the United States are worlds apart in terms of fundamental social values and underlying cultural assumptions. With his characteristically rhythmic prose, Carlos Franqui, an early revolutionary leader who later broke with the regime, remarked that both nations were so close "yet so remote and different in everything else. . . . One is a continent, the other is an island. One is Anglo-Saxon Protestant in character and based on the industrial revolution, power, and wealth. The other is Latin, Spanish, Black and Chinese."[3]

These differences and the tensions resulting from them have been exacerbated by decades of U.S. interventionism and neocolonial domination and by a stubborn incapacity to understand and respect the strong Cuban sense of honor. The fact that U.S. military, political, religious, business, and intellectual leaders have generally viewed Cubans as inferior and treated them condescendingly and paternalistically has fueled Cuban nationalism, a major factor in the victory, consolidation, and survival of the revolution. Early in the revolution, both countries broke economic ties and diplomatic relations, and they have remained enemies ever since, but geography forces them to contend with one another, like a broken couple forced to live as next-door neighbors after a nasty divorce.

The Pendular Revolution

The thread of a pendular revolution is not an original contribution of this book. In fact, as far back as 1978, Carmelo Mesa-Lago recognized pendular shifts, cycles of alternating socioeconomic-political formulas, and since then many other students of the revolution have resorted to pendular swings between idealism and pragmatism to periodize the revolutionary trajectory.[4] My contribution consists, rather, in bringing the periodization of pendular shifts up to date and combining the standard short-cycles periodization model with a three-part, long-phase periodization consisting of an idealist phase (1952–70), a personalistic institutionalization phase (1971–89), and a survival phase (1991–). These long phases, which correspond to the three parts into which this book is divided, encompass several short, alternating cycles as represented in table 1. As decades passed, however, the revolutionary pendulum slowed down, producing less dramatic swings between idealism and pragmatism.

The periodization of the Cuban Revolution and that of the diaspora it pushed away are, of course, interrelated. Numerous social scientists have created and used typologies based on distinguishable waves of exile and emigration. Recently, sociologist Susan Eckstein applied a different analytical approach, recognizing "cohorts" instead of waves. From that

Table 1. Chronology of the Cuban Revolution: long phases and short cycles

Long Phase	Years	Short Cycle	Years
I: Idealism	(1959–1970)	Heroic idealism	(1959–1962)
		The Great Debate	(1963–1966)
		Compromised idealism	(1967–1970)
II: Personalistic Institutionalization	(1971–1990)	Institutionalized pragmatism	(1971–1985)
		Institutionalized idealism	(1986–1990)
III: Survival	(1991–)	Survivalist pragmatism	(1991–2000)
		Survivalist idealism	(2001–2006)
		Survivalist pragmatism II	(2007–)

perspective, Eckstein divided the Cuban diaspora into two groups: the "exile cohort," those who left Cuba between 1959 and the end of the 1970s, and the "New Cubans" who have migrated to the United States since the 1980s. In a similar vein, Alejandro Portes has more recently periodized the Cuban diaspora into two long phases divided by the "bifurcation" of the Miami enclave, which he sees taking place beginning in 1980.[5]

The "cohorts" perspective and "bifurcation" thesis offer multiple benefits, particularly when studying relations among different immigrant cohorts settling in South Florida at different times. I propose, however, an alternative periodization that recognizes three rather than two immigrant cohorts and two bifurcations instead of one.[6] Based on sociopolitical culture criteria, this book offers a periodization that consists, first, of those individuals who were socialized under capitalism before Fidel Castro took power (roughly the cohort that left from 1959 through the 1970s) along with their parents and children; second, the children of the revolution, those who were socialized during the first two decades of the revolutionary process but whose parents' generation had lived through and had been socialized in pre-revolution Cuba (this is roughly the Mariel cohort and others going into exile during the balance of the 1980s); and third, the revolution's grandchildren, those whose parents and themselves were socialized during the revolution (roughly the *balsero* cohort, since 1990).

In spite of their many differences, all three cohorts share the common experience of enduring two traumatic shocks; first the trauma of departure, immediately followed by the trauma of resettling in an environment that was sharply different from the one left behind, in which each new cohort experienced a clash of culture and values with the host community.[7]

The Art of Triangulation

One of the explanations for the Castros' longevity in power and their many political successes over more than half a century is Fidel Castro's extraordinary ability to recognize and apply triangulation strategies to pit individuals, groups, nations, and even superpowers against each other to gain, consolidate, and expand power. This book traces the thread of triangulation from Fidel Castro's days as a student activist, through the struggle against Batista, and throughout his long dictatorship. When he saw opportunities for triangulation, he exploited them; if they were not there, he created them. He also used them repeatedly to divide his enemies in exile.

The Revolution's Third Man

Since the triumph of the revolution until the present, a Castro has ruled supreme: Fidel up to 2006–8 and his brother Raúl since then. Up to that seventeen-month-long transition, it was perfectly clear that Raúl Castro was the number two man. He was popularly nicknamed *el número dos*, a triple-entendre appellative hiding two insulting characterizations of him.

The question of the revolution's "third man"—whoever was next in power behind the Castro brothers—is yet another valuable thread that serves as a window onto ideological and political shifts taking (or about to take) place. Thus, the selection of the revolution's "third man" is discussed throughout the text, from Guevara during the early years of revolution until Raúl Castro's recent selection of Miguel Díaz-Canel as first vice-president and de jure second man. Generally speaking, Cuba's third men have played key roles in either the domestic or the international arena. And for the sake of their survival, they have had, first of all, to prove absolute loyalty to the Castro brothers; second, to avoid casting even the slightest shadow on them; and last, to demonstrate extraordinary effectiveness when carrying out their assigned tasks.

The Persistent Plantation

This book's most useful and overarching thread is the thesis of the persistent plantation, a view of Cuba's history, social organization, and culture as profoundly shaped by the sugar agroindustrial complex and its concomitants: coercion of labor, rigid social hierarchy, land concentration, foreign dependence, and the like.[8] While generations of scholars have viewed sugar as the source of the island's most endemic problems, students of the revolutionary era have either ignored or downplayed the crop's enduring negative repercussions. The revolution originally set out to free the island and its people from the grip of the sugar plantation and its insatiable demand for vast extensions of land, cheap labor, and expensive imported technology. It soon became evident, however, that Cuba would indefinitely remain trapped by the sugar plantation and continue to taste its bitter by-products.

A corollary to this thread is the persistent counterplantation. As evidenced by the historical record of the Caribbean and wherever a plantation system was erected, those forced to toil under slavery or some other form of coercion resisted and contested that system in a variety of ways. Some resisted passively: slowing down at work, pretending to be sick, deliberately breaking work tools, and mocking their masters in stories, fables, and jokes; others violently: staging revolts, burning cane fields, or killing overseers; yet others, spiritually, brewing potions or casting spells. Others sought to escape the system altogether, some through legal mechanisms such as self-purchase, others by becoming maroons in remote wilderness locations or in Havana, some returning to Africa, the most desperate committing suicide.

In the aftermath of the abolition of slavery (1886), a persistent counterplantation culture fueled much of the resistance against Spanish colonialism, oppression, and manifold forms of exploitation during the republican era and Batista's two regimes. In all three instances, rebels resorted to the wholesale burning of sugarcane fields. As demonstrated throughout this book, counterplantation defiance, in old and new forms, has persisted since 1959.

An Exile and a Scholar

The Cuban Revolution elicits passions that oftentimes produce distorted views of reality, hence the creation of a body of works that, in great measure, is both politicized and polarized. Among the distortions that have plagued the literature on Cuba, its revolutionary era in particular, we find a teleological view of history that reduces the pre-1959 era to a mere prologue to the revolution; a before-and-after framework that obliterates the manifold continuities tying the pre-revolutionary era to the era of the revolution; and a static depiction of the revolutionary period that lends itself to misleading generalizations applied to a period five and a half decades long. While over the past two decades Cuba specialists have produced scores of serious contributions to the field, these distortions still characterize the way most people speak, write, and teach about Cuba.

I do not claim to be free from bias. The historical processes that I study here have impacted and continue to impact my life and that of my family in numerous ways. We endured the indignities of state-organized harassment, my father was forced to resign from his job, all of our property—even family photo albums—was confiscated, and we were forced into a painful and prolonged exile, away from everyone and everything we loved and held dear. That said, I hold no bitterness toward the revolution, and whatever biases I may have are no less correctable than those of Castro sympathizers the world over. Besides being a lifelong exile, I am a scholar, and as such, I am bound by the rules of academic honesty and integrity and the moral obligation to seek and tell the truth, regardless of consequences.

Precisely for these reasons, I made a concerted effort to be attentive to and correct instances of partiality and bias in my writing and enlisted some colleagues and friends to assist me with that task. As a result, I believe that I have written an honest book that at the same time applauds the democratic, social justice, and anti-neocolonialist aspirations of tens of thousands of Cubans who fought and supported efforts to topple Batista in the 1950s, celebrates the idealism and manifold social achievements of the first few years of revolution, and criticizes the Castros' imposition of repressive and authoritarian rule. Likewise, I am critical of U.S. domination and exploitation of Cuba during the 1950s as well as of the more benign, but arguably no less insidious, dependency structures the Soviet Union fostered until 1989. The same holds true for the most extremist, violent, and undemocratic members of the opposition in exile.

I am well aware that this book will not please everyone. Some of what I say here will actually enrage some readers. This work will not resonate with either "Viva Fidel!" readers or the Cuban regime's most right-wing opponents. I have taken to heart, however, the advice of historian Louis A. Pérez Jr.: "As long as readers come out with the impression that you have been fair, it will be fine." In the end, I wrote the book I wanted to write, the way I wanted it to be.

PART I

Idealism, 1952–1970

1

History Will Absolve Me

The Rebellion, 1952–1958

I took to the hills.
My real independence was the maroon slave's palisade
and I rode among the troops of Maceo.

Only a century later,
along with my progeny,
from a blue mountain,

I descended from the Sierra.

Nancy Morejón, "Mujer Negra"

On March 10, 1952, at 4:00 a.m., Cuba's democratically elected president, Carlos Prío Socarrás, was hastily awakened at his luxurious La Chata estate on the outskirts of Havana. He woke up to the distressing news that troops under the command of former president and army strongman Fulgencio Batista were mobilizing to stage a coup d'état. One hour later, Prío—his trademark smile erased from his face—arrived at the Presidential Palace, where some of his close associates and supporters had begun to gather, among them a group from the Federación Estudiantil Universitaria (Federation of University Students, FEU) who requested weapons to fight the seditious troops. It soon became evident that the vast majority of the military supported the coup and that the populace would not step up to defend Prío's corrupt and demoralized government. Prío himself posed no resistance, seeking instead political asylum in the Mexican embassy and fleeing to Mexico four days later. The coup was virtually bloodless, its sole casualty a policeman who was shot down by guards as he drove menacingly toward the Presidential Palace while pointing a gun.[1]

Scores of jubilant soldiers and midlevel officers gathered around Batista in Camp Columbia, showering him with praise, cheering him, patting him on the back. A photograph of that moment shows him surrounded by jubilant soldiers (figure 1.1). He wears an open-collared white shirt and an unthreatening khaki gabardine jacket, his shiny black hair characteristically combed back with gel. Above, on the wall, an iconic photograph of Cuban patriot and intellectual José Martí hangs tilted forward, as if the martyred poet were watching in silent indignation. Thus ended Cuba's short-lived and troubled democratic experience: a dozen years of uninterrupted constitutional governments elevated to power via honest, regularly scheduled elections—a period, nonetheless, in which demagoguery, administrative corruption, and political chicanery blossomed.

A rebellion against "man on horseback" Batista began almost immediately. It was a rebellion with deep historical roots dating as far back as the island's conquest and colonization in the early 1500s. "Juana," as Columbus originally named Cuba, was Spain's third-oldest American colony after Hispaniola and San Juan de Puerto Rico. Following over three years of U.S. military rule, Cuba finally gained its independence in 1902. It was a mediated independence, however, limited by the humiliating provisions of the Platt Amendment (1902), which gave the United States the legal right to intervene in Cuban internal and foreign affairs; by the economic restrictions of the Reciprocity Treaty (1903), which granted generous preferential trade concessions to the United States; and by a string of U.S. military interventions between 1906 and 1933. Thus, by 1952, Cuba had endured almost four centuries of Spanish colonialism and its consequences—political subordination, mercantilist exploitation, spoliation of its natural resources, repatriation of profits; and an additional half-century of neocolonial domination by the United States, which imposed its own brands of political and economic subordination.

From its inception, the sugar industry had depended on and flourished under the auspices of state subsidies, loans, and legal protections. Cuba's first wave of sugar mill construction resulted from a royal loan in 1600 to seventeen planters. That same year, planters received the *privilegio de ingenios*, which protected their land, equipment, and slaves from seizure for failing to pay debts to commercial lenders. The reciprocity treaty of 1903 gave Cuban sugar preferential access to the U.S. market and beginning in 1934, the United States granted sugar quotas to the island at above-market prices.

As a sugar-based export economy throughout much of its history, particularly since the 1840s, Cuba had developed social structures and cultural patterns that grew out of the sugar plantation: a powerful oligarchy,

Figure 1.1. Batista and supporters celebrate the successful coup of March 10, 1952. A portrait of patriot José Martí hovers over the festive scene. Photograph by Harold Valentin. Courtesy of AP.

a labor force subjugated through slavery and other forms of coercion, racialized social stratification, and the institutionalization of violence to keep the laboring masses from subverting the hierarchical social order.

While foreign powers dominated Cuba politically and economically, generations of Cubans fought against foreign oppression and social injustice, beginning with rebel Taino Indians led by Chieftain Hatuey and with generations of defiant slaves, who resisted oppression by revolting, becoming maroons, even by committing suicide. Nineteenth-century freedom fighters continued the struggle, including former slave and abolitionist José Antonio Aponte, patriot-priest Félix Varela, planter-lawyer Carlos Manuel de Céspedes, the mulatto general Antonio Maceo, and José Martí. In the twentieth century, individuals such as communist student leader José Antonio Mella, labor leader Jesús Menéndez, and progressive, anti-communist politician Eduardo Chibás led the intertwined struggles for national sovereignty and social justice. With the exception of Varela, who died in exile in St. Augustine, Florida, all of these men became martyrs. Cuba, indeed, erected a huge pantheon of heroes and developed an ingrained warrior culture. The heirs of that history, as Cuban poet Belkis Cuza Malé lyrically put it, inhabited "an island in the tropics of war, / an island where all the glasses are broken, / an island on horseback."[2]

This was the culture inherited by what came to be known as the Centennial Generation (or Generation of 1952)—so named for the hundredth anniversary of Martí's birth—a generation whose coming of age was marred by Batista's coup. Paradoxically, during his first period of rule (1934–40) Batista had paved the way for future constitutional and democratic governments. Elected president in clean elections in 1940, he stepped down at the end of his term, yielding the reins of government to rival Ramón Grau San Martín of the progressive Partido Revolutcionario Cubano-Auténtico (Authentic Cuban Revolutionary Party, known as the Auténticos). While politically progressive, Grau San Martín, his successor Prío, and many other Auténtico leaders, were notoriously corrupt, and their aspiration for a more just society was rife with contradictions of race, class, and region, a vision that seemingly accepted the marginalization of blacks, urban and rural laborers, and vast regions of the interior. This led to the emergence of a splinter party in 1947, the Partido del Pueblo Cubano (Cuban People's Party), more commonly known as the Ortodoxos. Eduardo Chibás and the new party's other leaders ran on a social justice, anticorruption platform. They adopted a broom as their emblem to underscore their agenda of cleaning up the government.

Students of Cuban history have long recognized a succession of political generations whose protagonists and followers have fought for sovereignty and the creation of a more just society. This succession began with the Generation of 1868, which launched the Ten Years' War (1868–78), a large-scale but ultimately unsuccessful rebellion to free Cuba from Spanish colonialism. The Generation of 1895, under Martí's leadership, took up arms in pursuit of the same goals but saw them frustrated by U.S. intervention and military occupation. Similarly frustrated was the Generation of 1933, whose revolutionary thrust against neocolonialism and oppression was thwarted by U.S. and domestic reactionary forces. Well aware of the failures of previous generations, the Generation of 1952 sought to avoid the mistakes of its predecessors.

The Mulatto Overseer

Government corruption and political violence blemished Cuba's young and fragile democracy. According to estimates, Prío alone stole over $90 million of public funds, the equivalent of one-fourth of the annual national budget. Grau San Martín is said to have looted almost as much money before Prío. Another grave problem was the seemingly unstoppable plague of violent confrontations among political gangs. Consisting of mostly young, trigger-happy activists, these armed *grupos de acción* (action groups) competed for political favors and government payouts. Some sixty of them routinely exchanged blows and bullets in the streets of Havana.[3]

A small group of midlevel army and police officers had planned the March 10 coup with the ostensible object of ending widespread corruption and political violence, but in fact the coup was Batista's shortcut back to the Presidential Palace. While Batista was a candidate for the presidency in the elections scheduled for June 1, it had become obvious that he would lose: polls had him standing a distant third behind Ortodoxo Roberto Agramonte and Auténtico Carlos Hevia.

Batista was born in 1901 in Banes, Oriente Province, to a poor farming family. Of mixed racial ancestry, he joined the army at 21, where he learned stenography and soon rose to the rank of sergeant. In 1933, he played the leading role in the Sergeants' Revolt, which eventually led to the formation of a short-lived reformist government led by Grau San Martín. Batista seized power in January 1934 and ruled Cuba directly or indirectly with an iron fist for the next decade.[4] Although he amassed considerable political power and wealth, Cuba's white elite rejected him racially and socially, as exemplified by their denying him membership in the exclusive Havana Yacht Club. The threads of the "many Cubas" and "the persistent plantation" are useful here: Batista and the elite belonged to different Cubas, and if Cuba was a sugar plantation, Batista was not its master planter; he was, rather, a hired overseer and as such drew his authority from the real masters, Cuba's elites and foreign interests. He was beneath them and served at their pleasure.

Once the "overseer" had reclaimed the presidency, he placed people loyal to him in the regime's highest offices.[5] Batistianos swiftly replaced Prío supporters holding appointments in the state bureaucracy. Batista solidified support within the army, police, and state bureaucracy by raising government salaries and condoning extortion, the collection of bribes, and other forms of graft. He himself managed to amass a personal fortune that was estimated to hover around $300 million.[6]

Batista's coup and the swift consolidation of his regime can be attributed in large measure to the influence and support of planters, *colonos* (sugarcane growers), and U.S. sugar interests concerned that the anticipated overproduction of sugar in 1953 would trigger a devastating fall in prices. Batista delivered: he capped the 1953 sugar harvest at five million tons, a move that favored sugarcane farmers and unionized sugar workers, whose salaries were adjusted according to world sugar prices.[7] Batista, however, did not achieve actual control of the largest and most powerful labor union, the Confederación de Trabajadores de Cuba (Confederation of Cuban Workers, CTC), especially in the countryside, where the proscribed communist party by the name of Partido Socialista Popular (People's Socialist Party, PSP) retained much influence among sugar and tobacco workers.[8]

An expanding, prosperous, and increasingly nationally owned economy made Batista's assault on democracy tolerable to many Cubans and solidified the regime's support from U.S. economic interests, the national bourgeoisie, and a considerable segment of the middle class. Economic expansion under Batista included the development of nonagricultural economic activities such as manufacturing, construction, and tourism. Tourism became intimately tied to gambling, prostitution, and organized crime, which delivered additional ill-gotten income to Batista and his kleptocracy. His government also favored powerful economic interests through legislation, keeping wages low and allowing utility rate hikes, for example. As a token of their appreciation, executives of the American-owned Cuban Telephone Company presented Batista with a gold telephone in March 1957. A photographer captured the moment. Dazzled by the gleaming gift, the strongman from Banes plays with the phone's dial with a boyish smile as other government officials look on with satisfaction.[9]

Opposition to Batista erupted almost immediately among students, intellectuals, workers, and segments of the urban middle class. University students organized public rallies to protest the coup. In tune with Cuba's tradition of preference for bullets over ballots, armed opposition prevailed over dialogue and peaceful solutions. Bringing together mostly students and young professionals seeking to restore democracy, the Movimiento Nacional Revolucionario (National Revolutionary Movement, MNR) was the first of many armed opposition groups. Its leader was Rafael García Bárcena, a popular university professor. On April 5, Easter Sunday, around sixty-five armed MNR militants went to Camp Columbia hoping to stir up a coup among army troops. The attempt failed miserably. García Bárcena and several followers ended up in jail.[10]

Later in the year, Justo Carrillo, who had presided over the National Agricultural and Industrial Development Bank during Prío's administration, founded the armed organization Acción Libertadora (Liberating Action), and former minister of education Aureliano Sánchez Arango organized the Prío-backed Frente Nacional Democrático (National Democratic Front), commonly known as Triple A (the acronym for Asociación de Amigos de Aureliano [Sánchez Arango]).[11] Among the brewing opposition groups was a movement led by Fidel Castro, then simply referred to as "the movement," and a Santiago-based organization named Acción Revolucionaria Oriental (Eastern Revolutionary Action) founded by José (Pepito) Tey and Frank País. The PSP, although proscribed by Batista, maintained a neutral—often-collaborative—position vis-à-vis the regime. The PSP, in fact, had collaborated with Batista during his first dictatorship (1934–40), when he ruled as a populist at a time when communist parties around the world pursued "Popular Front" alliances with noncommunist parties. Batista rewarded communists in 1940 by giving them control over the CTC and appointing communist leaders Juan Marinello and Carlos Rafael Rodríguez to his cabinet.

While they included militants from all regions of the island, these armed groups were concentrated and staged most of their attacks and sabotage actions in and around large cities such as Havana and Santiago. Their leadership and the bulk of their ranks consisted of white, middle-class individuals, many of them hailing from professional fields: education, law, medicine, and administration. The army, for its part, was overwhelmingly composed of darker-skinned Cubans of poor social extraction, and its leadership increasingly included officers of low social origins whose loyalty to Batista afforded them expedited upward mobility within the ranks. One of the most baffling paradoxes of the 1950s civil war was the fact that a mestizo of poor social background fought for the preservation of a status quo that favored the discrimination and exploitation of his kind, while a white scion of the landed elite, Castro, led the struggle to limit—and later destroy—the economic and political power of his own kind. Significantly, the revolutionary struggle against Batista and his troops had obvious racist overtones. The caudillo was often represented in editorial cartoons with simian features and referred to as *el negro* and *el mono*.[12]

Castro, the Moncada Attack, and the 26 of July Movement

Castro was born in 1926 into a wealthy landowning family in Birán, Oriente Province, about thirty miles from Batista's poverty-stricken birthplace. Ironically, both Batista's and Castro's fathers began as manual workers employed by the powerful United Fruit Company. While the Batistas remained poor—Fulgencio later joining his father in the cane fields—the Castros accumulated a fortune. By the time Castro was born, his father owned an extensive farm, Manacas, which supplied sugarcane for one of the United Fruit Company's mills.[13]

Although his father amassed much land and wealth, Castro did not fully enjoy the benefits of his father's class standing. He grew up with a foot in one Cuba and the other in the other Cuba. He and all but two of his siblings were born out of wedlock, to Lina Ruz, a maid at the Castro household. When they were young, Ángel Castro's illegitimate children suffered numerous indignities and vicissitudes such as being barred from their father's home and spending time as foster children with a Haitian family in Santiago. His authoritarian father finally recognized Castro at age seventeen. As a young boy, he developed a reputation for bullying and challenging authority, sometimes violently, once punching and biting one of his teachers. He received a privileged education, including studies at the Christian Brothers' De la Salle School first and later at Jesuit-run schools Colegio Dolores in Santiago and Colegio Belén in Havana. Later, he earned a law degree from the University of Havana, where as a student leader he joined the Unión Insurreccional Revolucionaria (Insurrectional Revolutionary Union, UIR), a violent university students' political gang that rivaled the Movimiento Socialista Revolucionario (Socialist Revolutionary Movement, MSR). With roots in the political turmoil of the 1930s, such groups fought for political patronage and control over FEU posts at the University of Havana.[14]

As a university student, Castro participated in the aborted 1947 Cayo Confites expedition against Dominican strongman Rafael L. Trujillo and in the bloody Bogotazo riots the following year in Colombia. Various sources claim that he was involved in the plot to kill rival political gang leader Manolo Castro of the MSR and that he murdered a University of Havana policeman. Whatever the case, Castro found political protection in Rafael J. Díaz-Balart, former mayor of Banes and legal advisor to the United Fruit Company, with whose daughter, Mirta, he had a romantic relationship. The couple married in October 1948. Around that time, Castro reportedly used his connections with the Díaz-Balarts to secure a meeting with Batista, who was a senator at the time. According to Senator Rafael L. Díaz-Balart, Castro, then only 22 years old, suggested that Batista stage a coup to expedite his return to the presidency.[15]

Castro's ideology included influences from diverse sources, including the ideals of Martí; the progressive agenda of Chibás, whose suicide in 1951 left a leadership vacuum among the Ortodoxos; and European fascism.[16] A founding member of the Ortodoxo Party, Castro saw his electoral political aspirations cut short by the cancellation of the 1952 elections, in which he was running for a legislative post in Havana. Though Castro would go on to become the leader of Cuba's revolutionary government, in 1952 he was neither a communist nor a particularly important player in the opposition to Batista. The young Castro's alleged communist sympathies and affiliation have been the subject of much debate, with many of his opponents arguing that his communist links dated back to the early 1950s. While Castro was familiar with Marxist literature, there is no concrete evidence, beyond his own inconsistent testimonies, that he was even a communist sympathizer; he actually disdained the PSP.

Castro's younger brother, Raúl, joined the brewing insurrectionist movement. Five years younger than Fidel, Raúl Castro was his closest and most trusted comrade. Of known communist sympathies, he was arrested in June 1953 upon returning from a tour of several socialist countries in Eastern Europe.[17]

Shortly upon his return, Raúl Castro joined his older brother, who had planned what turned out to be the most significant and dramatic military action against Batista's government: an assault on the Moncada army garrison in Santiago, two other nearby civilian targets, and the Céspedes army camp in Bayamo. The attacks took place on July 26, 1953, hence the name of the rebel movement it later inspired: the 26 of July Movement (M-26-7).[18] The Moncada attack forces consisted of around 160 untrained and poorly armed combatants. The rebels hailed mostly from Havana and the town of Artemisa, where Fidel Castro recruited a substantial number of rebels. The rebel force included several Ortodoxos, mostly young men, and a handful of university students; two young women, Melba Hernández and Haydée Santamaría, also joined. The social composition of the rebels ranged from members of well-to-do families such as the Castros and Santamarías to middle-class individuals such as physician Mario Muñoz Monroy to manual laborers such as black bricklayer Juan Almeida Bosque. Its ranks, however, were mostly made up of men of modest backgrounds.[19]

Castro commanded the attack on Moncada, the country's second military installation; his younger brother took charge of the occupation of Santiago's courthouse; and a third detachment of twenty-one rebels under Abel Santamaría, Haydée's brother, occupied a nearby hospital. At the same time, seventy-five miles away, twenty-five other rebels led by Raúl Martínez Ararás struck against the Céspedes army camp in Bayamo. Government troops repelled all the attacks. Nine rebels and nineteen soldiers died in battle.[20]

The immediate aftermath of Moncada was far bloodier. Approximately sixty-eight rebels were tortured and killed. Soldiers under the command of Colonel Alberto del Río Chaviano reportedly pulled out eyes and mutilated bodies. The Castro brothers and other survivors were hunted, captured, tried, and eventually sentenced to prison terms ranging from thirteen months for the two rebel women to fifteen years for Fidel Castro (figure 1.2). Had it not been for the intervention of Lieutenant Pedro Sarría and later of archbishop of Santiago Enrique Pérez Serantes, Castro and the other survivors would likely have been summarily executed. Unlike Batista, Castro was a member of elite Cuba, and that membership afforded him special privileges.[21]

While it failed to accomplish its military objectives, the armed assault on Moncada became a source of inspiration for the continuation of the struggle against Batista. It exposed the vulnerability of the armed forces. It produced dozens of martyrs and catapulted Castro to national prominence. Later on, the Moncada trial provided Castro with a platform—he served as his own defense lawyer—from which he launched a scathing critique of Cuba's economic, social, and political ills and outlined a program of reforms. His lengthy self-defense speech was later published with its closing words for a title: "History Will Absolve Me."

In the speech, Castro painted a grim picture of an impoverished island trapped by sugar monoculture and languishing under a corrupt, brutal, and illegitimate government. He saw the hoarding of huge plots of land by a few owners and corporations as the root of most of the island's economic

Figure 1.2. Castro and fellow rebels under arrest following the failed attack on Moncada. Castro is flanked by Colonel Del Río Chaviano (*right*) and Major Morales (*left*). *Source: Bohemia*, January 11, 1959.

and social problems. Castro enumerated them: chronic unemployment and underemployment, squalor, inadequate housing, and a disease-ridden population with little access to education and medical services. In a hyperbolic twist of rhetoric, he claimed that contemporary Cubans were "living in worse circumstances than were the Indians Columbus discovered."[22]

The speech also outlined a reformist agenda whose first item was the return to a constitutional, democratic government. Castro's most salient proposal was an agrarian reform that would give land to landless peasants. To industrial workers he promised profit-sharing plans, and the urban poor were offered affordable, better-quality housing. Significantly, while Cuba's revolutionaries and reformers had historically blamed the United States for many of the island's ills and tribulations, Castro did not even mention Cuba's neighbor to the north. Well versed in Cuban history, he recognized that antagonizing the United States would condemn his brewing movement to certain failure.

In the aftermath of Moncada, Batista retained political and military control by cunningly balancing repression with the promise to restore democracy, including elections and the full reinstatement of the Constitution of 1940. He effectively manipulated divisions among his opponents. With the help of the state's repressive apparatus, including the Servicio de Inteligencia Militar (Military Intelligence Service) and the CIA-created Buró de Represión de Actividades Comunistas (Bureau for the Repression of Communist Activities), the regime cracked down on clandestine armed groups, crushing its leading opponents by the spring of 1954. Once Batista had suppressed the armed opposition, he proceeded to temporarily loosen the grip of his repressive apparatus.

During 1954 and 1955, peaceful civilian opposition to Batista re-emerged. Political party leaders, however, were divided in their trust of his promise of a return to democracy. Those seeking change through the ballot box hoped that Batista would once again accept the voters' will, as he had done during his previous period of rule, when he had even accepted the defeat of his hand-picked successor in 1944. Both the Auténticos and the Ortodoxos split into factions, one optimistic about the elections scheduled for November 1954 and the other seeking to topple Batista by force. As the balloting drew closer, however, leading opposition party candidate Grau San Martín withdrew from the race, allowing a virtually unopposed Batista to win the intimidation-ridden, fraudulent elections.

Following this mockery of the electoral process, a number of prominent civil society figures led by War of Independence veteran and renowned diplomat Cosme de la Torriente formed the Sociedad de Amigos de la República (Society of Friends of the Republic), an organization seeking to engage the government in a civic dialogue for the restoration of democracy. The society included a broad range of voices from different political parties and organizations, as manifested by the participation of leaders as diverse as former presidents Grau San Martín and Prío, renowned conservative intellectual Jorge Mañach, communist university professor Juan Marinello, and Catholic student leader José Antonio Echeverría. Batista proved unwilling to negotiate, however; the dialogue failed and the society soon disbanded.[23]

Batista, once again feeling firmly in control, signed into law the May 1955 General Amnesty Bill, which allowed the release of the Castros and other rebels from the Isle of Pines model prison; they had served less than twenty months of their sentences. By then, Fidel Castro's marriage had ended in divorce. His former brother-in-law, Rafael L. Díaz-Balart, had been the most strident voice among those opposing the amnesty that freed the Castros and their comrades-in-arms.

In July, the Castro brothers sought exile in Mexico, where they began to organize and train for an armed expedition. A few months later, while visiting New York City, Fidel Castro ominously declared: "In 1956 we shall be free or we shall be martyrs." By then, he had all but formally broken ties with the Ortodoxo party, though he continued to hold on to Chibás as a symbol of the struggle for democracy and social justice. Numerous other followers of the martyred Ortodoxo leader, including his brother, Raúl Chibás, joined the ranks of the M-26-7.[24]

The fiasco of the 1954 elections and the failure of the Civic Dialogue of 1955–56 prompted a reemergence of insurrectionist strategies against Batista's illegitimate rule. The M-26-7 was one among several armed organizations that resurfaced at the time; another one was the Havana-based armed movement Directorio Revolucionario (Revolutionary Directorate, DR), which emerged in 1955 under the command of youthful, charismatic student leader José Antonio Echeverría. Mainstream politicians also embraced the "island on horseback" option, as their predecessors had done since the birth of the republic in 1902. This was particularly evident among Auténtico veterans of the 1933 revolution against dictator Gerardo Machado, men such as former National Bank president Justo Carrillo, leader of Acción Libertadora, and deposed president Prío, who was at the helm of Organización Auténtica (Authentic Organization, OA), an armed faction of the Auténticos.[25]

While they shared the goal of toppling Batista, these anti-Batista organizations operated independently of one another. What little collaboration occurred among the groups mostly consisted of opportunistic moves by individual leaders to either gain control of the armed struggle or secure a portion of the spoils in the anticipated event of the regime's collapse. Prío, for example, spent part of his war chest to support the M-26-7. Carrillo also provided funds for Castro's movement. In turn, Castro pretended to recognize the leadership of Carrillo, whom he considered a likely successor to Batista, to the extent that in September 1955 he practically implored Carrillo for the mayoralty of Havana following Batista's fall. Echeverría and Castro formally agreed to collaborate when they signed the Mexico Pact in September 1956, but in reality, their respective groups continued their rivalry.[26] País was the only major rebel figure to sacrifice a leadership position when his Acción Nacional Revolucionaria (National Revolutionary Action) merged into the M-26-7.

Anti-government plots intensified in 1956, and state repression increased accordingly. A group of officers and enlisted men led by Colonels Ramón Barquín and Joaquín Varela Castro and Major Enrique Borbonet plotted a coup against Batista. Plans about the conspiracy were leaked, and Los Puros (the Pure Ones), as the plotters were called, were apprehended on April 4.[27] Later that month, Prio's OA launched an attack on the Goicuría army garrison in Matanzas. Informed about the plot, government forces met the rebels with heavy fire. Ten of them died during the confrontation, and another five were summarily executed by order of the post's infamously brutal commander, Pilar García.[28]

Rebels retaliated for the Goicuría massacre. At 4:00 a.m. on October 28, four armed rebels walked into the plush Montmartre nightclub, assassinated military intelligence service chief Colonel Antonio Blanco Rico and wounded Major Marcelo Tabernilla Palmero. Later that day, national police chief Rafael Salas Cañizares stormed the Haitian embassy, where the suspected plotters were thought to have found sanctuary along with six survivors of the Goicuría attack. Policemen killed all ten of them. Severely wounded in the gun battle, Salas Cañizares died two days later.[29]

The *Granma* Expedition and the Santiago Revolt

In Mexico, meanwhile, Castro's men continued to prepare for an armed expedition. Castro met, befriended, and recruited Ernesto "Che" Guevara, a 27-year-old Argentine revolutionary who had studied medicine. Guevara had fled Guatemala in the aftermath of the 1954 CIA-backed toppling of leftist president Jacobo Arbenz.[30] Spanish Civil War veteran Colonel Alberto Bayo helped train the guerrilla force. The planned expedition was set back, however, when at Batista's insistence, Mexican police arrested Castro and around fifty associates in June, keeping them in custody for about five weeks. With funds provided by Prío, Castro purchased the 60-foot yacht *Granma* to transport his rebels to Cuba. Among the eighty-two expedition members, the Castro brothers and twenty others were Moncada veterans.

The *Granma* landing was scheduled for November 30 to coincide with a planned revolt in Santiago led by Frank País, a popular and courageous 21-year-old Baptist schoolteacher. The revolt's main objective was to divert the attention of government troops away from the anticipated rebel landing. According to various sources, País reluctantly agreed to stage the revolt on that date in spite of the fact that he needed more time to prepare; but Castro insisted on keeping his promise of freedom or martyrdom in 1956.[31]

On November 30, nearly 300 armed M-26-7 insurgents attacked several army and police installations. Josué País, Frank's brother, and Léster Rodríguez led a failed assault on the Moncada garrison. Several rebels died during the attack on Santiago's national police headquarters. Other rebels rose up in the eastern cities of Guantánamo and Holguín, while around 100 others, led by peasant leader and reputed rural bandit Crescencio Pérez and Celia Sánchez, mobilized toward Niquero to support the *Granma* landing.[32]

Due to bad weather, the *Granma* was delayed until December 2, when the vessel finally reached Los Cayuelos mangrove swamp, a mile south of Playa Las Coloradas. The expedition's second-in-command described the inauspicious arrival as more of a sinking than a landing.[33] The rebel force marched toward the Sierra Maestra mountains until December 5, when government troops launched a combined air and land offensive at Alegría del Pío. Those who survived and escaped capture dispersed into several small bands. About half of them disappeared. The rest wandered for two weeks, avoiding detection by government troops until they regrouped in the foothills of the Sierra Maestra. Revolutionaries later created the myth of the twelve survivors—to mirror the twelve apostles—but the truth was that sixteen or seventeen survivors, perhaps more, formed the initial guerrilla nucleus.[34] In the aftermath of the *Granma* landing and the Santiago revolt, Batista's forces arrested and executed twenty-three M-26-7 and PSP militants between December 23 and 26, hence the infamous episode's name Pascuas Sangrientas (Bloody Christmas).[35]

Castro's band would most likely have perished had it not been for the crucial support it received from peasant leader Crescencio Pérez and his extended clan, who provided intelligence, provisions, and peasants armed with shotguns known as *escopeteros*. Batista's heavy-handed tactics, which included civilian massacres, indiscriminate bombings, and the forced relocation of peasants, strengthened the region's peasantry's support of the rebel cause.[36] Castro had expected, perhaps unrealistically, that Echeverría's DR forces would also join the M-26-7 insurrection following the *Granma* landing; had the DR done so, its rebels would have likely been wiped out. Fuming, Castro wrote an angry missive to Echeverría, accusing him of treachery and his followers of cowardice. It was now very clear that both leaders could no longer collaborate.[37]

The *Sierra* and the *Llano*

The literature on the rebellion, and therefore common perceptions on the subject, has privileged the role of the *sierra* (highlands) and its protagonists (the Castros, Guevara, Cienfuegos) over that of the *llano* (lowlands) and its leaders (País, Echeverría, Ramos Latour). A fair assessment of the roles of the *sierra* and the *llano*, however, points to the fact that urban clandestine movements were larger, more effective in causing harm to Batista's regime, and suffered far greater casualties than the shorter-lived, relatively small, and better-protected *sierra* forces. The fact that the Sierra Maestra–based rebel army was eventually responsible for the collapse of Batista's forces should not detract from the protagonist role played by the urban underground during most of the rebellion. However, the general public is broadly familiar with the roles of Fidel and Raúl Castro and Guevara but is unlikely even to recognize the names of urban martyrs such as Echeverría and País.[38]

During 1957, violence escalated as government forces intensified their efforts to crush the rebellion and the rebels expanded the fighting by opening new combat fronts. By then, the M-26-7 was the best organized and the largest of the armed opposition movements. It was strongest in the larger cities, such as Santiago and Havana; Castro's miniscule military contingent—eighteen rebels in January—represented only a tiny portion of M-26-7 forces. The Echeverría-led Directorio Revolucionario operated mostly in urban centers, and in Havana it was stronger than the M-26-7. Another major opposition player was deposed president Prío, who enjoyed the support of the most radical faction of the Auténticos and controlled the OA and the Directorio Obrero Revolucionario (Workers' Revolutionary Directorate).[39]

While small in numbers, Castro's nomadic guerrilla force became an important source of inspiration in the struggle against Batista. The rebel leader's status rose to mythical proportions as his guerrillas mocked the army's attempts to wipe them out. Aware of Castro's growing leadership, Batista falsely declared that army troops had killed him shortly after the *Granma* landing. The guerrillas won their first victory on January 14, when they captured the La Plata army post by surprise. This victory provided Castro's guerrilla force with desperately needed weapons, ammunition, and supplies; it also boosted the rebels' morale and reputation.[40]

New York Times reporter Herbert L. Matthews visited the M-26-7 guerrilla camp on February 17. His reports, accompanied by several photographs, dispelled claims that Castro was dead. Matthews presented a very favorable portrayal of the guerrilla leader. It was precisely the kind of image Castro wanted to be disseminated in the United States: that of a reasonable, democratic leader who harbored no anti-Yankee feelings. Castro conveyed to his interviewer, "We have no animosity toward the United States and the American People." Matthews reported, "He has strong ideas of liberty, democracy, social justice, the need to restore the Constitution, to hold elections." Some have credited the publication of Matthews's stories as the publicity stroke that opened the road to rebel victory. While helpful to the rebel cause, those stories did not play such a crucial role that Castro could claim "I got my job through the *New York Times.*"[41]

Meanwhile, in the *llanos* of Oriente, País's rebels continued to carry out sabotage and other clandestine operations. His organizational skills, his tremendous popularity, and his recognition as a courageous fighter allowed him to operate largely independently of Castro. Indeed, País, a strong believer in the primacy of civilian rule, was partially successful in subordinating Castro's *sierra* troops to the authority of the M-26-7's *llano*-based National Directorate. In July 1957, he notified Castro that the directorate would set the movement's policies and establish the insurrection's strategies.[42] Among País's independent initiatives was the formation of the Movimiento Resistencia Cívica (Civic Resistance Movement), an organization that recruited professionals and businessmen. He also founded the labor organization Frente Obrero Nacional (National Workers Front) with close ties to the M-26-7. País even opened a short-lived second guerrilla front in the Sierra Cristal of northern Oriente without Castro's consent.[43] País stands out in the annals of Cuban history as the individual who most emphatically and successfully challenged Castro's desire for absolute control.

By most accounts, including Castro's, the conditions endured by underground rebels who were operating in Santiago and Havana, where Batista's repressive forces were more numerous and effective, were far more dangerous than in the highlands. On one occasion, Castro expressed to Sánchez that he admired "the heroism being shown by our men in the underground," adding that "at times one feels ashamed of being in the Sierra. It is much more commendable to be there than to be here."[44] Sierra Maestra rebel troops were in fact relatively well-protected from army and police forces. In urban contexts, meanwhile, rebels faced a greater degree of surveillance, persecution, and violence. Several thousand anti-Batista militants were imprisoned, and hundreds—perhaps thousands—were tortured or executed.

On March 13, 1957, Echeverría's DR, along with some OA militants, staged a daring—arguably suicidal—armed assault on the Presidential Palace. Led by Carlos Gutiérrez Menoyo, the assailants came close to their objective of killing Batista. Echeverría, who briefly captured the CMQ radio station, and twenty-nine other rebels were killed during the four-hour-long gunfight. On April 20, police lieutenant Esteban Ventura Novo, on a tip from a young communist, massacred four survivors of the palace attack. The carnage took place at 7 Humboldt Street, near the splendid entrance of the University of Havana. The failed attack and its bloody aftermath dealt a severe blow to the DR and OA: several of their principal leaders—Echeverría, Carlos Gutiérrez Menoyo, and Menelao Mora among them—died in action, and most of the DR's weapons were captured by the police, while others ended in the hands of the M-26-7. This was payback time for Castro, who had actually ordered M-26-7 members not to provide any assistance to the DR.[45]

Later in the year, DR operatives regrouped in the southern highlands of Las Villas, where Gutiérrez Menoyo's younger brother, Eloy, opened another combat front in El Escambray. In February 1958, DR leader Faure Chomón landed on Cuba's northern coast with fifteen guerrilla fighters; and they proceeded to join rebel forces at El Escambray. Once there, they had a confrontation with Gutiérrez Menoyo, who insisted on being guerrilla chief, broke with the DR and created his own guerrilla force, Segundo Frente del Escambray (Second National Front of El Escambray).[46]

Two months after the abortive attack on the Presidential Palace, Prío's OA suffered yet another tragic setback. The deposed president intended to form an anti-Batista guerrilla nucleus to rival Castro's. Twenty-six OA militants under the command of labor leader Calixto Sánchez landed off the *Corynthia* at a location in Oriente Province near Mayarí on May 23. They marched toward the Sierra Cristal with the intention of establishing a guerrilla foothold. The plan ended disastrously when a few days later, government forces intercepted and killed sixteen of the rebels, Sánchez among them.[47]

Eager to expand the insurrection's popular base and demonstrate that it had the support of a broad spectrum of prominent political leaders, País arranged a meeting in the Sierra Maestra between Castro and some anti-Batista leaders of proven progressive and democratic convictions.

The meeting's timing in early July was auspicious: the OA and DR had just suffered major defeats, leaving the M-26-7 as the undisputable leading anti-Batista force. Ironically, Batista's forces had cleared the way for Castro's primacy. Among those participating in the Sierra meeting were Ortodoxo Party president Raúl Chibás; Enrique Barroso, head of the Ortodoxo Youth; Roberto Agramonte Jr., son of the Ortodoxos' former presidential candidate; and economist Felipe Pazos. Castro, Chibás, and Pazos signed the Sierra Manifesto on July 12, 1957, calling for the formation of a broad-based civic revolutionary front to develop a common strategy to topple Batista. The manifesto rejected the possibility of an electoral deal with Batista as well as any mediation in the conflict by third nations—namely, the United States—and any form of transitional government by a military junta. The document also promised a return to constitutional government and national elections within a year of the rebels' victory.[48]

On July 30, Colonel José Salas Cañizares gunned down País in a Santiago street. Just a few days earlier, País had reported on the increasingly dangerous environment: "The other day we had a miraculous escape from a police trap." País also voiced his distrust of Castro loyalist Vilma Espín, whom some have blamed for compromising the secrecy of his safe house. His death sparked huge popular mobilizations and an outcry against the regime's increasing violence; over 60,000 attended his funeral. Massive rallies, strikes, protests, and waves of sabotage followed.[49] With País out of the way, Castro could now impose full authority over the M-26-7's urban and lowland ranks. He appointed new leaders who lacked the independent spirit of País and the popularity and stature that had allowed País to keep Castro's authoritarian inclinations in check.

To guarantee the primacy of the *sierra* over the *llano*, Castro imposed the policy that his guerrillas become the primary recipients of the movement's resources. Seemingly never satisfied with the amount of funds and war matériel arriving in the *sierra*, he repeatedly accused the M-26-7's *llano* of failing to follow his directives. In August, he ordered Sánchez firmly: "All guns, all bullets, and all supplies to the Sierra!" On several other occasions, he scolded fellow rebel leaders for allegedly withholding weapons and other resources from the Sierra Maestra.[50]

While Castro had become the undisputed leader of the M-26-7, other anti-Batista organizations remained independent of his leadership, and even some M-26-7 militants—particularly those exiled in the United States—retained some degree of autonomy. Tensions between Castro and other opposition leaders peaked in November 1957, when representatives of eight organizations, including the Auténticos, the OA, the Ortodoxos, the FEU, and the DR, signed the Miami Pact and formed the Junta de Liberación Cubana (Cuban Liberation Junta).

Two members of the M-26-7, Pazos and Léster Rodríguez, signed the pact. Prodded by Guevara and Raúl Castro, the elder Castro protested their signing of the Miami Pact. On policy and strategic grounds, the Castros and Guevara objected to the pact's failure to explicitly reject any form of U.S. intervention to facilitate Batista's removal and the participation of Cuba's military in the subsequent power transition. Guevara and Raúl Castro used the occasion to further undermine the dwindling authority and relative independence of the M-26-7's National Directorate. They attributed conservative and even pro-U.S. sentiments to some *llano* leaders. Guevara called Pazos a "criminal" and scorned urban rebel leader Armando Hart as subservient to the United States. Raúl Castro blasted: "Even shooting these two gentlemen [Pazos and Rodríguez] would not be enough to repay them for what they've done."[51]

During this period, Guevara became increasingly open about his Marxist ideology, which he shared with Raúl Castro. Both pressed Fidel Castro to take a more aggressive stance against the Miami Pact, the *llano* leadership, and the moderate voices within the movement. Castro, meanwhile, employed his skills as master triangulator to pit the moderate *llano* against the increasingly radical *sierra*, which he favored.[52]

As stated earlier, Castro was not even a communist sympathizer. The animosity was mutual: the PSP had decried the Moncada attack as putschist and adventurous and derided its leaders as petty bourgeois, some even "implicated in gangsterism"—an allusion to Castro.[53] Moreover, the bearded guerrilla chief was sensitive to domestic and foreign accusations that he was a communist. Castro, nonetheless, recognized the strategic value of gaining PSP support. He pursued a "good cop, bad cop" strategy, giving Guevara and his brother liberty to attack the M-26-7's moderate wing and pursue more radical initiatives, including alliances with the PSP, while he appeared neutral, even publicly condemning communism.

In early 1958, Castro made yet another concerted effort to portray his movement as democratic, pro-United States, and capitalism-friendly; this was the Cold War and the tail end of the McCarthyist era and he sought to avoid even the appearance of having communist sympathies. Once again, he enlisted the U.S. media. *Look* and *Coronet* magazines published interviews in which he assured readers of his democratic plans. He told *Look*: "We'll set up a provisional government, whose heads are to be elected by some 60 Cuban civic bodies, like the Lions, Rotarians, groups of lawyers and doctors, religious organizations." "Within a year," he promised, "this caretaker regime would hold a truly honest election." Castro also pledged that he had "no plans for the expropriation or nationalization of foreign investments." Indeed, he said, "Foreign investments will always be welcome and secure here."[54]

Violence Escalates

In 1958, Batista's regime faced imminent collapse as guerrillas gained control over more and more territory, the economy took a turn for the worse, and the United States and other traditional regime allies, such as the Church, reduced or withdrew their support. Batista responded with brute force.

The M-26-7's underground and the rebel army began a strategy to disrupt the Cuban economy and thereby impair the government's ability to finance its military and repressive apparatus. According to some, 1957 had been the Cuban economy's best year ever.[55] The successful preservation of productivity in Cuba's sugar plantations seemed to assure the survival of Batista's regime. Thus, the strategic destruction of economic targets such as sugar plantations, mines, and factories, many of them backed or owned by U.S. capital, became a primary strategy of the rebels. Castro explained that it was necessary to burn the entire sugarcane crop. "It is the very importance of the cane crop," he said, "that compels us to destroy it."[56] Setting cane fields on fire actually had a long history; generations of rebellious slaves, separatist patriots, and disgruntled sugar workers had resorted to such tactics. Historically, the persistent plantation had generated equally persistent forms of resistance.

In 1958, the state unleashed a brutal campaign of terror. On March 12, Batista suspended civil liberties once again and further tightened press censorship; the regime imprisoned suspects by the hundreds and in many instances subjected them to gruesome tortures and even execution. The list of confirmed and reputed government assassins and torturers was extensive and included the likes of Alberto del Río Chaviano, Esteban Ventura Novo, Jesús Sosa Blanco, and Pilar García.[57]

The regime's repressive and murderous actions drew attention from the U.S. government. African American congressman Adam Clayton Powell led a successful campaign to stop the sale of weapons to Cuba that culminated with the imposition of an arms embargo in March. While the Cuban military filled the gap by purchasing British weapons and warplanes, these sanctions, which proved that U.S. support for Batista was not unconditional, had a profoundly demoralizing effect on the regime.[58] Around that time, the guerrillas received crucial supplies of weapons and ammunition from Costa Rica. Rebel leader Huber Matos, a teacher and rice farmer from Oriente, had acquired the weapons there with the assistance of left-of-center president José Figueres.

While *sierra* forces prepared to confront advancing government troops, the movement's *llano* leadership organized a general strike to further debilitate the regime and, they hoped, topple Batista. The strike, which took place on April 9, was poorly coordinated and failed to produce a nationwide work stoppage. The absence of the PSP from among its participants hampered its effectiveness. Former PSP member David Salvador was partly to blame: he had become a staunch anticommunist and rejected any communist participation in the strike. The PSP, for its part, continued to keep its distance from and sometimes even sabotaged M-26-7 efforts; some communists actually provided the government with intelligence about the planned strike.[59]

Ostensibly enraged by the failure of the general strike, which he had called for but failed to support, Castro used the occasion to solidify further his control over the movement by removing or reassigning key *llano* and exile leaders, replacing them with individuals he trusted and over whom he could exercise greater control. He summoned the *llano* leadership to a meeting on May 3 at a location in the Sierra Maestra called Altos de Mompié. Guevara led the assault against labor leader Salvador, whom he accused of "sectarianism" for his refusal to coordinate the strike with the PSP.[60] At Mompié, Castro secured absolute power over the movement and consolidated both military authority as commander-in-chief of the rebel army and civilian authority as head of the newly created Executive Committee.[61] After Mompié, Castro was free to pursue his two paramount goals: subordinating the remaining anti-Batista organizations and then toppling Batista.

The rebel army implemented a new offensive military strategy that included the creation of additional columns and fronts and the appointment of several officers, beginning with the promotion of Guevara and Raúl Castro to the rank of comandante (major). In late February, Castro ordered the formation of two new columns, besides his own First Column and Guevara's Second. He appointed comandante Juan Almeida Bosque, a black, working-class veteran of Moncada and the *Granma*, to lead Column

Figure 1.3. Raúl Castro and Che Guevara in the Sierra Cristal rebel encampment, June 1958. Photograph by Andrew St. George. Courtesy of AP.

Three and named his brother, Raúl, head of Column Six.[62] In March, Raúl Castro's hundred-men-strong column marched toward the Sierra Cristal (figure 1.3), where it established the Frank País Second Oriente Front. Almeida's column, meanwhile, relocated near El Cobre, not far from Santiago. There was even an all-female platoon named Mariana Grajales that engaged in combat in several battles.[63]

As late as May 1958, the number of M-26-7 troops remained low, at an estimated two to three hundred combatants in the First Front and roughly the same number in the Second Oriente Front. Another 1,000 peasant *escopeteros* reinforced each front.[64] As these fronts expanded the area under their control, rebel leaders created social programs and issued revolutionary decrees. They opened schools and medical facilities to serve the peasantry. Raúl Castro enacted an agrarian reform, and Guevara established schools, training facilities, and factories to produce uniforms and other war matériel. Unlike the government's soldiers, the rebel army treated peasants with respect and protected them from potential abuses at the hands of rogue rebels.[65]

The Regime Unravels

On May 25, Batista launched his most aggressive military offensive up to that time. Code-named "Fin de Fidel," it aimed to crush all highland rebel fronts. General Eulogio Cantillo, one of the regime's ablest and most respected officers, led 10,000 troops in the offensive. Having learned from his mistake in the Moncada attack, in which he had divided his forces to pursue four different targets, this time Castro consolidated the bulk of his troops into one single front. The army's ten-week offensive failed, in part, because government recruits lacked proper training and had become increasingly demoralized. Desertions ran into the thousands.[66] During the offensive, the rebel army won several battles, most importantly El Jigüe on July 21, considered the war's turning point.

On the Second Oriente Front, meanwhile, Raúl Castro responded to news that the United States continued to arm Batista's troops secretly by kidnapping around thirty Guantánamo-based U.S. military personnel, who became human shields of sorts. The rebels also kidnapped a group of U.S. and Canadian engineers from the Moa Bay Mining Company. The kidnappings, while controversial, proved effective, as the Cuban Air Force discontinued its bombing raids over the Sierra Cristal. In this matter, again, the younger Castro was cast to play "bad cop."[67]

The rebel army's success on the battlefield emboldened Castro to establish dominance over other anti-Batista organizations. On July 20, representatives of the various organizations of the Junta de Liberación Cubana met in Caracas, Venezuela, where they signed a unity pact that Castro had drafted. Signatory organizations of the pact included the M-26-7, the OA, the DR, the Agrupación Montecristi, the Partido Revolucionario Cubano Insurreccional, the Resistencia Cívica, the Partido Demócrata Independiente, the FEU, and Unidad Obrera. Conspicuously absent was the PSP, whose participation was unanimously blocked by the coalition, composed mostly of groups with ties to anti-communist Prío. In addition to recognizing Castro as the insurrection's leader, the pact ratified his selection of Judge Manuel Urrutia as future provisional president. Urrutia had gained widespread respect after he issued a dissenting ruling when he voted to absolve 151 individuals accused of participating in the *Granma* expedition and the November 30 revolt. However, he lacked both administrative and political experience. The signatories to the pact elected Havana Bar Association president José Miró Cardona, a moderate, as junta coordinator.[68]

Having stopped Batista's army's advance, Castro proceeded to launch a multipronged westward offensive. In August, he ordered Comandante Guevara's Column Eight to march east toward Las Villas Province along Cuba's south coast and Comandante Cienfuegos's 120-man-strong Column Two to proceed onto Pinar del Río along the north coast, roughly the same path taken by War of Independence hero Antonio Maceo, in whose honor the column was named. Another column, led by Comandante Jaime Vega, followed Guevara's but was defeated by army forces. By mid-October, Guevara's column had reached El Escambray mountain range in Las Villas; there, it joined forces with a contingency of 120 DR rebels operating in the region under Faure Chomón and Rolando Cubela.[69]

Guevara proved partial to the inclusion of communists into the guerrillas. At El Escambray, he formally incorporated around twenty PSP fighters under the command of Félix Torres, upon whom he immediately bestowed the rank of comandante. He also selected militant communist Armando Acosta as his top aide. Another communist leader, geography professor Antonio Núñez Jiménez, joined Guevara's forces in early December. Although some communist party members had had a presence in the Sierra Cristal for some time, the PSP did not officially establish collaboration with the M-26-7 until November 1958, when their respective labor organizations merged, forming the Frente Obrero Nacional Unido (National United Labor Front). More communists joined in late December as it became evident that Batista's army was on the run. The short length of their beards distinguished these latecomers from those guerrillas who had been fighting for a long period of time.[70] (figure 1.4)

Raúl Castro had also incorporated communists into the war effort. In July, Carlos Rafael Rodríguez, a high-ranking member of the PSP, had traveled to the younger Castro's camp, where he was warmly welcomed. Later, he met with Fidel Castro in the Sierra Maestra, where he faced hostility from anticommunist rebels. Rodríguez later reminisced that he found "nothing but understanding for the Communists" in the Sierra Cristal, but in the Sierra Maestra, "the understanding had changed to suspicion."[71]

Comandante Cienfuegos's westerly march through Camagüey lasted a month, during which time his men reportedly ate only eleven times. Handsome and charismatic, Cienfuegos earned the reputation of being a fearless fighter. Guevara once wrote admiringly: "Camilo did not measure danger, he was entertained by it, played with it, approached it like a bullfighter, he lured it and handled it."[72] The most important battle of Cienfuegos's march was the ten-day siege and capture of the Yaguajay army garrison. Once a student of sculpture, the always-colorful Cienfuegos

Figure 1.4. Editorial cartoon by Silvio Fontanillas mocking those who joined the rebellion in its latter stages. The short-bearded "retaguardia" rebel is a veiled allusion to the communists. *Source: Bohemia*, February 8, 1959.

concocted a flame-throwing tank from a tractor with reinforced plates. Nicknamed "Dragón Primero," the improvised armored vehicle was part of the arsenal that forced the garrison's surrender on December 31. By then, the Antonio Maceo column had grown to 450 troops. With the rebel army's increasing success, the strength of its forces islandwide had swollen to over 7,000.[73]

By the second half of 1958, both U.S. economic interests and the U.S. government realized that Batista had become a dangerous liability and that he had to be replaced before the rebels ousted him. The overseer, it became obvious, was about to let the plantation go up in flames. Little hope was placed on the presidential elections scheduled for November 3, in which Grau San Martín once again ran for his faction of the Auténticos, Carlos Márquez Sterling ran for the new Partido del Pueblo Libre, and Andrés Rivero Agüero campaigned as Batista's handpicked successor. As expected, Rivero Agüero won the fraudulent elections, an outcome that was unacceptable to armed rebels, civilian opponents, and even the U.S. government. Batista insisted on holding on to power, however. The U.S.

government clearly rejected Castro as the leader of a post-Batista Cuba and viewed Batista's refusal to step down as increasing the odds of that unwelcomed scenario. Castro and the vast majority of the opposition fully rejected any electoral solution while Batista was still in power. Castro went to the lengths of threatening politicians who ran for office with a thirty-year ban from government positions and those who committed fraud with the death penalty.[74]

The U.S. government displayed a clumsy, arrogant Cuba policy of too little, too late. It had supported and armed Batista for over six years. Now, with the regime facing imminent defeat, it pursued negotiations for a peaceful transition to preempt Castro's ascent to power. On December 9, secret U.S. envoy William D. Pawley, a former ambassador with a long history of dubious business dealings in Cuba, tried to persuade Batista to resign in favor of a civilian-military junta, offering him and his family political asylum in the United States. In line with the United States' historic disregard for Cuban self-determination, Pawley presented the U.S. government's selections for the junta: Colonel Barquín, Major Borbonet, retired general Martín Díaz Tamayo, and Pepín Bosch, co-owner of Bacardí Corporation. Adamant about staying in power, Batista angrily rejected the offer. On the eleventh, Ambassador Earl E. T. Smith communicated to Batista that he could no longer count on U.S. support and would not be granted asylum in the United States.[75] Having failed to persuade Batista, U.S. envoys pursued secret negotiations with high-ranking officers who had come to realize that the regime would soon collapse. Actually, Generals Tabernilla Dolz and Díaz Tamayo and other officers had begun to conspire months before.[76]

As a last, desperate military offensive, Batista deployed an armored train laden with troops and weapons to reinforce his dwindling forces in Oriente. The operation failed miserably. Guevara's guerrillas derailed the train in Santa Clara on December 31, forcing the troops to surrender.

That New Year's Eve, the besieged strongman held a dinner party at his Camp Columbia residence, where elegantly attired guests welcomed 1959 with a toast. The mood was definitely not festive. Batista had summoned his most trusted officers and associates, inviting them to bring their families. Nearly 100 had reached the army camp by 2:00 a.m., when he announced his decision to resign and flee and invited the remaining guests to board two awaiting DC-4 airplanes. A stampede-like scramble for the planes ensued, and other planes landed over the next few hours. According to Colonel Orlando Piedra, who traveled with Batista, his plane first flew in the direction of the United States, then changed course fifteen minutes into the flight and began heading toward the Dominican Republic, where fellow tyrant Trujillo confiscated part of his loot.[77] U.S. authorities had denied him permission to land, as Ambassador Smith had warned they would.

The exile party did not leave empty-handed: Batista took with him over $300 million, while Tabernilla carried $40 million that he had pillaged from the army's retirement fund. A year earlier, the popular magazine *Carteles* had denounced twenty high-ranking government officials who held individual Swiss bank accounts each valued at $1 million or more. After the sacking, less than $100 million remained in the nation's vaults.[78]

The bloody seven-year struggle against Batista and the regime's repressive responses produced a heavy toll of thousands of casualties and depleted Cuba's finances. In the process, traditional political parties lost whatever legitimacy they may have had and the military shrank into a band of defeated, ineffective, and demoralized soldiers; likewise with the police force that had systematically brutalized rebels and opponents alike. These circumstances amounted to a virtual vacuum in both political and military leadership. This facilitated the ascendancy of Castro's followers and the rebel army, which I analyze in the next chapter.

Was Cuba Ripe for Revolution? Was a Revolution Necessary?

Revolutions are immensely complex historical processes that erupt in response to multiple, oftentimes contradictory social, political, and economic forces. Cuba's case was no exception: the rebellion against Batista responded to numerous structural problems, among them persistent poverty, chronic unemployment, and landlessness among rural workers, as well as contingent factors, such as the protracted rule of an illegitimate government and the economic crisis of 1958. Views of the Cuba of the 1950s varied then and continue to vary widely, with some depicting it as paradise and others as hell, leaving little or no space for a middle ground.

During the second half of the 1950s, Cuba endured numerous structural problems. Its export-dependent economy relied upon the production of a single crop, sugar, and on trade with one partner, the United States. The "longest ninety miles" manifested themselves in Cuba's heavy dependence on U.S. capital, which dominated 90 percent of mining activities, 80 percent of utility services, 75 percent of arable land, and 40 percent of sugar production. Total U.S. investments rose during the 1950s from $712 million in 1950 to $1.1 billion in 1958.[79] Cuba's "persistent plantation," meanwhile, generated a host of social ills, among them the concentration of landownership in few hands, landlessness for a large proportion of rural workers, unemployment, underemployment, rural poverty, and political and economic subordination to the United States.

Geographer and historian Leví Marrero and others have pointed out, however, that the island was slowly but surely moving away from its dependence on producing sugar for the U.S. market toward industrialization, economic diversification, and a larger proportion of national ownership of agricultural land and various industries. Marrero highlighted that in 1950, industrial workers composed 24 percent of the workforce, the island produced over 75 percent of the food it consumed, and sugar, while accounting for 80 percent of all exports, generated only 25 percent of the national income.[80]

Marrero and others have also demonstrated that Cuba's economic and social indicators compared favorably with those of Latin America's most prosperous nations and in some cases even with those of industrialized European countries. Its per capita production ranked third among Latin American nations. Caloric intake levels were the third highest in Latin America. Its literacy rate was the fourth highest in Latin America, at 75 percent. With one physician for every 980 inhabitants, Cuba ranked second in Latin America in access to medical care. Life expectancy was high at 58.8 years and infant mortality was low, 32 per 1,000 births, the lowest in Latin America. Cuba also had a large, comfortable middle class comprising, according to Marrero's estimate, 22–33 percent of the population, and its consumption patterns resembled those of its U.S. counterpart. Cuba had one television set per eighteen inhabitants (first in Latin America) and one automobile per twenty-seven inhabitants (third in Latin America).[81]

Historically, however, Cubans—particularly those in the middle and upper classes—did not compare themselves with their southern neighbors but rather with those to the north. While urban, middle-class Cubans enjoyed numerous advantages, such as affordable health care clinics, good private schools, recreational clubs, excellent public transportation, and a high-quality higher education system, their income levels stagnated during the 1950s and fell further behind those of their U.S. counterparts, producing frustration and a sense of vulnerability. Real wages actually fell between 1953 and 1957. Not surprisingly, the insurrection's leadership and much of its support came from the middle class.[82]

By Latin American standards, class differences between the upper and lower classes were not abysmal, but they were nonetheless significant. The Auténticos' 1952 party platform denounced the fact that Cuba had more millionaires than England. Reportedly, Havana had the world's highest per capita rate of Cadillac ownership. A vestige of its long and relatively recent colonial past, Cuba was home to twenty-three marquises, twenty-two counts, and one viscount.[83]

Sharp distinctions were also evident between regions and between urban and rural areas. Havana, sometimes described as a First World capital of a Third World country, was the wealthiest and most privileged part of Cuba. The capital city's opulence and favorable social and economic indicators bucked national trends. While the national literacy rate was a respectable 75 percent, illiteracy was four times higher in rural areas than in cities. Likewise, Cuba's high doctor-per-inhabitant ratio masked the unequal distribution of medical care: 1 per 227 in Havana versus 1 per 2,423 in Oriente Province. Approximately 70 percent of all hospital beds were located in the capital city.[84]

During the late 1950s, land concentration was extreme: 3 percent of landowners controlled 56 percent of the land. Landlessness among peasants, however, was not a widespread problem—over 90 percent of peasants had legal use of the land they worked—but in eastern regions, such as the Sierra Maestra, landlessness was chronic. Cuba's agricultural workers endured the worst conditions. According to a 1957 study, 64 percent of agricultural workers' houses lacked toilets, 60 percent had dirt floors, and 42 percent consisted of only one room to accommodate an average family of six.[85]

Cuba was, indeed, actually two Cubas, many Cubas: one poor, one prosperous; one eastern, one western; one rural, one urban; one white, one black and mulatto. The anti-Batista insurrection pitted these Cubas against one another. Was Cuba ripe for revolution? Was a revolution necessary? It depends on which Cuba we ask.

2

▼

Fatherland or Death!

Setting the Revolution's Foundations, 1959–1962

1959—Year of Liberation
1960—Year of the Agrarian Reform
1961—Year of Education
1962—Year of Planning

I fixed the errors of your government,
I distributed the bread and befriended the poor.
Yes, it is true: in the process, I raided our house.
There is nothing left in it. I gave away
our goods, distributed our inheritance,
to the last items, the amphorae,
the textiles, the skins, the wheat, the spoons.
Our house stands empty, and still
there was not enough for everyone.

Antón Arrufat, *Los siete contra Tebas*

When the rebels ousted Batista, very few—if any—observers could have imagined that Castro's rise to power signaled the beginning of a prolonged new era of increasingly radical political and social transformations that would soon culminate with the establishment of a Marxist-Leninist regime. Even less imaginable was the scenario that in a matter of months and in the context of the Cold War, the Soviet Union would displace the United States as Cuba's main political ally and trading partner. Those who fled Cuba during the first four years of the revolution believed that their exile would be temporary; they rationalized that the United States would not allow the new order of things to go on much longer and would soon intervene to oust Castro.

This chapter looks at the decisive first four years of the Cuban Revolution, tracing and analyzing the manifold challenges it faced domestically

Figure 2.1. Directorio Revolucionario *guerrillas* wearing assorted headgear. *Source: Bohemia*, January 11, 1959.

and in the international arena, as well as its accomplishments and short-comings. By 1963, almost every aspect of Cuba—including its political system, social structure, foreign relations, trading partners, and cultural production—had been transformed profoundly. This was a period of heroic idealism, of grand social and economic programs, of feverish adventures.

It was a time of young bearded guerrillas in power, a photogenic moment that produced iconic black-and-white images of a baseball-capped Castro pitching a ball, of Guevara under his trademark black beret, of the ever-smiling Cienfuegos wearing a broad-brimmed cowboy hat. Photographers feasted on the profusion of photogenic moments. One captured an image of Camilo Cienfuegos on the day he assumed control of the Presidential Palace; it shows him standing defiantly on top of a ripped oil painting of Batista's wife. Another photograph immortalized a DR rebel soldier of humble background crowned with a lustrous top hat, most certainly looted from the closet of some wealthy partisan of Batista's (figure 2.1). The image captured the very essence of revolution: a poor man wearing a rich man's hat. Like Napoleon a century and a half before, this anonymous rebel had crowned himself in defiance of the old order.[1]

Guerrillas in Power

After Batista's unceremonious resignation and departure in the early hours of January 1, 1959, General Cantillo assumed control of the military. Colonel Barquín, who had been in the Isle of Pines penitentiary since the failed Los Puros conspiracy of 1956, and M-26-7 *llano* leader Armando Hart, who was also incarcerated there, were released and immediately flew to Camp Columbia. Arriving on New Year's Day still dressed in prison garb, Barquín assumed temporary charge over the camp, only to release it the following day to comandante Cienfuegos. Guevara and his troops also reached Havana on the 2nd with orders to capture La Cabaña fortress.[2] DR forces led by comandante Rolando Cubela, meanwhile, had already occupied the Presidential Palace and the University of Havana. To the east, Gutiérrez Menoyo's guerrillas had taken the city of Cienfuegos, Chomón's men occupied the picturesque city of Trinidad, and Víctor Mora's troops assumed control over the city of Camagüey.[3]

On January 1, Castro called for a general strike, which was widely observed throughout the island. As the day drew to an end, Castro, Matos, and a large group of rebels marched triumphantly into Santiago, where a festive multitude greeted them in euphoric jubilation. Streams of people flooded country roads and city streets, celebrating Batista's fall, the end of civil war, and the advent of a new political era. Dozens of businesses and organizations purchased large ad spaces in newspapers to congratulate the triumphant guerrillas. Among them was one ad in *Revolución* by Bacardí Corporation that read: "Because of your sacrifices and efforts we can once again say in Cuba how lucky we Cubans are."[4] Unbeknown to both victors and the vanquished, warriors and spectators, the rich, the poor, and those in between, this was the beginning of a profound, prolonged, contentious, and distinctively Cuban socialist revolutionary process.

Leaving Raúl Castro in command of rebel forces in Oriente, Castro began his triumphal caravan to Havana. Clad in olive-green fatigues and sporting beards of varying lengths, the guerrillas rode across the island with Castro leading the way in. Cheering masses lined the Central Highway as the undulating Jeep convoy roared its way toward the capital. On the night of the caravan's triumphant arrival in Havana—it was January 8—Castro addressed a crowd of 10,000 gathered inside Camp Columbia. His message was simple and his style conversational, often resembling the call-and-response pattern so characteristic of much of Cuba's popular music. He engaged the festive audience in a dialogue. "What are the

Figure 2.2. Rebels and patricians share a banquet in celebration of Batista's fall. Photograph by Carlos Núñez. Courtesy of Gustavo Arvelo.

people interested in?" Castro asked. In unison, the crowd chanted back, "¡*Libertad!* ¡*Libertad!*" Castro spoke about the need for the new government to monopolize all weapons and denounced "elements within a certain organization"—an obvious allusion to the DR, which had amassed an arsenal of its own. Then he asked the audience: "Weapons for what? To fight whom? Against the Revolutionary Government, which has the support of the entire people?" "¡*No!*" retorted the multitude as a single voice. White doves appeared on the scene. Two of them landed on the podium, and one perched on Castro's left shoulder (figure 2.3). The throng cheered in amazement; some saw it as a supernatural sign of divine approval, perhaps from an Afro-Cuban deity. Close, slow-motion examination of the film footage that captured the moment reveals a more earthly explanation: a man standing a few feet from the podium pushed the doves directly toward Castro.[5]

The new government's first order of business was the elimination of all remnants of the defunct regime. Many of Batista's collaborators fled; those who did not were eventually captured and imprisoned. Some endured the spontaneous wrath of looting mobs, and their properties became targets of sacking. Scores of Batista soldiers and policemen were charged with war crimes. Some did not have the chance of a trial; those who did, became part of Roman circus–like spectacles in crowded stadiums. One of the most notorious public trials was that of Colonel Jesús Sosa Blanco, a 51-year-old Batista henchman. Hundreds of thousands watched from their TV sets as the manacled Sosa Blanco clad in denim prison clothes trembled as his victims' relatives showered him with vociferous accusations. The grimace on his face was undecipherable, a strange combination of terror and mocking defiance. A military tribunal found Sosa Blanco guilty of 108 murders and sentenced him to death.[6]

A disturbing development in the administration of justice was Castro's personal intervention in judicial matters. In March, a revolutionary military tribunal had absolved nineteen air force pilots along with ten gunners and sixteen plane mechanics charged with dropping bombs on rebel forces and civilian populations. Disappointed with the outcome, Castro ordered a retrial and the new tribunal found the defendants guilty, sentencing the nineteen pilots to thirty years and the gunners to shorter sentences. Historian Lilian Guerra and others have underscored the fact that while

Figure 2.3. Castro's victory speech in Havana, Camp Columbia, January 8, 1959. Camilo Cienfuegos stands behind him. *Source: Bohemia*, January 11, 1959.

troubling, the execution of "revolutionary justice" had an enormous galvanizing effect, given the virtually universal hatred that Cubans had toward Batista's military and police forces.[7]

The elimination of the remnants of the Batista regime proceeded swiftly. Laws passed in January established the death penalty and expanded the list of capital crimes to include murder, rape, espionage, and treason. Strident crowds demanded executions to the rhythmic chant of "¡Paredón! ¡Paredón!" (To the wall!). Estimates of executions in the first couple of months ranged between 200 and 700, most of them carried out under direct orders from comandante Guevara. A privately conducted survey indicated that 93 percent of the population favored the executions.[8]

Upon assuming power, the revolution's leaders filled the political vacuum. Castro was by far the most popular and powerful of the revolutionary leaders, his stature reaching near-messianic proportions. A culture that venerated strong military caudillos allowed him to assume the new era's highest political standing. He retained his positions as head of the M-26-7 and commander-in-chief of the Rebel Army. The mild-mannered and politically naive President Urrutia posed no threat or challenge to Castro's authority. The revolution's first cabinet, ostensibly selected by Urrutia but with strong input from Castro and Carlos Franqui, was a showcase of some of the nation's most talented and respected professionals. Among them were Prime Minister José Miró Cardona, former president of the Havana Bar Association; Minister of Public Works Manuel Ray Rivero, a distinguished civil engineer; Minister of State Roberto Agramonte; and Minister of Social Welfare Elena Mederos. The cabinet also included five rebel army comandantes and several members of the underground movement.[9] Visibly missing from cabinet-level positions were individuals associated with rival armed organizations such as Prío's OA, the DR, and the Second National Front of El Escambray. Also absent were representatives of the PSP and, for that matter, individuals with communist leanings, with the exception of the aristocratic Minister of Revolutionary Laws Osvaldo Dorticós Torrado, whose communist credentials were tenuous at best.[10]

The original cabinet was socially homogeneous, composed of middle- and upper-middle-class professionals. It had no working-class representation, nor did it include one single black or mulatto. Despite the fact that several women had played key roles in the struggle against Batista, only one woman, Mederos, held a ministerial post. The cabinet projected an image of moderation—that of a team of able, politically moderate individuals acceptable to the Cuban middle class and the watchful eyes of the United States. Notably, it did not include anyone from Castro's inner circle, which mostly consisted of survivors of the Moncada attack and *Granma* landing. The absence of Castro's most trusted men from the cabinet foreshadowed the marginal and short-lived role he had in store for the body.[11]

At the same time, Castro formed a shadow government consisting of far more radical individuals, among them Guevara, Raúl Castro, Antonio Núñez Jiménez, Carlos Rafael Rodríguez, Vilma Espín, and Oscar Pino Santos. In contrast to the de jure cabinet members, these individuals were all either communists or communist sympathizers. This shadow government gathered quietly in Cojímar, east of Havana, the fishing village made famous by Ernest Hemingway in *The Old Man and the Sea*. Other PSP leaders often participated in these meetings. Meanwhile, Raúl Castro loyalists of communist proclivities gradually assumed important positions in the military.[12]

On February 7, the cabinet replaced the 1940 Constitution with the new Fundamental Law of the Revolution. This body of legislation gave all legislative power to the cabinet and executive power to Urrutia. By mid-February, however, it had become obvious that Urrutia had been reduced to a figurehead, while Castro governed informally from his Havana Hilton penthouse suite. Protesting the diminishing authority of the Council of Ministers, Prime Minister Miró Cardona resigned on February 13, striking an unexpected blow to the image of revolutionary unity that Castro sought to cultivate. Castro assumed the vacant premiership, further reducing Urrutia's power. Displeased with Castro's mounting authoritarianism, Urrutia tendered his resignation on February 17. Castro refused to accept it, avoiding further impressions of a government in disarray. Minister of Agriculture Humberto Sorí Marín resigned in May when the government unveiled an Agrarian Reform Law, which he had not been even allowed to contribute to. Most the cabinet's moderate voices were dismissed or resigned that year.[13]

The first few months of the revolution were characterized by the absence of a coherent guiding ideology. In April 1959, Castro vaguely defined the nature of the revolution as "Bread without terror, freedom with bread, neither leftist nor rightist dictatorships: Humanism."[14] The primary force sustaining the new government was, in fact, Fidelismo, the adoration of Castro by the masses. Most Cubans saw Castro as a larger-than-life, charismatic hero who listened to the people and seemed genuinely interested in the improvement of their lot. A February poll by the popular weekly magazine *Bohemia* reflected that more than 95 percent of the population embraced the course of the revolution.[15] The slogan "Comandante, *ordene*" (Commander-in-chief, order us) and ubiquitous house placards reading "*Esta casa es tuya, Fidel*" (This house is yours, Fidel) symbolized the intense admiration that many had for the Maximum Leader.

Capitalizing on high levels of popular support, Castro managed to centralize power around him. Reformist and redistributive legislation made the gradual demise of democratic practices and institutions seemingly acceptable to the populace; Cubans, in fact, had lived without democracy for most of their lives. Early in January, the government banned all political parties, curiously with the exception of the PSP. In early April 1959, Castro postponed the promised elections. "Revolution first, elections later," the slogan went. The following year, he told a crowd of about one million people that there would be no elections, claiming that Cuba had instituted a direct form of democracy.[16]

The new government further solidified its support among the populace and the middle class through a combination of progressive social legislation and the promise of major social and economic reforms.[17] Revolutionary leaders released a flurry of legislation aimed at raising the standard of living for most Cubans. New laws brought about a substantial improvement in the material conditions of the lower and middle classes. Among the myriad progressive measures was Law 135, which reduced house, apartment, and room rental costs by between 30 and 50 percent. Another law cut the price of medicines substantially. Bus fares went down following the nationalization of bus companies, and the American-owned Cuban Telephone Company had to cut its rates. Electricity rates were slashed 30 percent. Law 142 raised the minimum wage for government employees to 95 pesos.[18] A second, far more radical Urban Reform Law (1960) limited ownership of housing units to just one property, prescribed the confiscation of rented houses and apartments, and established that occupants would henceforth pay rent to the state and would eventually receive titles to those properties.[19]

The Agrarian Reform Law of May 1959 was the most far-reaching and comprehensive legislation enacted by the revolutionary government during its first year, which it officially named the Year of Liberation. Minister of Revolutionary Laws Dorticós was quick to point out that in no way did this law deny the right to private ownership. "It is not an agrarian reform with a socialist orientation like the Soviet Agrarian Reform," he explained. The law limited land ownership to thirty *caballerías* (approximately 1,000 acres), excepting land units whose productivity exceeded the national average by over 50 percent, in which case it set the maximum at 100 *caballerías* (approximately 3,300 acres). It made allowance for compensation for nationalized lands payable in twenty-year bonds at 4.5 percent interest. The application of the Agrarian Reform Law fell under the purview of the National Agrarian Reform Institute (INRA), a powerful agency under Fidel Castro's direct orders that not only oversaw the nationalization and distribution of land but also took responsibility for numerous rural programs, including housing, education, and infrastructure construction and eventually the administration of the sugar industry.[20]

Large segments of the rural population welcomed the agrarian reform, even well-to-do *colonos*, who in some instances benefited from the land redistribution. The weekly *Bohemia* quoted the leader of the cane growers' association saying, "This is our law and we will defend it come what may." Even some owners of small sugar mills applauded: "Forward Cubans, with the Agrarian Reform!" remarked a leader of the small mill owners' association.[21]

By the end of summer, INRA had expropriated some 2.5 million acres of ranch land. In 1960, sugar land nationalizations reached 3.1 million acres belonging to U.S. companies and 2.2 million acres owned by Cubans.[22] The largest of these properties were not broken up into smaller plots but were rather turned into farms run by the state or government-controlled farmer cooperatives. By the end of 1961, there were approximately 600 cooperatives and 500 state farms. The number of peasants receiving actual property titles was small, 31,500 during 1959 and 1960. Three to four times as many peasants nonetheless gained access to land without formal property rights.[23] Labor conditions within nationalized plantations improved with the granting of certain protections that did not exist before 1959, most notably guaranteed twelve-month employment, which sharply contrasted with the historic practice of laying off most sugarcane workers during the extended "dead season" following the end of each harvest.

The Colossal Neighbor to the North

Developments in Cuba met with skepticism in Washington. The U.S. government's distrust of Castro dated back to his early days in the Sierra Maestra. U.S. authorities viewed him as an unpredictable, authoritarian figure who harbored anti-U.S. sentiments. After having supported Batista's illegitimate government for six years, however, the United States was morally obliged to recognize Castro as head of Cuba's new government. It did so almost immediately, on January 7.

Early U.S. policy toward the new government can best be summarized as a combination of apparent harmony, vigilant concern, and reluctant restraint. Exchanges between the two nations were mostly cordial during the first few days of revolution. In a conciliatory move, the Eisenhower administration recalled Ambassador Earl E. T. Smith, who had been a strong supporter of Batista, replacing him with Philip W. Bonsal, a career diplomat of more liberal inclinations. One of the reasons for the United States' relative restraint was the lingering damage its international image suffered in 1954 for supporting a military coup in Guatemala primarily to protect the corporate interests of the United Fruit Company. The CIA had backed the coup against leftist president Jacobo Arbenz in retaliation for his reformist measures, most saliently his land reform initiative, which included the nationalization by purchase of vast extensions of land belonging to the United Fruit Company.[24] While the backlash from the heavy-handed U.S. intervention in Guatemala may have made the United States somewhat gun-shy toward Cuba, it taught Guevara, who had been in Guatemala at the time, and other revolutionaries that the survival of the revolution required the elimination of the Batista-era military and police forces that could be used to ignite a U.S.-backed counterrevolutionary war.

The flurry of executions of Batistianos taking place in Cuba provoked accusations from the United States. Some members of Congress protested and proposed sanctions, including banning travel to the island. *Time* magazine's January 26 edition denounced the mounting violence of the revolutionary government. The story, which included gruesome photographs of executions by firing squad, quoted Castro's defiant response to U.S. criticism: "If the Americans do not like what is happening, they can send in the Marines; then there will be 200,000 gringos dead." The White House, while disapproving of the executions, kept silent on the matter to avoid appearing hostile to the new government. As early as March, however, the U.S. National Security Council reached the conclusion that Castro had to be removed from office, and the sooner the better.[25]

Castro visited the United States in April 1959 as a guest of the American Association of Newspaper Editors. He arrived in New York City accompanied by several top officials and businessmen, an interesting mix of bearded warriors in fatigues and clean-cut gentlemen clad in tailored business suits. On the 19th, in Washington, D.C., Castro met with Vice President Richard M. Nixon. Eisenhower's decision to skip town for a golfing trip was indeed an insult to Castro and his delegation. The meeting with Nixon did not go well. Castro came out visibly angry, complaining that "this man has spent the whole time scolding me." Following his conversation with Castro, Nixon expressed uncertainty about the rebel leader's ideology. He was "either incredibly naïve about Communism," Nixon said, "or under Communist discipline."[26] Nixon was either incredibly ignorant about Cubans and their deep sense of honor or knew exactly what he was doing.

The subject of U.S. economic assistance was of paramount importance to Cuba. Castro did not wish to come across as a beggar, however. As he told one of his top economic advisors, "I don't want this trip to be like that of other Latin American leaders who always come to the U.S. to ask for money." While some have speculated that Castro rejected an offer of U.S. economic support, there is no indication that any such offer was made.[27] If that was, indeed, the case, it was an incredibly costly missed opportunity and mistake on the part of the Eisenhower administration. Unbeknown to U.S. authorities, and apparently even to his older brother, Raúl Castro had requested Soviet economic aid, and on April 23, only four days after the ill-starred Castro-Nixon meeting, the Soviet Presidium approved the funding.[28] The Rubicon may have very well been crossed on that fateful week in April 1959, farther extending the long ninety miles of the Florida Straits.

Despite Ambassador Bonsal's best efforts and the United States' ostensibly conciliatory approach, Cuba-U.S. relations quickly deteriorated, in great measure due to the wholesale confiscation of U.S. properties, including plantations, ranches, mines, banks, and other businesses.

Another matter of serious concern to U.S. officials was Cuba's involvement in guerrilla activities beyond its borders. The revolutionary government began to train, arm, and sponsor guerrilla groups seeking to topple right-wing regimes in the Dominican Republic, Haiti, Nicaragua, and Guatemala. Before the end of 1959, Guevara had spearheaded the creation of a "Special Missions" section. Directed by Manuel Piñeiro Losada, the unit coordinated and aided guerrilla efforts around the globe.[29] Castro was vocal in his support for aggressive internationalism. In July 1960, he grandiosely proclaimed that Cuba's example would "turn the Andes into the Sierra Maestra of the American Continent."[30]

Reflective of the desire of revolutionary leaders to distance Cuba from

U.S. culture, particularly its consumerism, Castro banned fellow *barbudo* Santa Claus, whom he denounced as representative of imperialism, before the end of 1959. *Bohemia* magazine, which was now controlled by the government, later published a cartoon that presented Santa Claus in a fiendish light, carrying two different gift bags, one marked "colored," the other one "white." Another cartoon on the same page represented Cuban Christmas: a smiling tree holding a rifle and capped with a Guevara beret.[31]

Demise of the Moderates and Rise of the Fidelista Communists

U.S. political leaders must have felt that the first year of the revolution validated their concerns about Castro as the government gradually moved toward a radical, authoritarian, and socialist path. "Bad cops" Guevara and Raúl Castro continued to push a radical agenda marked by open hostility toward Cuba's political moderates and the United States and the fostering of closer ties to the PSP. Paradoxically, leaders of the Soviet-aligned PSP favored a more moderate course and recognized the importance of maintaining a strong national bourgeoisie. Communists were disciplined, and the party's leaders had not been marred by scandal and corruption. They also enjoyed established relations with the Soviet Union, an increasingly valuable asset as relations between Cuba and the United States soured.

Throughout this period, the master triangulator cunningly applied divisive strategies to purge the military, the cabinet, labor unions, the media, the Church, political parties, and other institutions; first from remnants of the old regime such as labor leaders loyal to Mujal, then moderate voices such as Miró Cardona and Humberto Sorí Marín, later anticommunist revolutionaries the likes of Huber Matos and David Salvador, and finally non-Fidelista members of the PSP, Aníbal Escalante, for example.

In the summer of 1959, Castro's position of apparent neutrality between the M-26-7 and the PSP tilted to the point that he no longer tolerated criticism of the integration of communists into the revolution and pitted the mostly moderate M-26-7 against the PSP and the official cabinet against the radical shadow government. When President Urrutia questioned and publicly denounced communist infiltration, Castro maneuvered to force his resignation: on July 17, Castro resigned from the premiership, and that evening he unleashed a virulent four-hour-long televised attack against Urrutia in which he explained that due to serious differences, they could no longer work together. This choreographed resignation accomplished its intended goal of mobilizing Fidelista crowds that angrily called for Urrutia to resign. "*¡Paredón! ¡Paredón!*, chanted a mob gathered in front of the presidential palace." Disguised as a milkman, Urrutia escaped and went into exile in New York. Castro designated another unthreatening individual, cabinet member Osvaldo Dorticós, as new president. A few days later, on the occasion of a mass gathering of peasants gathered in Havana to celebrate the anniversary of the Moncada attack, Raúl Castro prodded the crowd to shout pleas for his brother's return to power. In no time, Fidel Castro assented and his brother proudly announced: "Cubans, Fidel Castro has decided to withdraw his resignation." The crowd exploded in jubilation.[32]

Despite their official titles, neither Urrutia nor Dorticós nor Chief of Staff of the Armed Forces Cienfuegos were the revolution's "second man"; that distinction belonged to Castro's baby-faced and pony-tailed brother Raúl. From the very beginning, Castro viewed his brother as his most loyal follower and heir. After the triumph of the revolution, Raúl became Fidel's life insurance of sorts. In the elder Castro's words, "If something ever happen[s] to me, Raúl will take my place." The younger Castro enjoyed that role; "If something happened to Fidel," he once reportedly threatened, "the Almendares River will be called the Red River; blood rather than water will flow through it."[33] The younger Castro officially became Fidel Castro's legal successor when he became deputy prime minister in 1962. Guevara, meanwhile, because of his enormous popularity, his ideological contributions to the course of the revolution, and his international connections, was the undisputed "third man."

Protesting against the increasing presence of communists in the armed forces, Air Force chief Pedro Luis Díaz Lanz defected in July. This was one of the first of many defections of men and women who had fought alongside Castro. Comandante Matos, who opposed growing communist presence and influence in the military, tendered his resignation on October 19, three days after the appointment of Raúl Castro as head of the newly established Ministry of Revolutionary Armed Forces (FAR), an appointment that abolished the post of Chief of Staff of the Armed Forces held by Cienfuegos.[34] A hero of the Rebel Army, Matos was very popular among his troops and throughout Camagüey Province, the region over which he took military charge. Castro dispatched Cienfuegos, along with Comandante Ramiro Valdés, to arrest Matos. Without resistance, Matos was detained, along with forty officers of the legendary Column 9. As a courtesy to his longtime friend, Cienfuegos did not handcuff him. Following a kangaroo court proceeding in which Castro directly intervened, Matos received a 20-year sentence for treason and sedition.[35]

A few days after Matos's arrest, Cienfuegos, who had reluctantly arrested his friend and had publicly stated that the revolution was not communist, perished in what the government described as an airplane crash caused by bad weather. The tragedy was shrouded in mystery, however, and neither the bodies nor the wreckage were ever found. The suspicious nature of his disappearance was fueled by a FAR report that Cienfuegos had been found alive, followed by another report denying the veracity of that information. Since then there has been much speculation about the truth about Cienfuegos's death.[36]

The radicalization of the cabinet continued. In the immediate aftermath of Matos's arrest, Manuel Ray and Faustino Pérez resigned. Osmany Cienfuegos, Camilo's older brother and a longtime card-carrying member of the PSP, replaced Ray as minister of public works, and navy officer Rolando Díaz Astaraín, who was married to Vilma Espín's sister, also joined the cabinet, replacing Rufo López-Fresquet as minister of finance. World-renowned economist Pazos was replaced in November by none other than Guevara, who lacked the most elemental knowledge about finances. By the end of the year, Hart was the only original cabinet member still holding his post.[37]

By the beginning of 1960, communists held important positions within the military and they had a strong presence in most ministries and within the powerful INRA. Tensions were apparent, however, between two generations. On one side was the old guard, doctrinaire, pro-Moscow faction, few of whose members—if any—had participated in the struggle against Batista; salient among them were Lázaro Peña, Carlos Rafael Rodríguez, and Aníbal Escalante. On the other side was the younger Fidelista communist faction, including Raúl Castro, Alfredo Guevara, and Flavio Bravo, among others.[38]

In the ongoing process of centralizing power, the revolutionary government also subjugated or eliminated the major institutions of civil society—the media, professional organizations, civic groups, unions, and churches. Just weeks after taking control, Castro castigated and demanded an apology from the publishers of the politico-satirical weekly *Zig-Zag* for an unbecoming editorial cartoon bearing his likeness.[39] Beginning in January 1960, the government systematically targeted the independent media. It started by imposing *coletillas*, brief comments and refutations that followed editorials and news stories. A typical *coletilla* read: "This article has been published in consideration of freedom of the press. However, the workers of this newspaper warn that this information does not reflect the truth, nor does it comply with the most fundamental journalistic practices." Editors and newscasters deemed hostile or just uncooperative endured harassment and eventually had no option but to resign. One by one, the regime took over or closed down all independent media. Wholesale closing of newspapers continued in 1960 with *Avance, El País, El Diario de la Marina*, and nearly all the rest. *Bohemia*, whose editor, Miguel Ángel Quevedo, had been a thorn on the side of Batista's regime, succumbed to government control in July. Television and radio stations endured the same fate, culminating with the nationalization of the popular CMQ Radio and TV in September. Only the PSP's *Hoy*, a nationalized *El Mundo*, and the M-26-7's *Revolución* survived.[40]

The government's assault on civil society included private institutions and independent associations. Immediately upon taking power, Castro closed several private universities. Later in 1959, he interfered in FEU elections in favor of comandante Cubela, a Guevara and Raúl Castro loyalist. By mid-1960, the regime had gained control of the previously autonomous University of Havana, imposing communist intellectual Juan Marinello as its new president and establishing a new governing board, despite the protest resignations of two-thirds of the faculty. A new university law of January 1962 ended university autonomy and the right of students to protest and go on strike. By then, university admission depended on political criteria.[41] In mid-1960, armed militias stormed the offices of the Bar Association and assumed control over that venerable institution. Months later, the government shut down two other powerful organizations: the Asociación Nacional de Hacendados (Sugarcane Planters Association) and the Asociación de Colonos (Sugarcane Growers Association).[42]

The revolutionary government also co-opted organized labor by applying triangulation strategies, first in January 1959, when M-26-7 labor leader David Salvador drove Eusebio Mujal's partisans out of the CTC leadership. Tensions soon flared up between M-26-7 union members and the PSP minority, and the two groups' respective newspapers, *Revolución* and *Hoy*, fired accusations against each other. At first, Castro seemed to favor the M-26-7, but he gradually revealed his support for PSP labor leaders. Castro ordered that the union's leadership be split evenly between both groups, in spite of the fact that M-26-7 workers accounted for the lion's share of the membership. In early 1960, communist labor leaders gained control of one union after another. By March 1960, Salvador was forced to resign; later that year, he was apprehended as he attempted to leave the island illegally and was sentenced to thirty years in prison. By 1961, communists held complete control over the CTC. That year, under the leadership of communist leader Lázaro Peña, who had served as General Secretary of the CTC (1939–47), the union was reorganized and renamed Central de Trabajadores de Cuba (Central Union of Cuban Workers). By then, the CTC had lost its autonomy and relinquished most fundamental workers' protections and rights, including the right to go on strike.[43]

Finally, the revolutionary state took on the Church. While not as powerful as its counterparts in the rest of Latin America, the Catholic Church was Cuba's strongest and largest nongovernmental entity.[44] The church's original stance vis-à-vis the revolution was mostly conciliatory. In response to the revolution's increasing radicalism and growing preponderance of communists, however, the church hierarchy and laity began to manifest open opposition. In August 1960, Cuba's bishops issued a pastoral letter in which they underscored the incompatibility of Catholicism and communism. Later that year, they issued an open letter to Castro that priests read from the pulpits. It denounced communist political indoctrination, systematic abuses of the clergy, the disruption of religious services, and Castro's insulting priests as *botelleros* (holders of no-show state jobs). A number of clergymen were detained after reading the letter, including Bishop of Santiago Pérez Serantes; this was the man who had intervened to save Castro's life seven years before. Catholic lay activists also manifested their opposition in mass rallies and marches. To the chant "*¡Fidel! ¡Fidel!*" they replied, "*¡Caridad! ¡Caridad!*"—referring to Cuba's patron, the Virgin of la Caridad del Cobre. Protestant denominations numbering some 150,000 adherents, for their part, mostly accommodated themselves to the new realities, generally supporting the revolutionary regime. Some U.S. pastors, however, were imprisoned. While the revolutionary government did not openly persecute Afro-Cuban religious practices, it viewed them as backward and tried to limit their visibility and influence. The Jewish community, for its part, was estimated at 15,000; over 90 percent of them left Cuba shortly after the revolution began.[45]

Communist-majority dominance in the revolutionary power structure was institutionalized through the founding of Organizaciones Revolucionarias Integradas Integrated Revolutionary Organizations (ORI). ORI, which became the only legal political party, was the precursor to the Cuban Communist Party. Created in July 1961 through the merging of the

M-26-7, the PSP, and the DR, ORI came under the leadership of old-guard communist Aníbal Escalante, the Soviet Union's point man in Havana. Now that the M-27-6 and DR had been disbanded through consolidation, the Maximum Leader proceeded to weaken the old communists. In March 1962, Castro accused old-guard communist Escalante of sectarianism for having allotted a disproportionate amount of power to the PSP within ORI. This was an odd accusation, given that Castro himself had used that very faction to push M-26-7 union leaders out of the CTC. In 1963, Castro forced Escalante, who had been a contender for the unofficial distinction of the revolution's "third man," to step down and banished him to a diplomatic post in Czechoslovakia. Veteran communist leader Blas Roca was also demoted at the time. Other old-guard communists maneuvered to survive politically by adapting to Fidelismo. The most salient example was Carlos Rafael Rodríguez, whose loyalty to Castro earned him the important post of INRA president.[46]

State repression played a critical role in the government's suppression of the opposition and the consolidation of centralized state power. Responsibility for Cuba's state security fell under the umbrella of the Ministry of the Interior (MININT), created in June 1961. Headed by comandante Ramiro Valdés, the MININT included the Directorio General de Inteligencia (General Directorate of Intelligence), whose primary task was gathering intelligence, carrying out counterintelligence operations, and supporting guerrillas abroad. Manuel Piñeiro Losada (aka Barba Roja [Red Beard]) was assigned to direct the MININT's dreaded domestic espionage unit, known as the G-2. By the end of 1960, Cuba held approximately 15,000 to 20,000 political prisoners, a number that swelled to 100,000 in April 1961. The official number of political executions had reached 550 by the end of June 1959; higher estimates from other sources claim three times as many executions for the same period and a total of 2,000 by early 1961.[47]

Mass Organizations and Social Goals

While the state eliminated or limited the freedom of the old institutions of civil society, it developed new revolutionary institutions. Upon the triumph of the revolution, Cubans took to the streets in support of Castro and the new government: tens of thousands gathered for large rallies in plazas, stadiums, or wherever the Maximum Leader convened them. The populace experienced a special bond with Castro, who made them feel as if power was in their hands. It was decision making by acclamation. He maintained that the revolution had replaced the previous "pseudo-democracy" with what he described as "direct government by the people."[48] New mass organizations were created to serve as vehicles of communication and collaboration between the state and its citizens and to play key roles in the implementation of numerous social programs.

The first mass organization was the Milicias Nacionales Revolucionarias (National Revolutionary Militias), created in October 1959. Within a few months, its ranks included 200,000 citizen-soldiers who were trained to combat any challenge to the revolution. In January 1960, the Asociación de Jóvenes Rebeldes (Association of Rebel Youth) emerged; two years later, it merged with the youth wings of the PSP and the DR and was renamed the Unión de Jóvenes Comunistas (Young Communists Union). It became a highly selective feeder organization for the future Communist Party. The biggest and among the most powerful of all mass organizations, the Federación de Mujeres Cubanas (Federation of Cuban Women, FMC), was established in August, following the forced disbanding of nearly 1,000 individual women's organizations. Castro charged Vilma Espín, who had recently married his brother, Raúl, with the task of creating this mass women's organization. She presided over the FMC from its inception until her death in July 2007. Over the next decades, the FMC played an important role in the mobilization of women for various government initiatives in education, health, and volunteer work. Its primary task, however, was to incorporate women into the workforce. The federation also served as a vehicle for women to voice their views on a variety of issues ranging from child care to health matters to expanded employment opportunities.[49]

The Comités de Defensa de la Revolución (Committees for the Defense of the Revolution, CDRs) emerged in September 1960. These neighborhood organizations served primarily to protect the revolution from foreign and domestic enemies. Its members were charged with monitoring suspected counterrevolutionaries and those who refused to integrate themselves into the revolution. CDRs also played social and political roles, such as harnessing support for the regime and its social programs. By 1963, according to government estimates, 1.5 million Cubans belonged to their local CDR.[50] Yet another mass organization was the Asociación Nacional de Agricultores Pequeños (National Association of Small Farmers, ANAP), formed in May 1961. Even schoolchildren had a mass organization of their own, the Unión de Pioneros (Union of Pioneers).[51]

One of the primary tasks of the mass organizations was providing so-called voluntary labor to help build the revolution. Guevara established the *domingos rojos* (red Sundays), during which volunteers spent part of the day working on agricultural or construction projects. Guevara also introduced the concept of "socialist emulation," a healthy form of "fraternal competition" among workers, who supposedly no longer aspired to the traditional monetary rewards of capitalism but instead for social rewards such as public recognition, medals, plaques, and certificates. In a 1962 cane cutters' emulation awards ceremony, for example, Guevara celebrated the exemplary accomplishment of two cane cutters from Matanzas: José Martín Alayón, who cut 800,000 pounds of sugarcane in fifty-six days, and Reynaldo Castro Yedar, who singlehandedly chopped down 1.4 million pounds. Both workers extended their calloused hands to receive their awards as fellow workers filled the hall with thunderous applause.[52] This kind of recognition came to be known as "moral incentives," which I discuss at length in chapter 3. Guevara's ideas about volunteerism, sacrifice, and socialist emulation were closer to the model of the Chinese Revolution than to orthodox Soviet Marxism, which proscribed the continuation of capitalistic rewards—"material incentives"—during the prolonged process of constructing a communist society.[53]

Since not everyone responded to nonmaterial rewards with the same degree of enthusiasm, soft coercion and social pressures were often applied. Vagrancy and absenteeism were publicly scorned as counterrevolutionary attitudes. Guevara also prescribed "compulsive measures" to ensure productivity: he had the dubious distinction of creating the first forced-labor camps, which were named in honor of his deceased friend Camilo Cienfuegos.[54]

Beginning early in 1959, the revolution set forth an ambitious, progressive legislative agenda. Its primary goal was the extension of education, health care, and other social services to the masses, particularly those segments of society most neglected by previous governments: peasants and the urban poor. Guiding the government's social agenda was the desire to redistribute wealth and provide access to services in a more egalitarian way among the entire population and the different regions and between urban centers and the countryside.

This far-reaching plan for social transformation required a profound restructuring of the economy and the eradication of an economic and political relationship that revolutionaries perceived to be at the root of Cuba's persistent poverty and dependency: the production of one product, sugar, for one market, the United States. Expressions of "sucrophobia" abounded. Shortly before the triumph of the revolution, Guevara stated that all Cubans were slaves to sugarcane, "an umbilical condition that binds us to the northern market."[55]

"The persistent plantation" and its bitter social and economic by-products had long been the target of progressive intellectuals. The first modern systematic analysis of the ill effects of the sugar monocrop was Ramiro Guerra's *Sugar and Society in the Caribbean* (1927). Better known yet is Fernando Ortiz's *Cuban Counterpoint* (1940), with its characterization of sugar as a bitter fruit deceptively wrapped in sweetness, the source of Cuba's chronic misfortunes: slavery, latifundia (large land units), a rigid social hierarchy, dependency, colonialism, neocolonialism, and dictatorship. Sugar, Ortiz concluded, was essentially un-Cuban.[56] Moreover, Ortiz and other scholars have underscored the impact of sugar on Cuban culture as manifested in enduring values, attitudes, and practices forged in cane fields, sugarhouses, planters' mansions, and barracoons.

The revolutionary government thus focused considerable energy on transforming Cuban agriculture, consequently naming 1960 the Year of Agrarian Reform. Early economic plans included the diversification of agriculture and the expansion of manufacturing to decrease dependence on imported foodstuffs and manufactured goods. Land previously devoted to sugarcane was planted with a variety of food crops for domestic consumption; by 1963, sugarcane acreage had fallen 25 percent from its 1958 level. Revolutionary economists planned import substitution initiatives, which had successfully spurred industrialization in other Latin American countries such as Argentina and Mexico. Minister of Industries Guevara envisioned that in a few years Cuba would produce a wide range of manufactured goods, including automobiles and cheeses that according to him would rival Europe's finest.[57] During the first three years of the revolution, Cuba's economy grew at a modest average yearly rate of 2.5 percent. Agricultural production in general rose 9 percent from 1959 to 1961, reaching a peak in 1960–61.[58]

The government made social matters a priority. Much investment and energy went into education. By May 1959, the percentage of children ages six to fourteen not attending school had been cut in half. Before the year was over, officials could boast that the government had built 3,000 schools, hired 7,000 new teachers, and enrolled 300,000 new students.[59] Education also expanded in a variety of nontraditional ways, such as through the creation of schools for peasants and former domestic servants, even a vocational training program for rehabilitated prostitutes. Responding to pressures from the FMC, in 1961, the government established low-cost daycare centers. It also set up Schools of Revolutionary Instruction to offer ideological training in three-month-long courses. By then, communists controlled the main branches of the Ministry of Education and had established a national commission to rewrite school textbooks.[60]

The Literacy Campaign of 1961 was the most ambitious and successful education program of the early years of the revolution. Beginning in January, an estimated 271,000 individuals, ranging from experienced teachers to students as young as 10 years old, were mobilized for the eradication of illiteracy. The literacy campaign was a huge success. According to government statistics, by the end of 1961 the illiteracy rate had fallen from 25 to 4 percent.

This unparalleled accomplishment also served the regime's effort to indoctrinate the population. Those being alphabetized learned to read by reciting sentences such as "The young and the old, united, pledge with Fidel: to defend Cuba. We will never be defeated." *Alfabetizadores* used the teaching supplement *¡Cumpliremos!*, an ideologically charged text that denounced the enemies of the revolution: "American electricity, telephone and oil monopolies exploited the Cuban people in a terrible way and year after year siphoned tens of millions of profit dollars away from Cuba," and highlighted the accomplishments of the revolution, real and imagined: "tortures and crimes are a thing of the past," "the people have weapons now," "the freedom to say the truth in the press," "the revolution is industrializing Cuba," and so on. *Alfabeticemos*, a manual for teachers, included a glossary with terms and definitions such as "*AP*. Associated Press: North American news service agency in service of Yankee imperialist interests"; "*Freedom of the Press*: The right to freely express thoughts through the press. The Cuban Revolution guarantees the freedom of the press insofar that it does not attack the people's interests"; and "*K K K*. Ku Klux Klan. North American racist organization that persecutes black citizens."[61]

The expansion of health services was yet another social priority. New health care facilities sprung up in poor, rural, and remote locations. In order to address disparities in the provision of medical care between rural and urban areas, the government established rural health services in January 1960. Outpatient clinics mushroomed throughout the country to provide a variety of general and specialized medical services. The number of public hospitals and hospital beds doubled between 1959 and 1961. Around half of Cuba's physicians left between 1959 and 1962, however, presenting a major obstacle to the goal of expanding the delivery of quality health care. Contagious diseases actually spread at a higher rate during the first few years of the revolution. The rate of tuberculosis, for example, almost doubled from 1959 to 1964. Mortality rates rose as well: infant mortality increased from 33.4 deaths per 1,000 infants in 1958 to 41.5 in 1962.[62]

Shortage and inadequacy of housing had plagued Havana and other cities for a long time. While the Urban Reform Law cut rents by as much as half, demand far outpaced the supply of housing units. Rural dwellers migrating to urban centers by the tens of thousands and the baby boom of 1959–62—the so-called *generación de Fidel*—further exacerbated the housing shortage. The government established a self-help housing program in 1960 that aimed to eradicate urban slums.[63]

Progress toward the goal of eradicating racial and gender inequality and discrimination was one of the notable social accomplishments of the period. The expansion of public health, educational, and other services improved circumstances and expanded opportunities for most blacks. Besides its concerted efforts to combat a lingering culture of racial discrimination, the government desegregated beaches, private clubs, and social associations.

Revolution and Culture

In its early years, the revolution also attended to the cultural needs of the populace, helping to promote creative energy and fostering a renewed enthusiasm for the arts and literature. Numerous exiled and émigré artists and intellectuals returned to Cuba, among them Alejo Carpentier from Caracas, Nicolás Guillén from Buenos Aires, and Alicia Alonso from New York. Painters, authors, dancers, playwrights, filmmakers, and musicians found unprecedented support as the revolutionary government created and generously funded new cultural institutions.

Among the many cultural institutions established in 1959 was the Consejo Nacional de Cultura (National Council of Culture). The Instituto Cubano del Arte e Industria Cinematográficos (Cuban Institute of Cinematographic Arts and Industry, ICAIC) played a vital role in revitalizing filmmaking, and it soon monopolized the making and distribution of documentaries and films. Most new films supported the revolutionary agenda—some trenchantly so. The short animated film *La prensa seria*, for example, denounced news coverage by independent newspapers, while the animated short *El Maná* chastised a fictional peasant for refusing to work and yet expecting to be fed. ICAIC elevated the making of movie posters to high artistic levels, drawing worldwide admiration. Also established in 1959 were the National Theater; the National Symphony Orchestra; the National Ballet, directed by internationally acclaimed prima ballerina Alicia Alonso; and Casa de las Américas, a cultural center and publishing house for the study and promotion of Latin American culture.[64]

The revolution also sparked a literary and publishing boom. In 1959, the state created a national press to publish various classic works of literature, among them a low-cost four-volume set of *Don Quijote* made of recycled sugarcane bagasse. One of the most vibrant and influential new cultural creations was *Lunes de Revolución*, the weekly cultural supplement of *Revolución*, edited by Guillermo Cabrera Infante. Both *Revolución* and *Lunes de Revolución* played a leading role in promoting Cuban and international art and culture. In 1960, Casa de las Américas began publication of the journal *Casa de las Américas*.[65]

The honeymoon between the intelligentsia and the state came to an abrupt end in 1961, however, when arts commissars, many of them doctrinaire communists, openly began to scorn the artistic establishment as bourgeois while insisting on the adoption of the exotic and insipid aesthetics of socialist realism, which put artistic expression in service of the revolution. Open confrontation erupted in June in what came to be known as the "*P.M.* affair." ICAIC head Alfredo Guevara denounced the documentary *P.M.* as demeaning to the revolution and lacking in revolutionary content. In essence, the controversial freestyle black-and-white documentary was a collage of scenes of black *Habaneros* drinking and dancing in somewhat shady night clubs. Because *Revolución* had helped fund the film, it became embroiled in the controversy.[66] Castro intervened in the dispute at a meeting of artists and intellectuals, where he uttered a vague but widely quoted admonition to the intellectuals: "Within the revolution, everything; against the revolution, nothing."[67] Soon thereafter, government authorities closed down *Lunes de Revolución*, and a few months later established the official Unión Nacional de Artistas y Escritores de Cuba (National Union of Cuban Artists and Writers, UNEAC) with Afro-Cuban poet Nicolás Guillén as its president.

Some of the first artists and intellectuals to endure official persecution were gay men, who were particularly targeted because they did not fit the stereotypical macho image of the model revolutionary, that of a virile militiaman, ready for strenuous fieldwork and the rigors and dangers of war.

To be sure, homophobia was not new to Cuba, where laws against homosexuality had been on the books for decades. Perhaps the most emblematic victim of the regime's homophobia was writer and playwright Virgilio Piñera. Despite his unquestionable revolutionary credentials, Piñera was accused of treason and thrown in jail. Chief domestic spy Ramiro Valdés responded to protestations by vowing to "finish off homosexuals and all that degeneracy."[68]

On balance, state involvement in literary and artistic creation and promotion was a mixed blessing. On the one hand, it created enormous opportunities; on the other, it permitted the government to monopolize and censor artistic production. One notable accomplishment of the revolution was the wide dissemination of the arts among the masses, not only as audiences but also as creators and performers participating in numerous local cultural centers, dance and theater companies, and other artistic endeavors.

Marching toward Socialism against the Backdrop of the Cold War

Nineteen-sixty was a year of profound transformation as Cuba moved decisively toward the establishment of a socialist system by nationalizing large estates and foreign and domestic businesses and redistributing land, properties, and wealth. Consequently, it was also a year when Cuba-U.S. diplomatic and economic relations deteriorated to the point of breaking down. As antagonism between the two countries increased, the rebel island cultivated friendly relations and stronger economic ties with the Soviet Union, China, and other socialist nations. Mastering the art of triangulation strategies in the context of the Cold War between the United States and the USSR served Cuba well, guaranteeing extraordinary Soviet support. Given the global polarization of the time, this was almost the default course for Cuba to follow. By the spring of 1960, it had become evident that the U.S. government was not only turning a blind eye to the deployment of Cuban counterrevolutionary forces and the shipping of weapons to Cuba from U.S. territory by belligerent exiles, it was actually providing intelligence and material aid to island-based counterrevolutionary organizations.[69]

The explosion of the French ship *La Coubre* in Havana Bay on March 4, 1960, was a pivotal episode in the breakdown of Cuba-U.S. relations. Laden with a huge cargo of Belgian-made ammunition, the ship blew up not far from where the famed USS *Maine* had exploded sixty-two years before. The explosion of *La Coubre* killed around 100 people, injuring another 200. The victims of the disaster were laid to rest in Havana's splendid Colón Cemetery. On that occasion, Castro immortalized the slogan "Patria o Muerte" (Fatherland or Death).[70]

That same day, Alberto Korda took the iconic picture of Guevara that has been recognized as the world's most famous photograph. The Argentine revolutionary appears pensive, with a melancholy gaze. His face puffed up from anti-asthma medication, he is crowned by his signature beret. An unkempt, dark mane frames the rebel's round face while his sparse moustache hangs over and around his mouth. Korda's photograph has since been reproduced thousands of times on coins, bills, pins, posters, T-shirts, and murals and in ads for everything from Smirnoff vodka and Converse tennis shoes to cigars and pizza.[71]

Given the unremitting wave of CIA-backed sabotage actions, Castro had a basis for blaming the United States for the explosion of *La Coubre*. Whatever the case, a few days after the tragic event, CIA director Allen Dulles provided Eisenhower with a plan for toppling the Castro regime. The president approved it immediately. It prescribed a propaganda campaign, the arming of the internal opposition, and economic sanctions, including discontinuing oil shipments and terminating sugar purchases. Some of the anti-Castro plots were outright bizarre, including a plan to place depilatory chemicals near the rebel leader so that his beard would fall off and creating an imaginary counterrevolutionary leader with exploits similar to those of the TV character El Zorro.[72]

In February 1960, Soviet deputy premier Anastas Mikoyan visited Cuba on the occasion of a Soviet trade exhibition. While in Havana, he negotiated a trade accord whereby the USSR agreed to purchase one million tons of Cuban sugar per year and provide the island nation with loans and crude oil shipments at reduced prices. The agreed-upon price for sugar was the current market rate of 3 cents per pound; this was significantly lower, however, than the preferential price of 5.35 cents per pound previously paid by the United States. In May, both countries established diplomatic relations, and soon thereafter, the first shipments of Soviet petroleum arrived in Havana. Later that year, a trade delegation led by Guevara visited China, where it secured a $60 million loan and China's pledge to purchase one million tons of sugar per year.[73]

Guevara ordered U.S. and British oil companies to refine Soviet oil imports, but they refused to do so following directives from the Eisenhower administration. In response, on June 30, Cuba nationalized its refining facilities and the processing of Soviet crude began. The United States retaliated by canceling the remnant of Cuba's 1960 sugar quota, which consisted of 700,000 tons.[74]

That summer marked the beginning of the socialization of the Cuban economy. Without much fanfare, Guevara announced in July that the revolution was "Marxist." Millions of acres of land had already been taken over by INRA. An escalating tit-for-tat ensued. In July, the government nationalized twenty-six American-owned firms, including the Cuban Electric Company, the Cuban Telephone Company, and several sugar plantations. In September, Chase Manhattan Bank, First National City Bank, and other U.S. banks met the same fate.[75] Numerous other foreign and domestic companies were confiscated in October 1960. One of them was Bacardí Corporation, whose owners must have wished that they had never supported Castro or welcomed his victory so effusively with an ad in the pages of Revolución less than two years before.[76]

The United States responded with the imposition of a partial trade embargo on October 19. Shipments of medicines, medical equipment, and nonsubsidized food products were still legal, however. Days later, Cuba seized 166 remaining American-owned businesses. On January 2, 1961, Cuba demanded that the United States reduce its diplomatic personnel to eleven. After consulting with president-elect John F. Kennedy, Eisenhower broke diplomatic relations with Cuba on the next day.[77]

In order to be fully understood, the increasingly radical course of the revolution must be seen within the larger geopolitical context of the Cold War. By the time Batista was ousted, tensions between the United States and the Soviet Union were explosively high and two major blocs of nations had formed, gravitating around each of the two superpowers. China was another power to be reckoned with, particularly because of its independence from and brewing tensions with the Soviet Union. While the Cuban Revolution was not imported from or imposed by the Soviet Union, as was the case in Poland, Hungary, and Czechoslovakia, the radical Cuban path to socialism would have not been possible—and certainly would not have lasted—without Soviet moral, economic, and military support. Castro in all likelihood would have not risked catastrophic U.S. economic sanctions, such as the cancellation of the sugar quota or the imposition of a trade embargo, had he not counted on the support of the Soviet Union and China. The gamble paid off. When the Eisenhower administration terminated the sugar quota, the Soviets immediately agreed to purchase the entire amount. The Chinese followed suit, purchasing another half-million tons.[78]

Within less than two years, the Cuban economy was extensively socialized and substantially integrated into the economies of the Soviet Union and the socialist camp. Before the end of 1961, the Cuban state controlled 85 percent of all production, the balance consisting mostly of crops produced by small independent farmers. By the following year, 60 percent of all Cuban workers were state employees. The Soviet Union and other socialist nations fully replaced the United States as Cuba's main trading partners. Whereas in 1959 Cuba's northerly neighbor absorbed 74 percent of its exports and delivered 65 percent of its imports, only two years later socialist nations received 73 percent of Cuba's exports and shipped 70 percent of its imports.[79]

The Opposition: Flight or Fight

The increasingly radical course of the revolution generated internal opposition, particularly within the middle and upper-middle classes. Opponents had two alternatives—flight or fight—and they began exercising both options early in 1959. One explanation for the rapid consolidation of Castro's government is that it was able to "export" to the United States most of the individuals who might have resisted and combated the revolution. Only ninety miles away, the United States served yet again—as it had since the 1800s—as a haven for the opposition and for political dissenters. The same proximity that made exile in the United States easy allowed armed exile groups to launch attacks, be they annexationist filibusterer expeditions in the late 1840s and early 1850s, anti-Spanish troop deployments in the 1890s, and later counterrevolutionary hit-and-run amphibious attacks in 1959 and beyond.

Whereas the very first exiles were primarily individuals with ties to the Batista regime, the ranks of the disaffected soon expanded as the government became more autocratic and veered further to the left and its decrees and legislation hurt an increasing number of citizens. In 1959 and 1960, the upper and upper-middle classes, in particular, endured severe economic losses stemming from nationalization of rental housing units, large plots of land, factories, retail establishments, and other properties. Soon thereafter, the professional and managerial middle class became increasingly alienated by the nationalization of American-owned businesses, the rise of communist influences, the closing of religious and lay private schools, the erosion of civil and human rights, and the systematic harassment of those who refused to be integrated into the revolution.

The emigration that had begun as a trickle in 1959 had turned into a torrent by the third quarter of 1962. Almost 250,000 left the island between January 1959 and October 1962, the vast majority resettling in South Florida.[80] These exiles constituted the first wave of a first cohort of exiles that would eventually include others who left Cuba during the balance of the 1960s and 1970s. Seen as a whole, the first wave of exiles did not mirror the general population: they were better educated and earned much higher incomes than average Cubans did. City dwellers, whites, professionals, and white-collar workers were noticeably overrepresented. Sixty-two percent came from Havana and another 25 percent originated in other large cities. In addition, while in 1953 only 4 percent of Cubans had attained a high school degree, 34 percent of the exiles held such credentials.[81] This brain drain had serious repercussions for the island. During the first four years of the revolution, approximately half of all teachers and physicians departed. Engineers also emigrated in large numbers, moving the government to plead with them to stay home. Most architects left as well. Two-thirds of all accountants and 270 of 300 agronomists also left.[82]

The government and its supporters equated exile with treason. Those seeking to leave the island were derided as unpatriotic, bourgeois, *gusanos* (worms), and worse. In February 1960, the government issued a law confiscating the assets of all exiles. Those applying for exit visas immediately lost their jobs, and militiamen inventoried and later confiscated their possessions, down to the last teaspoon and cloth napkin. Not even wedding rings or family picture albums were spared. In her first novel, *Dreaming in Cuban*, Cuban-born writer Cristina García employed the intensely brutal metaphor of rape to dramatize the trauma of exile. As was customary, revolutionary militiamen took an inventory of all properties belonging to the family of one of the novel's protagonists, Lourdes Puente. The sense of violation felt during the confiscation of all her family's assets, including even the most private items, was accompanied by the actual knifepoint rape of Lourdes by one of two militiamen who served her with the confiscation documents.[83]

CDRs, government-controlled unions, and other government organizations carried out *actos de repudio*, the systematic harassment and taunting of families seeking to emigrate. Such humiliations included egging homes, chanting slogans and expletives, and, at times, physical assaults. Abuses continued all the way to the airport, where departing passengers were often subjected to grueling interrogations and strip searches. They could not take money or valuables with them, only a few personal items. A Cuban friend who left as a child by himself shared with me the traumatizing experience of having his toy airplane and train confiscated at the airport; half a century later, the militiaman's words still echo in his mind: "You will not need these where you are going."[84]

Following the agony of departure, Cuban exiles faced additional traumatic experiences as they settled in South Florida and other destinations. These included the shock of arrival in a different country with a different language and culture, the pain of separation from homeland and family, and the overnight loss of all material possessions and social status. While they were generally welcomed as refugees fleeing from a Cuba under increasing Soviet influence, many faced a hostile reception from some Florida residents. As political scientist María de los Ángeles Torres has pointed out, there was no shortage of rental signs that read "No Children, No Pets, No Cubans."[85]

In February 1961, the Miami Cuban Refugee Center opened its doors. By mid-June, 43,000 Cubans had registered there, receiving food, clothing, shelter, and medical services (figure 2.4). The Miami Catholic Welfare Bureau, for its part, provided meals and services to thousands of Cuban exiles.[86] One of the great ironies exiles confronted was the fact that while they had escaped a regime that sought to impose an egalitarian society, their resettlement abroad had some temporary equalizing effects of its own. Stories abound of exiled physicians washing dishes in cafeterias and engineers working as late-shift custodians. One often-repeated story is that of a formerly wealthy Cuban who had been a frequent guest at the luxurious Fontainebleau Hotel; upon arriving penniless in Miami, he found employment there as an elevator operator.

One of the most dramatic and painful chapters of the Cuban exodus was Operation Pedro Pan, through which over 14,000 unaccompanied minors were flown to Florida between December 1960 and October 1962. The operation was sparked by widespread rumors that the government intended to take over parental rights and send thousands of children to be educated in the Soviet Union. Monsignor Bryan O. Walsh led the Miami-based operation that provided temporary shelter for the arriving children, many of whom were resettled in other states in foster homes. While most of the Pedro Pan children found refuge in safe and caring foster families, a few endured abuse at the hands of those entrusted with their protection.

Figure 2.4. Cuban Refugee Program building in Miami, later named "Freedom Tower."

The ranks of Pedro Pan alumni include notable individuals such the musical couple Willy Chirino and Lissette Álvarez, the late artist Ana Mendieta, author Carlos Eire, scholar Miguel A. Bretos, and former U.S. senator Mel Martínez.[87]

Letters written by Pedro Pan children reflect mixed feelings about their experiences as exiles, which included cultural adaptation and cultural clashes, and their feelings about the future of their homeland. In a letter dated April 30, 1962, one child wrote about cultural differences: "I am trying to adapt and I am having a good time even though their customs are so different from ours. . . . Deep down inside they are not bad even though they believe us to be uncivilized, we who have enough to teach them!" Another Pedro Pan, F. González, writing from Marquette, Michigan, described the place as "wonderful," adding that they lived at the monsignor's house, where, believe it or not, "we are considered members of the high life here." From Denver, Colorado, another child wrote that he "only [got] sad and worried" when he thought "of the problem of our homeland, which is really huge now, and my whole life is over there." In a more pessimistic tone, another child wrote that he did not know "when Fidel is going to topple." "About this," he remarked, "I have a bad feeling that never, because he is very strong and every time I think of that I go crazy and so furious."[88]

While most exiles preferred to remain close to Cuba in the Miami area, the refugee program made a concerted effort to resettle a portion of them in other parts of the country. Over 130,000 were relocated outside of South Florida: 37,000 to New York, 19,000 to New Jersey, another 14,000 to California, 13,000 to Puerto Rico, and even one exile to frigid Alaska. While many of them returned to South Florida as soon as they could, others formed significant exile settlements in places such as Union City, New Jersey, and San Juan, Puerto Rico; thousands more gravitated to other countries, including Mexico, Canada, Spain, and Costa Rica, to name but a few.[89]

While some boarded airplanes, others mounted their horses. Armed opposition to the revolution began as soon as the rebels assumed power. The first counterrevolutionary organizations were conservative pro-Batista groups. In January 1959, from exile in New York, Castro's nemesis and former brother-in-law Rafael L. Díaz-Balart organized a Batistiano force called La Rosa Blanca. Another anti-Castro group, the Liga Anticomunista, organized a failed military invasion in the summer of 1959 with the support of Dominican tyrant Rafael L. Trujillo. Yet another counterrevolutionary force was Masferrer's infamous paramilitary organization, Los Tigres. This group engaged in numerous armed actions in 1959, including sabotage and the landing of vessels with counterrevolutionary forces from South Florida.[90]

Other opposition groups emerged, many of these under the leadership of former Castro allies. In the early part of 1960, two former revolutionary cabinet members organized Movimiento 30 de Noviembre, which derived its name from the failed Santiago insurrection led by Frank País in 1956. Two other former Castro government officials formed the Verde Olivo revolutionary group. The island was on horseback again.[91]

In the fall of 1960, peasants in the El Escambray mountain region or-ganized several guerrilla bands to fight the revolutionary government. Sparsely supplied by the CIA, these guerrillas faced unremitting attacks from militia troops with virtually unlimited weapons and reinforcements. The first cleanup operation in the so-called fight against the bandits be-gan in March 1961, when a massive army of 60,000 to 70,000 militia and regular forces pursued the rebels, whose numbers hovered at around 700. Some 500 were either captured or killed. The survivors regrouped under the leadership of Osvaldo Ramírez and continued fighting government forces.[92]

Meanwhile, anti-Castro exiles continued to work within existing or newly formed Miami-based paramilitary organizations. These included older movements, such as Agrupación Montecristi and the Triple A, and new ones, such as Antonio Varona's Movimiento de Rescate Revolucio-nario (Revolutionary Rescue Movement), the Movimiento Demócrata Cristiano (Christian Democratic Movement), and the Movimiento de Re-cuperación Revolucionaria (Revolutionary Recovery Movement). The CIA arranged for these five groups, all of which had ties to the disbanded Au-téntico Party, to coalesce under the banner of the Frente Revolucionario Democrático (Revolutionary Democratic Front) in June 1960.[93]

Storm over the Bay of Pigs

When Kennedy assumed the presidency in January 1961, he inherited an aggressive policy that included planning and executing numerous plots against Cuba, from supplying weapons and ammunition to counterrevo-lutionary rebels to assassination attempts against Castro and other revo-lutionary leaders. The most ambitious project was the training of exiles for a large-scale operation that eventually became the Bay of Pigs invasion, known in Cuba as Batalla de Girón.[94]

The CIA-trained and -armed exile force, named Brigade 2506, eventually numbered around 1,500 men. It included a wide array of recruits, ranging from former Batista soldiers and policemen (even some known torturers) to the sons of prodigiously wealthy families to the sons of prominent exile leaders, such as Varona and Miró Cardona. The brigade's top Cuban com-mander was José (Pepe) Pérez San Román. Erneido Oliva served as his deputy commander and Manuel Artime as the brigade's political chief. The Frente Revolucionario Democrático originally served as the civilian wing of the growing exile army, but it later joined the more liberal Movimiento

Revolucionario del Pueblo in a broader opposition coalition named Concilio Revolucionario Cubano (Cuban Revolutionary Council, CRC), with Miró Cardona as its president.[95]

"The longest ninety miles" that for decades had made for difficult relations between Cubans and North Americans became evident during the planning and execution of the Bay of Pigs invasion in spite of the fact that both exiles and CIA operatives were supposedly on the same side. In a fashion similar to how U.S. leaders had treated Cubans for decades, several CIA officers exhibited utter disregard for the exiled civilian and military leadership's input on matters relating to the invasion plan. The most costly instance was the refusal of Frank Bender (aka Gerry Droller), who was in charge of organizing and training the exile force, to listen to repeated warnings that the Ciénaga de Zapata region was an inauspicious landing site due to its swampy conditions (*ciénaga* actually means "swamp"), its geographic isolation, and the reefs that surrounded the area. Bender knew better, however: he claimed that underwater shadows captured by aerial photographs were algae, and for practical purposes, algae they stayed.[96]

The views of CRC leaders were also regularly dismissed. They were sequestered days prior to the invasion, which they took as a serious affront. Almost unbelievably, CRC leaders found out about the invasion through radio newscasts. Even though the Movimiento Revolucionario del Pueblo had numerous militants on the island who were ready to join the fight, they were not even notified in advance of the invasion. As the CIA inspector general later recognized, "Some of the contract employees, such as ship's officers, treated Cubans like dirt."[97]

With input from the State Department and the Joint Chiefs of Staff, CIA agent Richard M. Bissell produced the Zapata Plan, named for the selected landing site. On April 14, 1961, Kennedy approved it, though not before reducing the number of planes to be used in preinvasion air strikes from sixteen to eight.[98] The Bay of Pigs invasion began as scheduled on April 15. At dawn, eight B-26s with fake Cuban Air Force markings flew out of Nicaragua to destroy Cuba's military airplanes, which were dispersed in three different airfields. The air strikes proved only partially successful: between a third and a half of Cuba's warplanes remained operational. Meanwhile, a force of 160 exile troops twice attempted a diversionary landing near Guantánamo. Both efforts failed.[99]

On the sixteenth, the invasion fleet gathered forty miles off of Playa Girón. Composed of four transport ships and two infantry landing vessels, the convoy transported around 1,400 members of Brigade 2506 along with supplies, ammunition, and weapons, including six M4 Sherman tanks. That night, at the urging of Secretary of State Dean Rusk, Kennedy cancelled the air strikes scheduled for the next day, further reducing the chances for success. Cuban authorities, meanwhile, preemptively arrested everyone suspected of potential counterrevolutionary inclinations. Nearly 100,000 suspects were rounded up with the help of CDR informers. Thirty-five thousand individuals were taken into custody in Havana alone. Some, like former agriculture minister Sorí Marín, were executed.[100]

On the morning of April 17, Brigade 2506 troops descended on Playa Girón. Another contingent landed on Playa Larga at the end of the Bay of Pigs. Battalion 5, whose troops landed later that day, closer to the mouth of the bay, endured the ripping welcome of Bender's "algae": piercing, jagged reefs that cut through vessel hulks and men's skins. Commander-in-Chief Castro immediately took control of all defense operations, ordering several battalions to mobilize toward the invasion sites. He also deployed a special unit of cadets from the School of Militia Officers under Captain José Ramón Fernández and Battalion 1 of the Special Forces of the FAR, led by Captain Aroldo Ferrer. In all, between 50,000 and 60,000 Cuban troops gathered to repel the invasion.[101] The Cuban planes that remained dropped a hailstorm of bombs and bullets on the invading force, disabling ships and knocking out three B-26s. These air attacks forced the remaining brigade vessels to retreat, making impossible the deployment of much-needed ammunition and equipment. Air strikes notwithstanding, brigade battalions pushed forward.[102]

While Cuban forces struggled for victory on the battlefields, Castro and Foreign Minister Raúl Roa fought to win over international public opinion. From the floor of the UN, Roa denounced the United States as the aggressor. Fed with false information, U.S. ambassador to the UN Adlai Stevenson adamantly denied U.S. involvement and was left holding the proverbial bag once Cuba presented indisputable evidence to back its accusations. The Soviet Union, meanwhile, offered Cuba more than moral support, as attested by Soviet premier Nikita Khrushchev's firmly worded missive to Kennedy: "As to the Soviet Union," Khrushchev wrote, "there should be no misunderstanding of our position: we shall render the Cuban people and the Government all necessary assistance in beating back the armed attack on Cuba."[103]

A dramatic episode during the fighting illustrates the brigade's precarious circumstances, the courage displayed by Cubans on both sides, and the broader Cold War context of the time. As a U.S.-made Sherman tank and a Soviet-made Stalin tank spewed metal and fire upon each other, the Sherman tank ran out of ammo. Its obstinate charioteer pushed forward, crashing against the Stalin. The tanks rammed each other repeatedly. They locked horns, neutralizing each other's push, until the Stalin tank sank into swampy soil.[104]

The brigade's situation at Playa Girón became untenable, as evidenced by Commander Pérez San Román's desperate radio communications. At dawn, he radioed: "Blue Beach [Girón] under attack by B-26. Where is promised air cover?" Three hours later, he pleaded with the CIA officer in charge of the operation: "Blue Beach under attack by two T-33 and artillery. Where the hell is jet cover?" The jet cover never materialized. Pérez San Román sent a final radio message at 4:32 in the afternoon: "Am destroying all my equipment and communications. Tanks are in sight. I have nothing to fight with. Am taking to the woods." Thus ended the ill-starred Bay of Pigs invasion.[105]

The death toll on the brigade's side was around 100, and another 1,197 were taken prisoner. On the Cuban government's side, the official deaths report listed 157 soldiers, but most other estimates range much higher, around 2,000. The most horrendous episode following the brigade's surrender was the death by asphyxiation of 9 out of 150 captives being transported to Havana by Osmany Cienfuegos' orders inside a truck's airtight container. The surviving prisoners were incarcerated and proceedings against them began soon thereafter; all were convicted and sentenced to serve thirty years. Following months of strenuous negotiation between the Cuban and U.S. governments, all but a few of the prisoners were freed in December 1962 in exchange for $53 million worth of medicine and food. As singer-song writer Carlos Varela later sang: "We exchanged mercenaries for shipments of baby food / back during Girón."[106]

For the Kennedy administration, Operation Zapata turned out to be an utter fiasco. Kennedy later referred to it as the worst experience of his life. To protect his administration from accusations of military aggression, he had condemned the operation to failure with the eleventh-hour reduction of essential air support. Poor logic stood behind the idea that the deployment of fewer planes and the cancellation of a second round of bombings would conceal U.S. involvement. As a result, Kennedy guaranteed the failure of the invasion, failed to hide U.S. involvement, and earned the distrust of thousands of exiled Cubans who felt betrayed. Kennedy publicly accepted responsibility for the fiasco but cautioned somberly, "Let the record show that our restraint is not inexhaustible"—a warning that the professed U.S. willingness to stay out of Cuban affairs had limits.[107]

Kennedy's low point was Castro's high point. Castro bragged that imperialism had "sustained its first great defeat in America." Victory at Girón strengthened the regime to the point of consolidation and elevated its international image. The Bay of Pigs also established the virtual impossibility of a cordial coexistence between Cuba and the United States. Castro now felt emboldened to move closer to the USSR and openly declare the socialist nature of the revolution. In fact, on the day following the first bombings, Castro referred to the revolution as "socialist" for the first time. On May 1, he again spoke about "our socialist revolution," and before the year was over, he stated in no uncertain terms that he was a Marxist-Leninist and would remain one until he died.[108]

Strengthened by the victory at Girón, the Cuban government now moved aggressively against its strongest domestic institutional adversary: the Catholic Church. The regime's antagonism and contempt toward the Catholic Church was so deep that the by-then-nationalized magazine *Bohemia* carried editorial cartoons mocking priests and associating them with the counterrevolution and extremist right-wing positions. Some depict priests in gowns adorned by fascist symbols (Franco's Fascism and German Nazism). One shows a kneeling priest taking communion (dollar bills) from Uncle Sam. Another one shows a masked priest donning a swastika instead of a cross and hiding a bomb behind his back.[109] In his May Day speech, Castro announced the nationalization of all private schools, most of which were run by priests and nuns. He was particularly angry at Catholic schools, like the ones he attended as a child, for "poisoning the minds of pupils." During the next few months, hundreds of priests and nuns were banished from the island by the planeload and shipload. Church-state tensions later abated, however, following the 1962 appointment of Monsignor Cesare O. Zacchi as the Vatican's chargé d'affaires; Zacchi took on the task of fostering conciliatory relations with the state.[110]

Mongoose to Missiles

Following the failed Bay of Pigs invasion and Castro's official declaration of a socialist revolution, the United States stepped up efforts to isolate Cuba further, both diplomatically and commercially. Moved in great measure by U.S. pressures, in January 1962 the Organization of American States (OAS) voted to exclude Cuba from the "Inter American System."[111]

U.S. aggression now took other forms, including an array of sabotage and destabilizing actions code-named Operation Mongoose. At the urging of Deputy Assistant Secretary of State for Inter-American Affairs Richard Goodwin, Kennedy created the oddly named Special Group—Augmented, which he charged with the planning and execution of covert operations against Cuba. The president's younger brother, Attorney General Robert F. Kennedy, assumed administrative control over the Group, while Air Force general Edward G. Lansdale took charge of the actual operations.[112]

Operation Mongoose was a large-scale, generously funded program with a staff of some 400 U.S. officers and 2,000 Cuban agents. Its projects included economic warfare, assassination plots, misinformation campaigns, and a wide range of sabotage activities, such as burning cane fields, spreading viruses among crops and animals, and destroying industrial equipment. Lansdale recommended several plans to destabilize the revolution, some of which were amusingly bizarre. "Operation Good Times," for example, consisted of dropping doctored photographs over Cuban territory of an overweight Castro surrounded by luxury and in the compromising company of two attractive women, a scheme that may have made sense in puritan North America but not in pleasure-loving Cuba.[113] The combination of this lack of cultural understanding and a crass underestimation of Cuba's intelligence and counterintelligence capabilities would continue to hamper the formulation of coherent and successful Cuba policies over the next five decades.[114]

Of all the known plans, the most extreme was Operation Northwoods. Prepared for and approved by the Joint Chiefs of Staff, it prescribed a series of actions aimed at provoking a war with Cuba, chief among them staging simulated attacks on the U.S. naval base at Guantánamo including a "Remember the Maine" incident that was to include funerals for mock victims. Plan documents stated that the publication of a casualty list in U.S. newspapers "would cause a helpful wave of national indignation." Another proposed action was the staging of a "Communist Cuban terror campaign" in Miami and the sinking, "real or simulated," of "a boatload of Cubans en route to Florida." Operation Northwoods was never implemented, remaining top secret until its documents were made public in 1997.[115]

In conjunction with Operation Mongoose, Kennedy expanded the U.S. trade embargo in February 1962 to include all U.S. exports with the exception of nonsubsidized food and medicines. A few weeks later, he further strengthened the embargo by banning all imports from Cuba as well as imports made with Cuban raw materials from third countries. The United States coerced other nations into compliance by threatening to terminate economic assistance to any country that aided or traded with the rebel island.[116] Not only did the embargo abruptly close the U.S. sugar market on which Cuba had become so deeply dependent, it also deprived the island of spare parts to maintain all kinds of U.S.-made machines, from refrigerators to automobiles to industrial sugar mill equipment.

The Soviet military presence in Cuba increased significantly, reportedly numbering 42,000 troops by October 1962. Likewise, the Soviet-built arsenal, which expanded with the deployment to Cuba of defensive surface-to-air missiles. In September 1962, Soviet freight ships delivered over two dozen medium-range ballistic missiles, nine of which were eventually fitted with nuclear tips. U.S. aerial photographs confirmed that missile bases were being built on Cuban soil and that these would soon become fully operational. As Cuban writer Antonio Benítez-Rojo put it, Cuba was building a "plantation of atomic projectiles."[117]

Although Kennedy was at first inclined to launch a major preemptive attack on Cuba, he delayed that option, declaring instead a "quarantine" of the island. Actually, it was a full naval blockade. Intense negotiations between Washington and Moscow ensued. On October 26, Khrushchev averted what seemed to be an imminent U.S. attack on Cuba when he offered to withdraw all missiles in exchange for a U.S. promise not to carry out the attack. Washington was ready to accept Moscow's proposition, but the next day Khrushchev added an unexpected additional demand: he now called for the removal of U.S. nuclear weapons from Turkey.[118] The crisis finally ended with a public accord: Khrushchev agreed to remove the missiles and Kennedy gave assurances that the United States would not invade or interfere with Cuba. Secretly, to save face, Kennedy also agreed to remove its nuclear weapons from Turkey. Three decades later, retired general Anatoly Gribkov testified that the Soviets had managed to transport over 100 nuclear warheads to Cuba.[119]

Unbelievably, Castro was disappointed with the peaceful resolution of the October crisis. Much to his chagrin, he had been relegated to the role of spectator. Not only had the Soviets imposed the installation of missiles on Cuban soil and kept control of the weapons, they also singlehandedly decided to remove them. In fact, Castro remained completely in the dark while the superpowers negotiated. Both Soviet and U.S. leaders viewed Castro—rightly so—as extremely belligerent and an obstacle to a peaceful resolution. Castro took it as an affront to Cuba's and his own honor.

When Soviet deputy premier Mikoyan arrived in Havana a few days after the end of the missile crisis, Castro demonstrated his displeasure by refusing to meet with him for two weeks.[120] This course of action was possible, to some extent, because Cuba enjoyed close relations with China and was able to leverage that to counterbalance the Soviet Union; this was a new triangulation scheme.

The Economy Falters

The economic accomplishments of the first three years of revolutionary government began to falter when 1962 ushered in an economic crisis, the result of multiple factors, including the effects of the nationalization of most of the land and all large businesses, the delayed effects of huge expenditures on wealth redistribution and radical social reforms during 1959–62, the flight of tens of thousands of professionals, managers, and skilled workers, mismanagement by revolutionaries, and the harmful consequences of the U.S. trade embargo.[121]

Contrary to the revolution's economic objectives, dependence on imports increased, as did trade deficits. The goals of strengthening the manufacturing sector and diversifying the economy failed as well. While the revolution had accomplished much domestically in terms of social and economic gains, its leaders could not liberate Cuba from its centuries-long status as a dependent, export-based economy; at best, they had been able to select what superpower to depend on and sell sugar to.

Because of the causes mentioned above, agricultural production fell considerably. The 1962 sugar harvest was disappointingly low. Food crop production fell too, with per capita output dropping by 40 percent over three years. Yields dropped drastically for rice, beans, and the tuber *malanga*, all staples of the Cuban diet.[122]

The economic crisis of 1962 had a deleterious impact on the government's attempts to raise the standard of living and consumption levels of the population. While significant achievements had been made in pursuit of these goals during the first three years of the revolution, the economy's sharp downward turn slowed and actually reversed those trends. Guevara acknowledged the dire circumstances and candidly stated, "This Revolution has given generously during its first years but today it cannot give as generously."[123]

The state responded to the food crisis by monopolizing food distribution through the *tiendas del pueblo* (people's stores) and by imposing a food rationing system that came to be known as *la libreta* (ration book). These measures helped guarantee an equitable distribution of dwindling food supplies and a basic level of adequate nourishment. Long queues to purchase rationed items such as rice, eggs, tubers, and even bars of soap became ubiquitous.[124] A black market emerged through which individuals could purchase food and other items in larger quantities by paying premium prices, as much as ten times the ration book cost. Protests against the ration system sprang up throughout the island, particularly among middle-class homemakers. The most memorable one took place in the city of Cárdenas, where women took to the streets banging pots and pans. Immediately, the government deployed tanks to silence the peaceful but cacophonous demonstration. In his characteristically unmerciful style, author Cabrera Infante, who broke with the regime in 1965, later wrote about the incident, "And the fearful general who had sent tanks to confront pots was deployed as ambassador to some African country—ever since he is known as the aluminum Rommel."[125]

Another consequence of the deepening economic crisis was an escalating trade deficit. Before the revolution, Cuba had generally managed to export more than it imported. For the period 1950–57, the trade balance had been positive every year except 1952. Trade balances for the four-year period 1959–63 were all negative, with export levels barely reaching 75 percent of imports. In 1962, the trade deficit rose to 237 million pesos. Soviet credits amounting to $100 million per year in 1960, 1961, and 1962 partially alleviated the impact of mounting trade deficits.[126]

A Balance Sheet, 1959–62

In just four years, Cuba experienced profound revolutionary changes that transformed society in almost every aspect. The political system went from a broken, authoritarian, and corrupt multiparty electoral system to a single-party dictatorship. This provided new mechanisms for mass political participation through organizations such as the FMC and the CDRs. The revolution's own guiding ideology mutated from humanism to socialism and shortly thereafter to Marxism-Leninism.

Defying all odds, the revolutionary government survived politically, mobilizing massive popular support, silencing its internal critics, and exiling, imprisoning, or executing its opponents. By the end of 1962, the threat posed by its mightiest foe, the United States, had significantly subsided given the failure of U.S. efforts to bring Cuba to its knees through the imposition of a trade embargo, a U.S.-led campaign to isolate the rebel island within the American hemisphere, an incessant barrage of sabotage actions, the ill-fated Bay of Pigs invasion, and the nearly cataclysmic missile crisis. What made this possible, besides the tenacity of the revolutionaries, was the willingness of the Soviet Union and, to a lesser extent, China to step in to become Cuba's benefactor states, immediately supplanting the United States as Cuba's primary commercial partners and political and military allies.

Within the revolution, Castro established individuals loyal to him as the core of political power. He did so through a gradual and calculated process of triangulation in which he targeted one group at a time: first pitting the M-26-7 against the moderates, later the PSP against the M-26-7, and finally younger Fidelista communists against older PSP leaders. Before long, only socialist Fidelistas remained standing. This triangulation strategy was paralleled in the media and organized labor arenas, where the M-26-7's *Revolución* newspaper and M-26-7 labor leaders such as David Salvador were used to displace pre-revolution media and Mujalista labor bosses, only to be soon squeezed out of existence and power by the PSP's *Hoy* and communist labor leaders.

The economy transitioned from capitalism to socialism more drastically and in a shorter period than any other case in history. In terms of foreign trade, the Soviet Union, China, and other communist nations replaced the United States almost overnight. Cuban black beans that had formerly been served with rice from the Carolinas were now eaten with Chinese rice; and box-shaped Soviet-made Ladas now shared Havana's streets with curvaceous 1950s Fords and Chevrolets. The initial goals of economic growth through diversification and development via import substitution failed, however, while sugar, Cuba's historic cash crop, suffered from neglect and inept management.

Built on the principles of egalitarianism and universal access to education, health services, and adequate housing, the revolution's social agenda made considerable advances. The number of children attending school skyrocketed, as did the number of schools, hospitals, and clinics, particularly in previously neglected remote locations. The urban reforms of 1959 and 1960 made housing more affordable. Salaries went up, and the state set up a basic safety net for its most vulnerable citizens. These social transformations, while improving the lot of Cuba's poorest, had a negative effect on the standard of living of the middle and upper classes: private schools were closed, higher-paying jobs in U.S. corporations disappeared,

Figure 2.5. Wreckage of the upscale El Encanto department store, destroyed by sabotage on the eve of the Bay of Pigs invasion. Photograph by Alberto Korda.

and foods as well as essential consumer items were now available only through the rationing system.

Not surprisingly, the middle and upper classes were overrepresented among those who left Cuba during 1959–62. They suffered an immediate loss of status as society ladies and gentlemen passed through the doors of Miami's refugee center, where they and other refugees queued for secondhand clothes, surplus cheese, and cans of Spam. Back on the island, their plush suburban homes sheltered new families, peasants-turned-rebels-turned-government workers who had difficulty figuring out how to use the electric appliances from Sears or La Vía Blanca. One former guerrillero's large family moved to a house in fashionable Miramar that belonged to a successful businessman. Not knowing any better, they used the refrigerator as a closet. The children learned to read and write at a school that was formerly the residence of a distinguished physician who now did menial jobs in Miami as he studied English and prepared for the medical board exams.

During the revolutionary process, Cuba's traditional elites lost their economic and political power. The island's bourgeoisie fled. Symbolic of its demise was the burning down of El Encanto (literally "the Enchantment"), Havana's most upscale department store, on April 13, 1961 (figure 2.5). It was an act of sabotage on the eve of the Bay of Pigs bombings.[127] Sergio, the hapless protagonist of Tomás Gutiérrez Alea's cinematic masterpiece *Memorias del subdesarrollo*, did not miss the metaphor: "Since the burning of El Encanto Havana resembles a provincial city," he remarked. "And to think that people used to call it the Paris of the Caribbean."[128]

3

▼

The Ten Million Will Happen

Expanding Socialism, 1963–1970

1963—Year of Organization
1964—Year of the Economy
1965—Year of Agriculture
1966—Year of Solidarity
1967—Year of Heroic Vietnam
1968—Year of the Heroic Guerrilla Fighter
1969—Year of the Decisive Effort
1970—Year of the Ten Million

The Medialuna cane, when wet, was treacherous; its slippery peel could deflect the mocha [machete], producing wounds in arms and legs. The mud covered their clothes and skin. Whites, blacks, and mulattos were all the same, the color of earth.

Jesús Díaz, *The Initials of the Earth*

This chapter traces the revolution's trajectory from "heroic idealism" in the early 1960s to what came to be known as the Great Debate among different socioeconomic models during 1963–66 to a "compromised idealism" formula toward the end of the decade, a phase epitomized by the epic drive to produce ten million tons of sugar in 1970.

Caught in the whirlwind of the Cold War, Cuba confronted several economic, political, and social dilemmas during the 1960s as it strove to find a balance between food production for domestic consumption and revenue-generating economic activities (i.e., sugar), between idealism and pragmatism, between principled internationalism and advantageous political alliances, and between a swift path to communism and gradual reformist socialism. Its leaders had to navigate—at times manipulate—tensions among the island's international partners: the Soviet Union, China, Third World allies, and liberation movements around the world. This was tied to the decision of which ideological formula to follow: orthodox Marxism-Leninism, the reformist socialist formula the USSR embraced at the time, Maoism or Cuba's own tropical socialist blend that was part Marx, part Lenin, part Stalin, part Mao, part Fidel mixed with Cuban-bred populism, nationalism, anti-imperialism, and caudilloism.

Recession and the Sugar Gamble

The economic crisis that began in 1962 spiraled into a recession in 1963, when the economy's annual growth rate experienced its first drop since the start of the revolution. The downturn was due primarily to diminishing agricultural production: 1963 levels reached only around a quarter of output in 1959. The 1963 sugar harvest was dismal at 3.9 million tons, the lowest since 1945. After rebounding briefly in 1965, agricultural production continued to drop through the balance of the decade.[1] The revolution's initial economic strategy of shifting away from dependence on sugar toward agricultural diversification and industrialization had the unintended effect of reducing Cuba's export capabilities and hence generating increasingly untenable negative trade balances, which soared to 238 million pesos in 1962, reaching further to a 324-million-peso deficit in 1963.[2]

The U.S. trade embargo—officially referred to in Cuba as *el bloqueo*—had undeniably damaging repercussions, and so did the hundreds of counterrevolutionary CIA-backed actions, including the burning of sugarcane fields and industrial sabotage. Guevara admitted in 1963, however, that Cuba's severe problems were not the result of the "blockade." "Our difficulties," he recognized candidly, "stem principally from our errors." He was referring to bureaucratism, labor absenteeism, and overall inefficiency.[3] Productivity fell sharply because of the collectivization of the vast majority of agricultural activities, especially on state farms, where output was only half the level of productivity achieved in private farms. Growing labor absenteeism was another major cause of production decline: French agronomist and Castro advisor René Dumont estimated that agricultural worker productivity fell by half between 1958 and 1963.[4] Even Mother Nature seemed to sabotage Cuba's economy, In October 1963, Hurricane Flora hit eastern Cuba, its circuitous path leaving an unprecedented trail of death and devastation.

In April 1963, Castro paid his first visit to the Soviet Union, where he received a hero's welcome. Before a crowd of 125,000 in Lenin Stadium, Khrushchev effusively praised the accomplishments of the Cuban Revolution: "You . . . have ignited the sacred fire of the Great October Revolution in the Western Hemisphere." Castro responded in kind, thanking his host for his friendship with Cuba. He closed his speech in Spanish: "Long live Communism! Fatherland or death! We shall triumph!" The crowd went wild: "Fee dell; Fee dell; Fee dell. . . ."[5]

While in Moscow, the Cuban delegation negotiated trade and economic accords. The Soviets agreed to purchase 24.1 million tons of sugar over the next five years at six cents per pound.[6] This agreement guaranteed a minimum price for Cuba's sugar while giving the island the option to sell part of its production in the world market whenever prices rose above what the Soviets had agreed to pay. When world sugar prices surged from 2.98 cents in 1962 to 8.5 cents in 1963, Cuba shifted a large portion of its exports to higher-paying markets; and when prices plunged during the second half of the 1960s, from 5.87 cents in 1964 to 2.12 in 1965, hitting bottom at 1.98 cents in 1968, exports flowed almost exclusively to the Soviet Union and East European markets, where they were valued almost three times higher than in the international market. To reciprocate the Soviets' preferential treatment of Cuban sugar, the island nation agreed to purchase Soviet exports at prices that often surpassed those of the international market.[7]

In February 1963, shortly before Castro's visit to Moscow, Guevara headed a trade delegation to China that secured a commercial accord for the exchange of one million tons of sugar for rice. The Chinese also matched the Soviet price for sugar. Guevara also negotiated a loan that he described as "unbelievable . . . interest-free, [with] no due date, and even no responsibility for paying it off." Such largesse must be understood, however, within the broader context of China's geopolitical interests: a Cuba fully dependent on Soviet trade and subsidies was a Cuba under the hegemonic influence of the Soviet Union, which was to China's disadvantage.[8]

Shortly after his return from the Soviet Union, Castro announced the implementation of a sugar-centered economic growth strategy. The newly created Ministry of Sugar formulated the Prospective Sugar Industry Plan with the goal of producing 47 million tons of sugar between 1965 and 1970, 23 million more than the Soviets had agreed to purchase.[9] At a cane cutters' mass rally in Havana, Castro underscored the renewed importance of sugar production. A massive billboard erected for the occasion draped the facade of the Ministry of Industries with the revolution's latest slogan: "We must turn all of Cuba's cane fields into sugar." Castro accepted, albeit reluctantly, that Cuba had not escaped the sugar trap that had held it captive since the early nineteenth century: "Without sugar," he said, "everything else is superfluous; if sugar is abundant, anything else is scarce." The plantation was, indeed, persistent.[10]

The implementation of the back-to-sugar strategy meant the reversal of the revolution's original economic strategy of industrialization, economic diversification, and self-sufficiency. Castro and other officials explained, however, that the renewed emphasis on sugar would be a temporary measure: larger volumes of sugar exports, they rationalized, would generate the necessary capital for a temporarily postponed industrialization. The Soviet Union and China's willingness to increase their sugar purchases allowed—actually spurred—Cuba's return to the monocrop economy.

The revolution changed most plantations' names—Hershey to Camilo Cienfuegos, Tánamo to Frank País, Arechabala to José Antonio Echeverría, and so on—but sugar remained sugar, and working conditions on the plantations were not much different from those in the nineteenth century. The return to a sugar-centered economy intensified the detrimental socioeconomic, cultural, and political consequences historically associated with the Caribbean plantation complex: dependence on coerced labor, including new forms such as the conscription of soldiers between the ages of seventeen and forty-four, who were forced into obligatory military service in 1963, precisely the year of the back-to-sugar strategy; dependence on foreign markets and imported foodstuffs; and an increasingly centralized authoritarian government to guarantee social order.

Heavy investment in sugar production translated into further sacrifices for the Cuban people. Food production was one of the most profoundly affected areas. Between 1962 and 1966, the production of rice, a primary staple of the Cuban diet, dropped 78 percent; bean production fell 23 percent; and *malanga* production levels plummeted, though other tubers (potatoes, *ñames*, and sweet potatoes) became more widely available. Eggs came to be an increasingly important source of protein and became a staple in the Cuban diet.[11]

Not everybody welcomed the return to sugar. Guevara was among those who opposed it as an abandonment of one of the core goals of the revolution. Indeed, many Cubans continued to associate sugar with exploitation and, not surprisingly, even the relatively well-paid sugarcane cutters fled the fields in search of less grueling types of work.[12] The brutalizing nature of cane-cutting labor was incompatible with the agenda of elevating the working classes and improving their lot. Higher levels of health, nutrition, and education among the population made the return to the cane fields more incongruous than ever before.

The passing of new laws and the implementation of novel programs helped secure the land demands of the sugar-based growth strategy. Back in 1962, the government had already turned the short-lived cooperatives into state-owned latifundia (large land units). In October 1963, the revolution enacted a second agrarian reform law, this time targeting privately owned plots of land exceeding 5 *caballerías* (167 acres). Through this legislation, the state expropriated 5.2 million acres from 11,215 farmers, thus securing control over 70 percent of all arable land and agricultural production.[13] This marked one of the early reversals of the revolution, whose leaders, since at least 1952, had voiced their hatred of latifundia, the sugar plantation, and its manifold ill effects.

Conflicting Partners, Contending Models, Competing Voices

The mid-1960s brought major political challenges. Cuba's leaders struggled to ensure the revolution's survival while seeking to maintain a mostly autonomous political course, one that befitted the island's unique material and cultural circumstances and that would be as independent as possible from the Soviets' reformist political prescriptions.

These goals, however, became hard to fulfill because of an increasingly complicated geopolitical context of heightened tensions between the Soviet Union and China. China's criticism of the USSR's abdication of Marxist-Leninist principles and the Soviets' failure to confront the United States fueled such tensions. Fundamental philosophical and strategic differences separated the Soviet and Chinese formulas for the construction of communism. For one thing, the Soviet model established that revolutions respond to objective material conditions in which a nucleus of organized industrial laborers and a radical vanguard party lead the revolutionary struggle. Upon gaining political power, they begin a long-term, gradual transition to socialism with the goal of eventually creating a communist society. According to Soviet Marxist-Leninist formulations, the retention of vestiges of capitalism, such as the market, wages, and private economic activities, are essential elements of the transition to communism. In contrast, the Chinese embraced a different revolutionary formula, one that begins with a rural-based insurrection. Instead of a prolonged transition to socialism, Mao believed in "jumping stages" and in the immediate eradication of capitalist institutions, practices, and values, along with the implementation of volunteerism and socioeconomic egalitarianism.[14]

Under such circumstances, collaborating and having simultaneous alliances with both the Soviet Union and China became increasingly difficult, but for the time being, Cuba sold sugar to both nations at subsidized prices while importing grain from the former and rice from the latter. The fact that pro-China and pro-Soviet factions coexisted on the island was critical for the balancing-act course Cuba pursued.

Against the backdrop of escalating Soviet-Chinese hostility, Cuba entered what came to be known as the "Great Debate," in which one faction of the leadership, headed by Guevara, sought closer relations with China and favored the Chinese revolutionary model, including a preference for economic centralization, radical egalitarianism, and the use of "moral incentives." This was, to use Carmelo Mesa Lago's term, the Sino-Guevarist model.[15]

Guevara put forth the idea of creating a "New Man" endowed with a revolutionary consciousness that would be manifested through a strong work ethic, discipline, and a spirit of sacrifice that placed collective needs above individual desires. This New Man would respond to revolutionary rather than capitalistic motivations. Instead of being motivated by material incentives, such as higher salaries, bonuses, and the acquisition of material goods, he would respond to "moral incentives," such as the reward of serving society and being publicly recognized for doing so.[16]

Another faction, under Moscow-aligned Aníbal Escalante, promoted even stronger bonds with the USSR and the implementation of its reformist brand of socialism that favored "material incentives" such as productivity bonuses and higher salaries for the most productive workers. Yet another faction led by Carlos Rafael Rodríguez and Raúl Castro pursued collaborative relations with the Soviet Union while embracing moderate orthodox Marxist policies and a combination of material and moral incentives.[17]

Throughout the early part of the debate, Castro appeared neutral. While sympathizing with the Chinese model, he recognized the vital importance of Soviet trade and military support. K. S. Karol succinctly captured the essence of his dilemma: "Fidel had his stomach in Moscow but his heart in Peking."[18]

Tellingly, however, as early as 1962, Castro signaled his preference for the sugar strategy, entrusting its implementation to Rodríguez, whom he appointed president of INRA, while reducing Guevara to Minister of Industries precisely when industrialization was no longer a primary goal. Rodríguez thus became the official plantation overseer.[19] Escalante, meanwhile, was politically rehabilitated after spending two years "exiled" in Czechoslovakia. Not coincidentally, he was welcomed back to Cuba and incorporated into the Partido Comunista de Cuba's (Cuban Communist Party, PCC) Central Committee in 1965, at a time of rapprochement with the USSR.[20] This was yet another triangulation process that pitted three factions against one another: Guevaristas, Soviet Union–aligned communists, and reformist Fidelistas.

There is no doubt that the Soviets had a much greater capacity to absorb Cuba's sugar exports and subsidize the island's economy. In 1964, 1965, and 1966, total sugar exports to China amounted to 1.4 million tons, whereas the Soviets absorbed 6.2 million tons, 4.4 times more sugar. In 1967 and 1968, the USSR purchased five times as much Cuban sugar as China did.[21] Moreover, the Soviet Union exerted dominance over several Eastern European socialist countries whose markets further expanded Cuba's export possibilities. Soviet assistance took many other forms, among them loans, loan extensions, trade credits, industrial and agrarian technology transfers, and the sale of underpriced crude oil, fertilizers, pesticides, technical support, and weaponry. Soviet expenditures on Cuba amounted to about $1 million per day. By 1970, the Soviet Union had transferred to its tropical ally $2.6 billion worth of trade credits, $940 million in the form of sugar price subsidies, and military aid valued at $1.5 billion.[22]

Revolutionary Internationalism

Internationalism, exporting revolution, and collaborating with national liberation movements throughout the Third World were early hallmarks of the Cuban Revolution. The Castro brothers and the majority of the Cuban leadership—Guevara more than anyone else—favored internationalist policies in Latin America, Africa, the Middle East, and Southeast Asia. Throughout most of the 1960s, Cuba engaged in a variety of foreign assistance projects, ranging from providing free education to international students and deploying medical missions abroad to arming and training revolutionaries in guerrilla warfare and rendering actual military assistance in the form of war matériel, training, and even ground troops. These activities were not motivated by pragmatism and the desire to gain benefits for the young revolution but were rather inspired by the flames of revolutionary idealism that had engulfed Cuba at the time. Cuba actually stood to lose much by pursuing an aggressive internationalist agenda.

As seen in chapter 2, within a few months of assuming power, the revolutionary government began to train, arm, and sponsor guerrilla expeditions seeking to topple right-wing dictators in various Caribbean nations. Cuba's first major internationalist military actions took place in Algeria in support of the National Liberation Front's insurrection against French colonial rule. The first Cuban shipments of weapons arrived in the port of Casablanca late in 1961, and by July 1962 Algeria had won its independence. Cuba and Algeria became close allies during the rule of Prime Minister Ahmed Ben Bella, who developed a personal friendship with his Cuban counterpart. In October 1963, Moroccan troops launched a military attack on Algeria, crossing the border and capturing portions of Algerian territory. Ben Bella requested military support. Cuba obliged, dispatching 686 volunteer soldiers and a vast arsenal. Cuba sweetened the deal—quite literally—with a donation of 4,744 tons of sugar. Cuban troops led by comandante Efigenio Ameijeiras were preparing to invade Morocco when a cease-fire agreement was reached on October 29. The island nation continued to support Algeria until Ben Bella's government fell during a coup in June 1965.[23]

Closer to home, in 1963, Cuba provided guerrillas operating in Venezuela with tactical support as well as arms and ammunition. A major inter-American crisis erupted late in 1963 when Venezuelan authorities discovered a three-ton cache of Cuban-supplied weapons and ammunition. This internationalist venture was significant because unlike earlier armed expeditions against circum-Caribbean military regimes, Cuba was targeting a democratic South American nation. Venezuela's progressive president, Rómulo Betancourt, had been a Castro ally as far back as 1958, but as the result of the establishment of a socialist dictatorship on the island, Caracas broke diplomatic relations with Havana late in 1961. So did Costa Rica, whose president, José Figueres, had supplied vital weapons and supplies to Castro's guerrilla force.[24]

Guevara was the driving force behind much of the internationalist activities. While guerrilla actions enjoyed Castro's blessing, Guevara retained a large degree of decision-making autonomy. Not since the days of Frank País had anyone else been able to exercise so much autonomy, let alone get away with publicly challenging the Maximum Leader. Historically, Castro had displayed a tendency to silence anyone whose popularity cast even the smallest shadow on him. As seen earlier, popular leaders Cienfuegos, Matos, and Franqui disappeared from the scene, the first in a plane accident, the second through imprisonment, the third dispatched to Italy in 1963 in an unofficial capacity from which he later resigned; he was literally removed from the revolution's iconography.[25] The politically powerful Escalante faced a similar fate in 1962, when he was forced into "exile" to Czechoslovakia. "Third man" Guevara's enormous popularity and his invaluable role as the main liaison with the Chinese made him indispensable and thus untouchable, at least for the time being.

Guevara was the consummate "man on horseback." He believed that the *foco* guerrilla model of building an armed movement in an isolated rural setting that had succeeded in the Cuban highlands could be replicated elsewhere. Guevara and journalist Jorge Masetti, a fellow Argentine, trained a small guerrilla force in Algeria, which remained the main foreign base from which Cuba launched guerrilla operations in Africa and Latin America. Disguised as Algerian diplomats, Masetti and a handful of revolutionaries (three of them Cuban) arrived in the northern Salta Province of Argentina in September 1963. Following Soviet directives, the Communist Party of Argentina denied them even minimal support, and Masetti's guerrillas were killed or captured by April 1964.[26]

In the first week of January 1965, Guevara began conversations with government officials in Congo-Brazzaville who were eager to enlist Cuban military support in anticipation of an invasion from rival Congo-Léopoldville.[27] Three months later, Guevara returned to Congo-Brazzaville with 130 volunteer Cuban troops, most of them black, and medical personnel. Several hundred Cuban soldiers fought during the summer and fall of 1965. They suffered a major defeat while trying to capture the city of Bendera and were forced to retreat in November along with their Angolan anti-colonialist allies of the Popular Movement for the Liberation of Angola (MPLA), whose headquarters were in Brazzaville. In 1966, Cuban military advisors began training MPL soldiers, a force led by Agostinho Neto that was fighting against Portuguese colonial rule. Other internationalist efforts in Africa included the deployment of medical and technical personnel to Guinea-Bissau, Ghana, and Tanzania.[28]

Internationalist ventures during the first half of the 1960s had numerous reverberations that affected Cuba in a variety of ways. For one, its support for revolutionary guerrillas in the Americas and beyond incurred the enmity of the United States and imperial European nations such as France and Portugal. The United States capitalized on Cuba's aggressive internationalism, denouncing the island nation not only as a regional nuisance but also as a serious threat to peace and stability in the hemisphere and beyond. Cajoled and pressured by the United States, Cuba's hemispheric neighbors rejected and combated its interventions in Argentina, Venezuela, Guatemala, and Bolivia. Cuba was already excluded from the "Inter-American system" as a result of its support for guerrillas in Venezuela, and in July 1964 the OAS voted to impose punitive diplomatic and commercial sanctions against it.[29] The United States succeeded in turning Cuba into the hemisphere's pariah. By the end of the year, all American states with the exception of Mexico and Canada had broken diplomatic relations with the rebel island.

The United States also forcefully asserted its determination to crush any further challenges to its hemispheric hegemony and to keep communism from spreading to other countries in the hemisphere. This was concretely demonstrated when the United States supported the 1964 coup against João Goulart's leftist government in Brazil and invaded and occupied the Dominican Republic in 1965. President Lyndon B. Johnson put it succinctly on May 2, 1965, when he reported on the political crisis in the Dominican Republic and denounced Cuban-trained radicals who allegedly sought to create another Cuba there. "The American nations," he sternly warned, "cannot, must not, and will not permit the establishment of another Communist government in the Western Hemisphere."[30]

Besides the stick of intervention, the United States used the carrot of Alliance for Progress foreign aid as a tool to stop the spread of leftist governments in the hemisphere. Paradoxically, back in May 1959, it was Castro who had advised the United States to develop a ten-year, multibillion-dollar program of aid to Latin America.[31] The actual Alliance for Progress program that began in 1961 stipulated that the United States would provide $20 billion in development aid over ten years; the countries of Latin America, Cuba excepted, pledged to contribute another $80 billion.[32]

Potentially more damaging was the risk that Cuba's persistence in exporting revolution would generate further tensions with the Soviet Union, the island's strongest ally and benefactor. While bound by political alliances and trade and military partnerships, Cuba and the Soviet Union held radically different views on internationalism. The biggest bone of contention was Cuba's insistence on offering military assistance to leftist rebels in various Third World nations, particularly in Latin America. This was the period of détente, a partial thawing of the Cold War during which the Soviet Union and the United States steered away from actions and provocations that could lead to the dreaded nuclear conflagration. The Soviet Union was also bent on improving its relations with the countries of Latin America and since the early 1960s had viewed Cuba's armed internationalist adventures as obstacles to achieving that goal.[33] Soviet pressures had actually fostered uncooperative relations between the region's communist parties and Guevara's guerrilleros.[34] While the Soviets rejected the strategy of aiding peasant revolutionary movements around the world, the Chinese government generally supported such actions, as in the case of Vietnam.

Numerous Third-World nations also welcomed Cuba's internationalism, among them Algeria, Vietnam, and Congo-Brazzaville. Moreover, the revolution became a source of inspiration to many leftist and liberation movements, ranging from Nicaragua's Frente Sandinista de Liberación Nacional (Sandinista National Liberation Front) and Colombia's Ejército de Liberación Nacional (National Liberation Army) to the Black Panthers in the United States and the Tupamaros of Uruguay. It also had a significant impact on the European and North American New Left and on youth and student movements the world over.[35]

Sino-Guevarism without China and without Guevara

The end of the Great Debate around 1966 ushered in a transitional period full of paradoxes and compromises in both the global and the domestic arenas. On the one hand, Cuba all but severed its bonds of friendship and collaboration with China at a time when the revolution recommitted to egalitarian, statist socioeconomic strategies and aggressive internationalism, policies that were in harmony with the Chinese model. On the other hand, as Cuba strengthened its economic, political, and military relations with the Soviet Union, its leaders moved away from the Soviet economic model of central planning, centralized budgets, and material rather than moral incentives. This was Sino-Guevarism without China and without Guevara, a hybrid formula that allowed Cuba to hold on to its core revolutionary pillars of socialism, egalitarianism, and internationalism while yielding in areas such as industrialization, economic diversification, and full autonomy in international affairs.

In 1964, overestimating the power of Cuba's international leverage, Castro began efforts to mediate between China and the Soviet Union. Before the end of the year, he dispatched Guevara on diplomatic missions to both countries. Guevara was unable to broker a rapprochement, however. The time for mediation, it became evident, had passed, and communist nations and communist parties around the world had to choose sides.[36]

For obvious pragmatic reasons, Cuba moved closer and closer to the more powerful Soviet Union, and consequently its relations with China quickly deteriorated. Shortly after the failure of Guevara's missions, Castro chastised China both privately and publicly. The Soviet reward arrived in no time: an additional $90 million loan. China decided to punish Cuba, announcing a reduction in its rice exports to the island to almost half the level of 1965. Castro responded virulently, accusing China of economic blackmail and economic aggression. In a televised rant in March 1966, a sweat-drenched Castro rebuked Mao as a "senile idiot." He later ordered that rice rations be cut in half and blamed China for the shortage.[37] Chinese officials should have learned from the failure of the big-stick approach of the United States. Instead of bringing Cuba to its knees, the imposition of trade quota reductions by the United States in 1960 led to a break in relations. In both cases economic blackmail pushed Cuba further into Soviet arms.

As Cuba and China grew increasingly distant to the point of hostility, Guevara's value as main interlocutor with China lost its value, and consequently his fortunes within the revolutionary leadership waned. For years he had openly criticized the Soviets' foreign and domestic policies. He denounced their trade agreements with smaller socialist countries, which in his view were unequal and fostered relations of dependency.[38] He found more to like in China's policies, which he viewed as supportive of Cuba's independence and its goal of attaining agricultural self-sufficiency.

When Guevara returned from Africa for a brief stop in March 1965, Castro reportedly scolded him for his harsh criticism of the Soviet Union and asked him to sever his ties with the Cuban government. Guevara obliged in writing: "I formally renounce my posts in the leadership of the Party, my post as Minister, my rank as comandante, my status as a Cuban citizen."[39] Guevara had grown increasingly distant from Castro and the Cuban regime as he watched the revolution diverting from its original course, first abandoning the goals of economic diversification and industrialization, and later embracing the Soviet Union while distancing itself from China. It was not until October 3, 1965, the precise day of the founding of the Fidelista PCC, that Castro made Guevara's resignation public. The timing of the announcement was not random, however; it was scheduled to mark Guevara's break with the revolution and to celebrate the foundation of a

Figure 3.1. Poster by Elena Serrano commemorating the Day of the Heroic Guerilla, OSPAAAL, 1968. *Source*: Lincoln Cushing, *¡Revolución! Cuban Poster Art* (San Francisco: Chronicle, 2003).

new government structure free from Guevara and his closest associates.[40] Once Guevara had lost his usefulness as chief interlocutor with China, he became dispensable and ceased to be the revolution's third man.

Guevara's internationalist admonitions, nonetheless, resonated loudly in Cuba and around the world. In January 1966, his famous speech on a worldwide guerrilla strategy was read to a large audience attending the First Havana Tricontinental Conference. We must create, an absent Guevara had written, "two, three . . . many Vietnams." The conference culminated with the creation of the Organización de Solidaridad de los Pueblos de África, Asia y América Latina (Organization of Solidarity with the Peoples of Africa, Asia and Latin America, OSPAAAL) (figure 3.1). Castro used the occasion as a platform to promote revolutionary internationalism and to assume the mantle of the world's leading internationalist. In that spirit, the government declared 1966 the Year of Solidarity, 1967 the Year of Heroic Vietnam, and 1968 the Year of the Heroic Guerrilla Fighter. If internationalism was a religion, Castro beatified the mysteriously disappeared Guevara as its patron saint while keeping for himself the role of highest priest.[41] This was another manifestation of Guevarism without Guevara, the pursuit of aggressive internationalist involvement in the absence of the mythical Argentine guerrillero.

Disguised as a bespectacled, bald, middle-aged businessman from Uruguay, Guevara arrived in Bolivia in November 1966. Along with a small number of guerrilleros, Guevara marched to Samaipata in Bolivia's southeast, where he met with Mario Monje, president of the Communist Party of Bolivia. To Guevara's chagrin, the pro–Soviet Union Monje withdrew support for the guerrilla operation, and as a result only a handful of Bolivians joined. The small guerrilla force soon came under the attack of special Bolivian military units.[42]

For months, Guevara and his rebels trekked through thick jungle. One of Guevara's men described the vicissitudes suffered by the guerrilla force, recalling "the extremely difficult life, the constant back-and-forth with supplies, building things, carrying knapsacks so heavy they sometimes make one's legs buckle under, the hunger that often stabs one's stomach like a sharp knife, the long marches over difficult terrain, and the constant possibility of falling into an ambush by soldiers." On October 8, 1967, Bolivian forces finally captured Guevara. They executed him on the next day. Thus ended the life of the legendary revolutionary.[43] Castro condemned the Soviet Union for having contributed to Guevara's martyrdom by forcing the Bolivian Communist Party to withdraw its support from him. Arguably, Castro also shared in the blame, given the minimal assistance Cuba gave to Guevara's guerrillas. Perhaps, as Bryan Latell and others have suggested, Castro even played an active role in his demise.[44]

Conversely, Carlos Rafael Rodríguez's star rose. He assumed very important positions in the newly created PCC as a member of the Economic Division of the party's Central Committee and its secretariat, replacing Guevara as the revolution's "third man." He was perfect for the role. He had demonstrated unfailing loyalty to the Castro brothers; back in 1959–60, he had been instrumental in the Castros' strategy of pitting the PSP against the M-26-7 with the object of debilitating the latter; and soon thereafter, he had played a similar role vis-à-vis the PSP's most pro-Soviet communist faction in order to advance the Fidelista faction. Rodríguez also lacked charisma and was unthreatening. No one would ever immortalize his image with a camera or wear a T-shirt bearing his likeness. Equally important, he was bright and astute and was well connected in Moscow.[45]

One of the signs of growing Soviet influence was the creation of a communist party that closely resembled the structure and prerogatives of the Soviet Communist Party. The creation of the PCC was yet another mechanism to strengthen Fidelista influence at the expense of the old PSP and Guevarist factions. Back in February 1963, ORI had morphed into a new organization: the Partido Unido de la Revolución Socialista de Cuba (PURS; United Party of the Cuban Socialist Revolution). In October 1965, Castro announced that the new PCC had replaced the PURS. The new party remained an elite body, however; its membership represented a mere one-half of 1 percent of the population.[46] Its leadership structure consisted of a 100-member Central Committee, a politburo of eight, and a six-member secretariat. Significantly, old communists constituted a small minority within the leadership structure. Fewer than a quarter of Central Committee members hailed from the ranks of the old PSP, among them a rehabilitated Escalante; and none belonged to the powerful Politburo, which included the Castro brothers and six confirmed Fidelistas. Only two old communists-turned-Fidelistas, Blas Roca and Rodríguez, served in the party secretariat.[47] Guevara supporters were also visibly absent from the party hierarchy. The armed forces, Raúl Castro's power base, had a preponderant presence within the PCC. Two-thirds of the Central Committee consisted of active members of the military, most of them high-ranking officers. Five members of the original Politburo held the rank of comandante; five years later, six army officers sat in the eight-member Politburo. At that time twelve men on horseback served as cabinet members.[48]

In spite of the fact that the revolution did much to eradicate gender and race discrimination and expanded educational and employment opportunities for women and blacks, their representation in the higher echelons of political power remained minimal. Only five of the original 100 PCC Central Committee members were women, and not one served in either the Politburo or the secretariat. Exemplary military service was one of the best ways to ascend to positions of political authority, and women did not have such opportunities.[49]

Black Cubans were poorly represented, not just in leadership positions but in most professional fields. While formal legal racial discrimination had ended early in the revolution and blacks were among the most loyal supporters of the regime, their integration into positions of authority proceeded slowly. Only 9 percent of the PCC's original Central Committee were blacks and mulattos, and whites—almost all male—dominated cabinet positions and leadership positions in the PCC.[50] Discrimination may have been formally outlawed, but sexism and racism could not be eradicated with the stroke of a pen.

Generous Soviet support strengthened Cuba's military, which was modeled after and designed for coordination with the Soviet military.[51] The Cuban armed forces had become increasingly professionalized, well trained, and well armed. From the beginning, the military had played a critical role in the consolidation of the revolutionary government, but its prestige grew further in the wake of the Bay of Pigs victory. Military service had become obligatory in 1963, expanding the military's ranks precisely at a time when soldiers were being called on to play a substantial role in economic activities such as cane cutting and construction. In 1965, a Sovietized FAR defeated the remnants of organized armed opposition when special army units exterminated the last of El Escambray's so-called bandits. Over 3,000 anti-Castro peasant guerrillas died in battle or by firing squads during the fighting in El Escambray. Surviving relatives were forcefully relocated to Havana and eventually resettled in various locations in the provinces of Pinar del Río and Ciego de Ávila. The removal of Cuban peasants to *campos de reconcentrados* (forced relocation camps) was a tactic used by Spanish general Valeriano Weyler, aka the butcher, in the 1890s, by Batista's army in the 1950s, and now by Castro.[52]

In spite of the fact that the Soviet Union had pulled Cuba into its orbit, tensions remained between the two communist nations. The Soviets used their economic power, particularly the lure of their vast sugar market, to coerce Cuba into submission and bring it closer to the Soviet line. In 1967, taking advantage of the Sino-Cuban rift, they cut Cuba's sugar quota by 20 percent, reduced oil shipments, withheld further arms shipments, and suspended negotiations for the next triennial trade agreement.[53] Castro demonstrated his indignation by shunning Premier Aleksei N. Kosygin during his June 1967 visit to Havana and by dispatching a third-tier government representative to the celebration of the fiftieth anniversary of the Bolshevik Revolution.[54] The Castro brothers also went after Escalante and his associates, whose loyalty to the Soviet Union and reformist ideas became increasingly intolerable in post–Great Debate Cuba. In late 1967, Escalante and another forty-two individuals were arrested and charged with treason and conspiracy with Soviet officials to undermine Castro's rule. On January 28, 1968, a tribunal purged Escalante from the PCC. A judicial process followed in which Escalante and thirty-six others were charged with conspiracy. Found guilty, Escalante was sentenced to fifteen years of hard labor, while the other members of his so-called microfaction received shorter sentences.[55] This was the culmination of the latest of Castro's domestic political triangulation strategies: eliminating the old communists who were loyal to the Soviet Union, people he had previously used to eliminate the civilianist and moderate branch of the M-26-7.

There were limits to how far anti-Soviet rhetoric and actions could go. Cuba had become extremely dependent on the Soviet Union, and the revolution's survival hinged on long-term Soviet economic, technical, and military support and the continuation of multiyear trade agreements that locked in favorable sugar prices. The days of successful triangulation of international powers were now over. Such strategies had worked when Cuba pitted the United States against the Soviet Union in 1959–60 and again when it pitted the Chinese against the Soviets in 1963–66, but now there was no world power that Cuba could pit against the USSR. In fact, unlike the United States in 1960 and the Chinese in 1966, the Soviets managed to bring Cuba into submission by threatening to cut import levels, financial support, and the supply of weapons.

The real test of Cuba's autonomy vis-à-vis the Soviet Union came in mid-1968. With mild Soviet economic sanctions in place and no weapons arriving in Cuban ports, Cuba's Maximum Leader had to make a difficult decision, and he once again prioritized his regime's survival over revolutionary and nationalist values. On August 20–21, 1968, Soviet and Warsaw Pact tanks roared into Czechoslovakia to smash the reformist government of Alexander Dubcek. Castro not only failed to condemn the Soviet invasion, he condoned it, justifying it as a "bitter necessity." The Soviets' not-so-gentle bear hug worked: when Castro openly defended the Soviets' crushing of Czechoslovakia's reformist government, Cuba was promptly rewarded with the restoration of previously agreed-upon trade levels and shipments of free weapons.[56]

In the domestic realm, the government also pursued Guevarism without Guevara, which included the quest for radical egalitarianism through the elimination of extant vestiges of capitalism, through the use of moral incentives, and through the promotion of volunteerism and the exaltation of the "New Man."[57] The time was ripe for Guevarism. Cuba was in the midst of a prolonged economic crisis and chronic shortages of consumer goods, and the government was no longer able to reward hard work and extraordinary efforts with material incentives, such as higher salaries and home appliances. Higher salaries would have proven ineffective, given the shortage of products available to those earning additional income for their extraordinary productivity.

Egalitarianism was another major tenet of Guevarism. During the second half of the 1960s, new policies and legislation further reduced income inequalities. New pay scales for government workers that were implemented in 1966 substantially narrowed the gap between the highest- and lowest-paying jobs; henceforward, top earners received a maximum of 450 pesos per month, while those at the bottom of the pay scale continued to be guaranteed minimum salaries of 95 pesos. Changes in salary structures also helped reduce socioeconomic inequalities between urban centers and the countryside. Between 1963 and 1970, average agricultural wages increased 54 percent, while salaries in industry and social services fell by 22 and 37 percent, respectively. Other sources of income disparity were phased out through the elimination of productivity bonuses, cash prizes, and remuneration for overtime work.[58]

Food rationing served as yet another equalizing mechanism, whereby the poorest citizens were guaranteed a modestly adequate diet similar to that available to those at higher income levels. At mid-decade, milk, coffee, beer, and other items were added to the rations list. Cubans increasingly depended on *la libreta*, particularly after the 1968 Revolutionary Offensive, when alternative sources of food, such as privately owned fruit and vegetable stands and restaurants, were closed down or nationalized.[59]

In an effort to create a more egalitarian society, the state expanded free social and public services, including health care, education, child care, bus transportation, sports events, and various utility services.[60] Health and education were the areas of greater expansion and transformation as the government pursued the goal of providing these services to all Cubans free of charge. The biggest innovation in the area of health care was the establishment of polyclinics throughout the island beginning in 1965. Each polyclinic served between 20,000 and 30,000 people in urban settings and around 7,500 in rural areas. Polyclinics provided basic health services and emphasized a close relationship between health care providers and their patients, preventive medicine, and health education.[61] Following a few early years of declining health statistics, due mainly to the exodus of half of the island's medical doctors, the overall health of the population improved dramatically, as demonstrated by the plunge in the rate of infectious and parasitic diseases from 94.4 per thousand in 1962 to 45.5 in

1970. But by 1970, infant mortality rates stood at 38.7 per thousand, 5.3 points higher than in 1958.[62]

In 1965–66, a program called Schools to the Countryside was unveiled in which secondary-level students were sent to rural boarding schools, where they had to provide "volunteer" agricultural labor. Starting with 20,000 participants in 1965–66, the program involved almost the entire high school population by 1970. In 1967, primary education became compulsory and educational efforts increasingly focused on the expansion of middle school enrollment and retention. Student enrollments in the primary grades more than doubled between 1958–59 and 1968–69 to 1,444,395, while at the middle and secondary levels enrollments grew at an even sharper rate, from 63,526 to 172,144. The number of primary school teachers tripled and the faculty ranks at the higher levels nearly quadrupled. The expansion of education, while commendable, had problems such as low rates of completion even at the primary level. Moreover, political indoctrination permeated the educational system at all levels.[63]

Housing showed the most lackluster improvements among the revolution's social agenda items. Population growth continually outpaced the construction of housing units. Because it continued to attract a steady flow of migrants from other provinces, Havana in particular suffered from intractable housing shortages. City planners and architects under the leadership of charismatic Pastorita Núñez developed the massive housing project of La Habana del Este, along with several other new residential projects, to alleviate the capital city's housing shortage.[64] Later, in the early 1970s, the government constructed an enormous apartment building complex east of Havana named Alamar. This complex eventually housed 130,000 residents, who were handpicked for their proven commitment to the revolution.[65]

The most radical Sino-Guevarist program of the period was the Revolutionary Offensive of 1968. Small businesses and individual professionals and artisans that had survived the nationalizations of the early 1960s came under attack in March 1968 when the government nationalized all remaining private businesses and virtually ended all forms of private employment. Private businesses were deemed to be not only obstacles to the creation of a communist society but also dangerous. Castro presented a detailed analysis of their evil effects when he unveiled the Revolutionary Offensive. He used as an example hot dog stand and pushcart owners, explaining that according to a government study, 95 percent of them were counterrevolutionaries. In addition to reaping huge profits, Castro explained, these individuals were "in constant contact with lumpen and other anti-social and counter-revolutionary elements." In no uncertain terms, he promised that "private trade, self-employment, private industry, or anything like it will not have any future in this country."[66]

In all, the Revolutionary Offensive affected around 58,000 small businesses ranging from TV repair shops and beauty salons and individuals ranging from cab drivers to peanut vendors. The remaining independent service providers were likewise banned from working on their own. Individuals engaged in such activities had been among the strongest supporters of the M-26-7 and the revolution during its early years. Whether veterinarians, locksmiths, or housepainters, all Cubans with the exception of a decreasing number of small farmers could henceforth work only for the government. The state now controlled 100 percent of industry, construction, retail, wholesale and international trade, transportation, banking, and education. Only 30 percent of agricultural production remained in private hands, but the sale and distribution of agricultural products became state monopolies. Before the decade was over, 86 percent of the workforce was on the state's payroll.[67]

In sum, with Guevara dead and Escalante behind bars, the only faction of the Great Debate left standing was Rodríguez's Fidelistas. He and other Castro loyalists would henceforward execute a hybrid formula that included the core Guevarist values of nonreformist socialism, egalitarianism, volunteerism, and internationalism while yielding to Soviet pressures to reverse the economic goals of diversification and industrialization and, eventually, the goal of full autonomy in international affairs. In global-strategic terms, these compromises secured Soviet economic and military support, which compensated for a sharp reduction in Chinese trade and aid.

Domestically, Cuba retained its relative autonomy from reformist Soviet practices such as opening spaces to for-profit private businesses and strengthened its emphasis on moral incentives. In short, the new revolutionary course was one of "compromised idealism" that allowed Castro—to expand on Karol's metaphor—to have his feet in Havana, his heart in Peking, his stomach in Moscow, and his hands throughout the Third World.

Homophobia, "Out of the Game" Poets, and Revolutionary Art

During the mid-1960s, Cuba's leaders redefined the nation's internal enemies. After vanquishing the last counterrevolutionary guerrilla forces of El Escambray and imprisoning nearly 20,000 individuals for political reasons, the state pointed its repressive apparatus toward gays, hippies, religious dissenters, and many writers and artists. Long hair for men and listening to "degenerate" capitalist music, such as the Beatles, became moral offenses against the revolution; it was viewed as extravagant behavior imported from the United States and Great Britain. Government agents rounded up thousands of so-called antisocial elements and conscripted them in what came to be known as Unidades Militares de Ayuda a la Producción (Military Units to Aid Production, UMAPs), penal labor camps created in 1965 ostensibly to reeducate social misfits for reintegration into society.[68]

Homosexuals endured systematic and fierce persecution. A sign at one UMAP camp welcomed them with the ominous message, "Work will turn you into men," chilling words reminiscent of the message adorning the gates of Nazi death camps, "Work will make you free." Jean-Paul Sartre, an early supporter of the revolution, once remarked, "Castro has no Jews, but he has homosexuals." The generally prudish Castro displayed a particular aversion to gay men: he once stated that they could live but would not be allowed to "pervert" others. His regime went to the lengths of establishing a segregated special center for the education of boys deemed effeminate or at risk of turning homosexual. Cuban psychiatrists began experimenting with Soviet and East European "conversion therapies," applying pain and testosterone injections to reduce male homosexual arousal.[69]

Jehovah's Witnesses, Seventh-Day Adventists, members of the Abakuá Afro-Cuban secret society, and other believers were also forced into UMAPs, famously among them a 30-year-old Catholic priest named Jaime Ortega who decades later would become Cuba's first cardinal.[70] The seven years following the arrival of Monsignor Zacchi as the Vatican's chargé d'affaires have been characterized as a period of "silence" for the Catholic Church. As Zacchi put it, his "principal task" was "to reduce the distrust between the Cuban clergy and the government." In 1967, he was elevated to bishop, and he continued to urge Catholics to integrate themselves into the revolution.[71]

Artists and writers whose works deviated from state-dictated norms endured harassment, termination of employment, and in some instances imprisonment. Cabrera Infante went into exile in 1965. His friend and colleague Carlos Franqui remained in Italy and finally broke with the regime in 1970.[72] In 1965, government authorities closed down El Puente, the only remaining independent scholarly publishing house. Members of the El Puente group and other nonconformist intellectuals were marginalized, and some endured systematic persecution and internment in labor camps. Antón Arrufat, for instance, lost the editorship of the prestigious journal *Casa de las Américas*, and painters Servando Cabrera and Raúl Martínez were dismissed from the faculty of the Cubanacán art school. Among the notable inmates of the labor camps were singer-composer Pablo Milanés—who was subsequently rehabilitated politically—and authors Virgilio Piñera, Walterio Carbonell, and Reinaldo Arenas. The government closed down the infamous UMAPs in 1968 in response to mounting protests from Cuban artists and writers, the UNEAC, and numerous foreign artists and intellectuals.[73]

The controversy surrounding UNEAC's 1968 national literary awards was emblematic of the growing difficulties many authors who were not fully integrated into the revolution faced. A jury that included both foreign and Cuban writers granted the national theater award to Arrufat for his version of Aeschylus's play *Los siete contra Tebas* and the poetry award to Heberto Padilla for his collection of poems *Fuera del juego*, both of which had plenty of veiled and metaphorical criticisms of the regime. Hard-line censors within the arts bureaucracy were quick to discover hidden critical allusions in Arrufat's play: the besieged city of Thebes represented Cuba during the Bay of Pigs invasion. A frustrated Eteocles, who stood for Castro, admitted the failure of the revolution: "I distributed the bread and befriended the poor. / Yes, it is true: in the process I raided our house. . . . / Our house stands empty, and still / there was not enough for everyone."[74]

They also objected to several of Padilla's poems, among them the collection's title poem, which contrasted a nonconformist poet who "refuses to play the game" with others who acted as "clowns" and "parrots" who "jump, / take a bow, / take a step back, / smile, / open their mouths," and say, "Well yes, / yes certainly, / of course, yes." "And," continues the poem, "they all dance well, / dance beautifully, / as they are asked to do."[75]

Under state pressure UNEAC directors reached a compromise. Following prolonged negotiations with the jury members, they proceeded to honor their commitment to publish the award-winning books but included a written denunciation of the volumes' alleged antirevolutionary nature, claiming that the awards "had been given to works built upon ideological elements in frontal opposition to revolutionary thought."[76] In the aftermath of the affair, Arrufat ended up at a small municipal library, where he was assigned the menial task of tying newspaper bundles. He could have no visitors, and his co-workers were instructed to shun him. Pablo Armando Fernández, whose *Los niños se despiden* won the 1968 Casa de las Américas award for best novel, was similarly punished, exiled to the bowels of a printing press.[77] Padilla faced better prospects, perhaps because of the protection afforded by his growing international reputation. He received an appointment as professor of literature at the University of Havana and continued to write poetry. He was not completely off the hook, however, as time would tell.[78]

While some writers and artists endured censorship and persecution, others flourished and developed new creative forms of expression. These included writers Alejo Carpentier (*El siglo de las luces*), Jesús Díaz (*Los años duros*), Nancy Morejón (*Richard trajo su flauta y otros argumentos*), and Miguel Barnet (*Biografía de un cimarrón*, an example of the *testimonio* genre he founded); filmmakers Gutiérrez Alea and Humberto Solás, directors of the acclaimed *Memorias del subdesarollo* and *Lucia*, respectively; musicians and composers such as Leo Brower, Harold Gramatges, and founders of the nueva trova movement Silvio Rodríguez, Pablo Milanés, Noel Nicola, and Sara González; painters Luis Martínez Pedro and René Portocarrero; photographers such as Osvaldo Salas and Alberto Korda; and artistic poster designers such as Félix Beltrán and Alfredo Rostgaard. One of the biggest cultural successes was in the area of classical ballet, where Alicia Alonso's Ballet Nacional de Cuba became one of the world's leading companies.[79]

Reaching all segments of Cuban society continued to be a primary goal of the revolution's cultural agenda. Traditional forms of art, such as novels, plays, art exhibits, and musical recitals, became increasingly accessible and affordable to the masses—not always, however, with the best results. In 1964, the lenses of Osvaldo Salas captured an example of some of the contradictions inherent in state-controlled arts. In one image, prima ballerina Alonso dances for an audience of young soldiers. Instead of wearing pointes, tights, and a tutu, she swirls clad in olive-green fatigues and army boots. Her loose, jet-black mane orbits around her head. The dance piece is called "The Advance Guard." The soldiers' dark-skinned, blank faces express indifference at best. Not one of them smiles; several hold their chins as if to keep their capped heads from falling over. It is obvious that they

Figure 3.2. Prima ballerina Alicia Alonso performs "The Advance Guard" for a group of soldiers. Photograph by Osvaldo Salas, 1964. *Source*: Gareth Jenkins, *Havana in My Heart: Seventy-Five Years of Cuban Photography* (Chicago: Chicago Review Press, 2002).

would rather be entertained by a flaming *rumba* dancer. (figure 3.2)[80] The revolution, nonetheless, successfully promoted popular forms of artistic expression: Afro-Cuban music and dance, nueva trova songs, testimonial literature, films, and poster art.[81]

Still Only Ninety Miles Apart?

The United States expanded its policy of isolating Cuba. In 1963 it banned U.S. citizens from traveling to the forbidden island, required special licenses for food and medicine exported to Cuba, and stopped all aid to countries that traded with Cuba. However, shortly before Kennedy's assassination the two countries began secret informal conversations with the object of easing hostilities. Upon becoming president, Johnson avoided further confrontation, and in April 1964 he ordered the end of covert activities against Cuba. Significantly, he also halted investigations into the alleged involvement of Cuban agents in his predecessor's assassination. In a recent book, Brian Latell presented testimony by high-ranking Cuban intelligence defector Florentino Aspillaga to the effect that Cuban intelligence "knew Kennedy would be killed" on the day that it happened.[82]

Since the early days of the revolution, the flow of exiles to the United States had served as an escape valve for the opposition and the disaffected. This flow decreased after the apocalyptic days of the Missile Crisis, precisely when the ranks of the disaffected were swelling due to the intensity of the economic crisis. Castro stopped flights to the United States and only about 80,000 Cubans were permitted to emigrate between October 1962 and November 1965.[83] Castro forced open the escape valve once again in the fall of 1965, surprising a massive audience gathered at the Plaza of the Revolution with an improvised plan for a boatlift to the United States for anyone who wanted to leave. Within a few days, a veritable flotilla departing from the Camarioca pier near Varadero began crossing the Florida Straits back and forth until close to 3,000 Cubans made it to the United States.[84]

That same year, Cuba and the United States negotiated a migration accord that brought order to what had turned into a chaotic situation. The agreement stipulated the creation of an airlift: two daily flights between Varadero and Miami, called "Freedom Flights" in the United States. The passage of the Cuban Adjustment Act by the U.S. Congress in 1966 marked yet another milestone in the history of Cuban emigration. This law gave Cuban émigrés who made it safely to the United States and spent two years there virtually automatic permanent residency status. The act was made retroactive to January 1, 1959, and applied to future exiles.[85]

The airlift ended on April 6, 1973, when its last flight landed at Miami International Airport. By then, over 300,000 Cubans had joined the "other Cuba" taking shape in Miami and its environs.[86] In contrast to the first wave of exiles (1959–62), which consisted of mostly professional and well-to-do people, those departing through the airlift represented a broader spectrum of society. While still overwhelmingly white, this wave included fewer professionals (only 12 percent); most were individuals employed in services, manufacturing, and agriculture.[87] Many had endured land confiscation mandated by the 1963 Agrarian Reform and the expropriation of all remaining private businesses during the Revolutionary Offensive of 1968. In spite of these socioeconomic differences, both waves belonged to the same cohort, made up of individuals and families who had been socialized during the prerevolution era. Most of those who left Cuba during the airlift had relatives already established in South Florida and elsewhere and benefited from the support networks created by earlier exiles.

An estimated 544,600 individuals of Cuban birth or parentage resided in the United States in 1970; of these, 250,406 lived in Florida, the vast majority in Dade County. Others were purposely dispersed throughout the country. A significant Cuban émigré community formed in the New York–New Jersey metropolitan area. Union City, New Jersey, had the area's highest concentration of Cubans, which earned it the nickname "Havana on the Hudson." Over 23,000 Cubans lived in Puerto Rico in that year. According to self-reporting, 97 percent of Cubans residing in the United States were white, the population's gender ratio was 89 men for every 100 women, and the median age was 28.2, just eight months older than the general U.S. population.[88]

While there were socioeconomic differences among the participants of sociologists Nelson Amaro and Alejandro Portes's three-wave periodization (upper and upper-middle class first, followed by the middle class, and then the "petite bourgeoisie"), it is also true that the exile experience—not unlike the revolution that pushed exiles away—had some equalizing effects. An exiled lawyer who, say, had escaped Cuba in 1960 and a plumber leaving the island in 1969 could very well end up living in the same Hialeah neighborhood and sending their children to the same public school. Such things would have been highly unlikely in prerevolutionary Havana or Santiago. While they would have been separated by different class cultures, the plumber and the lawyer would have shared the same fundamental characteristic of being members of the same exile cohort, one whose formative experiences occurred under a capitalist system. Most of the participants in later exile cohorts, by contrast, had grown up and were socialized into a socialist system.

After the failure of the Bay of Pigs invasion, many Cuban exiles lost faith in the support of the U.S. government; some actually felt betrayed and never forgave the Kennedy family. In addition, anti-Castro organizations proliferated. According to the CIA, 415 such groups were active in 1962.[89] A handful of them were paramilitary organizations. Alpha 66, which was founded in Puerto Rico in 1961, was the most daring of these armed groups. It launched numerous commando operations inside Cuba in the 1960s and 1970s. Among those captured by Cuban forces during a 1964 landing was Eloy Gutiérrez Menoyo, who broke with the revolution early on and fled Cuba in January 1961. Other small exile organizations resorted to terrorism and extortion. Orlando Bosch's group, Poder Cubano (Cuban Power), carried out a wave of bombings that targeted Cuban, Mexican, Japanese, British, and Polish vessels and consulates and tourist offices on U.S. soil and abroad. The hard-line group Representación Cubana en el Exilio (Cuban Representation in Exile) included among its leaders Luis Posada Carriles, who would later be charged with and convicted of heinous acts of terrorism, and Jorge Mas Canosa, a businessman who eventually became a multimillionaire and founder of the powerful Cuban American National Foundation (CANF), serving as its president from 1981 until his death in 1997. Miami too had become "an island on horseback" where extreme elements resorted to violence against the revolutionary regime and even against fellow exiles with more conciliatory views.[90]

"Sucropsychosis" and the Ten-Million-Ton Harvest

Nothing shaped the course of Cuba's history during the second half of the 1960s more than the preparation for and pursuit of the heralded ten-million-ton *zafra* (sugar harvest) of 1970. Cuba's leadership cast that goal as essential to the revolution's survival and turned it into a single-focus national obsession. Castro said that producing ten million tons of sugar in 1970 was "more than an economic goal," it was "a yardstick by which to judge the capability of the Revolution." On another occasion, he equated the struggle for the ten million tons with "defending the honor, the prestige, the safety and self-confidence of the country." Castro and other leaders sold the ten-million-ton goal as a critical objective that would allow the economy to expand and would liberate Cuba financially. Sugar, Castro stated, would become Cuba's greatest benefactor, the key to ridding Cuba once and for all of the evil weeds of the persistent plantation. In the same vein, Rodríguez promised that "the ten-million-ton *zafra* will guarantee our country's second liberation."[91] The master planter and his overseer were on the same page in terms of how to run the colossal plantation that Cuba was about to become.

Canadian economist Archibald R. N. Ritter coined the term "sucrophilia" to describe the country's initial back-to-sugar period of 1963–65.

As the march toward the ten million tons intensified, his diagnosis became more severe: "sucropsychosis."[92] The ten-million-ton target was not set because of scientific deliberations or agro-industrial feasibility studies; rather, it was an arbitrary goal set by Castro, who later admitted that ten million was a nice round number. Experts, including Minister of Sugar Orlando Borrego, doubted that it would be possible to meet the ten-million-ton goal, but few dared question Castro's projection. When Aníbal Escalante did so, Raúl Castro chastised him publicly, mocking him as a conspiring prophet.[93] The Castros and other revolutionary leaders continued to defend the viability of harvesting ten million tons even in light of the country's failure, year after year, to meet the incremental quota. A few months before the end of the 1970 *zafra*, in a televised speech, Castro predicted optimistically, "We think that no one will work past July 15." Cuban workers, seemingly on track to reach the sugar production goal, deserved a rest.[94]

In 1966–70, Cuba once again became a virtual sugar plantation; it was the persistent plantation at its peak. A considerable segment of the budget was devoted to sugar production at the expense of social services and investment in other sectors of the economy. Resources in land, labor, energy, and transportation that had previously been applied to other economic activities were now redirected toward sugar. The government invested heavily in the modernization of sugar *centrales* (mills): 40 percent of them dated to the nineteenth century, and the newest one had been built back in 1927.[95] Much of the sugar machinery had to be imported from the Soviet Union, as was the case with fuel, fertilizers, pesticides, tractors, and other vital resources.

While the rationing system had the positive effect of guaranteeing a basic food supply for the entire population at generously subsidized prices, it offered mostly low-quality foodstuffs, and even rationed foods were often unavailable as monthly rations went regularly unfulfilled. In 1969, new consumer goods such as bread and malt drinks and Cuba's historical export staples of sugar and cigars were added to the list of rationed products. Per capita monthly rations for that year included 4 pounds of rice, 1.5 pounds of beans, 9 pounds of tubers, 3 pounds of meat, 2 pounds of fish, 6 pounds of sugar, 1 pound of fat, 15 eggs, and a few other items. Each family was also entitled to a medium-sized pack of detergent, two and a half bars of soap, a roll of toilet paper, and a small tube of toothpaste. By 1970, the rationing system controlled 95 percent of all food sales, but in a 1971 survey 98 percent of respondents said that food rations did not last until the end of the month, and 88 percent stated that rations sufficed for three weeks or less.[96]

As food supplies fell, the population's diet deteriorated. In 1970, calories and proteins consumed by the average Cuban dropped well below pre-revolution levels. According to Claes Brundenius's calculations, from 1958 to 1968 the index of food and beverage availability barely increased, from 100 to 102. Meanwhile, economist Jorge F. Pérez-López calculated a substantial decrease in the availability of rice, beef, beans, fish, and chicken for the same period. Six years into the revolution, per capita consumption of calories was only slightly above the FAO's recommended level (2,700), while protein levels reached only 66 grams, 5 fewer than recommended.[97] Studies conducted by the Cuban government in 1967 and 1969 demonstrated that pockets of malnutrition persisted. Nonetheless, extreme levels of malnutrition had been eradicated throughout the countryside.[98]

Two major initiatives in the second half of the 1960s pushed Cuba further toward full socialization of the economy in preparation for the epic harvest of 1970. First, in 1966 the government established new mechanisms to acquire small, privately held farms and deprived government plantation and farmworkers of access to the small plots of land on which they produced food for their own consumption.[99] This move increased the dependence of rural workers on the state, made them more vulnerable to its insatiable demands for labor, and expanded the amount of land under government control.

Next, in 1967, came the creation of the Cordón de La Habana (Havana's greenbelt). This project aimed to force Havana's urban and suburban population to work in fields around the city planting coffee—a projected eighty million seedlings. One of the campaign's slogans speaks volumes: "*Para tomarlo, hay que sembrarlo*" (If you want to drink it, you must cultivate it).[100] The project turned out to be one of the most disastrous of the revolution's agricultural schemes. For one thing, it required the deforestation of the area where the coffee trees were to be planted; this included tearing down trees that had provided a wide variety of fruits to the population of Havana. Coffee trees take around five years to begin bearing fruit, and hence the *cordón* provided no immediate gains to offset the loss of the fruit trees or to reward *Habaneros* for their backbreaking labor. To make matters worse, the *cordón* was located in hot, low-elevation terrain suitable only for the cultivation of poor-quality robusta beans; the higher-quality arabiga variety requires both higher elevation and the protection of shade trees.[101] A common Cuban saying fits the *cordón* experiment:

"*Acabaron con la quinta y con los mangos*" (they destroyed both the farm and the mangoes).

The 1968 film *Coffea Arábiga* used irony and the juxtaposition of images, words, and sounds to denounce the absurdity of the *cordón* project. The film ends with a not-so-veiled attack on Castro, with the Beatles singing "The Fool on the Hill." The film's director, Nicolás Guillén Landrián, nephew of poet laureate Nicolás Guillén, was arrested and sent to a hard labor camp.[102]

The late 1960s was an inauspicious time to demand more sacrifices and extraordinary labor output from the Cuban people. Gone were the early revolutionary years, when workers received substantial pay increases and experienced a rapid improvement in their material circumstances. Gone too were the material incentives of the early 1960s. Income actually fell at a yearly rate of 2.6 percent between 1962 and 1967, continuing to drop during the balance of the decade. By 1970, workers' wages had sunk below 1959 levels.[103] As rationing expanded and consumer goods became increasingly scarce, the government established austerity programs to keep the population from spending money on nonessential goods and services. Bars were closed down and the lottery was abolished, for example.

After the abolition of slavery in the nineteenth century throughout the Caribbean sugar islands, former slaves generally fled as far as possible from sugar plantations. This was also the case in revolutionary Cuba, where skilled sugarcane cutters abandoned the government-owned plantations en masse. This was understandable, given improvements in education and health and the creation of a stronger safety net for Cuba's poorest. In 1958, an estimated 370,000 individuals were categorized as professional sugarcane cutters; five years later, precisely the time when Cuba returned to sugar, their numbers had fallen to 210,000. The flight of *macheteros* continued: only 88,000 worked the 1969 harvest.[104]

Because of the decreasing supply of sugarcane workers, finding alternative sources of labor became imperative. Volunteers—actual and so-called—were incorporated in large numbers. Many were high school and university students. Women were recruited to take over urban jobs in order to liberate men for work in the cane fields. Castro's 1966 call for the incorporation of one million women into the workforce was only partially successful, however, due to cultural notions of gender roles, the absence of economic incentives, falling wages, and other factors. The percentage of women participating in the labor force increased only a negligible

1.4 percent from prerevolutionary times to 1968. According to a 1969 government study, despite the opportunity to do so, 75 percent of women decided not to join the workforce. Curiously, in 1970, the percentage of Cuban women in the labor force was three times bigger among exiles than among island residents.[105]

The labor shortfalls of the late 1960s were supplemented by coerced labor. This included conscripted soldiers, who were forced to work under military discipline; penal labor; and individuals who had applied for visas to leave the island. Stories abound of physicians whose hands were rendered useless in the operating room after years of cane cutting and of former administrative and clerical workers who succumbed to premature death or permanent disability as a result of forced labor in the countryside. Some workers resorted to self-inflicted wounds to escape the seven-day-a-week brutalizing labor; workers enjoyed a break only on Sunday afternoons.[106] The government also put in place numerous mechanisms to subjugate workers and force them to be more productive, including issuing labor cards to workers that were a record of any form of misbehavior. Labor dossiers, implemented in 1969, included details about individuals' work performance and even about their political attitudes.[107] After a decade of revolution, sugar was still king, and the persistent plantation continued to depend, to a large extent, on coerced forms of labor.

Following the practice of giving an emblematic name to each year, 1969 became the Year of the Decisive Effort and 1970, not surprisingly, the Year of the Ten Million. Accordingly, the year's battle cry was "*Los diez millones van*" (The ten million will happen), an optimism echoed in the lyrics of "Cuba va," the harvest's anthem composed by nueva trova singer-songwriters Milanés, Rodríguez, and Nicola: "Some machete may / get caught up in the undergrowth, / some nights may be / dark and starless, / we may have to cut through the jungle / with our bare arms, / but in spite of these sorrows, no matter what: / Cuba will go forward! Cuba will go forward!"[108]

The 1968 harvest that was scheduled to produce 8 million tons reached only 5.2 million. The planter blamed the overseer, Minister of Sugar Borrego, and fired him. The next harvest was even smaller, the lowest since 1963. At 4.5 million tons, it was half of the projected output. A disappointed Castro referred to it as "the agony of this country."[109] The low output was partially due to a redirection of resources toward the attainment of the 1970 goal: some of the cane slated for harvest in 1969 remained standing for the following year's *zafra*. Authorities purposely shortened

Figure 3.3. Seminarians from the San Carlos Seminary work the 1970 *zafra*. Courtesy of AP.

the 1969 harvest to 86 days, while the 1970 harvest (which actually began in mid-July 1969) was stretched through to July 26; the 1970 harvest was 52 days longer than the average length of the previous five *zafras*.[110]

A total of 1.2 million Cubans (14.5 percent of the entire population) worked in the 1970 sugar harvest. This included around 80,000 professional cane cutters, hundreds of thousands of volunteers and so-called volunteers, and 100,000 military troops (figure 3.3). While the role of women consisted essentially of moving into urban jobs left vacant by men working in the fields, thousands volunteered for sugar work, including a group that organized into the all-female Centennial Youth Column of Camagüey.[111] Penal laborers, exit visa applicants, and peasants forcibly

Table 2. Cuban sugar: production, exports, and prices, 1962–1970

Year	Production level planned by Cuban government, tons	Amount that the USSR agreed to purchase, tons	Production in thousands of tons	Exports in thousands of tons	Soviet import values, U.S. cents per pound	World market price, U.S. cents per pound
1962	—	1.0	4,882	5,131	4.14	2.98
1963	—	1.0	3,882	3,521	6.23	8.5
1964	—	1.0	4,475	4,176	6.04	5.87
1965	6.0	2.1	6,156	5,316	5.90	2.12
1966	6.5	3.0	4,537	4,435	6.17	1.86
1967	7.5	4.0	6,236	5,683	6.14	2.03
1968	8.0	5.0	5,155	4,613	6.12	1.98
1969	9.0	5.0	4,459	4,799	6.12	3.37
1970	10.0	5.0	8,538	6,906	6.11	3.75

Sources: Mesa-Lago, "Economic Policies and Growth," 302; Pérez-López, *Economics of Cuban Sugar*, 49, 126–28, 140, 143; Duncan, *The Soviet Union and Cuba*, 31.

relocated from El Escambray, the last stronghold of armed rural opposition, were also forced to work in the sugarcane fields. Solidarity work brigades from all over the world arrived to help with the *zafra*, including three Venceremos (We Shall Triumph) brigades from the United States.[112]

In spite of the over one million workers employed, the billion pesos invested, the extraordinary extension of the harvest season, and the consequent virtual paralysis of other economic activities, the 1970 *zafra* reached only 8.5 million tons; other estimates placed the harvest at 7.5 million tons. "One pound under 10 million tons," Castro had declared in October 1969, "would represent a moral defeat!" In 1970, Castro fired the new minister of sugar, who had replaced Borrego two years before.[113]

A major cause of the failed *zafra* was insufficient labor: it was estimated that only 89 percent of the required workers were employed.[114] Since the labor force mostly consisted of workers without agricultural experience, productivity levels were low and absenteeism rates were high. The workforce of the late 1960s and 1970 lacked both the revolutionary enthusiasm and Guevarist spirit of the early years of revolution and access to the material incentives that might have motivated them. As Lilian Guerra put it, the *zafras* led to "political exhaustion."[115] Guevarism, for all its merits, had no place in the cane fields.

The government had counted on the mechanization of sugarcane harvesting and loading to meet the ten-million-ton goal. While the loading of cut sugar cane became highly mechanized, increasing from only 1 percent in 1963 to almost 85 percent of the harvest in 1970, the mechanization of the labor-intensive harvesting phase failed. Government officials had hoped to produce or import enough combines to mechanize 30 percent of the harvest. Instead, only 1 percent of the cane was harvested by machine in 1970; the rest was cut manually using sixteenth-century technology.[116]

The imprisoned Escalante, who probably did some cane cutting of his own in fulfillment of his hard-labor sentence, must have found some satisfaction in the failure of the *zafra*, which he had prognosticated years before. Opposition writer Reinaldo Arenas was forced to cut cane at a Pinar del Río plantation and, adding insult to injury, was compelled to write a book glorifying the ten-million-ton harvest. Eventually, exiled in New York City, Arenas wrote rancorously about the failed harvest: "The country had been devastated; thousands upon thousands of fruit trees and royal palms, even forests, had been felled in the attempt to produce those ten million tons of sugar. The sugar mills, trying to double their production, were run into the ground; a fortune would be needed to repair the machinery and resume agricultural production. The whole nation, completely ruined, was now the poorest province of the Soviet Union."[117]

Neither hurricanes nor droughts or floods nor plant diseases—not even CIA sabotage—could be blamed for the shortfall. Land allotments were adequate, as was the amount of cane on the fields, and the workforce cut as much cane as was needed to fulfill the production target. Simply put, the agricultural phase of the 1970 harvest was successful. The failure was mostly due to lack of adequate coordination among the various stages of production, including the precise synchronization of cutting, transport, and processing. Once sugarcane is cut, it must be milled and processed immediately; if this is not coordinated carefully, the cane loses sucrose content. Thus, delays between the agricultural and industrial phases were costly. There were reports that some cane was milled a month after it was harvested, by which time its minimal sucrose content rendered it useless.[118] The primary blame should rest on those in charge of directing, managing, and coordinating the *zafra*: namely, state officials. Castro dramatized his acceptance of blame in his speech of July 26, 1970, when he offered the forlorn crowd the option of replacing him. Not surprisingly, the crowd shouted "*¡No! ¡No!*" and then "*¡Fidel! ¡Fidel!*"[119]

Because the revolution's leadership had turned the ten-million-ton harvest into a matter of national honor, the failure to reach the goal came to represent a moral defeat, the failure of the New Man, and a blow to Castro's prestige. The sucropsychosis that enveloped Cuba had serious long-term consequences. The revolution's second failure to create a basis for industrialization pointed to the impossibility of autonomous, self-sustained economic development. The neglect of other sectors of the economy during the sugar frenzy further debilitated agriculture, mining, and manufacturing. Dependence on sugar production was no longer a temporary evil but rather the country's only feasible option. The plantation was, indeed, persistent, and so were its socioeconomic consequences.

The First Decade on Balance

Some of the revolutionary promises of 1953–58 were eventually fulfilled—rents were cut and ill-gotten cash and properties were recovered from Batistianos, for example—and some were discarded, including elections, the reestablishment of the 1940 Constitution, and the pursuit of economic self-sufficiency. Others were significantly expanded. For example, the 1953 promise to nationalize foreign-owned utilities was extended to the nationalization of all corporate and business properties, foreign and national, large and small; not even hot dog vendors on the street were spared. As new realities emerged—the trade embargo, economic crises, U.S. intervention, Soviet subsidies, and the elimination of the bourgeoisie—new radical goals emerged, among them full socialization, militarization, and, eventually, the Sovietization of Cuban society.

The revolutionary leadership aspired to create a more equitable society by elevating the poorest and limiting the wealth and economic power of the formerly privileged. Over several years, the government eradicated unemployment, raised wages for the lowest income earners, established a salary scale that sharply reduced income inequality, and put the state in control of the distribution of food, housing, education, and health services. It also redistributed wealth and channeled funds, goods, and services toward rural areas.[120] The government generally succeeded in improving quality of life and expanding social services in the first decade of the revolution, particularly in the key areas of education and health care. Its performance in the areas of food distribution, nutrition, and housing was less than stellar, however. While centuries of inequality could not be undone in little over a decade, the revolution successfully eradicated extreme differences between the two Cubas that coexisted on the island prior to 1959. Two Cubas remained, however: one had sailed away on-board the pontoon of exile, and the other remained sandwiched between the Atlantic Ocean and the Caribbean Sea.

The system that emerged cannot be considered democratic according to the consensus definition used by political scientists around the world or the one spelled out in the Universal Declaration of Human Rights, which requires respect for basic human and civil rights; free and fair elections in which various political groups are able to participate; division of powers between independent executive, judicial, and legislative branches; and the existence of a civil society free from state control. The regime, meanwhile, offered its own definition of democracy, in which discrimination on the basis of race and gender had been outlawed and sharply reduced, the en-tire population's most basic social needs were met, and traditional elec-tions had been replaced by new means of popular participation, such as public acclamation in rallies and through the voice of mass organizations like the CDRs, labor unions, and the FMC.

In 1963, the government postponed and then in 1970 discreetly dis-carded the much-heralded goal of industrializing Cuba. By then, the economy was less diversified than it had been in 1958. In fact, the pre-ponderance of sugar among all exports during 1966–70 (80 percent) was equivalent to its proportional importance in 1954–58.[121]

Gross domestic product statistics clearly demonstrate that the econ-omy grew at negligible rates: 1.5 percent between 1961 and 1970. Dur-ing 1966–70, it froze. When population growth is factored in, it becomes clear that the economy actually shrank during the first twelve years of revolution.[122] At the same time, the foreign debt grew exponentially, from $45.5 million in 1959 to a whopping $4.2 billion in 1972. Cuba's cumula-tive trade deficits skyrocketed, reaching $1.5 billion in 1970.[123]

While Cuba's major trading partners were entirely different from those of the prerevolutionary era, its dependency on foreign trade and on a sin-gle product for a single market persisted.[124] Whereas in 1958, 67 percent of Cuba's exports had headed to the United States and the United States had absorbed 70 percent of Cuba's exports, by 1968, Cuba was sending 44 percent of its exports to the Soviet Union and 19 percent to the other Warsaw Pact nations (a combined total of 63 percent) and was receiving 61 percent of its imports from the USSR and 11 percent from Eastern Europe.[125]

The failure of the ten-million-ton harvest was a major turning point in the history of the revolution. Cuba's attempts to achieve economic independence and then national sovereignty had failed not once but twice. During the tortuous push toward the ten million, the revolution lost its ability to choose among conflicting allies and trading partners, among contending ideological models, and among competing voices. The struggling regime was seemingly left with no option other than the persistent plantation, no option beyond increasing its dependence on the Soviet Union and its allies, and no power to assert its domestic and foreign policy independently from the dictates of the Soviet Union, which included reversing the primacy of national sovereignty, adopting the goal of accelerated social egalitarianism, using the strategy of moral incentives, and providing military support for guerrilla movements throughout the world. Growing Soviet pressure soon led Cuba to embrace—albeit reluctantly—the Soviets' reformist formula, which combined a rigidly planned centralized economy, the continued use of market mechanisms, and some private capitalist ventures. Cuban-born sociologist Marifeli Pérez-Stable has claimed, and others have agreed, that such changes marked the end of the revolution: "Indeed," she stated, "the year 1970 poignantly marked the end of the revolution."[126] While the revolution may not have ended, it was a far cry from what it had been during its "heroic idealistic" phase in 1959–62. By decade's end, actually, the shift toward "compromised idealism" had already reversed radical and egalitarian aspects of the revolution.

PART II

Personalistic Institutionalization, 1971–1990

4

▼

We Must Turn the Setback into Victory

Sovietization, Institutionalization, and the Expanding Cuban Diaspora, 1971–1985

1971—Year of Productivity
1973—Year of the Twentieth Anniversary of Moncada
1974—Year of the Fifteenth Anniversary of the Revolution
1975—Year of the First Congress of the Cuban Communist Party
1976—Year of the Twentieth Anniversary of the *Granma*
1977—Year of Institutionalization
1978—Year of the Ninth Festival
1979—Year of the Twentieth Anniversary of the Victory
1980—Year of the Second Congress of the Cuban Communist Party
1981—Year of the Twentieth Anniversary of Girón
1982—Year of the Twenty-Third Anniversary of the Revolution
1983—Year of the Thirtieth Anniversary of Moncada
1984—Year of the Twenty-Fifth Anniversary of the Triumph of the Revolution
1985—Year of the Third Congress of the Cuban Communist Party

> Rumors circulated that someone had boiled and eaten the ambassador's cat. People were tearing leaves from the trees and eating them—the mangoes had long been gobbled up. Some made soup from fish bones and drank warm water seasoned with salt to alleviate their hunger. . . . The people of Cuba would rather suffer inhumane conditions, eating pets and shrubbery to survive, than live in a communist paradise.
>
> **Mirta Ojito, *Finding Mañana***

On July 26, 1970, Castro addressed the Cuban people who had gathered to commemorate yet another anniversary of the Moncada attack; authorities had purposely scheduled the end of the *zafra* for that date to use the occasion to celebrate the anticipated success of the ten-million-ton harvest. Back on May 19, however, Castro had somberly announced that production would fall short of the much-heralded goal. With little to celebrate on July 26, he instead recognized the country's dismal economic situation and, in passing, accepted part of the blame. Castro called for a fresh start and coined the slogan "We must turn the setback into victory." He emphasized the need to expand the national workforce and increase worker productivity and outlined major structural reforms to spread authority beyond the top party leadership and the Council of Ministers, expand the influence of the mass organizations, and grant more economic decision-making power to managers at the production level.[1]

In the aftermath of the 1970 harvest setback, Cuba embarked on a wide array of ideological, social, and economic transformations that closely resembled the Soviet reforms of the mid-1960s, which Castro and other leaders had previously disparaged as reactionary and capitalistic. In the process, the government officially reformulated several of the revolution's foundational principles for the sake of a new model of economic growth that was dependent on the Soviet Union and Eastern Europe. New laws and programs actually reversed wealth redistribution, the pursuit of egalitarianism, and the application of moral incentives to motivate productivity by reinstituting material incentives that led to increased productivity but also produced growing income inequalities. While the revolutionary regime itself did not end, its post-1970 orientation differed substantially from what its leaders had envisioned and promised during the early revolutionary years. The 1970 watershed separated the early idealist phase of the revolution from a new fifteen-year period of pragmatic institutionalization during which a sugar-centered economy, Soviet-style reforms, dependent development, and material incentives became guiding policies. Students of the Cuban Revolution have referred to this period as one of institutionalization; but that term implies that institutions become more powerful than (and independent from) particular leaders. Because the Castro brothers and other revolutionary leaders retained more power than the institutions they created or formalized, I use the qualifier "personalistic" in reference to the process of institutionalization.

The most emblematic leaders of the revolution's new phase were Carlos Rafael Rodríguez, who in 1970 took on the powerful post of head of the newly created Inter-Governmental Soviet Cuban Commission for Economic, Scientific, and Technological Cooperation, and Soviet-trained economist Humberto Pérez, who as head of the Sistema de Dirección y Planificación de la Economía (System of Direction and Planning of the Economy, SDPE), created in 1976, directed Cuba's planned economy in coordination with the Soviets. Rodríguez demonstrated an unmatched ability to adapt to whatever socioeconomic formula Castro embraced at any given time: humanism, then socialism, then orthodox Marxism, then reformed Marxism, and toward the end of his life back to orthodox Marxism. Guevara, for his part, was all but forgotten; his "New Man" model of self-sacrifice, community spirit, and volunteerism lay buried in the cane fields where the battles for the ten million tons were fought and lost.

During the 1970s, Cuba entered a process of political institutionalization that aligned both its government and military structures with those of the Soviet Union and further formalized economic relations between the two countries. In the 1970s and the first half of the 1980s, the revolution also increased its presence in the international arena; Cuba gradually reintegrated itself into the hemisphere's commercial and diplomatic systems. Indeed, the island nation gained ascendancy as an important international political and military player in Africa, the circum-Caribbean region, and among the nations of the Non-Aligned Movement (NAM), which remained formally independent from the major powers' military alliances.

While many of these shifts can be understood as having successfully "turned the [1970] setback into victory," managing as they did to stabilize the national economy and to win Cuba a more prominent place among world nations, many old problems lingered and new ones arose that created the conditions that led to the massive exodus through the port of El Mariel in 1980, thus swelling and profoundly transforming the exile community in South Florida.

Sovietization of the Economy

Since a scarcity of labor had been partially to blame for the failure of the ten-million-ton harvest, the government sought to expand the labor force and increase its productivity. Accordingly, 1971 was dubbed the Year of Productivity. The Cuban leadership used a variety of strategies to attract all able-bodied men and a higher percentage of women to the workforce. These ranged from implementing material incentives to passing coercive antivagrancy legislation to charging for previously free or heavily subsidized goods and services. Castro repeatedly stated that the moral incentives of the late 1960s had worked poorly and that a new version of egalitarianism had to be implemented, once complaining that moral incentives had become "a pretext for some to live off the work done by others."[2] The government began to offer a range of Soviet-inspired material incentives reminiscent of the capitalist, individualistic vestiges the Cuban leadership had vehemently denounced during the 1960s. "Third man" Rodríguez, who had long pushed for the adoption of material incentives, became the architect of the new strategy of Sovietization, and his stature and power within the government rose astronomically.

Beginning in the early 1970s, a new productivity incentive program called the *normas* system offered bonuses to production units, factories for example, that exceeded their established production goals. By 1973, two million workers (80 percent of the labor force) were working under this system. At first, the government allowed units to set their own production goals and determine their rewards, but it turned out that the *normas* system and the rewards it established did not require much additional effort by the workers. When higher authorities eliminated or tightened most of them, the number of participants in the *normas* system decreased. During the late 1970s and first half of the 1980s, however, the ranks of workers under that system expanded once again.[3]

The state also introduced wage increases to stimulate worker productivity. Beginning in 1974, when the government allotted 132 million pesos to raise wages for managers and technicians, salaries for these categories of workers grew disproportionately. The wage gap between managers and laborers expanded further in 1981, when a new pay scale widened the difference between top and bottom earners from 4.67 to 1 to 5.29 to 1, still a remarkably low income differential. To motivate managers to extract higher productivity from their subordinates, the government offered them the opportunity to purchase automobiles and have access to other privileges. Meanwhile, rank-and-file workers demonstrating extraordinary effort received lesser rewards, such as resort vacations and privileged access to the purchase of television sets and other consumer products. Pay for overtime work similarly encouraged productivity at the expense of egalitarianism.[4]

Two new forms of material incentives emerged in 1979–80. Extraordinarily productive and efficient production units received cash bonuses called *primas*. To avoid excessive income differences, however, the government capped *primas* at 30 percent of each worker's basic salary. *Premios*, a profit-sharing system, also went into effect: *premios* allowed state firms to keep part of their profits to distribute among their workers, invest in social projects, or reinvest in their firms. Overall, the number of workers eligible for material incentives went from practically zero in 1970 to encompass the vast majority of the workforce in 1985, when the government spent 91 million pesos in *primas*, 71 million in *premios*, and millions more in *normas*.[5]

In addition to these carrots, the government wielded sticks to boost labor productivity. Just months after the failure of the ten-million-ton harvest, labor minister Jorge Risquet proposed legislation forcing all able-bodied men to work. Passed in 1971, the so-called antivagrancy law established harsh penalties for the willingly unemployed, slackers, and those who were regularly absent from their workplaces. Men who refused to work could be—and in some instances were—sentenced to forced labor camps. Underproductive workers and chronic absentees faced the threat of losing their vacations and other privileges, including access to social services and other benefits.[6]

In order to force reluctant laborers into the workforce, the state reduced and eliminated subsidies for various social and public services and consumer goods. Beginning in the mid-1970s, bus transportation; phone, water, and electric service; sporting events; and day care services, all formerly free, began to require some payment. The government also raised the price of cigarettes, beer, movie tickets, restaurant meals, household appliances, and other nonessential consumer goods.[7] Moreover, the population now had to pay for an ever-larger share of the food it consumed. The availability of rationed food decreased and its importance as a food source correspondingly declined: while rations made up 95 percent of the Cuban diet in 1970, they counted for only 30 percent by 1980. Meals in workplaces and school cafeterias partially made up for the gap and became increasingly important sources of nutrition. This helped reduce absenteeism by giving workers and students an additional incentive to show up for work and school. Although workplace meals were originally distributed free of charge, by the mid-1970s they cost 50 Cuban cents. Given all these changes, individuals found it hard to survive outside the labor market.[8]

The move toward material incentives actually produced a combination of material and moral incentives that did not quite reach the extent of the Soviet and East European cases, where material incentives played a more significant role. At their peak in 1985, all material incentives combined amounted to only 11 percent of worker income. The USSR and the Soviet bloc, by contrast, had higher proportions of material incentives, ranging from 15 percent of regular wages in Hungary to 36.4 percent in the USSR to 55 percent in East Germany. In other words, while the average highly productive East German could earn over one-third of his salary through various forms of material incentives, his Cuban counterpart could expand his income by little over 10 percent.[9]

The most far-reaching and overarching institution of the economy's Sovietization was the SDPE. Under Humberto Pérez's direction, the SDPE institutionalized economic reforms that mirrored those previously implemented in the Soviet Union. Besides establishing the material incentives and market mechanisms mentioned above, the SDPE created a more efficient planning system built around the five-year-plan model (the first one in 1976–80) and decentralized the economy by granting decision-making powers to individual production units while demanding that they operate on a self-financing model, independent of the national budget.[10]

Beginning in the mid-1970s, the government escalated its economic reform program by beginning to reverse the almost complete socialization of the economy carried out during the idealist 1960s. Through these new, radical reforms, the state partially reprivatized some sectors of the economy, allowing individuals to work on their own for profit and encouraging foreign corporations to become co-investors in various state firms to a maximum 49 percent of ownership. A new law passed in 1978 made it possible for citizens to engage in limited, highly regulated, and heavily taxed forms of self-employment, most salient among them house construction, trucking, food production, and the sale of handicrafts.[11]

To address the persistent housing deficit, the government issued licenses to individuals that permitted them to build houses and apartments. An estimated 63 percent of all dwellings constructed between 1981 and 1986 were independently built. Around 10,000 truck owners, meanwhile, provided cargo services *por cuenta propia* (on a self-employed basis). The most widespread and successful type of nongovernment enterprises were the *mercados libres campesinos* (free farmers' markets), which began selling fresh fruits and vegetables in 1980. These *mercados* expanded the availability of food, albeit at much higher prices than the shrinking, subsidized, and unreliable rationing system. By 1981, 200 *mercados* were in operation, fostering a noticeable increase in food production and accounting for nearly 10 percent of consumer food purchases.[12] Furthermore, the General Housing Law of 1984 allowed homeowners to rent properties on a short-term basis and to swap houses and apartments through a cumbersome system called *permutas* that was masterfully satirized by filmmaker Juan Carlos Tabío in *Se Permuta* (1984). These measures chipped away at two major idealist-phase programs: the Revolutionary Offensive and the Urban Reform.[13]

Produce sold at the *mercados* was so expensive that it was beyond the reach of most families. An increasingly ubiquitous black market made foodstuffs available at even higher prices. To combat the resulting price inflation, the government created its own nonrationed food distribution system, which came to be known as the parallel market. In 1982–83, authorities imposed new regulations on the *mercados*, along with virtually confiscatory fees and taxes. State agents, meanwhile, cracked down on profiteering, the diversion of state property, and black market activities.[14]

The numerous mechanisms the state employed to expand the labor force and raise its productivity had positive results. Their success was particularly evident in the increased incorporation of women into the labor force: the proportion of employed women rose sharply from 25 percent in 1970 to 45 percent in 1979. By 1979, women made up 30 percent of the workforce, a proportion that jumped to 38 by 1984.[15] While worker productivity grew moderately during the 1970s, it boomed in the first half of the 1980s, when the most generous material incentives and self-employment reforms took effect. Economist Carmelo Mesa-Lago calculated that productivity increased a substantial 41 percent between 1981 and 1985 alone.[16] This was solid confirmation that material incentives were more effective than all the patriotic harangues, motivational speeches, public recognitions, plaques, medals, and threats and punishments combined.

While the state was Sovietizing the economy, it received vast amounts of Soviet aid. When Cuba was on the verge of bankruptcy in 1970, the Soviet Union bailed out the struggling island nation through a substantial aid package. Meanwhile Vice-President Rodríguez successfully negotiated Cuba's admission to the Council for Mutual Economic Assistance (CMEA, also known as COMECON) in July 1972. The CMEA included the USSR and eight other socialist nations. Its main purpose was to integrate and coordinate the economies of its member nations and facilitate trade and barter among them. Also in 1972, Cuba benefited from a generous adjustment in the terms of Soviet loans. The Soviets agreed to postpone Cuba's loan repayments until 1986 and froze interest on loan principals. To round out the aid package, the Soviets raised their subsidized price for Cuban sugar in 1973 from 6.11 to 11 cents per pound. The five-year-plan trade agreement of 1976–80 hiked the price of sugar to 30.4 cents; it increased again in 1985 to 52 cents, over twice the world market level.[17]

While the Soviets had supported Cuba financially since 1961, the level of aid the USSR provided had been sufficient only to ensure the most basic needs of the populace. This changed during the 1970s and early 1980s, when the USSR decided to turn Cuba into a showcase of successful socialist economic development under Soviet hegemony.[18] The United States pursued a similar strategy with neighboring Puerto Rico, where massive economic aid had turned the poor, mostly rural, agriculture-based colony into a prosperous, predominantly urban, industrial, autonomous commonwealth of the United States.

Soviet aid flowed in under a variety of guises. Some of it was "repayable," including trade credits, trade aid, and loans. "Nonrepayable" aid included trade subsidies for selected Cuban exports and imports, namely, sugar, nickel, and crude oil. During the 1970s, Soviet economic assistance grew at an accelerated pace. Total Soviet aid in 1971–75, exclusive of military aid, reached $3.5 billion, an amount equivalent to the total Cuba had received from 1960 to 1970. Aid levels further increased to $14.2 billion in 1976–80 and $22 billion in 1981–85.[19]

The 1970s were an auspicious period for sugar-exporting nations. Prices climbed to dizzying heights, particularly during the early part of the decade. Prices grew nearly tenfold in just four years, from 3.75 U.S. cents per pound in 1970 to 29.96 cents in 1974. World prices fell thereafter, averaging 13.2 in 1976–80 and 8.61 in 1981–85.[20] But Cuba was protected from the volatility and unpredictability of the world market because of its five-year-plan agreements with the USSR and the CMEA.

Cuba and other Soviet Union allies also benefited from a reliable and heavily discounted supply of oil. While much of the world endured the devastating effects of the oil crisis of 1973–74, Cuba barely felt its impact. Beginning in 1974, the Soviet Union sold oil to Cuba at discounted prices. As stipulated by the 1976–80 five-year plan, Cuba acquired Soviet oil at 70 pesos per ton, considerably cheaper than the world market average of 200 pesos. When a second oil crisis struck in 1979–81, not only was Cuba cushioned from skyrocketing prices, it actually profited from them. The Soviets allowed Cuba to re-export oil and to export Cuban-refined gasoline to other markets. Unbelievably, Cuba even sold part of its oil reserves back to the Soviet Union. Such exports earned Cuba between $200 and $500 million a year, which represented nearly 9 percent of all its exports.[21]

While sugar continued to rule supreme, other economic activities expanded more rapidly, including manufacturing, the fishing industry, and

Table 3. Cuban sugar: production, exports, and prices, 1971–1985

Year	Production, thousands of tons	Exports, thousands of tons	Exports to socialist nations, percent	Exports to the USSR, percent	Exports to other markets, percent	World market price, U.S. cents per pound	Soviet price, U.S. cents per pound
1971	5,950	5,511	59	29	41	4.53	6.23
1972	4,688	4,140	55	27	45	7.43	6.09
1973	5,383	4,797	61	35	39	9.63	12.34
1974	5,926	5,491	59	36	41	29.96	19.69
1975	6,427	5,744	70	55	30	20.50	28.69
1976	6,151	5,764	74	53	26	11.57	27.90
1977	6,953	6,239	75	61	25	8.09	28.30
1978	7,662	7,231	71	54	29	7.84	36.92
1979	7,800	7,269	70	53	30	9.66	38.16
1980	6,805	6,191	64	44	36	28.67	49.03
1981	7,926	7,072	67	45	33	16.89	37.20
1982	8,040	7,743	80	57	20	8.41	36.70
1983	7,460	6,792	75	49	25	8.47	49.72
1984	7,783	7,017	79	52	21	5.20	51.04
1985	7,889	7,182	76	52	24	4.05	48.93

Source: Pérez-López, Economics of Cuban Sugar, 49, 126–28, 140, 155.

medical products development. Cuba began to build a considerable proportion of its sugar-processing machinery along with trucks and buses, and it actually came close to becoming self-sufficient in pharmaceutical products. By the mid-1970s, the government was investing more in industry than in agriculture.[22] Some of this industrial investment flowed toward the mechanization and modernization of the sugar industry. Whereas harvesting machines cut only 1 percent of cane in 1970, this figure reached 62 percent by 1985. The modernization of old *centrales* and the construction of new ones was even more challenging and expensive.[23]

The combination of generous Soviet aid and subsidies, consistently high sugar prices, increased worker productivity, and heavy investments in the industry led to growing sugar output and gave sugar a higher proportional importance among exports. The volume of sugar exports rose from a yearly average of 5.4 million tons in 1971–75 to 6.5 million in 1976–80 to 7.2 million in 1981–85. The plantation persisted and thrived.[24]

The stabilization and strengthening of the Cuban economy from 1971 to 1985 was an odds-defying accomplishment. Rates of growth surpassed those of the rest of Latin America. The economy grew at an astonishing annual rate of 14 percent between 1971 and 1975. The growth rate slowed down during the second half of the decade, actually hitting a brief recession in 1979–80, but then it grew again at a respectable 7.3 percent yearly average from 1981 to 1985.[25] Cuba was also spared the dramatic economic swings that plagued its neighbors in the Caribbean and Latin America; it avoided the ballooning inflations that hit other countries in the hemisphere and the concomitant shock treatments so liberally inflicted by the World Bank and the International Monetary Fund. None of this would have been possible without the massive economic aid provided by the Soviets.

Yet Cuba paid a price too. Its trade deficits and foreign debt skyrocketed, its economic reliance on the export sector doubled in three decades, and its devotion to King Sugar spread: sugar made up 87 percent of agricultural exports in 1975–79. Similarly, its dependence on one market—the USSR and the CMEA—surpassed 64 percent between 1976 and 1984.[26] Although the revolution freed the island nation from its neocolonial ties to the United States, Cuba could not escape the suffocating sugar trap, and the economic reforms of the 1970s increased its dependence on the Soviet Union. Instead of being self-sustained, the island's manufacturing spurt depended on the USSR and the CMEA.

It is curious that despite a substantial and prolonged Soviet and East European presence in Cuba and the tens of thousands of Cubans who spent time studying in the various countries of the socialist bloc, such nations had a barely perceivable cultural impact on the Cuban people. One interesting exception was the 1970s fad of giving Cuban children Russian names. Names like Pavel, Vladimir, Ivan, Nadezca, and Tatiana became as common as Carlos or María. There are some odd examples of the Soviet influence on child-naming practices, including Aurica, the brand name of Soviet-made washing machines, and Rosía, the name of a Moscow hotel frequented by Cuban travelers. Toward the end of the decade, a new naming fad spread as many children received names that started with the letter Y; some like Yuri, Yulieski, Yuriorkis, and Yevgeny, were or sounded Russian.[27]

Political Institutionalization

As the Cuban economy became Sovietized, the revolution embarked on a parallel process of political and military institutionalization, a restructuring of government bodies and the armed forces with the goal of aligning them more closely to Soviet institutions. Discussions of the transformations to come began as early as 1970 within the highest echelons of the PCC. The general goals of institutionalization included strengthening the PCC, creating a new constitution and electoral system, and decentralizing power by modestly expanding the participation of the citizenry in governance.

Although the PCC had been a rather weak and marginal institution since its birth in 1965, its membership grew rapidly as it increased its power and influence. Its ranks nearly doubled from 1969 to 1970, reaching 100,000 members. Party membership doubled twice more by 1982, reaching 434,000. PCC members had a virtual monopoly on the highest posts in the state apparatus and in the military.[28]

The First Party Congress was a major step in elevating the PCC's influence and power—significant enough that the government named 1975 the Year of the First Congress of the Cuban Communist Party (figure 4.1). The party leadership agreed to strengthen the PCC by expanding its Central Committee from 100 to 112 members and its Politburo from 8 to 13.[29] Among the matters approved during the congress were the revision of the party platform and the restructuring of geographic administrative divisions by expanding the number of provinces from six to fourteen and consolidating the existing 407 municipalities into 169. More importantly, the congress approved the 1976–80 economic plan and the draft for a new constitution created by a commission of government, party, and mass organization delegates.

Following the party's acceptance of the draft constitution, the general population approved it virtually unanimously through a referendum, and on February 24, 1976, it became the law of the land. The Constitution established that the Republic of Cuba was a democratic socialist state guided by Marxism-Leninism. Some of its articles were pulled almost word for word from the current Soviet Constitution, which dated to 1936. It recognized the primacy of the PCC as the "guiding force of society and the State."[30] It also established a government structure in which the National Assembly of People's Power served as the "supreme organ of the state" and had direct legislative and indirect administrative powers.[31]

Figure 4.1. Poster commemorating the First Congress of the Cuban Communist Party, 1975.

The National Assembly was theoretically the peak of a complex, multi-level electoral system of representation. The assembly's powers, however, were restricted by provisions prescribing that the body meet only twice per year; in practice, those sessions lasted only two or three days. Actual legislative power, thus, lay with the 31-member Council of State. Modeled after the USSR's Presidium of the Supreme Soviet, the Council of State monopolized lawmaking during the 360 or so days when the National Assembly was not in session.[32]

The first nationwide elections since the Batista-rigged electoral contest of November 1958 took place on October 10, 1976. Around 5 million Cubans participated. This was a limited and indirect election process. The electorate voted directly only at the municipal level; voting for higher-level delegates was restricted to elected municipal delegates, who then selected provincial-level delegates, who in turn held the exclusive right to vote for delegates to the National Assembly.[33]

The National Assembly chose old-time communist Blas Roca as its president, a sign of his rising importance given Cuba's increasingly close relations with the USSR. As expected, the assembly selected Castro as president of the Council of State and his younger brother as vice-president, both unanimously.[34] The Council of Ministers, which the Constitution recognized as the "maximum executive and administrative body," was ostensibly selected by the Council of State, but in his capacity as president, Castro had the power to nominate and therefore select the ministers.[35] The judiciary remained constitutionally subordinate to the National Assembly and Council of State, which appointed the judges who sat on the Popular Supreme Court, the highest judicial body.[36] Political institutionalization thus was clearly personalistic, the Castros retaining power over the institutions they created.

Chapter 7 of the Constitution spelled out the rights granted to the citizenry. Many of these were social rather than individual rights. They include the right to employment, to the benefits of the social security system, to education, and to health care—even, curiously, the right to physical education, sports, and recreation. Also mentioned, albeit with many caveats, were limited individual freedoms of the liberal Western tradition: speech, press, worship, association, and the like. These individual rights were applicable only insofar as "they conformed to the objectives of socialist society." The state controlled all media; freedom to gather, to engage in demonstrations, and to form associations were only possible through state-sanctioned mass organizations; and freedom of worship was limited to government-regulated religious institutions and only when religious beliefs and practices were not in conflict with the goals of the revolution and were not "exercised in opposition to the Constitution and the laws, or against the existence and goals of the socialist state, nor against the decision of the Cuban people to build socialism and communism."[37]

As far back as 1959, real power had rested with the Castro brothers, and their dominance over the government, the PCC, and the mass organizations grew with the reorganization of the political system in 1976. The Constitution endowed Castro with official dictatorial powers, through which he controlled all branches of government. As commander-in-chief of the armed forces and FAR minister, the Castros also combined civilian and military authority. Fidel Castro also reigned supreme over the PCC, serving as first secretary of the party and its Politburo.[38]

A lingering shortcoming of the political system was its poor record of incorporating women and blacks and mulattos at the higher echelons of authority. From the beginning, the revolutionary leadership was almost exclusively male and white. In 1975, ten years after its creation, the party's Central Committee included only six women out of ninety-five members, and women constituted just 13 percent of the party's membership. The 1976 elections yielded a small proportion of women delegates at all levels: 8 percent in the municipal assemblies, 14 percent at the provincial level, and 21 percent in the National Assembly. Blacks and mulattos continued to be underrepresented in the ranks of elected officials: 28 percent at the municipal level and 38 percent in the National Assembly. Blacks and mulattos constituted only 7 percent of the membership of the PCC's Central Committee.[39]

Given the National Assembly's limited powers outlined above, any growing gender and racial diversity was merely symbolic. Where power really mattered—at the head of ministries, in the party secretariat and Politburo, and in the high ranks of the military—both women and blacks remained virtually absent. Comandante Juan Almeida was the token black in the government and the party hierarchy. The miniscule group of women holding ministerial or other high-ranking positions consisted of Castro's companion, Celia Sánchez, secretary of the Council of State (1976–80); Vilma Espín, Raúl Castro's wife and founding president of the FMC; and a handful of women who held vice-ministerial appointments. It is important to note, however, that the expansion of the Central Committee in 1980 permitted the appointment of a larger number of women to its ranks, and by 1985 18 out of 143 members were women. Female representation in national-level mass organization leadership, while increasing, remained low.[40]

The FMC, in contrast, expanded its membership and reach, becoming an increasingly important vehicle for voicing and addressing women's concerns. Its ranks swelled when membership became compulsory in 1968, incorporating 80 percent of all women of eligible age. The federation played a leading role in the creation of the Family Code of 1975 that sought to end discrimination against women and reformed laws pertaining to maternity leave, divorce, alimony, child support, and abortion. Most interestingly, the new code dictated gender relations within the home setting, including controversial and unenforceable provisions that demanded that husbands take on equal domestic chores and child-rearing responsibilities. Access to free abortion services expanded and consequently the ratio of abortions per live births rose from 65:100 in 1975 to 84:100 in 1985. Divorce rates also grew, reaching 44 divorces per 100 marriages in 1989.[41]

Persistent Repression and the Emergence of Dissent

The Soviet system's imprint extended beyond economic and political influences. The 1970s brought a state-imposed Stalinist rigidity on cultural matters and increasing persecution and punishment of nonconformist intellectuals, homosexuals, some religious individuals, and political dissenters. The years 1971–76 came to be known as the *quinquenio gris* (the gray five-year period), during which the government tightened its grip on intellectual and artistic expression. During those years, under arts commissar Luis Pavón Tamayo, the National Culture Council (NCC) unleashed a purge of intellectuals, beginning with what came to be known as the Padilla Affair.[42] The arrest of renowned poet Heberto Padilla in March 1971 for allegedly plotting against the authority of the state and his subsequent detention, torture, and forced confession drew indignation and criticism from intellectuals the world over, many of whom had been staunch supporters of the revolution.[43] Another major blow to cultural expression was the government's closing in 1971 of the monthly journal *Pensamiento Crítico* and the University of Havana's Philosophy Department, under whose auspices the journal had been published since 1967. Western New Left theoretical discussions and critiques of Soviet Marxism had profoundly influenced the journal. Artistic repression softened somewhat, however, after the appointment of Armando Hart in 1976 to head up the new Ministry of Culture, a body that replaced the NCC.[44]

Persecution of gays also increased, and homosexuality came to be seen as an illness and social pathology. The PCC banned gays from its ranks, and in May 1973, homosexuality officially became a crime "against the normal development of sexual relations." Laws banned gays from teaching or pursuing medical careers.[45] Tomás Gutiérrez Alea and Juan Carlos Tabío's acclaimed film *Fresa y chocolate* (1993) masterfully depicts and criticizes official homophobia during the late 1970s. Miguel, a university student and macho militant of the Union of Communist Youth, recruits his roommate, David, to spy on Diego, an openly gay artist who is the antithesis of the revolutionary "man on horseback" and is disaffected with the regime. What starts as a spy-versus-spied-upon relationship eventually turns into a close friendship. One afternoon Diego offers David a glass of "the enemy's" spirit (whiskey), and he toasts their friendship, "Clink, clink. For this encounter"[46] (figure 4.2).

Since the early days of the revolution, Cuba had had a large penal population. More than 50,000 were in prison in the mid-1980s, including

Figure 4.2. Diego (Jorge Perugorría) and David (Vladimir Cruz) toast in a scene from Tomás Gutiérrez Alea and Juan Carlos Tabío's film *Fresa y chocolate* (1994). Courtesy of Instituto Cubano del Arte e Industria Cinematográficos (ICΛIC).

individuals convicted of rather minor offenses: a young man serving three years for illegally selling beer, another serving ten years for selling gasoline coupons diverted from his place of work, and five workers who dared to plan an independent labor union in 1983.[47] The number of political prisoners had declined substantially to an officially recognized 4,500 in 1978; this was due in part to the implementation of the so-called Progressive Plan, which reduced sentences of counterrevolutionary convicts who agreed to participate in an ideological reeducation program. An estimated three-fourths of all political prisoners joined the program. Many of those who remained defiant, called *los plantados* (the planted ones), refused even to wear prison garb as a way of challenging the dictatorship that held them captive under often Dantesque conditions.[48]

Although organized opposition to the revolution had been crushed back in the mid-1960s, new manifestations of dissent emerged in 1976 with the formation of the Comité Cubano Pro Derechos Humanos (Cuban Committee for Human Rights, CCPDH), led by university professor Ricardo Bofill and physician Marta Frayde. Both were soon imprisoned. Three years later, Frayde was forced to leave the island, but Bofill continued leading the movement, only to be reincarcerated in 1980. From behind bars, Bofill; Gustavo Arcos, a veteran of the Moncada attack; and other members of the Committee for Human Rights worked diligently to inform the outside world about atrocities occurring in Cuba's prisons, which included beatings, torture, and executions.[49] One of the best-known political prisoners, Armando Valladares, had been in jail since 1960, according to him for refusing to place a card on his desk bearing a communist slogan. The government's version incriminated him with terrorist activities. After enduring twenty-two years in various prisons, where he was routinely deprived of food and water, humiliated, and tortured, he was finally freed in 1982. Following his release, Valladares published several accounts of his experiences as a political prisoner, most famously the book *Against All Hope*.[50]

While repression in general increased, the state loosened its grip on religion. Around 1969, the officially atheist state began to recognize the benefits of friendlier relations with the Catholic Church and other faith communities, especially because of the growing popularity of liberation theology in Latin America, a reinterpretation of the Christian faith with an emphasis on delivering the poor and powerless from socioeconomic and political oppression. The Chilean, Nicaraguan, and Salvadoran revolutionary experiences also demonstrated that Christian base communities and progressive Catholic priests such as Ernesto Cardenal, who became the Sandinistas' first minister of culture, and archbishop of San Salvador Oscar Romero, who was executed in 1980 by a right-wing death squad, could play critical roles in revolutionary struggles. Beginning in 1979, Cuba allowed a greater degree of religious openness to the Catholic Church, Protestant denominations, and Afro-Cuban religions such as Santería.[51]

Cuba as an International Power

In July 1984, Kenneth N. Skoug Jr., director of the Office of Cuban Affairs of the U.S. Department of State, keenly observed of Cuba, "It is a small island, but it has the foreign policy and the military establishment of a major power."[52] Indeed, beginning in the middle years of the 1970s, Cuba had reformed, expanded, and further professionalized its military, restructuring it to resemble more closely that of the Soviet Union. In the period of détente, when the United States and the USSR avoided direct confrontation, smaller nations aligned with each of the two superpowers and fought in proxy wars around the world under varying degrees of command, guidance, and support from their respective patron powers.

Cuba's foreign policy closely followed the Soviet Union's, and the military establishments of the two nations reached a high degree of coop-eration and coordination. Soviet shipments of weapons and war supplies increased in the 1970s, reaching $3 billion between 1971 and 1976. Cuba doubled its military budget between 1974 and 1978, and by 1975 the FAR was 200,000 troops strong.[53] Cuba's military involvement in Africa, which began in 1975, and later in Central America, demanded further expan-sion of troops, weaponry, and funding. In 1980, the government reacti-vated the civilian militias whose ranks reached 500,000 by 1982. In 1985, when its troop levels peaked, Cuba had the largest number of combat-ready troops of any Latin American country, surpassing those of Brazil, Argentina, and all others combined. Cuba had over 1.7 million men and women, including reservists, militias, and MININT forces.[54] There were more Cubans on horseback than ever before, and they were ready to fight way beyond the island's natural borders.

While Cuban soldiers had been deployed to Algeria, the Congo, and other hot spots since the early 1960s, actual FAR units did not see battle until 1973, when several hundred regular troops—Israeli intelligence claimed as many as 4,000—fought in the Yom Kippur War between Israel and a military coalition led by Egypt and Syria, a strong ally of the Soviet Union. According to a FAR spokesperson, 800 Cubans drove and rode So-viet tanks, and all of them returned safely in spite of the massive carnage that characterized that war. Cuba broke relations with Israel and culti-vated alliances elsewhere in the Middle East, developing close relations with Iraq and Yemen and playing a significant role training Yasser Arafat's Palestinian Liberation Organization guerrillas.[55] Cuba also developed col-laborative relations with Iran following the 1979 Islamic revolution that brought Ayatollah Khomeini to power. Shared anti-U.S. sentiments ce-mented the unlikely alliance between the officially atheist socialist state and the fundamentalist Muslim theocracy. Castro rationalized the alli-ance, stating that there existed no "contradiction between revolution and religion."[56]

The focus of Cuban military engagements in the 1970s was not the Middle East, however, but sub-Saharan Africa. In 1975–76 Cuba launched a military operation in Angola that was code-named Operación Carlota. The name was highly symbolic; it referred to a Yoruba slave named Carlota who in 1843 turned her machete into a weapon and co-led a slave revolt. Manuel Moreno Fraginals, at the time Cuba's most renowned historian, wrote a short essay for *Granma* in 1976 about Manuel, an Angolan slave baptized in Guanabacoa in 1685 that underscored the centuries-long and

Figure 4.3. Cuban soldiers train at a camp in Angola, 1976. Photograph by Manuel Munoa. Courtesy of AP.

intimate blood, cultural, and historical ties between Cubans and Angolans. That same year, César Leante published the historical novel *Los* guerrilleros *negros* about slave rebellion in Cuba. The message of these publications was clear: the costly and prolonged military engagement just beginning in Angola was more than an act of international solidarity, it was a response to racial and ethnic bonds that tied black Cubans to the continent of their ancestors. Black Cubans constituted a disproportionately high number of troops sent to fight in Angola.[57]

Since 1966, Cuba had provided military training to the People's Movement for the Liberation of Angola (MPLA), a communist-leaning coalition of political organizations fighting to gain independence from Portuguese colonial rule (figure 4.3). In the spring of 1975, as Portuguese troops were preparing to withdraw from Angola, MPLA leader Agostinho Neto requested military assistance from Cuba to confront the expected aggression of the National Front for the Liberation of Angola (FNLA), which was supported by Zaire, South Africa, and the CIA, and yet another Angolan guerrilla force, the National Union for the Total Liberation of Angola (UNITA). Although Cuba's decision to intervene in Angola was independent of Soviet designs, the USSR provided Cuba and the MPLA with weapons and supplies, while China and the United States covertly backed and armed the FNLA-UNITA alliance. In response to a combined South

African-Zairian invasion in October 1975, Cuba dispatched regular troops and special forces, around 36,000 by April 1976. Without Cuban support, FNLA-UNITA forces would have literally pushed the MPLA into the Atlantic Ocean. Cuban troops successfully repelled the invading troops and forced them to retreat from Angolan territory before the end of March.[58]

A year later, Cuba became embroiled in the Ogaden War between Ethiopia and Somalia. Chaos and a bloody civil war had spread in Ethiopia following a successful coup against Emperor Haile Selassie in 1974. The new Ethiopian leadership embraced Marxism-Leninism and became the beneficiary of Soviet aid. In July 1977, neighboring Somalia sent troops to Ethiopia's Ogaden territory, occupying 60 percent of its area in just two weeks. During the Ogaden War, the Soviet Union and Cuba fought in perfect coordination against Somalia: the Soviets provided MiG fighter planes, weapons, and supplies, while Cuban soldiers served as trainers and combat troops. Cuban military advisors arrived in Ethiopia in May 1977, and troops—some 12,000—began arriving in January 1978 at the request of the Soviet Union. General Arnaldo Ochoa, a highly decorated veteran of the Sierra Maestra, the Battle of Santa Clara, the Bay of Pigs, and a guerrilla intervention in Venezuela commanded the Cuban troops. By March, the combined Ethiopian-Cuban-Soviet military offensive had pushed all Somali troops out of the Ogaden.[59]

Back in Angola, South African troops made repeated incursions into MPLA-held territory throughout the late 1970s and the 1980s. Cuba sent additional fighting units to repel those troop movements. The most significant of these confrontations was the Battle of Cuito Cuanavale, where Cuban troops stopped a combined UNITA–South African offensive against that key Angolan military installation. This battle had produced tensions between the Castro brothers, who insisted on a higher troop concentration at Cuito Cuanavale, and General Ochoa, who, following his own strategic instincts, decided to strengthen other troop encampments. Following months of negotiations, the warring parties finally agreed on a cease-fire in August 1988. Before the year was over, Cuba and Angola signed an agreement for the removal of all Cuban troops by July 1991.[60] Civil war and bloodshed continued until 2002, however.

Cuba's role in the war not only kept Angola from potentially falling under South African control, it helped debilitate South Africa's own apartheid system, which the African National Congress (ANC) had been battling for decades. International pressure on South Africa mounted, and within months of the end of the war, its government began negotiations to abolish apartheid. The racist legal system and white rule ended when Nelson Mandela and the ANC won the elections of 1994. During his inauguration ceremony, a grateful Mandela embraced Castro and reportedly whispered in his ear "You made this possible."[61]

What had started as a post-independence civil war turned into a regional conflict and soon thereafter into an international war buttressed by dueling ideologies: Marxist-Leninists, reformed Chinese communists, free market capitalists, and South African white supremacists. The three major world powers, while abstaining from sending troops of their own, supported each of the contending sides. For thirteen years, Cuban descendants of Angolan slaves fought with and against their distant cousins. In all, over 300,000 Cubans saw combat, while another 50,000 served in civilian capacities as teachers, engineers, doctors, and the like.[62] When all was said and done, expansive regions of the green continent lay smoldering after years of napalm showers, rays of fire spewed from dueling flamethrowers, missiles fired by Soviet MiGs and French-made Mirages, and exchanges of projectiles of all imaginable calibers. An estimated half a million people lost their lives during the 27-year-long civil war. Official estimates of Cuban deaths reached 2,077, a figure that some have challenged as exceedingly low.[63]

Much has been written about whether Cuba made its own decisions to join the African wars or served as the Soviet Union's proxy in Angola and Ethiopia. While critics of Cuba's military interventions have claimed that it acted as the Soviet Union's proxy, others have argued that it acted independently and oftentimes at odds with the USSR's wishes. In the case of the Somali-Ethiopian War, Cuban and Soviet armed forces clearly coordinated efforts in support of Ethiopia. In Angola, on the other hand, Cuba decided to send troops without even consulting the Soviet Union. Nonetheless, from the very beginning of Cuba's military involvement, the Soviets provided weaponry, supplies, and strategic support.[64] Cuban-born political scientist Samuel Farber recently distinguished between involvement in Angola, which he views as an autonomous "war of duty," and intervention in Ethiopia, a "war of choice," a response to the Soviet Union's Cold War global strategy. While Cuba had traditionally supported the Eritrean nation's quest for independence from Ethiopia, after Selassie was ousted, Cuba openly sided with the new pro-Moscow Ethiopian government seeking to suppress Eritrean nationalist aspirations.[65]

Paradoxically, while pursuing a largely Soviet-dictated foreign policy, Cuba managed to increase its reputation and influence within the

Non-Aligned Movement. This was, in great measure, the result of Cuba's sustained international diplomacy, which included deployment of medical teams and other forms of aid to dozens of Third World countries. In the early 1970s, Cuba had normalized diplomatic and commercial relations with several Latin American countries, the traditional sphere of influence of the United States. During that decade, Cuba's hemispheric isolation began to crumble as new leftist and progressive governments came to power throughout the continent, first in Peru in 1968 and then in Chile in 1971. Nine other Caribbean and Latin American nations reestablished relations with Cuba by 1975, when the OAS voted to lift sanctions against the communist island. By 1985, three other nations established relations with Cuba.[66]

Cuba's courage in standing up against the mighty United States, its partially successful economic system, its military victories in Angola and Ethiopia, and its generous assistance to underdeveloped countries throughout the world helped improve its international standing, which peaked when member nations of NAM elected Castro as the movement's chair for the 1979–82 term. When Soviet troops invaded Afghanistan in 1979, however, Cuba supported the USSR, voting against a UN resolution condemning the aggression against a fellow member of NAM. Because of this, Cuba lost some stature and credibility as leader of the movement, and it failed to get the necessary votes to gain a temporary seat on the UN's Security Council.[67]

Cuba's expansion in the international arena went far beyond its military presence in various theaters of war. In 1977, the Isle of Youth, formerly known as the Isle of Pines, became an educational center for thousands of international students who received free training in a variety of professional and technical fields. By 1984, 18,000 foreign students were enrolled in its various programs. At the same time, Cuba maintained a large international presence of tens of thousands of citizens throughout the Third World, including 4,500 teachers, 3,000 doctors, and numerous technicians. According to estimates, in 1985 Cuba deployed one international worker for every 625 Cubans. Cuban funding also helped build schools, hospitals, and infrastructure around the world, from Jamaica to Angola to Vietnam.[68]

Cuba's increasing economic and political international profile did not escape notice in the United States. For much of the 1970s, U.S.-Cuban relations improved modestly. In 1974, the embattled administration of Richard M. Nixon took the first steps toward loosening the U.S. economic embargo by allowing the importation of Cuban cultural products, such as books, magazines, recordings, and posters. Several members of the U.S. Congress maneuvered to improve relations with the rebel island, led by Senator Edward M. Kennedy, who called for the lifting of the trade embargo his brother had imposed thirteen years before. In August 1975, the United States further relaxed the embargo by allowing subsidiaries of U.S. companies in Latin America to sell products to Cuba. In the same vein, the U.S. government ended sanctions against countries that traded with Cuba. This process, however, came to a halt later in the year, when Cuban troops first arrived in war-torn Angola.

A curious connection existed between the covert efforts of the United States to destabilize and topple the Castro regime in the 1960s and the Nixon administration's use of criminal tactics that threatened the U.S. democratic system and eroded the people's trust in their government. The so-called Watergate plumbers, who operated under direct White House orders, were led by E. Howard Hunt, one of the principal planners of the Bay of Pigs Invasion. Three of the five burglars who broke into the Democratic Party's headquarters at the Watergate building to copy confidential documents and install listening devices were Cubans (Virgilio González, Eugenio Martínez, and Bay of Pigs veteran Bernard Barker) who had been trained by the CIA to carry out sabotage and espionage activities against Cuba. A fourth burglar, Frank Sturgis, had connections to Cuba. He had long been a gunrunner, first for Castro's rebel army and later for the opposition. He had even participated in a failed attempt to kill Castro. The fifth burglar, James McCord, was a former CIA agent who had planted listening devices in Cuba and had been tasked back in 1961 to spy on the pro-Castro Fair Play for Cuba Committee. The Watergate incident, as will be seen later, would not be the last time when CIA operatives trained to subvert socialist governments abroad would also carry out illegal operations at home.[69]

In January 1977, Jimmy Carter ascended to the presidency and immediately revamped U.S. policy toward Latin America, emphasizing human rights and withdrawing support for right-wing military regimes that had taken root throughout the hemisphere. Carter viewed the thawing of U.S.-Cuban relations as an opportunity to push the island to improve its human rights record. During his first year in office, Carter lifted the travel ban to Cuba and allowed U.S. citizens to spend money while visiting the island; he even allowed Cubans residing in the United States to send remittances to their relatives. In September, both countries opened interest sections offices: Cuba through the embassy of Czechoslovakia in Washington, D.C., and the United States through the Swiss Embassy in Havana.[70] Of all the U.S. presidents who had had to contend with Cuba, beginning with William McKinley, who sent U.S. troops to intervene in the Cuban War of Independence in 1898, Carter was the first to treat Cubans honorably and to prove willing to negotiate differences with them as among equals. He did much to shorten the ninety miles of separation, but unfortunately, his headstrong Cuban counterpart did not reciprocate.

Progress toward normalizing relations slowed down in 1978, after Cuba deployed several thousand troops to Ethiopia. U.S. diplomats had already asserted that the withdrawal of troops from Africa was an essential requisite for the normalization of relations.[71] Despite this setback, the Carter years opened up opportunities for dialogue, not just between Cuba and the United States but also between Havana and representatives of a small segment of the Cuban population in the United States seeking closer ties with Cuba. A formal dialogue between the government and a delegation of exiled Cubans in 1978 (which I examine later in this chapter) led to the release of 80 percent of Cuba's political prisoners and the visit to Cuba of over 100,000 exiles in 1979 alone.

In 1979, Cuba-U.S. relations took a decisive turn for the worse, however. First, on March 13, Maurice Bishop, leader of the Marxist New Jewel Movement, took power by force in the Caribbean island of Grenada. Later that year, after almost a decade of insurgency, the socialist Frente Sandinista de Liberación Nacional (Sandinista National Liberation Front) took over control of Nicaragua in the wake of Anastasio Somoza's resignation and flight. Cuba had been funding, training, and arming Sandinista guerrillas for more than a decade, and that support facilitated the Sandinistas' military victory in 1979. Not since the guerrilla victory in Cuba two decades earlier had a popular uprising led to the formation of a socialist government in the hemisphere. Cuba also provided training and weapons to leftist guerillas in neighboring El Salvador.[72] Cuba moved quickly to support both the Sandinistas and the New Jewel Movement's People's Revolutionary Government. Before 1979 was over, more than 1,200 Cuban civilians were laboring in Nicaragua as teachers, medical personnel, and military advisors. Cuba also sent considerable resources for developmental aid to the Sandinista government and hosted thousands of Nicaraguan students.[73] Hundreds of additional civilian and military advisors and, reportedly, actual combat troops were deployed in the next few months as opposition forces organized beyond Nicaragua's borders and launched military attacks against the Sandinistas. When an all-out civil war broke out in El Salvador in 1980 and various rebel organizations coalesced as the Frente Farabundo Martí para la Liberación Nacional (Farabundo Martí National Liberation Front), they received generous economic and military support from Cuba to fight against the U.S.-backed governing junta.[74]

Cuba supported Bishop's revolutionary government in Grenada on a much smaller scale. It offered some weapons, intelligence, and strategic military support; deployed a medical mission; and provided funds for scholarships for study in Cuba and civilian and military monetary grants. The primary task of Cubans in Grenada was the construction of a new airport, the Point Salines International Airport, which, when completed, had the capacity to land both fighter planes and large jet liners for tourism.[75]

The Carter administration opposed Cuba's involvement in Central America and Grenada and the fact that in 1979 the Soviet Union increased its military presence on the island. The United States responded with a threatening show of force, carrying out a training invasion exercise in which 1,800 marines landed at the Guantánamo Naval Base in October 1979.[76]

The Cuba policy of the United States became openly hostile when Ronald Reagan became president in 1981; his secretary of state, the bellicose Alexander Haig, was a vocal proponent of "going to the source," by which he meant confronting Cuba militarily for its support for various guerrilla movements. The Reagan administration poured huge amounts of money, much of it illegally, into supporting the conservative military forces, known as Contras, who were fighting against the Sandinista government and to maintaining its allies in power in El Salvador and Guatemala. In retaliation for Cuba's involvement in the region, the United States terminated the concessions it had made during the brief rapprochement of 1977. In 1982, it tightened the trade embargo, refused to extend the fishing accords, restricted travel to the island, and reduced the amount of money U.S. citizens could spend while visiting.[77]

In 1982, as part of the U.S. policy of containing the spread of leftist governments in the Americas, 7,000 U.S. troops invaded Grenada on October 25, just a few days after a radical faction of the government led by Deputy Prime Minister Winston Bernard Coard staged a coup against Bishop's government. Bishop was executed and several of his supporters were killed. One of the targets of the invading forces was the new airport being built by a Cuban brigade. Both construction workers and the few dozen regular soldiers encamped at the site combated U.S. forces.

Twenty-four Cubans died in action, while the remaining 750 or so surrendered, much to Castro's indignation. They had received orders not to surrender under any circumstance. Upon the brigade's return to Cuba, they were welcomed as heroes. However, the brigade's commander, Colonel Pedro Tortoló, was court-martialed, demoted to the rank of private, and deployed to Angola.[78]

The Reagan administration's illegal efforts to topple the Sandinista government of Nicaragua became public in 1986 and led to the scandal known as the Iran-Contra Affair. The administration's strategy, which was directed from the White House by Lieutenant Colonel Oliver North, consisted of illegally selling weapons to Iran and using the proceeds to illegally arm and supply the Contras. Not unlike the previous major government scandal, Watergate, there was a Cuban connection; at least two CIA-trained exiles played major roles in the Iran-Contra Affair. Convicted and fugitive terrorist and longtime CIA operative Luis Posada Carriles served as direct supplier of weapons for the Contras; another CIA-trained Cuban exile with a long history of covert actions around the world, Félix Rodríguez, also dropped shipments of war matériel for the Contras. This was yet another example of how the United States' illegal and covert actions abroad resulted in criminal behavior at the highest levels of government. In both Watergate and the Iran-Contra Affair, there was a direct connection between American CIA agents and Cuban exiles trained to carry out covert operations and commit crimes against the Cuban regime.[79]

The Cuba Outside Cuba

Following the discontinuation of the air bridge that transported over 300,000 Cubans to the United States between 1965 and 1973, the flow of refugees dropped substantially to around 11,500 per year during 1973–75 and to fewer than 4,000 a year between 1976 and 1979.[80] The Greater Miami area continued to be the primary magnet not just for new exiles but also for exiles relocating from Europe and other parts of the United States. According to census data, 806,200 Cubans and individuals of Cuban origin lived in the United States in 1980. More than half of them resided in Dade County, Florida, where Cubans constituted around 70 percent of all Hispanics and a quarter of the county's total population.[81] The nation's second largest concentration of Cuban exiles was in Union City and West New York in New Jersey. Significant Cuban and Cuban

American populations also resided in major urban areas such as New York, Tampa, Houston, and Los Angeles. Substantial Cuban nuclei also emerged throughout the world, in Madrid, San Juan, Caracas, Mexico City, and beyond.

Northern-based Cubans tended to flow to Miami as soon as they had the chance to do so. A scene in León Ichaso and Orlando Jiménez-Leal's acclaimed film *El Súper* (1979) speaks volumes. It is a cold winter day and heavy snow covers the sidewalks of New York City. The protagonist, Roberto, an embittered exiled building superintendent, returns to his basement apartment after taking out loads of trash. "The whole thing's absurd! Everything in this city!" Roberto exclaims angrily. He throws his gloves and tools on his work desk and continues his tirade: "Can't go on living this way. We must go to Miami and fast!" In the film's closing scene, a visibly distraught Roberto tells his friend Pancho: "I am going to Miami. *To Miami*. I can't stand it any longer." Driving south to Miami and beyond to Key West is actually a common motif in Cuban American literature as well as a recurrent dream—an actual dream—for many an exile. The protagonist of Virgil Suárez's *Going Under* went even further. After reaching Key West's southernmost point buoy, he "turned to the sea and, clothes and all, dove off and plunged into the water. He went under, opened his eyes to the sting of the salt, held his breath and swam. . . . In pursuit of the unattainable, Xavier Cuevas was swimming home." Pilar, the protagonist of Cristina García's *Dreaming in Cuban*, felt the same urge and made plans to go to Key West and reach Havana from there.[82]

Many factors attracted Cubans to the Greater Miami area. Climatic similarities were, of course, an important one, and so was proximity to their beloved island. In Miami, they sought to create another Cuba, a substitute enclave for the homeland, where Cuban culture flourished, at times almost as a caricature of the original. Hundreds of old Cuban businesses, products, and institutions resurged throughout Greater Miami: the restaurants La Carreta and La Esquina de Tejas; retail stores such as La Casa de las Guayaberas (traditional Cuban shirts), La Canastilla Cubana (baby products), and La Moderna Poesía (books); the Caballero Woodlawn and Rivero funeral homes; products such as the soft drinks Materva and Ironbeer, Hatuey and Polar beers and *malta* drinks, Bustelo and Pilón coffee, Nela condensed milk, and Conchita guava paste; institutions such as Belén Jesuit Academy, FEU in exile, the Auténtico and Ortodoxo political parties, and even the Association of Former Employees of El Encanto department store; and places of worship, such as the Chapel of Cuba's patron la Caridad del Cobre off Biscayne Bay and the Shrine of Saint Lazarus in Hialeah.[83]

With the population growing and the passing of time, economic prosperity came to Miami. Cuban entrepreneurship created thousands of businesses, ranging from small coffee windows and fruit and vegetable stands to supermarket and retail chains such as Sedano's and Navarro and financial institutions such as the Continental National and Republic Federal banks. All this was possible, in great measure, because the first exile cohort established solidarity networks and mechanisms to help each other out. This included business loans that required neither credit history nor collateral.[84] According to census information, in 1977 there were nearly 9,000 Cuban-owned businesses in Florida alone. When compared to all other Hispanic groups, Cubans had much higher rates of educational attainment, income, and home ownership. By 1980, Cuban families were earning a median income of $18,245 per year, around 10 percent less than the median of $19,917 for the country as a whole. Meanwhile, the percentage of Cuban and Cuban American families under the poverty line was 11.7, only 2.1 percent higher than the national average. When looking at these statistics it is important to keep in mind that Miami consistently ranks as one of the poorest major U.S. cities, with lower incomes and higher poverty rates.[85]

As a growing number of Cubans became eligible to vote, exile politicians began to gain and wield power at the local, state, and national levels. Between 1975 and 1980, the number of Hispanic voters in Dade County doubled, and in the townships of Hialeah and Miami they became the majority of the electorate. In the 1970s, Cuban exiles were already being elected to judgeships and school board seats. One sign of their growing power was the declaration of Dade County as officially bilingual in 1973. Cuban electoral power became increasingly evident during the 1980s, as reflected by the election of Raúl Martínez as Hialeah's mayor in 1981 and four years later the election of Xavier Suárez as mayor of Miami.[86] By 1981, three of the seven municipal commissioners of Hialeah were Cuban.[87]

Cuban and Cuban American voters were overwhelmingly Republican, in great measure because they identified with the conservatism and Cuba-hostile policies of the Republican Party. In the 1980 and 1984 elections, 90 percent cast their votes for Reagan.[88] Their conservatism should not be read as a sign of blind Yankeeism, however, particularly in cultural matters. While some Cubans embraced U.S. mainstream culture to the point of changing their last names to Anglo surnames—Wilson or Johnson, for example—most clung tenaciously to their identity and culture, and not a few refused to become U.S. citizens and learn the English language. As Susan Eckstein has stated, "Cuban Americans [were] making it in America while only partially acculturating and assimilating."[89]

While most turned to the ballot box to express their political views, a few extremists employed intimidation and violence. New radical terrorist anti-Castro groups emerged in the mid-1970s and carried out hundreds of violent actions on U.S. soil and abroad, including bombings and assassinations. Notorious among these groups was Omega 7, founded in New Jersey in 1974 by Eduardo Arocena. Omega 7 was responsible for scores of bombings, various assassination attempts, and at least two killings between 1975 and 1983. Their bombing targets included Cuban diplomatic offices in New York, Washington, D.C., and other places that they deemed symbolic of solidarity with communist Cuba. Following the arrest and conviction of most of its members between 1983 and 1985, Omega 7 disbanded.[90]

Two of the most notorious Cuban exile terrorists of the period are Orlando Bosch and Luis Posada Carriles. In 1976, they founded the terrorist umbrella organization Coordinadora de Organizaciones Revolucionarias Unidas (Coordinator of United Revolutionary Organizations, CORU), which included Bosch's Acción Cubana and Guillermo Novo Sampol's Movimiento Nacionalista Cubano (Cuban Nationalist Movement). These extremist men on horseback organizations were responsible for a rampage of terrorist actions, most infamously the 1976 bombing of a Cuban commercial plane en route to Barbados that resulted in the death of all seventy-three persons on board. In coordination with Chilean authorities they also assassinated former Chilean diplomat Orlando Letelier.[91]

The most dominant of the nonviolent exile groups was the Cuban American National Foundation (CANF), founded in 1981 by Bay of Pigs veterans Jorge Mas Canosa and Raúl Masvidal. It soon became the largest, best organized, and most successful Cuban exile group. The organization and its political action committee, the Free Cuba PAC, pursued lobbying strategies similar to those employed by the American Israeli Political Action Committee. CANF achieved a high degree of influence with U.S. politicians of both parties and consequently on U.S. foreign policy. Among its accomplishments were the creation of the federally funded Radio Martí (1983) and TV Martí (1990), which beamed anti-communist programs to Cuba, the strengthening of the embargo through the Torricelli (1992) and Helms-Burton (1996) Acts, and the banning of remittances (1994–98).[92]

A number of smaller exile organizations to the left of CANF sought to establish friendlier relations with the Cuban government and foster links through cultural exchanges, travel opportunities, and family reunifications. In 1974, Rutgers University sociology professor Lourdes Casal and a few other young exiles founded the magazine *Areíto*, a quarterly publication focusing on cultural and political topics. The group of young Cuban-born exiles linked to *Areíto* took steps to travel to Cuba. Fifty-five of them organized as the Antonio Maceo Brigade and traveled to the island in December 1977; for most of them, this was their first visit since they had left. More than a dozen Maceo Brigades traveled to the island over the next few years. The first brigade's most significant accomplishment was its preparation of the stage for a dialogue with the Cuban regime.[93] The juncture was propitious. Carter was eager to improve relations with Cuba, and Castro was eager to generate new sources of revenue through the visits of tens of thousands of exiles for brief family reunions. In 1978, after decades of scorning exiles as "scum," "traitors," and *gusanos*, Cuban authorities coined a kinder term to refer to those who had left since 1959; they were now referred to as "the Cuban community abroad."[94]

At the same time, the Cuban government was pursuing another avenue for rapprochement. Cuban agents made contact with Bernardo Benes, a Miami-based Cuban banker known for his moderate political stances. They invited him to a meeting with Castro. With the consent—even encouragement—of the U.S. government, Benes accepted the invitation and agreed to head a commission of seventy-five exiles to begin a formal dialogue with Cuban authorities.[95] The dialogue began in Havana with two meetings between the exiles and a delegation of government officials, one in late November and the other in early December 1978. The exile delegation was overwhelmingly composed of professionals, including numerous intellectuals and college professors. It also included several clergymen and a few laborers, among them a handful of Key West fishermen. The Cuban government carefully selected the members of the exile delegation; it included many left-leaning exiles, a minority of politically moderate voices, and not a single hard-liner or conservative.[96]

Immediately following the dialogue, the government agreed to release 3,600 political prisoners and allow Cubans abroad to visit their families. Among those released by the government were Huber Matos, on the exact day on which he finished his twenty-year sentence; Eloy Gutiérrez Menoyo; and Ramón and Polita Grau-Alsina, the former coordinators of the Pedro Pan children's exodus. Around 100,000 exiles traveled to Cuba for seven-day visits in 1979. They contributed an estimated $100 million to the Cuban treasury with money spent on airfare, overpriced hotel accommodations, meals, and purchases at special dollar-only stores, created to capture hard currency.[97]

The dialogue and its results gave Castro yet another opportunity for triangulation, this time by fomenting divisions among exiles. Many among the Miami exile community harshly criticized the dialogue, insisting instead on a hard-line approach to the Castro regime. Participants and their sympathizers were scorned as *dialogueros*, and some individuals who traveled for short family reunifications were criticized and even threatened. Omega 7 and other radical groups launched a campaign of terror, bombing the homes and businesses of dialogue participants.[98]

The Mass Exodus of El Mariel

The family reunification visits of 1979 had some unforeseen and explosive ramifications. Through direct contact with their exiled relatives, island residents witnessed, heard stories about, and saw pictures of the much better material circumstances their kin enjoyed in the United States and their freedoms and rights. Cubans visiting the island bore presents; brought pictures of their homes, cars, and vacation trips; and bought gifts at the dollar stores that residents were not even allowed to enter. More importantly, islanders confirmed firsthand that exiled Cubans were not the selfish, cruel monsters they had been painted to be by the official propaganda. These temporary family reunions alerted Cubans to the life they could aspire to in the United States. This knowledge, coupled with a severe economic downturn in 1979, spurred many to leave Cuba. In fact, in 1979 and 1980 Cubans made a number of attempts to seek asylum in foreign embassies, and seagoing vessels and aircraft were hijacked by those seeking to flee.[99]

The most dramatic and far-reaching asylum-seeking attempt occurred on April 1, 1980, when a driver crashed his bus through the gates of the Peruvian embassy in Havana. Peru's ambassador immediately granted asylum to the driver and his five passengers. Angered, Castro responded by withdrawing police protection for the embassy and declaring it open. This action led another 10,850 asylum seekers to pack into the embassy grounds, where the lack of water and food—as Mirta Ojito put it, "eating pets and shrubbery to survive"—the absence of bathroom facilities, widespread dehydration and cases of fainting, and an epidemic of

Figure 4.4. Peruvian Embassy grounds overcrowded with asylum seekers, 1980. Courtesy of AP.

gastroenteritis all contributed to pandemonium on the embassy grounds (figure 4.4).[100]

Within a few days, Peru, Costa Rica, the United States, and Spain agreed to take in a few thousand of the asylum seekers. In the meantime, in South Florida, hundreds of individuals prepared a ragtag flotilla to pick up relatives and friends, ignoring repeated warnings by the U.S. government that such actions violated the law.

The government denigrated and systematically harassed the crowd gathered inside the embassy. On April 19, through the coordination of the CDRs, it mobilized nearly one million people to march in repudiation of the crowd. "*¡Que se vayan! ¡Que se vayan!*" (Go away! Go away!) chanted the marchers.[101] The next day, Castro announced that those wishing to leave could do so and opened the port of El Mariel so vessels could come to fetch them. The government used the opportunity to deport thousands of so-called "undesirables." They are "the scum of the country," Castro blasted in his May Day speech, deriding them as "antisocial homosexuals, drug addicts, and gamblers." Among those prodded to leave was a chronically lazy resident of Playa, Marianao. When he learned that in the United States he would have to work, he decided to stay home.[102]

During the first fifteen days of the Mariel exodus, 16,000 refugees arrived in Key West. Despite the U.S. government's attempts to stop the frenzied back-and-forth flow of vessels, the Mariel flotilla continued to transport boatloads of individuals. Because of his humanitarian response to the crisis, Carter actually encouraged the illegal arrival of exiles when he stated on May 5: "We'll continue to provide an open heart and open arms to refugees seeking freedom from Communist domination and from the economic deprivation brought about by Fidel Castro and his government." The following day, he declared a state of emergency in Florida. The exodus lasted over five months, until Castro decided to close the port on September 25. When the last vessel reached Key West, over 125,266 refugees had crossed the Florida Straits.[103]

While the Mariel exodus served as an escape valve to release mounting frustration and rising anti-government feelings, it backfired because it hurt Cuba's international reputation. The prolonged Mariel exodus and intense international media coverage of the event became a source of embarrassment for the revolutionary government. If the revolution was as successful as its leaders claimed, why were so many Cubans—particularly working-class and darker-skinned individuals—so desperate to escape?

Commonly called *marielitos*—a diminutive term that can suggest either endearment or derision—those who left Cuba through El Mariel constituted a second exile cohort that differed substantially from earlier exiles.[104] Their average age was thirty-four years, and a high proportion of them had been born after 1959 or were small children at the time.[105] As children of the revolution, they had been raised in a socialist system that included the experience and expectation of the revolution's social benefits as well as the limitations it imposed on individual rights and economic opportunities.[106] They were more familiar with Russian cartoons and military parades than with Hollywood films and 1950s carnival parades. Revolutionary Cuba was the only Cuba they knew.

Besides being younger, Mariel refugees differed from earlier exiles in other sociodemographic traits. They were predominantly male (70 percent) and single, and their ranks included a larger proportion of nonwhites (18 percent) and a much lower proportion of professionals and administrators. Unlike members of the first cohort, who tended to have established relatives in the United States, only half of Mariel entrants had at least one relative to help ease their settlement in Miami and elsewhere.[107]

The Cuban government's hand selection of a portion of the Mariel refugees had an impact on the overall composition of the exodus and consequently on how they were perceived in the United States. In a systematic fashion, authorities encouraged and at times forced "undesirables" to leave, including hundreds of prison inmates, mental patients, lazy individuals, homosexuals, individuals who refused to work, and religious dissenters, particularly Jehovah's Witnesses and Seventh-Day Adventists.

While the U.S. media sensationally exaggerated the proportion of so-called undesirables, the actual number of Mariel entrants who were criminals and mental patients was small. While some 26,000 had criminal records of some sort, these were mostly for minor offenses that would not be considered crimes outside of Cuba. According to official immigration records, the total number of actual criminals and mental patients was lower than in the general U.S. population.[108]

Artists and intellectuals were overrepresented among Mariel exiles. Notable among them were writers Reinaldo Arenas, Roberto Valero, and Andrés Reynaldo; painter-writer Juan Abreu; and painters Carlos Alfonzo and Juan Boza. In 1983, Arenas, Valero, and a few other Mariel intellectuals founded the journal *Mariel, revista de literatura y de arte* as an outlet for works whose voices and aesthetics differed sharply from those of previous refugees. It is revealing that many Mariel-cohort intellectuals found propitious creative spaces only outside of Miami, in New York, for example.[109]

While poorer than the first cohort of exiles, those who arrived via El Mariel also had to leave all their material possessions behind and suffered the trauma of separating from their families and friends, not knowing when, or if, they would ever see them again. Compounding the trauma of their exit, Mariel entrants confronted an inhospitable reception from both the U.S. government and society in general. The United States was in the midst of an economic recession that featured high unemployment and soaring gasoline prices. The U.S. government began to differentiate between Mariel refugees, officially referred to as "entrants," and earlier exiles, denying the latter automatic political asylum and residency status within one year. New asylum seekers had to provide evidence that they would face persecution if forced to return to Cuba.[110]

All entrants had to be processed by immigration officials. Those who had local sponsors could leave the processing camps, but several thousand were retained in a makeshift detention camp inside the Orange Bowl stadium and later transferred to a tent city under the overpass of Interstate Highway 95. Another 60,000 or so were relocated to special refugee camps in the Florida Panhandle, Arkansas, Pennsylvania, and Wisconsin.[111] In the Arkansas and Florida camps, the Ku Klux Klan organized hate parades.

How ironic that the same individuals who a few weeks before had been derided as *gusanos* (counterrevolutionaries) by rabid Cuban mobs were now being chastised as "communists" and insulted with racist epithets by hooded white supremacists. Some of the imprisoned Mariel exiles rioted and others escaped.[112]

Because of the chaotic nature of their exodus, their vilification by the Cuban government and U.S. media, and the crime wave sweeping through Miami in 1980–81, the Mariel cohort became the victim of negative stereotypes and discrimination. Hollywood, with its historic penchant for depicting Hispanics in the worst possible light, contributed to their denigration through films such as *Scarface* (1983), the story of a fictional *marielito* who becomes a brutally violent drug dealer. Less violent but equally stereotypical and demeaning was *The Perez Family* (1995), a comedy about a group of Mariel refugees who pretend to be a family to expedite their release from a refugee camp.[113]

The established South Florida first-cohort Cuban community resented the fact that these newcomers were tarnishing its image. A 1982 Roper survey demonstrated that the Cuban exile community in general was no longer viewed as a "model minority" and as "golden exiles." In that survey, Cubans ranked first in negative perceptions about immigrant groups (59 percent of respondents) and last in positive perceptions (9 percent of respondents), behind Haitians (10 percent), Puerto Ricans (17 percent) and Mexicans (25 percent). A similar national Gallup poll placed Cubans near the top of a list of least desirable neighbors, just behind cult members.[114]

Relations between those who had left Cuba in the 1960s and early 1970s and their recently arrived compatriots were strained and marked by discrimination against the latter by the former. It became obvious that two decades of exile for one group and two decades of socialist revolution for the other had separated them ideologically, financially, and to some extent culturally. Thus, the Mariel exodus brought about an uneasy reunion of two exile cohorts with different class perspectives, values, concepts of the work ethic, and political and social views. Most Mariel exiles entered the picture as subordinates who were generally employed in low-paying, menial tasks under the supervision of established Cuban bosses. Incredibly, some expected the new exiles to cut cane in Florida plantations under horrendous work conditions alongside semi-enslaved Haitian seasonal workers. A 1983 survey of Mariel exiles showed that 75 percent believed that earlier-established Cubans discriminated against them, and 52 percent said that they had personally been victims of discrimination. Portes has argued that the arrival of exiles via El Mariel marked the beginning of the bifurcation of the Miami enclave because the so-called "historic" exiles did not welcome the *marielitos* into existing social, financial, and commercial networks.[115]

Author Reinaldo Arenas, perhaps the best known of all Mariel exiles, wrote bitterly about his experiences in Cuban Miami. He found his compatriots to be extremely materialistic, uninterested in literature and the arts, and obsessively politicized. As he later reminisced, "I did not want to stay too long in that place which was like a caricature of Cuba, the worst of Cuba: the eternal gossip, the chicanery, the envy." With his characteristic acrimony, Arenas once remarked, "If Cuba is Hell, Miami is Purgatory."[116] Soon he left for New York City in search of a more auspicious intellectual environment.

Still in Revolution?

The term "revolution" evokes images of violence, movement, change, rapid and profound transformations, one social class losing power to another, a group of leaders replacing another, institutions destroyed and institutions created, statues demolished, new ones erected. Revolutions bring new laws, new aesthetics, new values, new textbooks and sacred texts: in short, a new ideological superstructure, to use Marx's term, to support a new social and economic structure. In Cuba, the revolutionary process was swift and far-reaching. As earlier chapters demonstrated, within a handful of years Cuban society underwent a profound transformation, from a U.S.-dependent, capitalist, stratified, bourgeois-dominated society to a Soviet-dependent, communist, egalitarian, collectivist nation ostensibly governed by workers.

The initial idealist revolutionary phase represented by people such as Guevara, Cienfuegos, and Franqui yielded to a pragmatist institutionalized phase represented by technocrats such as Humberto Pérez and Carlos Rafael Rodríguez. Significantly, the official names given to the revolutionary years 1971–85 are backward looking and bland in comparison to those of the early years: the government named eight of those fifteen years for important revolutionary anniversaries and another three for party congresses.

By contrast, the term "institutionalization," the process Cuba underwent during the period covered in this chapter, evokes images of stability, inertia, absence of change; the freezing in time of an established ruling elite; the end of experimentation and improvisation; conservatism and re-action—in short, the opposite of revolution. Over the course of the 1970s and early 1980s, the Cuban government managed to survive—arguably thrive—by adopting Soviet economic, political, and military models while receiving vast amounts of Soviet aid to stabilize and improve the economy and raise its international profile. In the process, however, Cuba ceased to be revolutionary.

5

▼

Now We Are Going to Build Socialism

Crisis and Rectification, 1986–1990

1986—Year of the 30th Anniversary of the *Granma* Landing
1987—Year Twenty-Nine of the Revolution
1988—Year Thirty of the Revolution
1989—Year Thirty-One of the Revolution
1990—Year Thirty-Two of the Revolution

One day somebody asked me
if I had read *Das Kapital*.
"Yes, but I didn't like it;
'cause in the end, the hero dies."
In fact, I hold a strong aversion
to the fictionalized economy
authored by Karl Marx.

Frank Delgado, "Konchalovsky hace rato no monta un Lada"

On January 8, 1989, on the occasion of the thirtieth anniversary of his triumphant speech at Camp Columbia, Castro addressed an audience composed primarily of students at the same compound, which had been renamed Ciudad Libertad. Thirty years older, his beard greying, his gesticulations slower, and his voice less strident, he wore olive-green fatigues and a cap almost identical to the ones he had donned on the commemorated occasion. He even had a small, seemingly fake white dove attached to his right shoulder, reminiscent of the one that rested briefly on his shoulder exactly thirty years before (figure 5.1). Castro spoke at length about the accomplishments of his generation—agrarian reform; the eradication of illiteracy; universal, free health care and education; socialization of the economy—and challenged the next generation to further develop

Figure 5.1. Fidel Castro speaking at the Ciudad Libertad education complex in commemoration of the thirtieth anniversary of the revolution, January 8, 1989. *Source: Granma*, January 9, 1989.

and perfect socialism, at a time, as he put it, when a "capitalist euphoria" was taking hold in "certain socialist countries."[1]

What Castro called euphoria exploded a few months later into a pandemonium that raged through Eastern Europe and beyond. Eastern European communist regimes fell like the proverbial row of dominoes: first Poland, then Hungary, East Germany, Bulgaria, Czechoslovakia, and Romania. This was just the beginning; by the end of 1992, ruling communist parties lost control in at least twelve other countries as disparate as Albania, Angola, Mongolia, Yemen, and Yugoslavia.

For a period of time in the long summer of 1989, even China seemed to be on the verge of democratic change: tens of thousands of protesters occupied Beijing's Tiananmen Square until the Chinese army violently dispersed them on June 4. It is almost impossible to forget the photograph of that lone protester, who with his extended hand stopped an entire tank convoy. He was removed from the scene, never to be seen or heard from again. His name and identity are still unknown. Within the next two years, the USSR collapsed and the seemingly unshakable Russian Communist Party was voted out of power. For Cuba, these dramatic changes represented the end of Soviet and CMEA financial support, trade subsidies, and military aid.

Though the revolution's top leadership may not have wavered, even those most sympathetic to the Cuban revolution must have contemplated the likely collapse of the three-decade-long revolutionary government. Scholars, journalists, and other observers wrote scores of articles, books, and editorial pieces on the subject, many of them pessimistic about the regime's future, some outright celebratory of a transition to democracy that seemed around the corner.[2] The state of Florida and Dade County prepared for a potentially chaotic political transition and mass exodus; Congress passed hostile legislation to accelerate the anticipated fall of communist Cuba; U.S.-based entrepreneurs, some of them Cuban, planned an all-out economic invasion of the island. Members of the Miami-based Asociación Nacional de Hacendados de Cuba (National Association of Sugar Mill Owners of Cuba, ANDHAC) made plans to reestablish themselves as the sugar aristocracy of postsocialist Cuba and even negotiated a labor contract with an exile union that included paltry daily wages of $7.46 for cane cutters and $12.88 for industrial workers—one third Kafka, one third Ionesco, one third Trespatines: a masquerade of grown men dressed up as planters, without plantations and union bosses, without workers. Constitutions for postsocialist Cuba were drawn and redrawn; exiles lined up to recover confiscated properties and assume political posts from the presidency on down;[3] and singer-songwriter Willy Chirino wrote what immediately became exiled Cuba's unofficial anthem, "*Nuestro día (ya viene llegando)*" (Our day [is coming soon]; 1991). He ends his song by enumerating the nations where socialist or communist governments had collapsed, each followed by a shout of *¡libre!* (free): "*¡Nicaragua. Libre! ¡Polonia. Libre! ¡Hungría. Libre!*" and so on. The song ends with the loud shout "*¡Cuba. Libre!*" followed by repetitions of the fading chorus: "*Ya viene llegando. Ya viene llegando . . .*"

This chapter examines the period 1986 through 1990, yet another swing of the pendular revolution during which the revolutionary leadership embraced an ideological and institutional form of idealism, whose goals and programs were diametrically opposed to those of the previous fifteen years, which had been characterized by pragmatism. It was a desperate top-down swing back to idealism, but not to the Guevarist brand of the 1960s; those who had inhabited the paradise of innocent idealism had since eaten the forbidden fruits of sugarcane and material incentives and had consequently been expelled from Eden. There would be no return to paradise. Rather, this was a period of institutionalized idealism, officially christened the "Rectification of Errors and Negative Tendencies Process." These were years when the sins of capitalism were purged through a revived cult of Guevara, the revolution's martyred patron saint of sacrifice, discipline, and selflessness. The lack of new ideas and grand initiatives that characterized the second half of the 1980s is evidenced by the bland and uninspiring official names given to those years: 1986 was dedicated to the thirtieth anniversary of the *Granma* landing, and the subsequent four years were named after the triumph of the revolution's anniversaries: Year Twenty-Nine, Year Thirty, and so on.

While the shift to rectification is widely recognized as a retreat from the extreme pragmatism of the previous fifteen years, there has been some debate about the motivations, reach, and extent of idealism behind that pendular swing. Two scholars, Carmelo Mesa-Lago and Susan Eckstein, held divergent positions on the subject. While Mesa-Lago viewed rectification as a sharp ideological and policy change, Eckstein characterized it as more ideological than idealist, and very selective as to which aspects of capitalism were retained and which ones should be turned back or eliminated. While I agree with Eckstein's conclusion about more ideology than idealism, I concur with Mesa-Lago's argument of a virtually 180 degree comprehensive socioeconomic policy transformation.[4]

Between the Cold War and a New World Order

The second half of the 1980s brought profound and unanticipated transformations to the Soviet Union. When Mikhail Gorbachev became general secretary of the Soviet Communist Party in March 1985, he inherited a dismal economic situation and widespread popular discontent. Both circumstances resulted in part from the country's prolonged, costly, and unpopular war in Afghanistan; from low oil prices around the world; and from multibillion-dollar expenditures to support Cuba and other allies and client states. These things notwithstanding, the USSR poured around $10 million every single day into Cuba alone.[5] Upon attaining power, Gorbachev initiated a process of far-reaching reforms known as *glasnost* (openness) and *perestroika* (restructuring). *Glasnost* included a series of political reforms to create a more open and democratic—and consequently less repressive—system. These reforms included what was previously unthinkable: allowing other political parties to compete with the all-powerful Russian Communist Party. Parallel economic reforms under the rubric of *perestroika* meanwhile expanded market mechanisms and private enterprise to stimulate productivity and economic growth.

During the same period, with Ronald Reagan serving his second presidential term, U.S.-Cuba relations became increasingly acrimonious. Among the major points of contention were migration control, the trade embargo, Cuban support for Sandinista Nicaragua and guerrilla forces in El Salvador, and the ongoing military intervention in Angola. With civil war still raging in Nicaragua, El Salvador, and Guatemala, and the Reagan administration's claims that a large number of Cuban military advisors were active in the region, the United States began to broadcast anti-Communist programming to Cuba through Radio Martí on May 20, 1985. The launching of Radio Martí infuriated Castro, who retaliated by abrogating the migration accord signed a few months earlier, which included provisions for the departure of liberated Cuban political prisoners and the return to Cuba of incarcerated Mariel exiles. Cuba also temporarily banned exiles from traveling to the island.[6]

The U.S. government used the growing rift between Cuba and the reformist USSR, with its concomitant damage to the island's economy, as an opportunity to launch a multifront strategy to further isolate and debilitate the beleaguered island. New regulations strengthened the long-standing trade embargo. The United States banned foreign imports of machines and equipment suspected of containing Cuban materials such as nickel and it pressured foreign nations and international business not to trade with or lend money to Cuba. Between 1986 and 1988, the United States intensified its monitoring of the illegal flow of U.S.-made products to Cuba via third countries, most commonly Panama, which had become one of Cuba's closest regional allies. U.S. authorities also further restricted the amount of cash and gifts exiles could take to the island or remit to relatives there and restricted travel to Cuba by U.S. citizens.[7]

Harsh treatment of Cuba continued during George H. W. Bush's administration (1989–92), in great measure in response to the successful lobbying efforts of the Mas Canosa–led CANF. In 1990, Congress passed legislation that included the controversial Mack Amendment, a law banning all trade between foreign-based subsidiaries of U.S. corporations and Cuba. Although Bush pocket-vetoed the bill, his administration applied heavy-handed pressure to keep other nations from trading with the rebel island.[8]

During the thawing of the Cold War, the United States and the Soviet Union engaged in negotiations to improve relations and work toward the common goal of nuclear disarmament. Soviet support of Cuba remained one of the thorniest points of contention. During a series of high-level U.S.-Soviet meetings in 1989–91, U.S. officials continued to pressure an unraveling Soviet Union to cease all aid and trade subsidies to Cuba. It worked. By 1992, all subsides had ended. A few months earlier, Russia had also removed its troops from Cuban soil, a process that was completed before the end of 1993.[9]

While *glasnost* was implemented in an attempt to save the Soviet Union and its socialist system, it had the opposite effect; it contributed to the weakening of the Soviet Communist Party, the collapse of the socialist bloc in 1989, and the disintegration of the Warsaw Pact, the CMEA, and even the Soviet Union two years later. Gorbachev himself became a victim of his own reforms—when the Commonwealth of Independent States replaced the former USSR in 1991 he was left without a country to rule.

Cuba remained practically isolated from the Western world. Trade with and travel to and from Europe and most of Latin America were very uncommon. This isolation had its origins in the early 1960s, in part due to U.S.-led efforts to crush the revolution, in part due to the regime's desire to prevent Western cultural and political influences. Oddly enough, this isolation, which was compounded with rigid state controls, had some positive effects. Cuba had been spared from some of the troubles many other nations endured. For example, the use and traffic of illegal drugs that plagued many Latin American and Western countries barely touched Cuba; neither did organized crime and the violence associated with drug activities. Likewise, Cuba had been spared from other social plagues such as gang-related crime, human trafficking, sex tourism, widespread political corruption, excessive consumerism, and even the systematic degradation of the environment.

However, in light of waning relations with the USSR and Eastern Europe, Cuba began to open itself gradually to the rest of the world. It cultivated diplomatic and commercial relations with other nations and opened the island to foreign tourists. Cuba and China embarked on a rapprochement after two and a half decades of virtual disconnection. In 1989, their foreign ministers exchanged visits, and later in the year they signed a trade agreement that in 1990 amounted to over $600 million. Significantly, the

Cuban government not only failed to condemn the bloody crackdown against Tiananmen Square protesters, it publicly accepted the Chinese government's justifications.[10]

Cuba also improved its relations with several Caribbean and Latin American neighbors. In 1986, a year that brought rapprochement with Argentina and Spain, Cuba established diplomatic links with Brazil. After nearly a decade of interruption, Cuba reestablished diplomatic relations with Venezuela in 1989 and with Jamaica in 1990.[11] At the same time, however, Cuba suffered two major setbacks in its hemispheric relations. In December 1989, U.S. troops deposed Panamanian strongman Manuel Noriega, who had facilitated the circumvention of the trade embargo via transshipment of U.S.-made high technology products. Two months later, Cuba's closest hemispheric alliance unraveled when an opposition coalition voted the Sandinistas out of office in Nicaragua.

Within a few short years, the nearly five-decade-long Cold War thawed, yielding to a so-called New World Order in which the United States became the sole surviving superpower. Against all odds, Cuba remained defiantly afloat in the otherwise warm Florida Straits, an iceberg calved off from the Cold War's glacial mass.

Economic Recession

The profound political and economic transformations that took place in the Soviet Union during the second half of the 1980s provoked the weakening and eventual demise of Cuba's long-standing, beneficial, and dependent economic relations with the Soviet Union and Eastern Europe. Cuba was particularly vulnerable because of its decades-long heavy dependence on trade with and aid from CMEA member nations. The island imported the lion's share of various essential foodstuffs, such as wheat flour, from the CMEA, as well as raw materials such as oil, cotton, and lumber and manufactured goods ranging from shoes to printing paper to buses.[12]

In 1986, the Soviet Union and Cuba signed their last five-year trade agreement. This time, the agreement included cuts in Soviet price subsidies. Later that year, crude oil prices plummeted from around $28 a barrel to barely over $11. Although prices recovered somewhat, they remained low over the next four years. According to some estimates, buying Soviet oil at above-market prices cost Cuba an additional 5 to 7 billion pesos during the period 1986–89.[13]

The combined effect of the end of Soviet trade subsidies, mounting indebtedness, spiraling trade imbalances, budget deficits, and falling production pushed the economy into a recession. Adjusting for population growth, the economy shrank at an annual rate of 1 percent during 1986–89.[14]

In the winter of 1989–90, the Soviet Union did not fulfill its commitment to deliver essential cargoes of grain and animal feed. The Soviets further cut oil shipments in 1990 and 1991. The mere 6 million tons of oil they exported to Cuba in 1992 were less than half of 1990 levels. This forced Cuba to cut the supply of gasoline and oil-generated electricity to government firms and the general population.[15] After the CMEA disbanded in 1991, Cuba had to conduct its trade with Eastern European countries and with what was left of the Soviet Union at world-market prices and in hard currency instead of rubles.

These foreign trade adjustments generated ballooning trade deficits that had devastating effects for the economy. Trade imbalances with the Soviet Union jumped from a yearly average of 639 million pesos in 1981–84 to 1,412 million pesos during the period 1985–88. Those trade deficits in turn reverberated in the national budget, turning a yearly average surplus of 135 million pesos in 1981–84 into a deficit of 549 million pesos in 1985–88.[16]

The economy also dragged the albatross of decades of mounting foreign debt, mainly with the socialist bloc but also with France, Japan, and other capitalist nations. In 1987, Cuba's debt to socialist countries peaked at $10 billion, while its debt to Western countries hovered at around $5.7 billion. Cuba had accumulated one of the hemisphere's most onerous debt levels in proportion to the size of its economy and the value of its exports.[17]

With mounting pressures from Western creditors and a rapidly approaching deadline to restart payment of debts owed to the Soviet Union, Castro and other government leaders denounced the stifling effects of chronic indebtedness among Third World nations. In fact, Castro assumed informal leadership of an international movement that sought to reduce or eliminate the crippling debts borne by poorer countries. In the summer of 1985, Cuba hosted a conference on the external debt of Latin America and the Caribbean in which Castro compared foreign debt to a deadly disease. "It is a cancer that requires surgery," he uttered ominously. A year later, Cuba stopped paying its short-, medium-, and long-term debt to Western banks and failed to start making payments on its Soviet debt.[18]

The Cuban government's reactions to *perestroika* and *glasnost* were mixed. Castro immediately attacked the Soviet reforms. Vice-President

Rodríguez, still Cuba's "third man," became the harshest critic of the reforms. Other Cuban leaders were sympathetic to Gorbachev's reforms,
among them third-man-in-waiting Carlos Aldana, who sat on the PCC secretariat, headed up the Ideology Department of the party's Central Committee, and was a close confidant of Castro; charismatic Union of Communist Youth leader Roberto Robaina; and physician Carlos Lage. Reformist
Soviet publications such as *Moscow News* and *Sputnik* gained popularity
throughout the island. Quite significantly, as Cuba-Soviet relations deteriorated toward the end of the 1980s, Cuba banned those publications
from circulation.[19]

Rectification of Errors

The economic and political changes Cuba implemented in this period ran
counter to those that were taking place in the USSR. While the Soviets
confronted their economic and political crisis by further reforming socialism, expanding market mechanisms, and promoting nonstate economic
activities, Cuba launched counter-reform measures known as the Rectification of Errors. Rectification condemned market ideas and practices
that had infiltrated the economy during the previous decade and a half
characterized by pragmatism, material incentives, and private economic
activities, which increased disparities in income and standards of living
and fostered a boom in corruption, black market trade, and other illegal activities. Increased centralization of power and government re-mo-
nopolization of the economy were other major hallmarks of rectification.
These counter-reforms targeted growing trade and budget deficits and
the spiraling external debt and sought to reduce dependence on imports
and foreign capital. The new economic strategy focused both on revenue-
generating export crops at the expense of consumer foodstuffs and on
investing in an incipient tourist sector, which the government saw as a
promising source of hard-currency income.

In February 1986, at the opening of the Third Congress of the PCC,
Castro launched a severe critique of the economy and unveiled an agenda
for rectification. "Now," Castro said, "we are going to build socialism." In
the next few months, as the rectification process began, Castro repeatedly
blasted bureaucratism, selfishness, laziness, and corruption, all the while
eliminating the capitalist practices and institutions that had fostered such
problems. According to political scientist Damián J. Fernández, rectification sought not only to solve the economic crisis but also to reformalize

a society that had widely recurred to informal practices of survival and resistance that included black market activities, cronyism, and adopting what came to be known as "double morality," essentially having a public persona that vocally supported the government while criticizing and undermining it in private.[20]

The rectification process was the latest in a succession of pendular swings between alternating formulas of idealism and pragmatism. Castro was convinced that during the early 1980s the pendulum had swung too far in the pragmatist direction and that this had brought on deleterious effects, particularly the resurgence of a culture of individualism, profiteering, and speculation. One major difference separated this new idealist phase from the previous one: it did not have grassroots support but rather was institutional and imposed from above. While Castro referred to the sudden shift away from pragmatism as the "Battle of Ideas," it clearly had more to do with ideology than idealism.

Echoing a somewhat forgotten Guevara, Castro called for the creation of a new man: "I believe that a new man, a socialist, communist man, has to be created." This was another moment of revived Guevarism without Guevara, when the government resurrected the revolutionary icon as a symbol of altruistic service to the revolution, motivation through moral incentives, and revolutionary consciousness. Twenty years after Guevara's death, Castro used him often as the ultimate model for rectification. On one occasion, he exclaimed, "Che would have been appalled if he had been told that money was becoming man's main concern, man's fundamental motivation." The regime revived the slogan "Seremos como el Che" (We shall be like Che) as it reintroduced moral incentives such as socialist emulation that were reminiscent of those championed by Guevara more than two decades before.[21]

Among the primary targets of rectification were the private economic activities that had been legalized during the first half of the 1980s. The first to be banned were the free peasant markets. Referring to these markets, Castro announced, "We will rectify what was undoubtedly a wrong decision." He repeatedly rebuked the markets as sources of speculation and excessive profiteering that had produced numerous farmer millionaires.[22] The rectification process also targeted private land ownership, construction companies, and permuta realtors. The state assumed control of additional private farms, which it turned into government-controlled cooperatives. Likewise, authorities shut down private construction businesses, which had partially alleviated chronic housing shortages but were notoriously corrupt. With private construction no longer an option, in 1987 the government revived the 1970s concept of volunteer microbrigades to build and repair housing units, schools, and day-care centers.[23]

One of the period's most significant counter-reforms was the eradication of most types of material incentives in favor of moral incentives. During the closing sessions of the 1986 Third Party Congress, Castro expressed the reasoning behind his antipathy toward material incentives and his intention to end them: "We really went from one extreme to another," he stated, "from a complete rejection of material incentives . . . to fetishism with money."[24] It is important to point out that this pendular swing away from material incentives, like the previous one in the mid-1960s, was linked to the island's deteriorating economic situation. Simply put, during times of economic hardship the government could not afford to spend large sums of money on productivity bonuses, premiums, and other forms of compensation. The state eliminated all *premios* by 1989. Not surprisingly, the abolition of material incentives provoked a reduction in worker productivity, a 10 percent drop between 1986 and 1989.[25]

Contrary to the tenets of *perestroika*, the Cuban state expanded its participation in the economy to the point that it regained a virtual monopoly of all economic activities. In 1986, the government set up special "diplomatic" dollar-only stores that were open only to foreigners with the object of collecting desperately needed hard currency. Two years later, it established the infamous "gold and silver stores," where individuals turned in jewels and precious metals in exchange for television sets, refrigerators, and other consumer goods. Citizens stood in long lines for hours holding wedding rings, old silver coins, or their grandparents' gold pocket watches to exchange them for a Soviet-made TV set or a Japanese boom box. Critics soon dubbed these stores "Tiendas de Hernán Cortés" in allusion to the Spanish conquest's exploitative exchanges of beads, bells, and mirrors for Aztec silver and gold treasures.[26]

Three years into the Rectification of Errors, counter-reform policies had failed to stimulate economic recovery and the impending end of Soviet aid and trade subsidies made the regime increasingly vulnerable.

Political Purges and Pseudo Glasnost

Just as economic restructuring and political openness were interconnected in the Soviet case, in Cuba economic counter-reforms were closely tied to the increased centralization of power by the Castro brothers and the PCC. During the late 1980s, as the Cuban government moved in a direction that was the opposite of *perestroika*, it also pursued political strategies diametrically opposed to the *glasnost* model.

In 1986, the System of Direction and Planning of the Economy, which had played a central role in setting economic policy during the previous decade, was transformed and stripped of many of its prerogatives, which were transferred to the Central Group of the Politburo of the PCC, headed by unconditional Castro loyalist Osmany Cienfuegos. SDPE chief Humberto Pérez became the crisis's most visible scapegoat; he was removed in July 1985 from the post he had held since 1979 and was simultaneously fired from his position as vice-president of the Executive Council of the presidency.[27] Back in 1979, Castro had entrusted production on the great plantation of Cuba to Pérez, and consequently the master planter fired his overseer when economic crisis befell the nation. Among the other victims of the political shakeup of 1986 were Ramiro Valdés, who was removed from his post as head of the MININT, and Guillermo García Frías, the first peasant to join combat in the Sierra Maestra. Both lost their vice-presidencies and Politburo seats. Three decades after the triumph of a revolution led by men and women in their twenties and early thirties, the Politburo was comprised of an entrenched, graying leadership, mostly veteran *sierra* combatants who now averaged 57 years of age.[28]

A new round of purges swept the island in 1989. This time, the primary targets were a group of MININT officers accused of coordinating and supporting cocaine trafficking between Colombia and the United States and a handful of FAR officers accused of corruption and smuggling ivory, diamonds, and gold from Africa. The crisis began to unfold in February 1988, when U.S. authorities apprehended Miami-based Cuban exile Reinaldo Ruiz and his son, Rubén, for drug smuggling. Ensuing investigations incriminated Cuban officials when evidence surfaced that Ruiz had conspired with his cousin, MININT captain Manuel Ruiz Poo. Cuban security agents and FAR members were involved with the transshipment of cocaine cargoes via a port in Varadero, and Cuban MiGs had even escorted drug-trafficking airplanes. The complicity of Panama's General Noriega also surfaced during the investigations.[29]

In June, authorities arrested General Arnaldo Ochoa. His status as a hero of the revolution, his popularity among his troops and the people, his inclination toward Soviet-style reforms, and the independence of action he had demonstrated in Angola made Ochoa a threat to the Castro brothers. The appearance of pro-Ochoa graffiti in Havana reading "8-A"

Figure 5.2. A somber-looking General Arnaldo Ochoa during his 1989 trial. Still image from footage of televised trial, Cuban TV.

(phonetically Ochoa) did not bode well for the three-star general, as it made his popularity increasingly obvious to the Castros. Among those accused of drug trafficking were the controversial bon vivant de la Guardia twins, MININT colonel Antonio de la Guardia and MININT brigadier general Patricio de la Guardia. Their commanding officer, José Abrantes, also came under arrest for his failure to prevent the drug trafficking, smuggling, and other forms of corruption among his underlings. Significantly, FAR Minister Raúl Castro, whose fighter planes routinely escorted drug planes landing in military airfields, was neither blamed nor punished for the crimes and corruption of his subordinates.[30]

During the televised trial, Ochoa appeared stoic, almost stonelike, with his Roman-centurion profile mostly tilted down, his eyes tired and devoid of expression (figure 5.2). Whether he was drugged remains a matter of speculation, but he was visibly not the same proud and undefeatable hero that Cubans had come to know. Ochoa made no effort to defend himself, instead accepting full responsibility for his actions: "I committed treason against the fatherland," he said in a soft voice, "and I tell you with full honesty, the payment for treason is death."[31]

International pleas for clemency notwithstanding, including a request from the pope, on July 13 a firing squad armed with AK-47s executed Ochoa. His final words were "I'm no traitor." That day, FAR captain Jorge Martínez Valdés, Colonel Antonio de la Guardia, and MININT major Amado Padrón Trujillo suffered the same fate. General Patricio de la Guardia received a 30-year sentence. MININT chief Abrantes was sentenced to twenty years; he died in prison in January 1991, officially of a heart attack, three days after he reportedly stated that Fidel Castro had personally ordered the drug trafficking and smuggling operations. Patricio de la Guardia was paroled in 1997. All in all, the 1989 purge included scores of individuals, the vast majority of them high-ranking MININT officials. Among them were the national fire and police chiefs, the Coast Guard commander, and the MININT chiefs of customs, intelligence, and immigration and naturalization. The Castros also purged the Western Army of officers even remotely suspected of pro-Ochoa sympathies.[32]

The firings, arrests, trials, prison sentences, and executions had more to do with politics than with crime. Two days after Ochoa's arrest, Raúl Castro publicly castigated the fallen general for his "unbridled populism." It was no secret that Raúl Castro, who had not seen battle since 1958, resented the popularity of his old friend, battle-seasoned Ochoa, who had successfully commanded forces in South and Central America, Africa, and the Middle East. Commenting on the Ochoa affair, the senior Castro stated, "At a time, as was said here, when people are questioning socialism and the Cuban Communist Party I believe that the courts have issued a warning." Indeed, it was a chilling warning: there would be zero tolerance for corruption, dissent, and, more importantly, potential challenges to the Castros' authority.[33]

The 1989 purge resulted in the reduction of personnel in and an overall weakening of the MININT, now commanded by Raúl Castro's close collaborator Abelardo Colomé Ibarra. In subsequent years, the armed forces played an increasing role in the higher echelons of power. High-ranking officers moved up to top positions in various key government bodies, such as the ministries of the sugar industry, fisheries and merchant marine, transportation, communications, tourism, and higher education and the office of the attorney general. FAR officers also assumed commanding roles in various economic activities, such as management of hotel chains, transportation, retail sales, and agribusiness.[34] Not all officers proved to be good managers, however. One notorious case of military management gone awry included a combat-seasoned officer who was put in charge of a shrimp-packing plant in southern Camagüey Province. His strategy for stopping the continuous theft of shrimp was to install a Vietnam war–style booby trap to kill or maim anyone who dared remove merchandise from the packing plant. Quite literally, in Camagüey, a bag of shrimp could cost an arm and a leg.

In the early 1990s, as Cuba expanded its commercial and political relations with Latin America, Canada, and Western Europe, it came under increasing pressure to democratize its political system and improve its human rights record, in response to which it implemented mild political reforms, a pseudo-glasnost of sorts. In 1990, the government experimented with secret voting at the lowest levels of the nominations structure. The Fourth Party Congress (1991) provided the opportunity for further reforms, including the decision to allow religious believers to join the ranks of the PCC. On that occasion, the party accepted locally nominated candidates for its 225-member Central Committee, for the first time. The secret voting that followed resulted in the renewal of the body with the election of 126 new members, many of them young. The party congress also agreed to reform the election of provincial assemblies and the National Assembly by allowing direct secret voting for their delegates.[35] Despite these reforms, the system was still far from democratic: the PCC remained the only legal party and there was only one candidate for each of the 1,190 provincial posts and 589 national posts.[36]

After fifteen years of institutionalization and pragmatic policies in a context of relative prosperity, the revolution reverted in 1986 to an idealist cycle that was top-down, bureaucratic, and institutionalized. Rectification was a contrarian shift, as the Soviet Union, Eastern Europe, China, even Vietnam moved in the opposite direction, opening the doors to individual entrepreneurship. The late 1980s turned out to be the preamble to the much harsher period of the early 1990s, when the cooling of Cuba-Russia relations produced a virtual severing of political and commercial relations, including the termination of Russian subsidies, a change that turned the economic recession into a profound and prolonged depression.

PART III

Survival, 1991–2013

6

Socialism or Death!

The Long Special Period, 1991 2000

1991—Year Thirty-Three of the Revolution
1992—Year Thirty-Four of the Revolution
1993—Year Thirty-Five of the Revolution
1994—Year Thirty-Six of the Revolution
1995—Year of the Centennial of the Fall of José Martí
1996—Year of the Centennial of the Fall in Combat of Antonio Maceo
1997—Year of the 30th Anniversary of the Fall in Combat of the Heroic Guerrilla Fighter and his Comrades
1998—Year of the 40th Anniversary of the Decisive Battles of the War of Liberation
1999—Year of the 40th Anniversary of the Triumph of the Revolution
2000—Year of the 40th Anniversary of the Fatherland or Death Decision

At night the area [around Hotel Deauville] is filled with *jineteras* and their pimps, transvestites, potheads, clueless folks from the provinces. Masturbators, peanut vendors, hustlers pushing fake rum and cigars, and real cocaine, young harlots recently imported from the provinces, street musicians with guitars and maracas, flower peddlers, rickshaws pedaled by jacks-of-all-trades, cops and aspiring emigrants. And some forlorn women, some of them old, and some children, the poorest among the poor, who beg incessantly for coins.

Pedro Juan Gutiérrez, *El Rey de La Habana*

The relatively abrupt termination of Soviet trade subsidies and other forms of aid beginning in 1989, the tightening of the U.S. trade embargo during the 1990s, and Cuba's temporary virtual withdrawal from international trade pushed the economy into a free fall. It hit rock bottom in 1993, when Cuba entered its deepest and darkest economic, social, political, and moral crisis. This profound and prolonged crisis proved more severe, damaging, and traumatic than any previous crisis of the revolutionary period.

In 1991, Castro somberly alerted the population of the looming disaster that came to be known by the euphemism "Special Period in Times of Peace" and announced a series of extreme contingency plans, the so-called Option Zero, in anticipation of the exhaustion of all oil reserves. Castro's ominous phrase "Socialism or death!" became the revolution's new guiding slogan, a clear signal of the revolutionary leadership's commitment to socialism, no matter how desperate the situation got. As late as mid-2007, Raúl Castro recognized that the Special Period had not ended yet.[1]

The government's primary objective was to survive at any cost. It embarked on yet another pendular swing, this time toward a survivalist form of pragmatism. The Special Period revealed the extremes to which both the revolutionary leadership and the citizenry would go for the sake of survival. It became evident, however, that the regime's political survival and the physical survival of the Cuban people were not in alignment and were often at odds. The extreme austerity measures imposed by the regime saved money in the national budget, but the population endured severe food scarcities and the deterioration of medical, educational, transportation, and other services.

The scarcities and hardships of the Special Period sparked the revolution's third great emigration wave: the *balsero* cohort, named after the *balsas* (rafts) in which tens of thousands left and continue to leave the island. These emigrants mostly belonged to a cohort two generations removed from pre-1959 capitalist Cuba. Raised in a socialist system and traumatized by the extreme austerity and indignities of the Special Period, this cohort adopted a survivalist culture, within or beyond legality. It had become mathematically impossible for most individuals and families to adequately feed and clothe themselves and put a roof over their heads, let alone face other expenses such as transportation and leisure activities. Many had to resort to theft at the workplace or perform private services for gain. The *balsero* cohort was also woefully unprepared to fit, assimilate, and succeed in Cuban Miami earlier waves of emigrants had built. Many in the *balsero* cohort, it should be noted, left not on board rafts but through a variety of other legal and illegal means, such as marrying a foreigner, seeking political asylum, or overstaying their visas in the United States, Spain, Canada, and other countries.

The Special Period went through three distinct phases. The first, Option Zero, which lasted until 1993, was a period of severe shortages of the oil and gasoline needed to keep the economy moving, maintain a functional transportation system, and provide at least a few daily hours of electricity. Government authorities applied draconian austerity measures in an effort to reduce expenditures and consumer spending levels; they also stimulated food production and sought to reduce dependence on imported oil. These emergency measures were implemented within the framework of a somewhat orthodox form of socialism.

The Special Period's second phase, structural reformism, began in 1993, the worst year of the crisis. At that time, the government started implementing profound structural changes that ran counter to those of the Rectification of Errors. These included attracting foreign investments, legalizing private economic activities, allowing the circulation of the U.S. dollar, and further expanding into new sectors of the economy, including tourism and mining.

The United States responded by strengthening its trade embargo as a weapon to derail the island's attempt to reintegrate itself into the world trade system as a path to economic recovery. The Helms-Burton Act of 1996, otherwise known as the Cuba Liberty and Democratic Solidarity Act, had profoundly deleterious effects on Cuba's economy and society because of its sanctions against foreign corporations and individuals that owned, used, or "trafficked" in properties formerly owned by U.S. nationals that had been confiscated by the Cuban government.

When the worst of the economic debacle was over, Cuba entered a new phase of recovery and retreat from reformism in 1997. Improving material conditions for some and the regime's proven capacity to survive the crisis enabled it to weaken or eliminate many of the structural reforms of the previous phase. This was not a return to idealism but rather a retreat from the extreme pragmatism of the mid-1990s.

The Onset of the Special Period

Numerous economic indicators dramatically demonstrate the cataclysmic proportions of the Special Period, most telling among them the sharp drop in GDP. During 1991, 1992, and 1993, the GDP fell by double digits; the total GDP collapse between 1990 and 1993 reached a whopping 35 percent, a greater fall than Cuba endured during the Great Depression. In addition, the budget deficit more than tripled between 1989 and 1993. Capital reserves were decimated to a meager $12 million in 1992, one-eighth of the amount Batista had left behind in 1959. The foreign debt, meanwhile, soared to unprecedented levels: $6.5 billion owed to Western creditors and 15 billion rubles to Russia.[2]

Production and trade volumes experienced parallel drops. Sugar output fell every year from 1988 to 1995, with the exception of 1990. By 1993, production had plummeted to only 4.3 million tons, nearly half the 1988 output. In 1995, at 3.3 million tons, the sugar harvest was the smallest in half a century. Due to falling international sugar prices, sugar earnings dropped at an even sharper rate. Output of other agricultural products declined as well, registering a nearly 50 percent decrease between 1990 and 1994.[3]

Trade statistics demonstrate the extent to which Cuba retreated from international commerce. Between 1989 and 1993, import levels decreased by 75 percent and exports fell by 80 percent. The destination of exports and the origin of imports changed drastically: the share of trade conducted with the Soviet Union/Russia dropped from 69 percent in 1988 to only 20 percent in 1993. Trade with Western Europe and Latin America increased from 7 and 4 percent, respectively, to a combined 60 percent. In 1998, the three principal destinations of Cuba's exports were Russia (22 percent), the Netherlands (13 percent), and Canada (13 percent), while its biggest sources of imports were Spain (22 percent), France (11 percent), and Canada (10 percent).[4]

The profound economic crisis had widespread negative reverberations in almost every aspect of life. While the government remained true to its aspiration of maintaining a basic social safety net, the extent of the economic collapse challenged its ability to deliver minimally adequate amounts of food, proper health care services, housing, public transportation, and electricity. Even Cuba's greatest source of pride, its education system, suffered from reduced funding and diminished resources.[5]

Abrupt reductions in Soviet and East European shipments of food, fertilizers, animal feed, and fuel to run agricultural machines led to severe food scarcities. The supply of basic staples such as bread, grains, and eggs fell sharply. Consequently, average daily caloric intake plummeted from 2,845 in 1989 to 1,863 in 1993, far below the FAO's minimum recommended levels. Cubans, facing starvation, took to foraging to put food on their tables and a cuisine of squalor took hold: a glass of sugared water, mocked as *sopa de gallo* (rooster soup), was not an uncommon meal; rich-in-protein stray cats disappeared as if raptured to cat heaven; and ground plantain rinds and old breaded washcloths became the substitutes of choice for beef. In some extreme cases, young men injected themselves with HIV-infected blood so they could be confined in medical compounds that assured them three full meals per day. Both physically and emotionally, Cubans showed signs of physical and emotional deterioration. On average, they lost twenty pounds; and bitterness, hopelessness, and depression prevailed among many. Cuba was not a happy place.[6]

The government developed emergency plans to confront the food crisis. It reduced *libreta* allocations of food and consumer products to all-time lows and raised food prices to keep consumption levels as low as possible. Generally, distribution of rationed food fell short of expected amounts and failed to arrive regularly at *bodegas*. The quality of rations also deteriorated; established rations did not provide sufficient food. According to one estimate, toward the century's end, *libreta* allocations provided consumers with only 61 percent of the recommended daily caloric intake, 65 percent of recommended levels of vegetable protein, and 36 percent of recommended levels of animal protein. Families had to purchase or acquire around half of all their food outside the rationing system, and thus the *libreta* ceased to be an effective nutrition equalizer.[7] Circumstances forced the citizenry to seek supplemental food at much higher prices through legal venues or the black market. Food hoarding and speculation aggravated scarcities and pushed prices further up. In 1993, a chicken cost the equivalent of an average monthly salary, and the cost of unrationed items such as powdered milk, clothing, and beer was similar to or higher than that in cities such as Paris, Toronto, and Miami.[8]

The government implemented new food production plans and developed new types of fares. Workers who had lost their jobs when industrial plants and mines closed were temporarily assigned to agricultural duties. Thousands of office workers, members of the armed forces, and party members joined them in the fields and other productive activities. Urban and suburban agriculture projects proliferated, including hydroponic and organoponic (raised-bed) farming, the so-called people's gardens, and suburban farms.[9] One experimental food production plan at a farm in San Cristóbal, Pinar del Río Province, was based on recycling and renewable sources practices: its tractors ran on coal made from locally produced wood; pigs and chickens were fed with corn stalks and sugarcane bagasse; pigs, chickens, and eggs were not only used as sources of food but also in other creative ways, for example to produce sealants from pig skin, soap from pig fat, and glue from eggshells; pig and chicken excrement was gathered to feed fish being bred at the farm pond; humans consumed the fish, eggs, and pork; and their bodily waste, in turn, fertilized the soil from which various crops were produced. In the summer of 1990, Castro reported that the food chain at the San Cristóbal farm was still being perfected.[10]

In light of the protracted scarcity of regular foodstuffs, the Food Industry Research Institute developed new food items, among them *masa cárnica*; *fricandel*; ground chicken mortadella; hamburger patties made of ground pork and soy (popularly ridiculed as McCastros); *cerelac*, a cereal concoction for senior citizens that had unintended laxative qualities; and *picadillo de soya*, part soy ground beef substitute, part usually inedible meat parts.[11] Celebrity TV chef, cookbook author, and nutritionist Nitza Villapol gave advice on how to reduce food waste and introduced a variety of affordable dishes, including meatless meatballs. With its traditional sense of humor, the population mocked the Special Period culinary innovations as *OCNIs: objetos comestibles no identificados* (unidentified comestible objects).[12]

The combination of poor nutritional levels among the population and budget cuts in health care had detrimental effects on public health. Old deficiency diseases resurfaced and new ones like optic myeloneuropathy reached epidemic proportions. The incidence of contagious diseases, such as tuberculosis, hepatitis, chicken pox, syphilis, and AIDS rose. Although the average infant birth weight dropped for the first time in decades, infant mortality rates actually improved every single year between 1989 and 1996. Death rates among those 65 and over, however, rose sharply from 40 per thousand in 1989 to 56 per thousand in 1993. The supply of medicines and medical supplies dwindled. In 1994, on my first visit to Cuba, I walked into a pharmacy that had no aspirins. It was basically stocked with healing herbs. The provision of medical and dental procedures declined as well; the number of surgeries dropped from 885,790 in 1990 to 486,067 in 1993.[13]

During the early years of the Special Period, public transportation dropped sharply. Vehicles disappeared from roads and streets as severe shortages of fuel and spare parts grounded most cars, buses, and trucks. Two-thirds of Havana's buses stopped circulating between 1991 and 1993. Outside Havana, bus services operated at only one fifth of their pre-crisis levels. One of the Special Period's most enduring and maligned symbols was the *camello* (camel), a Cuban-made bus consisting of a truck pulling a humped-back container crudely habilitated to transport 300 persons (figure 6.1). Riding on crowded *camellos* was such a denigrating and suffocating experience that their patrons referred to them as "The Friday night

Figure 6.1. *Camello* bus roaring through the streets of Havana. Photograph by Celestino Martínez Lindín, 2001.

movie; Warning: contains sex, violence, and foul language." Legions of clunky Chinese-made bicycles flooded Havana's otherwise empty streets, and oxen, horses, and mules hauled plows and wagons in rural Cuba as diesel-gulping tractors and trucks went idle.[14]

The quality and reach of education dropped, as did the motivation of youngsters to continue onto high school and pursue post-secondary degrees. Why bother with school? many wondered, when even doctors fail to earn a living wage. A hustler, a black marketer, or a prostitute could make ten times or more than a surgeon. Books and school materials became scarce, school campuses deteriorated, and the recruitment and retention of teachers became increasingly difficult.[15]

Housing, which had never been adequately addressed by the revolutionary government, became increasingly scarce, and the condition of houses and apartments deteriorated further. It became a routine occurrence for a building to collapse in Havana and elsewhere. A 1999 study concluded that 60 percent of urban dwellings were in good condition, while 40 percent were in fair or poor condition. In Havana, 75,000 buildings had to be propped up and another 4,000 were in imminent danger of collapsing. The situation in rural areas was much worse: only 32 percent were in good condition; 36 percent were in fair condition and 32 percent were in poor condition.[16] The dearth of housing forced many people to live in multigenerational households, which put further strains on married couples and contributed to an increase in domestic violence and divorces. In 1992 the divorce rate hit 5.1 per thousand inhabitants. By 1998, the cumulative effect of a sustained high divorce rate had translated into the extraordinarily high ratio of 61 divorces per hundred marriages, among the highest in the world.[17]

All this contrasted sharply with the early 1960s, when the general population had experienced a substantial improvement in its material conditions and standard of living as medical services, education, and better sources of food became widely available to previously neglected segments of the population, particularly rural dwellers and the poor. Revolutionary leaders rightfully took pride in these accomplishments and regularly broadcasted statistics about the revolution's achievements. In their speeches, Castro and other leaders routinely recited litanies of statistics to demonstrate that unemployment and illiteracy had been virtually eradicated, school enrollment had increased, free medical services were universally accessible, the infant mortality rate and rates of infectious diseases had declined, nutritional levels had improved, and the economic and social differences between those earning lower salaries and those working in better-remunerated professions had decreased.

However, many of these laudable accomplishments were reversed during the economic crisis of the 1990s. Moreover, with the passing of time, other Caribbean and Latin American nations, even some of the poorest ones, matched and in some cases surpassed Cuba's advances in education, health care, and nutrition. Cuba's high literacy rate, for example, was no longer exceptional by 1995, when six Latin American and Caribbean countries had literacy rates higher than Cuba's 95.7 percent. Another telling indicator, the proportion of students attending universities and other postsecondary institutions, dropped 5 points in Cuba from 1980 to 1997, while the comparable statistic increased by 5 percentage points in the Dominican Republic and 9 in El Salvador.[18] Likewise, by 1995, Cuba's high life expectancy rate of 75.7 years was no longer extraordinary when compared with those of several of its Latin American and Caribbean neighbors.[19]

In all fairness, however, the government took steps to prevent much higher drops in health, education, and nutritional indicators during the Special Period. As indicated by 1995 UN statistics, while Cuba's average GDP index was that of a "developing country" (0.48, less than half that of the United States), its life expectancy and education indexes were still in line with those of wealthy nations: close to those of the United States and equivalent to those of Luxembourg.[20]

The State Confronts the Crisis: Structural Reforms

In 1993, with the economy still in decline and the population enduring serious deprivations of food and consumer goods and reductions in social services, the government embraced a new and drastic strategy to pull the economy out of the depression. The pendular swing toward pragmatism that had begun at the onset of the Special Period went further as Cuba implemented a series of structural reforms that represented a 180-degree turn from the Rectification of Errors of the late 1980s. Castro accepted the new package of reforms reluctantly as a temporary, last-resort effort to keep Cuba afloat and himself in power. Raúl Castro was more pragmatic, effectively convincing his brother of the urgent need to implement far-reaching structural reforms. While the elder Castro's rhetoric continued to defend socialism—"We cannot privatize anything. On the contrary, we must gradually socialize"—the government moved decisively toward market-oriented reforms on a path similar to the Chinese model, whereby the state opened spaces within the economy for private investment, economic ventures, and profits without yielding an inch of political power.[21] The reforms were a diluted and rigidly controlled version of *perestroika*— some jestingly referred to it as Péreztropical—that also did not go as far as the Chinese economic reforms that began in the late 1970s under Deng Xiaoping and intensified during the 1980s and 1990s.

Among the early leading reformists was the revolution's new third man, Carlos Aldana, who fell into disfavor with the Castros because of his reformist ideas and was fired from his posts as head of the PCC's ideology and foreign relations departments in 1992. Like Escalante decades earlier, Aldana's star fell at a time of distancing between the Kremlin and Havana.[22] Within a few months, when the economy hit rock bottom, reformism became more widely acceptable and another reformist, Carlos Lage, was named vice-president of the powerful State Council, from which position he spearheaded major structural reforms, which included legalizing private individual business, allowing the circulation of U.S. dollars, providing for increased foreign investment and business, implementing new taxes and import fees, and diversifying the economy through the expansion of tourism, mining, biotechnology, and dollar-only sales of food, other consumer items, and services.

Between 1993 and 1996, various laws legalized, regulated, and taxed private employment and small businesses, activities that had, in many cases, been practiced illegally for years. Law 141 approved over fifty types of self-employment through which individuals could earn income and make profits. The number of self-employment job categories tripled by 1996. These ranged from bicycle parking attendant and dog groomer to hairdresser and disposable lighter refiller.[23] The motivation behind these reforms was twofold. On the one hand, self-employment created sources of work and income for the growing ranks of the unemployed and under-employed, retirees, and others at the margins of the official labor struc-tures. Unemployment peaked in the early 1990s, when it was estimated that over 8 percent of the labor force had no job and about 25 percent was underemployed. This was very different from the 1960s guarantee that anyone who wanted to work could find a job.[24] On the other hand, private employment generated income and supplied essential goods and services that the state was unable to provide (figure 6.2).

The ranks of the *cuentapropistas* (self-employed) peaked in 1995–96 at around 200,000. Not only did they produce and provide necessary goods and services, they also generated revenue for the state, which collected monthly license fees that ranged from 20 pesos for oxen drivers to 40 pe-sos for plumbers to 80 pesos for hired auto drivers. The state also collected progressive income taxes at rates of 5 to 50 percent. However, taxes were difficult to collect due to underreporting by the self-employed.[25] Others found nongovernment employment with partially foreign-owned joint venture companies. In such ventures, foreign investors paid the govern-ment in hard currency for the right to employ Cuban nationals. This prac-tice became a crass form of labor exploitation as foreign companies paid the government in hard currency, say $200, while the state paid the work-ers in national currency, 200 pesos. In 1995, the official dollar-to-peso exchange rate hovered around 1:32; during the balance of the decade, it remained stable at about 1:21.[26]

In 1994, when generalized malnutrition became imminent, two major reforms legalized private agricultural markets (*mercados libres agropecu-arios*) and markets that sold artisanal consumer products: shoes, hand tools, even rudimentary espresso coffee machines. Raúl Castro was in-strumental in the opening of the peasant markets, reportedly once tell-ing his older brother: "Beans are more important than cannons."[27] These markets helped alleviate the food crisis and stimulated domestic produc-tion of foodstuffs. By all accounts, the new *mercados* were a success. In

Figure 6.2. Self-employed woman selling food at the door-front "Daisy" cafeteria. Photograph by Celestino Martínez Lindín, 2001.

their first four months of operation, they sold 600 million pesos' worth of goods and generated 10 percent of that amount in tax revenue. Supplies of vegetables and fruits expanded when the government lent state lands to private farmers and turned more than 3 million hectares of state farms (7.4 million acres) into cooperative-like units called Unidades Básicas de Producción Cooperativa (Basic Units of Cooperative Production) in 1993.[28]

When self-employment legislation was passed in 1993 that opened several job categories related to the preparation and sale of snacks and meals, a host of eateries ranging from coffee stands to elegant restaurants immediately emerged throughout the island. Some charged in pesos while others accepted only U.S. dollars. By 1994, there were 4,000 family-owned and -operated restaurants called *paladares*. The government regulated them heavily, limiting dining areas to twelve chairs, banning the sale of lobster and other luxury foods, prohibiting the hiring of nonfamily employees, forbidding advertisements, and imposing onerous fees and taxes, as much as 50 percent of profits. Frequent, unannounced visits by government agents often led to fines, confiscation of forbidden foods, and restaurant closings. Some *paladares* operated clandestinely; I recall visiting one of them in 1994, a shady windowless establishment with great service and a broad menu of exquisite forbidden food.[29]

One of the most surprising, important, and far-reaching Special Period reforms was the legalization of the U.S. dollar in July 1993, which resulted in the dollarization of the domestic economy. This move, which the old guard revolutionary leadership embraced reluctantly, allowed the government to increase its access to hard currency and stimulated a sharp growth in the flow of remittances from Cubans living abroad. Remittances, which soon became the nation's second most important source of hard currency, reached an estimated yearly average of $670 million in the period 1995–2000.[30] When Cubans received remittances, that money flowed into the economy and ended up in the hands of a state that desperately needed hard currency. A substantial portion of remittances was spent in government-owned, dollar-only supermarkets, appliance stores, and general stores. A 1995 law created the *peso convertible* (convertible peso), a currency that was artificially set as equivalent to the U.S. dollar.[31] The economy's dollarization actually created two parallel economies, one with higher-quality products and services in which only dollars were accepted, the other for peso-holding customers. The photographic lens of Ángel Antonio de la Rosa captured the irony of the dual monetary system

Figure 6.3. "*No pase. Acceso limitado*" (Do not enter. Restricted access.) Photograph by Ángel Antonio de la Rosa.

in which Cuban pesos are not welcome in most establishments. The photograph includes a counter with a large image of a Cuban peso with Guevara's image; behind it is a closed door with a sign that says "Do Not Enter: Limited Access" (figure 6.3).

In order to recover, the economy needed vast amounts of capital to build infrastructure and production facilities and to acquire the resources necessary to expand into new economic activities. With international sugar prices low and preferential sugar prices gone, the economy moved aggressively into the areas of tourism and mining, particularly nickel mining, which was carried out by Moa Nickel, a partnership between Sherritt International of Canada and the government.[32]

Legislation dating as far back as 1982 allowed foreign investments in the form of joint ventures in which Cuba retained at least 51 percent of ownership. Foreign investments had barely trickled into the island during the 1980s, however. When the Special Period was officially declared in 1991, only two joint ventures were operating. New laws passed in the early 1990s further stimulated and facilitated the establishment of joint ventures. Law 77 of 1995 permitted full foreign ownership of enterprises and allowed the creation of free trade zones. In 1996, Cuba opened its real estate market to foreigners and passed new laws to protect foreign investments.[33] The number of joint ventures rose sharply, from 11 in 1991 to 404 a decade later. Among the largest foreign investors were Sherritt

International (nickel), Grupo Sol Meliá of Spain (hotels), Telecomunicaciones Internacionales de México (phone service), and Pernod Ricard of France (rum). All told, foreign investments amounted to almost $5 billion in 2000.[34]

With the help of foreign investment capital, Cuba moved aggressively to develop the tourism sector, which had virtually disappeared in previous decades. In 1989, Cuba had an inadequate number of tourist-quality hotel rooms; even the island's most luxurious hotels had deteriorated to embarrassing levels, as attested by Maurice Halperin's description of conditions in the Havana Libre hotel, formerly the Havana Hilton: "The mattresses in the twin beds were thin and worn. . . . The faucet for potable water in the bathroom sink worked sporadically . . . the toilet stopped flushing. . . . More disconcerting were the cockroaches." He did mention, however, that "the chambermaids . . . were cheerful and joked."[35]

Beginning in 1989 the island developed its tourism capabilities, building scores of new hotels, refurbishing existing ones, establishing tour companies, and expanding air travel and bus service. Early tourism development focused on the splendid colonial architecture and rich cultural life of Havana and on the beach resort areas of Varadero, Cayo Coco, and Cayo Largo. The number of international tourists remained relatively small during 1989–93, averaging about 300,000 per year. In 1991, Cuba's share of Caribbean tourism was a paltry 3.6 percent, though Cuba is by far the largest island of the chain.[36] But over the decade, tourism became the primary engine behind Cuba's economic recovery, surpassing sugar in 1994 as the main economic sector. The number of tourist visits grew consistently thereafter from 745,000 in 1995 to 1.2 billion in 1997 to 1.8 billion in 2000. Tourism-generated revenue shot up accordingly: $1.1 billion in 1995 and $2 billion in 2000.[37]

Most numerous among tourists were Canadians, Italians, and Spaniards. U.S. legislation barred U.S. citizens from traveling to Cuba unless they fell into specific categories such as Cubans traveling to visit relatives, journalists, research scholars, or those traveling for humanitarian purposes. The quality of foreign tourists varied widely, ranging from the wealthy and sophisticated who spent liberally on hotel rooms, meals, and shopping to what Cubans call *turistas de medio pelo* (riffraff tourists), who are mostly interested in sexual tourism.

Yet another tourism variant is medical tourism. Foreigners visit Cuba to receive medical treatment for a variety of conditions and diseases at prices way below what they would pay in their home countries. Cuban scientists and physicians have gained international recognition for the quality of their medical services and their development of innovative health treatments and medicines. Visitors paid bargain prices for hysterectomies, organ transplants, plastic surgeries, and treatments for Parkinson's disease, vitiligo, various forms of cancer, and substance abuse. Cuba also developed a wide range of biomedical products such as interferon to treat tumors, epidermal growth factor to stimulate the growth of skin in burn or wound patients, inexpensive HIV test kits, and vaccines against meningitis and hepatitis B. PPG, a cholesterol-lowering medication whose side effects remedied erectile dysfunction, became widely available both in pharmacies and on the street. The privileged access to treatments and medicines that foreigners enjoyed became a source of resentment for Cubans who were unable to receive them.[38]

The expansion of tourism had disturbing side effects of its own. It produced growing disparities between tourist-sector workers, who have access to hard-currency tips, and the rest of the labor force. Most odious was the emergence of "tourism apartheid," whereby Cuban nationals were denied access to hotels, tourist beaches, and other tourist facilities that were open only to foreigners and dollar-paying visiting Cuban exiles. Even locals who could afford to pay were barred from such facilities. This added to the growing feeling among regular Cubans that they had become second-class citizens in their own country, legally barred from enjoying many of the island's best beaches and resorts and thus from access to services and amenities reserved for tourists. While tourism provided much-needed hard currency and generated employment, it brought a heavy baggage of corrupting influences, particularly through riffraff tourism, which created a market for prostitution, illegal drugs, trafficking in stolen or fake cigars, and even the exploitation of minors.

Aware of the growing importance of tourism to Cuba's economic survival, foreign-based anti-Castro terrorists launched a bombing campaign in 1997. Seven bombs exploded in Havana hotels and tourist facilities, leaving eleven wounded and one Italian tourist dead. Two Salvadorians were soon apprehended and sentenced to death in 1999; years later, the government reduced the penalties to thirty years' imprisonment. Notorious exile terrorist Posada Carriles admitted involvement in the bombing plans and in an interview with *New York Times* reporters implicated the leadership of CANF, a charge that has never been substantiated.[39]

Men on horseback played a fundamental role in the structural economic reforms of the mid-1990s. The FAR created and managed a large number of state businesses, which were administered as profit-making capitalist ventures. The corporations FAR managed included Gaviota and Cubanacán, which provided tourist services such as hotels, tours, and car rentals; Cubalse, which ran retail store chains; agricultural development programs; and banks and financial institutions. Even the sugar industry came under military discipline when General Ulises Rosales del Toro became the new overseer of the persistent plantation as minister of the sugar industry in 1997.[40]

One of the Special Period's austerity measures was the reduction of military expenditures and the transfer of military personnel to productive endeavors. The FAR was uniquely positioned to take on a substantial role in the economy, having earned widespread popular admiration for its accomplishments in Africa, Central America, and elsewhere. The military was also highly disciplined and loyal to the Castro brothers. Perhaps more importantly, hundreds of officers had spent time in Europe receiving training in managerial and business skills.[41] The military's leading managerial role not only strengthened the FAR, it also gave its officers a strong stake in the preservation of the regime and further guaranteed their loyalty to the Castro brothers. These measures counterbalanced U.S. efforts to lure the Cuban military into staging a coup against the Castros with the promise of allowing them to retain power in its aftermath.[42]

The extreme austerity measures of the early 1990s and the economic reforms of 1993–96 paid off. After hitting its lowest point in 1993, the economy began to rebound with a negligible 0.7 percent GDP increase in 1994, followed by a modest 2.5 percent increase in 1995. By 1996, it was clear that the economy was on a path to recovery; the GDP annual growth rate had increased considerably to 7.8 percent. Over the next few years it continued to improve, albeit more slowly, averaging growth rates of 3.9 between 1997 and 2000. In spite of this progress, the GDP level reached in 2000 was still 12 percent less than what it had been in 1989.[43] Budget deficits also shrank from 34 to 2.5 percent. Between 1994 and 1996, exports rose 72 percent and imports jumped 80 percent. Still, by 2002, export levels were 26 percent lower than 1989 levels and import levels had reached only half of 1989 levels.[44]

Other indicators further demonstrated the economy's lingering vulnerability. In 1998, the nation's external debt mounted to $11.2 billion and Cuba's credit ratings were reduced to among the lowest in the world. In that year, the trade deficit was a shocking -$2.7 billion.[45]

As soon as the economy showed signs of sustained growth, the pendulum began to swing away from the extreme pragmatism of the mid-1990s, as the government reversed many of the reforms that had helped spark the recovery. Self-employment and sources of individual income and profit were among the first targets of the counter-reforms of the late 1990s. When *cuentapropistas* had to re-register in 1996, their license fees went up. In addition, government authorities created more effective mechanisms for collecting income taxes and curbing illegal profits. *Paladares* endured further scrutiny and higher license fees. The state curtailed or eliminated other private economic activities such as *permuta* real estate transactions and the rental of rooms to tourists.[46] In his closing speech to the Fifth Party Congress in 1997, Castro used language eerily reminiscent of the language of his Rectification of Errors Campaign. "We do not want to create a rich class in this country through privatization," he stated. Such a class, he warned, "would acquire too much power and conspire against socialism," just like the "counterrevolutionary" hot dog vendors of 1968 and the maligned greedy millionaire farmers of 1986. The new round of counter-reforms reduced the ranks of the self-employed from 200,000 in 1996 to 160,000 two years later. Likewise, in those two years the number of *paladares* shrank from 1,562 to 416. Only 253 were still in operation by 2000.[47]

As they had in previous policy reversals, the Castros changed the composition of the political leadership, including the Politburo and the cabinet. In 1997, they replaced eight Politburo members with six new ones when the size of the body was reduced from 26 to 24. Among those who left the Politburo—in his case due to old age—was 84-year-old Carlos Rafael Rodríguez, who died later that year.[48]

From Embargo to Blockade?

During the 1990s, as Cubans endured the calamities of the Special Period, the United States expanded the trade embargo that had been in place for the past three decades by passing new legislation with extraterritorial reach. The new restrictions sought to further isolate Cuba, discourage foreign investments, and accelerate the anticipated collapse of the regime. While the Cuban government has long referred to the U.S. embargo as a blockade, technically it was only an embargo since other nations could trade freely with Cuba. The passage of two pieces of legislation with coercive extraterritorial provisions, however, gave some credence to the use of the term "blockade."

In February 1992, U.S. Democratic congressman Robert Torricelli of New Jersey introduced a bill that eventually became the Cuban Democracy Act. It included provisions to stop all trade with Cuba by U.S. subsidiaries based in third countries and to curtail trade between Cuba and other nations by imposing quarantines on cargo vessels that had recently called on Cuban ports. It also imposed further limits on monetary remittances by U.S. citizens and residents. Torricelli's Democratic colleague, Senator Bob Graham of Florida, presented an identical bill in the Senate. Not wishing to alienate powerful corporate interests whose subsidiaries sold products to Cuba, President George H. W. Bush opposed the bill, instead ordering the Treasury Department to ban ships with Cuban cargoes from docking in U.S. ports.[49] Democratic presidential candidate Bill Clinton saw an opportunity to gain political capital among Cuban and Cuban American voters by endorsing the bill, and his endorsement forced Bush to follow suit. The president signed it into law on October 23 at a CANF event, just eleven days before the presidential election.[50] The Torricelli Act further aggravated Cuba's dire economic situation by increasing the cost of trading with foreign nations, thus jacking up the price of its imports.[51]

A bill introduced in 1995 by archconservative senator Jesse Helms of North Carolina and Representative Dan Burton of Indiana, both Republicans, further strengthened sanctions against Cuba. It spelled out how the United States would help in the event of Cuba's transition to democracy; made foreign nationals who owned, used, or "trafficked" in properties of U.S. citizens that had been confiscated by the Castro government liable to lawsuits; and denied U.S. visas to corporate officers and shareholders with controlling interests in foreign companies that held or trafficked in assets confiscated by Cuba.[52]

The bill had little promise of becoming law prior to the dramatic events that unfolded in the Florida Straits on February 24, 1996.[53] Since 1991, the exile organization Hermanos al Rescate (Brothers to the Rescue) headed by Bay of Pigs veteran José Basulto had regularly flown civilian aircraft missions to spot and rescue *balseros* in the Florida Straits. Toward the middle of the decade, the group became more aggressive, flying repeatedly into Cuban airspace and occasionally dropping political leaflets over Havana. Cuban authorities protested such provocations and warned U.S. authorities that they would treat further violations of Cuban airspace seriously, possibly shooting down intruding planes. U.S. authorities relayed these warnings to Hermanos al Rescate. On February 24, 1996, three Hermanos al Rescate planes notified Havana Center of their intention to enter Cuban airspace and were told that such action would put them in "danger." When they proceeded, Cuban fighter jets destroyed two of the three planes, killing four South Florida Cubans, three of whom were U.S. citizens.[54] The attacks violated international regulations that allow for the downing of unarmed civilian vessels only as a last resort. A subsequent investigation by the International Civil Aviation Organization concluded that the two downed planes had never even crossed into Cuban airspace, while the third plane, flown by Basulto, whose crew survived, had indeed flown into Cuban jurisdiction.[55]

Castro's decision to shoot down the planes made no political sense, given improving U.S.-Cuba relations and his desire to have the United States reduce or end the embargo. It was a decision based on his impulsive way of making foreign policy and his hyper sense of honor. The result proved costly for Cuba. Less than three weeks after the downing of the planes, Congress passed the Helms-Burton bill, which Clinton signed into law on March 12 of that election year. By signing the bill, Clinton gave away much presidential control over the embargo. No longer could a president singlehandedly lift the embargo; the matter was now mostly in the hands of Congress. Clinton did exercise his presidential prerogative, however, to suspend Title III of the act, which would have allowed U.S. citizens to sue individuals and corporations that held or trafficked in properties they lost decades earlier through nationalization by the Cuban state.

Clinton's successor, Republican George W. Bush, did not permit the implementation of Title III either. His administration did, however, use Title IV provisions against some executives and owners of a few corporations that benefited from confiscated properties. Upon the passage of the Helms-Burton law, the U.S. government sent letters of exclusion to executives of five corporations, including Sherritt International and Grupo Domos, a Mexican telecommunications corporation that prevented them from entering the United States. There is evidence that several companies have since decided against investing in Cuba and others have divested their holdings there because of the threat of U.S. sanctions.[56]

The Torricelli and Helms-Burton Acts reflected the unremitting arrogance of U.S. policy and added the insult of humiliation to the injury of economic sanctions. Indeed, the expanded embargo with its extraterritorial clauses echoed provisions of the Platt Amendment of 1902, a document that dictated the terms under which the United States Congress would permit the withdrawal of U.S. troops and grant Cuba the independence that so many Cubans had given their lives for. Like the odious Platt

Amendment, which was in force until 1934, the new embargo legislation sought to block or limit Cuba's ability to enter commercial and financial agreements with foreign nations. The longest ninety miles became longer yet.

During the 1990s, the United States and Cuba attacked each other in the United Nations. The United States presented yearly resolutions to the UN Commission on Human Rights denouncing human rights violations in Cuba, and Cuba sought UN condemnation of the U.S. trade embargo every year beginning in 1992. The United States presented its first resolution in Geneva denouncing Cuba's human rights abuses in 1987. The resolution failed to pass that year, as did similar resolutions presented in 1988 and 1989. This changed, however, in 1990, and the U.S. resolutions passed every year after that until 1997. In 1998, following Pope John Paul II's visit to Cuba and the subsequent release of over 100 political prisoners, the resolution against Cuba failed to pass, although similar resolutions passed in 1999 and 2000.[57] During this period, the United States stood virtually alone in its defense of the embargo: the number of nations that voted with the United States against the condemnation of the embargo ranged from one to three, Israel always among them.[58]

The international community, including some of the staunchest allies of the United States, among them Canada and the United Kingdom, and international organizations such as Amnesty International and Human Rights Watch joined Cuba in condemnation of the Helms-Burton Act. While the strengthening of the decades-long trade embargo fell short of the definition of "blockade," the recourse to extraterritorial economic and diplomatic coercion backfired. The world rallied in opposition to the Torricelli and Helms-Burton Acts, as attested by UN voting patterns. Every year the number of nations condemning the embargo in the UN increased, surpassing the 90 percent mark in 1998. Not coincidentally, on the heels of the passage of the Helms-Burton Act, the European Union (EU) softened its position, implementing the Common Position on Cuba, a policy of fostering dialogue and engagement with the island as long as it made progress in human rights and democratization.[59]

No es fácil: Cubans Endure the Special Period

While Special Period measures achieved some success in lifting the economy out of its depression, several of them had profound and lasting detrimental social and moral effects. They led to widespread pauperization, particularly for women and children; larger social and economic gaps; a surge of racism; sharper regional inequalities; and the splitting of social services and recreational facilities into three systems, one for wealthy foreigners, a second for the military and political elites, and a third for regular citizens. The population became increasingly frustrated, apathetic about the political process, angry with party and government leaders, and more willing to engage in forms of defiance that ranged from illegal activities such as petty theft and black market transactions to joining or supporting dissident movements to fleeing in makeshift rafts.

During the Special Period, state salaries remained low and the peso lost much of its value as the economy became increasingly dollarized. In 1995, salaries averaged 185 pesos (US $5.78) per month. Four years later, mean state wages had risen modestly to 222 pesos, the equivalent of $11. These incomes were actually lower than in any other country in the hemisphere, except Haiti, which did not lag far behind.[60] Moreover, at forty-eight hours, Cuba had the longest work week in the hemisphere. Because of the population's growing dependence on food, transportation, and services such as plumbing and television repair purchased with dollars, the cost of living skyrocketed. One study concluded that from 1989 to 1995 the price of basic goods jumped 660 percent.[61] Many workers, like their enslaved ancestors, labored at minimum capacity, played sick, appropriated workplace supplies, and sabotaged machines and tools. Such behaviors were easily rationalized. As a common joke goes: the government pretends that it pays me and I pretend that I work.

A portion of the population, meanwhile, saw its income rise: those working in bonus-paying or tip-earning jobs, such as cigar makers and bartenders; the self-employed; those engaged in illegal activities like black marketeering or prostitution; individuals working for joint venture companies; and recipients of dollar remittances. As a result of this, the income gap between the highest-earning and the lowest-earning workers grew to a ratio of 829 to 1, which was still small by world standards but far removed from the ratio of 4.6 to 1 that had been achieved in 1966.[62] The amount of income going to the wealthiest top 5 percent of the population jumped from only 10 percent in 1986 to 31 percent in 1995. By decade's end, the top 20 percent of income earners received almost 60 percent of all income, while the lowest 20 percent earned only 4 percent of all income.[63]

These developments had a particularly negative impact on blacks and mulattoes, who were less likely to find employment in the higher-paying tourist sector and to receive remittances from relatives abroad, as the vast majority of exiles were white. According to estimates for the year 2000, although nearly 44 percent of white households received remittances, the percentage among blacks was only 23. Thus, the income pyramid became increasingly racialized so that by century's end, 58 percent of the white population was in the top dollar-earning stratum and only 31 percent of mulattoes and 10 percent of blacks fell in that category. The disproportionate pauperization and marginalization of blacks led to other problems such as a highly visible overrepresentation of blacks in illegal activities such as black marketing and prostitution and a higher rate of incarceration among them.[64]

Women of all races bore a disproportionate share of the impact of Special Period calamities. Because of chronic food scarcities, women carried the bulk of increased responsibility for putting food on their families' tables. This required more working hours to supplement family income, more time and energy for securing ingredients either legally or illegally, and more ingenuity in preparing meals with dwindling and unorthodox ingredients. Because of skyrocketing divorce rates, more and more women took on total responsibility for feeding, clothing, and providing other necessities for their families, which oftentimes consisted of elderly parents and young children. In addition, men were more than three times more likely than women to be self-employed, and thus women were less able to supplement their incomes through such opportunities.[65]

The Special Period also exacerbated regional disparities that the revolution had successfully reduced over the decades. As the capital, the most important city, and the nation's center of business and tourism, Havana was the biggest beneficiary of opportunities and income stemming from joint business ventures, tourist expenditures, remittances, and self-employment. Although Havana's population represented roughly 20 percent of the island's total, 40 percent of government stores were located there, and its residents received 60 percent of all remittances. Specialized health care services and even simple ones such as the dispensing of contraceptive pills or contact lenses became increasingly concentrated in the capital. Consequently, Havana became a magnet for internal migrants, mostly from the eastern provinces, who gravitated there by the tens of thousands. Government authorities viewed this mass migration as a threat. In derision, some *Habaneros* referred to eastern migrants as *palestinos*, while the government, which was led by two easterners, set in motion policies to discourage further migration.[66]

The Counter-Plantation: Dissidence, *Jineterismo*, and Cultural Transgression

The crisis of the Special Period further eroded popular support for the regime and pushed an increasing number of citizens into open opposition. Others engaged in everyday forms of resistance. A 1990 survey conducted by the PCC found that nearly 60 percent of Cubans lacked trust in their government leaders. In another contemporary survey, only one in ten said they would vote for a candidate who was a PCC member.[67] An incipient dissident movement with roots in the second half of the 1970s expanded and gained visibility and strength. Scores of private organizations surfaced that attempted to challenge the government's more than three-decade-long monopoly over state-sanctioned mass organizations, or what passed for civil society in Cuba. Human rights groups proliferated, as did independent press agencies, professional associations, labor unions, women's organizations, and even nonrecognized political parties, all of which were illegal.

Meanwhile, tens of thousands confronted the crisis and the regime through *jineterismo* (literally, horse riding)—engaging in a host of illegal activities such as hustling, selling and buying in the black market, and informal variants of prostitution. Others resisted through artistic expression such as poems, songs, films, and paintings or through everyday passive counter-plantation practices such as labor absenteeism, telling antigovernment jokes, engaging in *choteo* (mockery of everything through humor), and even naming their children with odd, subversive-sounding names.

The most dramatic manifestations of popular resistance were the unprecedented spontaneous riots that broke out in the summer of 1993 in Regla and Cojímar, the latter spurred by the killing of three unarmed *balseros* by policemen. An even larger riot erupted the following summer in Havana's Malecón (the Seafront), hence its name: *el maleconazo*.[68]

Human rights activists and those seeking political reforms organized and mobilized during the Special Period. After spending five months in prison in 1986–87, Elizardo Sánchez Santacruz, one of the leaders of the CCPDH, formed his own organization, the Comisión Cubana de Derechos Humanos y Reconciliación Nacional (Cuban Human Rights and National Reconciliation Commission, CCDHRN). Ricardo Bofill, Samuel Martínez Lara, and Tania Díaz along with other dissidents founded the Partido Pro

Derechos Humanos de Cuba (Cuban Human Rights Party) as the political arm of the CCPDH.[69] Another new major opposition group was the Movimiento Cristiano de Liberación (Christian Liberation Movement, MCL), an organization founded in 1989 by Oswaldo Payá. By 1990, nearly 100 dissident, independent, and human rights organizations were functioning, and many established collaborative links with exile groups based in Miami, Madrid, San Juan, and New Jersey. Some received modest financial support from the U.S. government.[70]

A major milestone of the opposition movement was the formation between late 1995 and early 1996 of a national coalition composed of over 100 independent and dissident groups under the banner of the Concilio Cubano (Cuban Council). The *concilio*'s original signatories included many of the island's leading dissidents, among them Arcos Bergnes, Payá, Rivero, and Sánchez Santacruz. Its founding declaration included four specific goals: peaceful transition to democracy, amnesty for all political prisoners, the defense of human rights, and the inclusion of all Cubans in the political process. The *concilio* was scheduled to have its first major congress on February 24, 1996, but before that could happen, scores of Concilio members were harassed, arrested, and in some instances convicted and sentenced to prison. As a result of heavy state pressure, the *concilio* lost strength and eventually disbanded.[71] The next major unity effort occurred in November 1999, with the formation of Todos Unidos (All United), an opposition coalition effort led by Payá and former fighter pilot Vladimiro Roca Antúnez (the son of legendary communist leader Blas Roca).

Numerous NGOs emerged during the Special Period. These included independent journalists' associations, such as CubaPress, Havana Press, and the Independent Press Bureau of Cuba. In the 1990s, civil society groups proliferated, including small independent professional associations for lawyers, physicians, teachers, writers and artists, and economists; labor unions; and independent libraries, whose collections included banned publications made available to the public.[72]

Opposition and independent organizations continued to press for change, and independent press agencies kept the world informed about human rights violations and the atrocious conditions endured by political prisoners. The MCL, led by Payá, initiated a drive to collect 10,000 signatures for a petition to the National Assembly asking for a referendum to guarantee freedom of expression, freedom of the press, the right to free association, and the right to establish private business enterprises. The petition, whose legality was recognized by the Constitution, also called for an amnesty for political prisoners and the enactment of electoral reforms.[73] In 1992, Payá tried to run for a national delegate post, but authorities arrested him two days before the nominations assembly. On election day, some voters used the opportunity to protest. Island-wide results showed that 7 percent of voters spoiled or left their ballots blank; the rate of spoiled and blank ballots in Havana was more than twice the national rate.[74]

Another dissident group that gained widespread attention during the second half of the 1990s was the Grupo de Trabajo de la Disidencia Interna (Internal Dissidence Working Group). Composed of Vladimiro Roca Antúnez, engineer Félix Bonne Carcassés, attorney René Gómez Manzano, and economist Martha Beatriz Roque, the group drafted the manifesto "La Patria es de todos" (the fatherland belongs to all of us) and sent it to the Central Committee of the PCC in June 1997. The document was a response to the draft of a document prepared for approval during the PCC's Fifth Party Congress that provided a falsified version of Cuba's history and celebrated the government's success in fighting the economic crisis of the Special Period. In a few days "La Patria es de todos" became international news, and later that year authorities arrested its four signatories. In 1999, they convicted and sentenced them to between three and a half and five years behind bars. This drew widespread criticism from around the world, including some from leftist organizations and longtime friends of socialist Cuba.[75]

The state responded to the growing opposition and independent movements with a heavy hand. Violent, government-organized mobs called rapid response brigades were routinely unleashed to harass and physically attack dissidents. These brigades, mostly composed of young, male militants and undercover MININT officers, stand on call for mobilization under direct orders from the PCC.[76] In 1991, when they were first organized, one brigade assaulted writer María Elena Cruz Varela and forced her to eat a paper containing a pro-democracy manifesto she had written; she later received two years' jail time. That same year, another rapid response brigade targeted Payá's home, ransacking it and defacing its front wall with graffiti that said "*Payá gusano* (worm)" and "Viva Fidel." This action and the unremitting harassment that followed put the dissident leader's signature-gathering efforts on hold for several years.[77] Hundreds, if not thousands, of other dissidents endured repeated arrests, interrogations, and imprisonment, in some cases for the most inoffensive actions.

One notable example was the arrest and sentencing of six members of Asociación Pro-Arte Libre (Association for Free Art), an independent arts organization, in October 1988 for laying a wreath at Martí's monument in Havana.[78]

Toward the end of the decade, when around twenty independent news bureaus were in operation, the government passed a stringent gag law aimed at penalizing independent journalists and other individuals who were providing information to foreign media or the U.S. government that could harm Cuba's economic interests. The law stipulated prison sentences of up to fifteen years.[79] Most independent journalists and private library operators have been arrested, beaten, or sentenced to prison terms under this law.

State repression would have been harsher had it not been for the increased global vigilance of foreign governments, human rights activists, and international bodies such as the International Red Cross, Amnesty International, and the United Nations. After almost three decades of refusing permission for outside monitoring of human rights and prison conditions, in the late 1980s Cuba allowed it for the first time. A 1988 report by Amnesty International denounced inhumane conditions prevailing in Cuban jails. A six-member team of the United Nations Human Rights Commission confirmed those findings. During its 1988 visit, the UN team documented over 2,400 incidents of human rights abuses. Only ninety individuals had an opportunity to testify before the team members.[80] Foreign recognition of Cuban dissidents helped encourage them in their struggle and provided some degree of protection for them and their respective movements. Payá, Sánchez Santacruz, Cruz Varela, and dozens of other Cuban dissidents and journalists received important international awards for their work in the cause of human rights.[81]

The Catholic Church also began to play a more energetic role in the defense of human rights. It also began to criticize the nation's material and moral decay. Church attendance increased significantly as the Catholic Church and new Protestant congregations, particularly Pentecostal groups, became an increasingly significant source of material support (medicine and clothing, for example), spiritual solace, and a sense of community. A September 1993 pastoral letter by Cuba's archbishops and bishops became a major milestone in the history of the revolution. The document denounced the island's deteriorating economic, moral, and political conditions. "Scarcities of the most basic material needs: food, medicines, transportation, electricity," the prelates proclaimed, "foster a tense

Figure 6.4. Banner of the Sacred Heart of Jesus draping the National Library as Pope John Paul II officiates Mass in the Plaza of the Revolution, January 1998. Photograph by Domenico Stinellis. Courtesy of AP.

environment that occasionally hides the Cuban people's nature[,] [which is] characterized by peace and cordiality." In an unprecedented action, the bishops denounced the regime's undemocratic practices: the exclusionary and omnipresent nature of its official ideology, its limitations on personal freedoms, the excessive control exercised by the state security apparatus, the large number of incarcerated individuals, and discrimination based on political, philosophical, and religious beliefs.[82]

Pope John Paul II's five-day visit to Cuba in February 1998 was one of the most significant events of the period. In anticipation of his visit, as a goodwill gesture, Cuba legalized the long-banned celebration of Christmas Day. During the pope's sojourn, he officiated at four massive outdoor masses, the last of which drew hundreds of thousands of people to the iconic Plaza of the Revolution. Almost surreally, the state allowed the display on the facade of the José Martí National Library of a huge banner with the venerated image of the Sacred Heart of Jesus, just a few hundred yards away from the Ministry of Industries building, which was adorned with a large metal sculpture of the revolution's secular patron saint, Che Guevara (figure 6.4). The pope's message resonated throughout the island

and beyond. One of his most memorable statements—"May Cuba, with all its magnificent potential, open itself up to the world, and may the world open itself up to Cuba"—reflected his balanced and fair critique of the Cuban situation. With that sentence, he called on Cuba to join the modern world and embrace pluralistic and democratic ideas and practices and invited the world, namely the United States, to end its hostile policy of isolating Cuba economically and otherwise. Thus, the pope was able to denounce both Cuba's shortcomings and the U.S. embargo, satisfying both the Vatican's agenda and that of the Cuban regime. The papal visit had the immediate result of the release of over 100 political prisoners.[83]

The poverty and desperation of the Special Period were such that the population adopted a survival mode that fostered *jineterismo*. Although the terms *jinetera* and *jinetero* are most commonly applied to women and men who exchange sexual favors for money or valuables, in their broader definition they also refer to those who challenge the system through a variety of illicit activities such as black marketing or running illegal gambling operations. Chronic scarcities of food and other essentials forced most of the population to engage in one form of petty *jineterismo* or another. A 2001 government study concluded that nine out of ten Cuban families were involved in illicit activities. Many government officials and presidents of neighborhood CDRs were among those who participated in such activities.[84] The prevalence of *jineterismo* and the population's growing resentment toward the government led to the so-called double morality. For example, the same CDR president who gives speeches against corruption and illicit activities is likely to satisfy half or more of her household food needs with black market merchandise.[85] What allowed such complex webs of illicit activities to flourish was the system of *sociolismo*, a slang term whose etymological root "*socio*" (partner or buddy), highlights the fact that for Cubans, survival hinged on the ability to cultivate affective relations with others for the informal—and often illegal—exchange of favors, goods, services, and information.

The combination of the state's incapacity to provide adequate food and basic consumer goods and services, the increasing number of foreign tourists visiting the island, and the dollarization of the economy produced a fertile ground for *jineterismo*. So-called *bisneros* (from the English word businessman), peddled ill-gotten goods such as gasoline, cooking oil and office supplies. They could sell tourists almost any product or service they wanted, from Cohiba cigars (real or fake) to PPG pills from island-wide tours that included lodging in shady clandestine motels to the services of a tag team of voluptuous, spandex-clad *jineteras*.

Prostitution, which had virtually disappeared during the first few years of the revolution, reemerged vigorously in the late 1980s and the 1990s. It became embarrassingly visible in resort areas such as Varadero, in Havana's Malecón, and even in Havana's most splendid boulevard, la Quinta Avenida, where provocatively dressed women; girls in their mid-teens; high-heeled, mini-skirted transvestites; and muscular male prostitutes (*pingueros*) waited to be picked up by dollar-paying clients. Singer-songwriter Silvio Rodríguez wrote his first actual protest song on the subject of teenaged *jineteras* cruising la Quinta Avenida. Its closing verses read: "Flowers under bed sheets with eyes / disposable flowers / cravings' hand bells / flowers without spring or season / flowers feeding off the leftovers of love." Another official intellectual, Miguel Barnet, later wrote a poem about an HIV-infected male prostitute who "was cast into oblivion, devoured / slowly by a disease / that was the scourge of the century."[86]

While some *jineteras* practiced their trade as full-time, pimp-managed, street-walking prostitutes, most engaged in more informal forms of *jineteria*. A college-educated divorcee with several children to feed might occasionally seek out a tourist to befriend and have sex in exchange for material benefits. At times, such liaisons develop into long-term relations and even marriage. One *jinetera* from the western province of Pinar del Río explained her status thus: "I am neither a prostitute nor a whore. I am a chemistry technician. But with my 200-pesos-a-month salary I can only afford a plate of rice and beans. What else can I do?" Castro, in one of his most disgraceful remarks ever, recognized on television that Cuba had a prostitution problem but joked that Cuban prostitutes were the best educated and healthiest in the world. While they were certainly educated, they may not have been that healthy, given the rise of sexually transmitted diseases, which reached epidemic proportions on the island during the 1990s. Even the leadership of the FMC, according to interviews conducted by Maxine Molyneaux, demonstrated insensitivity toward the rising prostitution problem, blaming it on the U.S. trade embargo and on *jineteras'* greed.[87]

Individuals also expressed their lack of support for and criticism of the government with nonconfrontational everyday actions not dissimilar to the counter-plantation practices of their ancestors, which James C. Scott, Damián J. Fernández, and others have called "everyday" or "informal" forms of resistance.[88] These included slowdowns and playing sick at work, sabotaging work tools and machines, creating alternative realities through jokes and storytelling, and engaging in symbolic acts of resistance such as wearing "subversive" clothes, and creating a new popular vocabulary of social criticism and resistance.

Some individuals escaped their harsh realities through suicide. Cuba's historically high suicide rate—which has been among the highest in the world since the nineteenth century—increased from an average of 16.4 per 1,000 during the 1970s to 22 per 1,000 between 1980 and 1988, falling slightly to 21 per 1,000 during the first five years of the Special Period. The rock-bottom year, 1993, registered the highest number of suicides ever: 2,374. When the economy rebounded during the second half of the 1990s, the suicide rate dropped to 19 per 1,000.[89]

Cubans have long used *choteo* to mock those in power and denounce social problems. The Castro brothers and the *mayimbería* (ruling elite) are continuous targets of jokes. One of the hundreds of such jokes goes like this: Castro's limousine drives by an extraordinarily long *cola* (queue). He orders the driver to drop him off to join the *cola*, thinking that the lined-up multitude is standing there for something very special. Suddenly all but one of the *coleros* disappear, and a puzzled Castro asks the one who remained in line "Why did everyone else leave?" The *colero* respectfully responds: "Comandante, this was the line to leave Cuba, and they must have thought that if Castro is leaving, there is no longer reason to flee." Another one tells of an attempt by Castro to elevate his popularity by fighting a bull. Castro, dressed in bullfighters' colorful attire, pink tights, red cape, and all, waits for the angry bull to come out. The bull charges toward the center of the rink. Castro whispers something in its ear and immediately the bull dies. The crowd goes wild: "¡Olé! ¡Olé! ¡Viva Fidel!" Another bullfighter asks the matador: "How did you kill the bull without even touching it?" Castro responds: "It was simple. I whispered in its ear 'Socialism or Death.'"

Low-quality products sold to the public during the Special Period also became targets of *choteo*: bad rum was *chispa 'e tren* (train spark), low-quality tennis shoes were *chupa meao* (urine absorbers), clunky Chinese bicycles were *chivos* (goats). *Choteo* allowed common citizens to channel frustrations and create temporary alternative realities in which they turned hierarchies upside down. They were not unlike those created by slaves and their descendants, whose jokes, stories, and sayings mocked masters and overseers.[90]

Figure 6.5. Satirical drawing poking fun at ill-equipped European sex tourist. Drawing signed "Narciso," circa 1994. Photograph by Luis Martínez-Fernández.

The Special Period also generated a rich lexicon of mockery and resistance. *El teque*, for example, refers to the stale rhetoric of government officials. *Yuma* means the United States but also a foreigner. A *turispepe* is a Spanish client of a *jinetera* (figure 6.5); an *ostinado* [*sic*] is someone in a state of malaise due to overwhelming daily problems; and *resolver* and *inventar* are used to refer to creative ways of gathering basic supplies such as food for the next meal.[91] The word *jaba*, a pre-Columbian Taino word for utility bag, is one of the most commonly used terms, given its ubiquity as a vessel for carrying food and other goods acquired at *bodegas* or through barter or illicit trade. The Cuban body, a joke goes, is composed of a head, a torso, extremities, and a *jaba*. A curious new form of symbolic resistance involved child-naming practices. Russian names such as Gorki and Nadezca went out of style, yielding, in some cases, to Yankeephile (and thus subversive) names such as Yusa, Usdolar, and Yankiel.

The arts became yet another vehicle for the expression of criticism and in some instances for manifesting outright opposition to the regime. Poets, painters, authors, filmmakers, and popular music composers used their talents to denounce the grave problems of the Special Period. Some even labored outside the margins of legality as members of dissident and opposition groups. Others developed new aesthetics in contraposition to those of the official arts establishment.[92] During the 1990s, the government expanded spaces for critical art, something that was unimaginable during the Stalinist 1970s. This was partially due to the state's inability to adequately fund and provide equipment and supplies to filmmakers, painters, and writers. Artistic creation not only survived but also experienced a boom as arts organizations and individual artists sought alternative means of artistic dissemination such as film co-productions, co-publications, and the active merchandizing and distribution of publications, films, music CDs, and concert tours abroad. These circumstances pushed Cuban artists to develop a less insular art, one with broader global appeal. The role played by Abel Prieto, who became minister of culture in 1997, is worth mentioning. He served as a strong advocate for artistic creation and succeeded at obtaining equipment, resources, and better salaries for artists. He has also been pivotal in opening up cultural spaces for Afro-Cuban artistic representations and new popular music genres such as hip-hop and reggaeton.[93]

Film, which had always played a major role in the revolutionary education of the populace, became a vehicle for the denunciation of social, political, and economic problems. Such was the case with the ethereal film *Alicia en el pueblo de Maravillas* (1991) directed by Daniel Díaz Torres, a scathing satirical critique of bureaucratism and governmental ineptitude. Because of the controversy surrounding the film, ICAIC authorities replaced their director, Julio García Espinosa, with former ICAIC director Alfredo Guevara, who remained in that position until 2000. Other noteworthy Special Period films were Tomás Gutiérrez Alea and Juan Carlos Tabío's *Fresa y chocolate* (1993) and *Guántanamera* (1995) and Fernando Pérez's *Madagascar* (1994) and *La vida es silvar* (1998). The latter three explore common Special Period subjects such as emigration, alienation, and survivalist behavior. *Guántanamera* was particularly controversial because of its veiled—but obvious—criticism of the regime. This acclaimed dark comedy was broadly screened even though Castro publicly called it a counterrevolutionary film.[94]

The 1990s also produced a torrent of literary works chronicling the social, economic, and moral decay of the time. Novelists Zoé Valdés (*La nada cotidiana*, 1996) and Pedro Juan Gutiérrez (*Trilogía sucia de La Habana*, 1998; and *El Rey de La Habana*, 1999), among others, have left poignant depictions of everyday struggles and squalor. Other authors such as Daína Chaviano and Leonardo Padura Fuentes, recurred to less direct genres to speak to the hardships of the Special Period, Chaviano through science fiction and fantasy (*Confesiones eróticas y otros hechizos*, 1994; *El hombre, la hembra y el hambre*, 1998) and Padura Fuentes through his series of four detective novels published between 1991 and 1998, collectively titled *Las cuatro estaciones*. Numerous authors left Cuba in the 1990s, settling in Europe, Latin America, or the United States. Such was the case with Valdés, Chaviano, Cruz Varela, Norberto Fuentes, Jesús Díaz, historian Manuel Moreno Fraginals, and print journalist Wilfredo Cancio Isla, among many others.[95]

The new openings the state created for painters and graphic artists to exhibit and sell their works in tourist sections in Havana and abroad and legislation in 1991 in the United States that made it legal for U.S. citizens to purchase paintings by Cuban artists sparked a boom in the plastic arts. While street art consisted mostly of lower-quality works with stereotypical themes—1950s cars, voluptuous nude or seminude women, and hackneyed rural landscapes—gallery works often engaged social and political issues such as racism, exploitation, and prostitution. Some plastic and performance artists tested the limits of official patience with critical and anti-government art. Performance artist Tania Bruguera, for example, published a few editions of the arts newspaper *Memoria de la Postguerra*, which was highly critical of social realities and included Cubans living outside the island among its contributors. State censors quickly banned it from circulation. A little-known young artist, Ángel Delgado, carried out an odd and daring installation: he defecated on a *Granma* newspaper inside an art gallery. He received a six-month sentence for "public scandal."[96] In 1989, at an art exhibition at Havana's oldest colonial fort, la Real Fuerza, co-painters Eduardo Ponjuán and René Francisco Rodríguez displayed a painting of a buxom Castro in drag. The exhibition was closed within five days and Marcia Leiseca, who authorized the exhibit, lost her job as vice minister of culture.[97]

It was artists like Ponjuán and Rodríguez rather than political dissidents and independent journalists who first dared cross the line by personally and publicly ridiculing the Maximum Leader. As a common phrase went, "one could play with the chain but not with the monkey." They yanked at the chain and ridiculed the monkeys.

"So near and yet so foreign": The Ongoing Havana-Washington-Miami Drama

During the 1990s, U.S. policy toward Cuba became deeply intertwined with the U.S. electoral process as CANF became an increasingly powerful lobbying force and Florida turned into a major battleground state in elections. U.S. presidents, presidential candidates, and numerous members of Congress supported aggressive measures against Cuba to court Cuban and Cuban American votes. Because of their geographic concentration in Miami-Dade County and high rates of voter participation, Cuban votes could very well decide the outcome of elections in Florida, and because Florida was such an important swing state with a large number of electoral votes, results there could decide national elections. Aware of this power, CANF proved willing to support candidates from both parties as long as they pursued a hard-line policy toward the Castro regime. While the majority of Cubans and Cuban Americans residing in the United States favored hostile actions toward Cuba, a growing minority preferred improving relations and ending the embargo.

As seen before, Bill Clinton backed the Torricelli Bill in 1992 to gain political support in Florida. This was the first serious effort by a Democratic presidential candidate to lure the support of Cuban and Cuban American voters.[98] Significantly, although George H. W. Bush carried Florida by two points, his margin of victory was only 86,000 votes, considerably less than the nearly one million-vote margin by which he had won the state in 1988. Senator Graham and Representative Torricelli, the main promoters of the Cuban Democracy Act, were reelected by large margins. At the state level, voters reelected Cuban-born Republican congresswoman Ileana Ros-Lehtinen and sent two other Cubans to Congress: Democrat Robert Menéndez of New Jersey and Republican Lincoln Díaz-Balart of Miami. Overall, while Cubans and Cuban Americans continued to vote overwhelmingly for Republican presidential candidates, they began to demonstrate a willingness to support Democrats who espoused strong anti-Castro positions.

CANF president Mas Canosa put it succinctly: "Although I'm voting for Bush out of loyalty, Clinton's decisive support of the Cuban Democracy Act turned the Cuban-American community around."[99]

One of the thorniest issues that affected the Havana-Washington-Miami love-hate triangle was migration control. The centrality of this matter became apparent once again with the explosion of yet another massive exodus that began in 1993–94. Twice before (in 1965 and 1980), Castro had managed to encourage and manipulate the mass departure of disaffected citizens to gain a bargaining chip with the United States and to provide an escape valve for mounting domestic tensions. The number of people leaving the island illegally, mostly on *balsas*, was small throughout the 1980s. It increased in the early 1990s, when a per annum average of 1,739 *balseros* reached the United States (1990–92). Nineteen-ninety-three was a record year of *balsero* activity, with 3,656 arriving in Florida; but in 1994 outmigration increased tenfold as tens of thousands of *balseros* left Cuba, 37,145 of whom made it safely to the United States.[100] The timing was no coincidence: popular discontent peaked in 1993 and 1994, the worst years of the Special Period, as Cubans struggled to put food on their tables and clothes on their backs.

Looking at the *balsero* phenomenon by counting heads, however, severely limits our understanding of the individual motivations and harrowing experiences of those who jumped on rafts, sometimes as rudimentary as an inner tube, seeking to escape the island they called home. A case of seven young men who embarked on a raft in the coastal town of Santa Cruz del Sur comes to mind. Years later, when I visited that town, a young woman told me that her husband and another six men had left on a raft. The townspeople never heard from them again and assumed that all had been swallowed by the ocean. The young woman was left alone to care for her infant twins.

Another actual case, the *balsa* flight of a family of circus performers, seems to have come out of the best literature of Latin American magical realism. Cecilio Rojo (fifty-five) owned and managed a circus in which his youthful wife, Yulina Rico (nineteen), performed on the tight rope and the unicycle; his son, Inti Rojo (twenty-three), swallowed fire and performed magic tricks such as making doves and eggs appear and disappear. The circus ran into difficulties during the lowest point of the Special Period. According to Alfredo A. Fernández's chronicle, their battered circus could no longer perform:

Due to the lack of fuel, it could not travel from place to place as before. The last pair of doves from Inti's prestidigitation act were sacrificed and eaten with rice. Because of the same lack of fuel, he could no longer breathe fire for the audience. The beautiful Yulina, high-wire artist, had to cancel her two sensational acts. . . . The unicycle she used had a flat tire, and they had no spare. . . . For want of the umbrella she needed to maintain her balance, she fell and broke her arm. She had to have it placed in a sling because the hospitals had no plaster to cast it.

"Frightening things happened," the narrative continues, "such as a robbery and the progressive loss of almost all the crystal they used in their juggling acts. . . . The pair of monkeys they exhibited, caged, somehow connived to stone and beat to death the old toothless lioness that was the relic of the Rojo Circus. . . . The monkeys devoured the lioness . . . after a week of intense hunger during which the owners had not been able to offer the monkeys even a banana." After witnessing that horrific scene, the circus family decided to join the *balsero* fleet. Rojo sold the patched circus tent along with what was left of the circus. With the proceeds he bought a small sailboat on which they sailed into an uncertain dark horizon on August 16, 1994.[101]

In marked contrast to the safe departure of previous exiles, who left on planes and seaworthy vessels, *balseros* faced the possibility of death as they tried to reach South Florida on floating devices that often consisted of just an inner tube and a rope-woven seat. *Balseros* braved long journeys, sea storms, blistering exposure to the sun, and the threat of voracious sharks. Estimates of deaths while attempting to cross the Florida Straits range from 30 to 70 percent.[102] The Florida Straits have become a veritable underwater mass grave.

Desperation sparked a rash of vessel hijackings in Havana and harsh responses from security forces. The most tragic of these occurred in the predawn hours of July 13, 1993, when a few individuals hijacked the wooden tugboat *13 de Marzo*, which transported around seventy passengers, including twenty children. The hijacked tugboat was heading north toward Florida, when two firefighter vessels approached and proceeded to sink the relic, which dated to 1879, with water hoses. The brutal attack caused twenty fatalities, eleven of them children. Two weeks later, one of the ferry boats that connected Havana and Casa Blanca, across the bay, was hijacked and taken safely into U.S. territorial waters, where the Coast

Guard rescued it. Only fifteen of the 200 passengers asked to return to Cuba. Yet another ferry was hijacked on August 4.[103]

Rumors circulated that on August 5 a large vessel would sail to Havana's Malecón and pick up anyone who wished to emigrate to the United States. A large crowd began to assemble there. It soon expanded into 20,000 to 30,000 people, and *el maleconazo* broke out, a riot the likes of which had not been seen since the fall of Batista. Protesters chanted: "*¡Libertad! ¡Libertad!*" and "*¡Abajo Fidel!*" (Down with Fidel!) and looted and destroyed stores and other establishments. Government forces including members of the notorious rapid response brigades violently dispersed the rioting crowd. Later that day, none other than the Comandante himself appeared at the scene. The nightly news broadcast downplayed the riot, misinforming the public by saying that the crowd consisted of only 700 people, but the public, well informed by *radio bemba* (word of mouth), knew better.[104]

Less than a week later, Castro instructed the police and the Coast Guard not to interfere with *balseros* fleeing the island. Pandemonium ensued, an echo of the crises of the Camarioca and El Mariel exoduses. Havana's streets were filled with surreal scenes as thousands gathered to witness the spectacle of hundreds of *balseros* marching toward the ocean along with an endless flotilla of rafts, makeshift sailboats, inner tubes of varying sizes, even wooden doors freshly pulled out of their frames.

When the *balsero* crisis exploded, U.S. mid-term elections were less than three months away. Having learned from Jimmy Carter's mismanagement of the Mariel crisis and remembering that *marielito* riots in detention facilities in Arkansas were partly to blame for his losing reelection as governor of that state, Clinton took immediate action to minimize the impact of the out-of-control flow of immigrants. Almost immediately, he gave orders that henceforward all *balseros* intercepted at sea be transported to the Guantánamo Bay Naval Base or U.S. bases in the Panama Canal Zone for processing and the possible granting of entrance visas. In early September 1994, U.S. and Cuban negotiators reached agreement on a formula to reduce the flow of *balseros*. Cuba agreed to crack down on flight attempts and the United States promised to issue 20,000 visas each year for those who wished to leave the island legally. Negotiations continued until both countries signed a formal migration accord in May 1995 whereby Cuba accepted the return of nearly 20,000 refugees encamped at Guantánamo and the United States reaffirmed its commitment to grant the promised visas.[105] In a great twist of irony, while U.S. and Cuban troops had never fought against each other, a few hundred *balseros* detained in a

U.S. camp in Panama escaped from that facility and engaged U.S. troops in a daylong battle—an actual battle. Armed with bricks, bottles, rocks, and other improvised weapons, the Cubans injured 236 U.S. soldiers.[106]

The new Cuban migration rules were a profound reversal of the historic policy of granting virtually automatic political asylum to fleeing Cubans. Clinton's new "wet foot/dry foot" policy required that those seeking asylum set foot (dry feet) on U.S. territory and prove that if forced to return they would face persecution, while those found at sea (wet feet) would not be admitted to the United States but would be returned to Cuba or temporarily interned in U.S. military bases on foreign soil.[107] The Cold War had ended and images of desperate individuals escaping communist Cuba were no longer valuable propaganda for the United States.

Early in the 1996 electoral year, the vast majority of Cuban and Cuban American voters supported the presidential candidacy of Republican senator Robert Dole. Clinton's signing of the Helms-Burton Act chipped away at Dole's support, however. In addition to Dole's lackluster campaign and charisma deficit, another factor that reduced support for the Republican candidate was the aggressive anti-welfare, anti-immigration, and "English only" policies his party embraced. Even conservative Republican legislators Díaz-Balart and Ros-Lehtinen rejected such extremist positions. Election results demonstrated that Republican presidential candidates could no longer count on the support of a solid Cuban electoral bloc that was focused on a single issue. In Florida, Dole received only 60 percent of the Cuban and Cuban American vote, while Clinton received 40 percent, nearly double what he got in 1992. Clinton carried Florida with 48 percent of the vote, garnering its coveted 25 Electoral College votes.[108]

Interestingly enough, while members of the *balsero* generation are sometimes at odds with first- and second-cohort South Florida Cubans, they enjoy generally good relations with their extended families and friends who are still on the island. In part, this is because they shared the difficult experience of the Special Period, embraced a common survivalist culture, and developed a lack of faith in politicians and ideologies, both on the island and abroad. More important is the fact that unlike the first two exile cohorts, émigrés in the *balsero* cohort—the revolution's grandchildren—have cultivated strong collaborative relations with those they left behind. They travel back to Cuba often and remit larger proportions of their income than earlier exiles. Because of these transnational connections, island residents hold *balsero*-generation emigrants in high esteem.[109]

In the aftermath of the 1996 U.S. elections, much to the chagrin of Miami's most radical exiles, Clinton embraced a conciliatory attitude toward Cuba. He continued to suspend the application of Title III of the Helms-Burton Act every six months through the end of his second presidential term. In 1998 the Clinton administration reauthorized remittances, relaxed travel restrictions, and increased the amount of money U.S. citizens could spend while visiting Cuba. The most conciliatory actions of the administration were several laws and provisions in 1999–2000 that expanded the number of airline flights between the two countries and allowed for even larger remittances and a larger maximum amount of money that could be spent on the island. Less than two weeks before the 2000 general election, Clinton signed into law the most far-reaching of his new Cuba policies, the Trade Sanctions Reform and Export Enhancement Act. The act made it legal for U.S. firms to sell medical and agricultural products to Cuba as long as such transactions were made in cash instead of through financing.[110]

The Elián González affair set the stage for a major confrontation among the Cuban exile community, Castro's Cuba, and the U.S. government. It became yet another opportunity for Castro to demonstrate his mastery over the art of triangulation, this time pitting the exile community against the U.S. federal government. On November 21, 1999, six-year-old Elián; his mother, Elizabeth Brotons; and another twelve *balseros* got into a small-engine boat and headed toward Florida.[111] During a heavy storm eleven of the *balseros* perished, his mother among them. Miraculously, Elián survived, his mother having tied him to an inner tube. On the 22nd—it was Thanksgiving Day—two men on a boat spotted Elián off the coast of Ft. Lauderdale and rescued him. This was the start of a prolonged, explosive controversy over whether Elián should remain in Miami under the custody of his extended family or return to his father in Cuba. The affair immediately turned into an international controversy as the father and the Cuban government demanded and fought in court to have father and son reunited. Quite significantly, the lead lawyer for the Cuban government was Gregory Craig, who became famous by leading Clinton's defense when he was impeached. The Elián affair embroiled all three branches of the U.S. government. His repatriation case reached the Supreme Court, whose justices decided not to hear it. The Department of Justice and the Immigration and Naturalization Service aggressively pursued the child's return to Cuba, while the U.S. Congress debated a bill to grant citizenship to Elián.[112]

Before dawn on April 22, a heavily armed team of Immigration and Naturalization Service officers broke into the house where Elián lived and forcibly removed him. This was a heavy-handed use of force that was justified, disturbingly, by false Cuban intelligence claiming that the house was heavily armed. A dramatic award-winning photograph by Alan Díaz captured the precise moment when ferocious-looking, SWAT-equipped operatives wrested a terrified Elián at the point of a machine gun from his Miami home. Following months of litigation, Elián was reunited with his father and returned to Cuba, to a heroes' welcome.

Once again, the exile community endured defeat and humiliation at the hands of Castro's regime. The other big loser was presidential candidate Al Gore, who was unable to distance himself enough from the Clinton administration's conciliatory Cuba policy and its handling of the Elián case. Clinton's amicable handshake with Castro at a UN meeting just weeks before the election did not help Gore.[113] Cuban and Cuban American voters punished Democrats and Gore at the ballot box, casting 82 percent of their votes in support of Republican candidate George W. Bush.[114] In large part thanks to Cuban and Cuban American votes, Bush won Florida, albeit by a paltry 537 ballots. Electoral fraud and voter intimidation also played a role in the outcome of the election. Florida turned out to be the deciding state in the election, sending another Bush to the White House despite the fact that nationwide he received almost half a million fewer popular votes than Gore. It was a great irony that the same Cuban exiles who had been humiliated by the Elián affair and who for four decades had been unable to have any impact on Cuban politics became a decisive political force that arguably allowed them to determine the outcome of an election in the United States.

The Cuban Diaspora Revisited

By century's end, an estimated 1.5 to 2 million Cubans resided outside the island. The 2000 U.S. census registered 1.24 million Cubans and individuals of Cuban descent (853,000 of them Cuban-born). This population was heavily concentrated in Florida (67 percent), especially in Miami-Dade County (52 percent). Among these exile Cubans, 20,000 had settled in Puerto Rico. At the time, another 150,000 Cubans lived in other nations of the hemisphere, most numerously in Mexico (around 40,000), Venezuela (around 30,000), Costa Rica, Canada, Panama, and the Dominican Republic. At the time, Spain was the European nation with the largest Cuban population (around 50,000), followed by Italy (around 8,000). In all, one out of ten Cubans lived abroad, among them one who settled in Egypt and earned a living giving camel tours.[115] Not all Cubans residing abroad left definitively; tens of thousands are on temporary loan to foreign countries by the Cuban government as medical personnel, sports trainers, musicians, and technicians.

During the 1990s, particularly since 1994, a third cohort of Cuban emigrants entered the scene. While most of them were *balseros*, thousands more left Cuba legally with U.S. visas in hand, and thousands more relocated to the United States from third countries, some crossing the border from Mexico or Canada. The average *balsero* is a young, male, poor laborer or unemployed individual without knowledge of the English language who left Cuba from Havana or Havana Province. The *balsero* population that arrived between 1991 and 1994 was 73 percent male and had an average age of 29. U.S. census data shed light on differences between those who arrived before and after 1990: 43 percent of the latter (25 and older) had less than a high school degree, and only 15 percent had held managerial or professional positions while in Cuba.[116]

The large influx of impoverished *balseros* during the second half of the 1990s lowered the Cuban population's traditionally high rate of income and increased its low rate of poverty. Statistics examined by Alejandro Portes clearly demonstrate those changes. By 1999, salaries for the entire Cuban and Cuban American population had dropped below the national average; ten years later, the poverty rate among all Cubans and Cuban Americans was close to 20 percent. At the century's end, the financial divide between the first and third migratory cohorts was enormous. Family income for the first cohort was almost twice as much as that earned by families who had arrived after 1990. In part because *balseros* were markedly poorer than earlier Cuban migrants and in part because they maintained strong transnational bonds with the island (i.e., frequent travel and remittances), their socioeconomic status and degree of connection with their host country are more like those of other immigrant groups such as Salvadorians, Mexicans, and Dominicans.[117]

The arrival of this wave of immigrants exposed the growing cultural rift between migratory cohorts, what Susan Eckstein has called "the Cuban American Divide."[118] The biggest differences that separated the most recent entrants from those of previous cohorts were cultural. While *balsero*-generation immigrants and earlier exiles shared a common Cuban identity, culturally speaking, they were worlds apart. The vast majority of *balseros* and other recent immigrants had been born after 1959 and thus were socialized into and educated in a socialist reality. They had no first-hand knowledge of pre-Castro Cuba and were too young to have witnessed the early accomplishments of the revolution. In addition, their parents, for the most part, had also been socialized into the revolution. What both generations witnessed was the pauperization and decay of revolutionary Cuba. In contrast, first-cohort Cubans residing in the United States had first-hand knowledge of pre-1959 conditions, and their children and grandchildren grew up in capitalist, socially conservative, and anti-communist Cuban Miami. By the time *balseros* began to arrive in large numbers, Mariel-cohort immigrants had not yet fully integrated themselves into Cuban Miami and exhibited significantly lower rates of English-language skills, high school and college graduation, employment, and income than members of the first cohort.[119]

In speech, diet, dress, values, work ethic, and many other aspects the most recent immigrants had little in common with earlier exiles and their Cuban American children. The cultural "Americanization" of stateside Cubans and Cuban Americans and the lumpenization of the island's culture during the Special Period weakened cultural common ground between those who had just left Cuba and those who had long been settled in the United States.

These social, cultural, and political differences have been obstacles to the integration of the *balsero* cohort into Cuban Miami. With less education, fewer work skills, and lower levels of English-language proficiency, most of those who have migrated since the 1990s have been forced into the lowest rungs of the social ladder, as dishwashers, construction workers, domestics, and workers in other low-paying jobs. Even those who brought college degrees and professional titles have found it hard to join the middle class. The Oscar-nominated Spanish documentary *Balseros* (2002) is illustrative. The film traces the lives of seven *balseros* from their departure in 1994 until 2001. Of the seven, all but one fared poorly: one succumbed to drugs and prostitution, another became a hustling gigolo, and another suffered a terrible accident and became disabled. All suffered varying degrees of cultural alienation.[120] I personally know a *balsero*-cohort plastic surgeon who had to trade his scalpel for a bread knife when he left Cuba and found employment in a cafeteria in Orlando, Florida, making Cuban sandwiches. At night he worked a second job as custodian at the university where I teach.[121]

However, immigrants belonging to the three different cohorts and

Cubans on the island and abroad still share not just aspects of material culture such as music and food but more importantly, nonmaterial aspects such as a deep sense of pride and honor; strong nationalist sentiments; creativity and entrepreneurialism; extraordinary valor, be it to fight a war or stop an abuse; proclivities to ostentation and hyperbole; a strong sense of family, both nuclear and extended; envy of the greenest hue; gregariousness and generosity; a penchant for verbosity; a peculiar type of irreverent, sometimes morbid, sense of humor; joie de vivre; hypereroticism; bossiness and admiration for caudillos; individualism, not in the American sense but an individualism with a strong sense of community and collaboration; spirituality and fatalism; and aversion to rigidity, bland aesthetics, *guatacas* (sycophants), traitors, hypocrites, and snow.

Cubans, unfortunately, also share a centuries-old culture of intolerance, authoritarianism, and political violence. While the Cuban regime institutionalized repression and the violation of civil and human rights, the most vociferous and intransigent exile leaders and some rogue operatives replicated similar intolerant, intimidating, and repressive practices in Miami. They created an atmosphere in which those who openly defied the hard-line position endured intimidation, harassment, death threats, and in some instances actual death. During the period when rapid response brigades were beating up independent journalists and destroying their communications equipment, a group of Miami thugs beat up an employee of Radio Progreso, a station that aired a program with alternative political views. As MININT-organized gangs forcibly closed down art exhibits throughout the island, one or more exiles placed a bomb at the Miami Museum of Contemporary Cuban Art because it was exhibiting works by artists living in Cuba.[122] While Castro purged hundreds of party and government officials for views that were not in line with his own, exile organizations such as the Bay of Pigs Veterans Association purged some of their members just for attending a conference held on the forbidden island. And as Raúl Castro sought to limit entrance to Cuban universities to those who were fully integrated into the revolutionary process, politically moderate Miami-based Cuban professors received repeated threats of violence. In Miami, it must be clarified, political violence and civil rights violations are not the norm, and when they do occur authorities treat them as serious crimes.[123]

The two Cubas that are reunited geographically in South Florida and other places, while sharing some cultural traits, have and continue to clash, embracing divergent social and political views. Established exiles saw their newly arrived brethren as having a poor work ethic, acting as if society and their relatives were responsible for providing for their needs and desires and holding on to a survive-at-any-cost culture. A Miami restaurant owner was shocked to see one of his employees wearing an expensive pair of shoes that he had just given to a newly arrived cousin; as it turned out, the cousin had sold the shoes for a few dollars to buy food. Recent immigrants, for their part, complain about the Americanized, materialistic, politicized, and selfish character of long-established exiles and their children and grandchildren. As one of them put it: "It's like they have the dollar sign on their forehead."[124]

Survival at Any Cost, but at What Price?

On November 9, 1989, when the border between East and West Germany suddenly broke open, tens of thousands of East Germans were able to visit the other side for the first time in nearly four decades. Cuba's state-controlled TV newscasts barely mentioned the day's momentous events. The footage consisted of late-night images of East Germans returning home to spend the night, the story spun to give the impression that while many left for the West, many others headed East. Cuban TV viewers knew better, of course. Other communist regimes fell, culminating with the Soviet Union's dismemberment and fall from superpower status. These events marked the end of the two-pole geopolitical reality of the over four-decade-long Cold War. Cuba, no longer the recipient of billions of annual Soviet aid, now had to function under a completely different set of rules. It had to adjust for the budgetary shortfalls caused by the termination of Soviet aid and subsidies; it had to pay for its imports with hard currency; it had to seek new trading partners; it could no longer completely ignore international denunciations of human rights abuses; and it had to face increasingly hostile treatment by the United States, spurred by what seemed to be the imminent collapse of the island's communist regime.

The Cuban government adopted numerous radical strategies—many of them contrary to the revolution's fundamental principles—as it shifted focus almost exclusively toward the primary goals of the survival of its socialist system and the continuation in power of its top leaders, who were ageing. The leaders embraced a delayed and watered-down version of *perestroika*. But the new policies would have been unimaginable a few years earlier: foreign investments were aggressively encouraged, the economy became dollarized, it became legal for individuals to own private businesses, and even foreigners could own Cuban real estate. These structural reforms saved the government from collapsing, but whatever was left of socialism had little in common with the egalitarian, classless society and government-monopolized economic system that had been built during the first decade of the revolution.

The combination of a profound economic depression and some of the government's reforms had profoundly detrimental social and economic consequences for the vast majority. Incomes were cut, as were services in food distribution, health care, education, housing, and transportation. Famine and malnutrition reared their ugly heads. The number of surgeries, dental procedures, and other medical services shrank. Fewer teachers were able to stay in their profession, and the number of high school, university, and technical school students fell by the tens of thousands. Scores of Havana's buildings collapsed due to lack of maintenance. During the first few years of the Special Period, Cuba's streets and roads became virtually deserted because of fuel shortages. Cuban ingenuity, however, created a surreal fauna of means of transportation: the maligned *camellos*, U.S.-made 1950s cars fitted with Russian-made engines and transmissions, Chinese bicycles by the hundreds of thousands, motorized bicycles, horse carriages, oxen-pulled truck cabins, rickshaws, and numerous other wheeled species.

While the majority suffered, some benefited, among them members of the military brass and political elite. The brunt of the crisis fell disproportionately on the backs of darker-skinned Cubans and residents of the eastern provinces, who were less likely to find employment in lucrative sectors such as tourism and to receive remittances from abroad. Women too suffered disproportionately because of fewer self-employment opportunities and added responsibilities to put food on their tables. The specter of two Cubas sharing the same island resurfaced: one extremely impoverished, one not so poor; one rural and eastern, one urban, mostly Havana-based; one black and mulatto, one white.

How did Cubans manage to survive? Some resorted to ingenuity and a latent entrepreneurial spirit, embarking on a host of independent employment options and businesses. Many put food on their tables and clothes on their backs thanks to remittances from relatives abroad. FE became the key to survival, not *fe* (Spanish for faith) but FE, the acronym for *familiares en el extranjero* (relatives living abroad). Some resorted to actual *fe*, finding spiritual consolation through religion, flocking to Catholic churches, joining Protestant congregations, or embracing Afro-Cuban religions. Others resorted to black market activities. Some became hustlers, sex workers, and common thieves. Others resorted to escapism: little bread and lots of circus—street concerts, steamy Brazilian soap operas on TV, plenty of cheap beer and liquor, nihilist music, and incessant *choteo*. Thousands committed suicide out of desperation. Tens of thousands played Russian roulette by embarking on makeshift rafts. Thousands of corpses now line the bottom of the Florida Straits.

How did the government survive? First, the authoritarian system and its repressive mechanisms allowed it to impose extreme austerity measures upon the population without the risk of popular uprisings. While support for the regime waned, resistance remained essentially pacifist and the *balsero* exodus, like previous exile waves, served as an escape valve for tens of thousands of frustrated and angry citizens. Moreover, the purge of scores of high-ranking military and MININT officials reduced the possibility of internal challenges to the Castros' leadership and sent a sobering message to anyone holding independent political aspirations. The government's survival was also the result of the application of profound economic reforms such as the expansion of state capitalism, the opening of the tourist sector, and the easing of the flow of remittances from abroad.

Paradoxically, the increasingly belligerent rhetoric and actions of the U.S. government and CANF and other hard-line exile organizations helped prop up the embattled socialist state. The exiles who most ardently agitated for Castro's fall actually helped strengthen his grip on power by spreading fear among Cubans that a post-Castro transition would bring about a rule by vindictive Miami-based Cubans, a socioeconomic reality similar to that of the Batista era, unbridled capitalism, and the return to exiles of all properties confiscated since 1959, including homes and apartments now inhabited and legally owned by those who stayed behind.

The government capitalized on such fears. One TV ad portrayed a man walking down a Havana street. His arrogant gait, flashy jewelry, and fancy clothing made for the stereotypical Miami *cubanazo*. As he walked down the street, he looked at the apartment buildings with covetous eyes as if plotting to gain ownership over them. One by one, women popped out of their balconies to shout at him "This is my home!" "Don't even think about it!" and so on. The women's shouts became louder and angrier, forcing the visibly terrified *cubanazo* to run away.

In spite of the scarcity of food and consumer goods, in spite of the lack of civil freedoms and the routine infliction of human rights abuses, and in spite of an authoritarian government increasingly disconnected from the masses, Cubans did not want to lose their homes, did not want to give up their rights to free and universal education and health care, did not want to return to conditions similar to those that prevailed under Batista, did not want the Miami-based National Association of Sugar Mill Owners of Cuba to "help in the reconstruction of Cuba," and certainly did not want to return to U.S. political and economic control.[125]

7

This Revolution Can Destroy Itself

Cuba at the Dawn of the New Millennium, 2001–2011

2001—Year of the Triumphant Revolution in the New Millennium
2002—Year of the Heroes Imprisoned by the Empire
2003—Year of the Glorious Anniversaries of Martí and the
　　　Moncada
2004—Year of the 45th Anniversary of the Triumph of the
　　　Revolution
2005—Year of the Bolivarian Alternative for the Americas
2006—Year of the Energy Revolution in Cuba
2007—Year Forty-Nine of the Revolution
2008—Year of the 50th Anniversary of the Triumph of the
　　　Revolution
2009—Year Fifty-One of the Revolution
2010—Year Fifty-Two of the Revolution
2011—Year Fifty-Three of the Revolution

> Ramón left the building, locked the door, and said to himself "Now let's see
> what happens," as he put up the sign that said, CLOSED FOR REPAIRS.
>
> **Nancy Alonso, *Closed for Repairs***

While the rest of the world celebrated the advent of a new millennium on
the eve of January 1, 2000, Cuba skipped the fanfare and the fireworks
altogether. Fidel Castro had imposed his will, arguing—correctly so—that
the new millennium did not begin technically until the following year. Accordingly, the government named 2001 the Year of the Triumphant Revolution in the New Millennium.

　　If the last decade of the previous century had been years of sacrifice,
survival, and partial recovery from the revolution's worst crisis ever, the

first decade of the new one tested Cuba's ability to achieve economic stability, provide for the population's most basic needs, maintain social order, and retain its socialist system. This was a tall order that required injections of foreign capital and the expansion of commercial relations with new and old partners. Fortunately for Cuba, Hugo Chávez's oil-rich Venezuela filled the lingering vacuum left by the termination of Soviet subsidies and oil shipments a decade earlier.

The year 2001 was also the forty-third year of the revolution and the year when Fidel Castro turned 75 and his brother 70. The elder Castro had perhaps forgotten that three and a half decades earlier he had ridiculed Mao Zedong, then 73, calling him a "senile idiot" and pledging that Cuban revolutionaries would not rule past the age of 60.[1] Not because he wanted to but because serious health problems forced him to do so, Castro temporarily stepped down from power in July 2006, yielding control to his brother. Less than twenty months later, in February 2008, the succession was completed when Raúl Castro formally assumed the presidency.

With very few exceptions, the top government, party, and military leadership consisted of individuals over 60. At the end of the century's first decade, the ruling inner circle remained almost exclusively made up of septuagenarian and octogenarian *sierra* veterans of the struggle against Batista: the Castros, Juan Almeida, José Ramón Machado Ventura, Ramiro Valdés, José Ramón Fernández, Julio Casas Regueiro, and José Ramón Balaguer Cabrera, among others.[2] In short, the Generation of 1952 had largely denied political ascendance to the two generations that followed. This not only deprived Cuba of new ideas and creative energy, it also broadened the distance between the rulers and the ruled, 76 percent of whom were either younger than eight or had not been born when Castro's rebels marched into Havana in 1959.

Cuba and the World

The twenty-first century heralded profound geopolitical and economic transformations around the world. These had far-reaching repercussions for a Cuba seeking new international alliances and trade and financial relations in an increasingly globalized world at a time of major power realignments. The end of the Cold War had produced a unipolar geopolitical configuration consisting of a single global military superpower, the United States, two secondary military powers with broad regional influence, China and Russia, and a host of nations with tertiary military strength of limited regional reach such as India, the United Kingdom, France, Brazil, North Korea, Iran, Iraq (until 2003), Israel, and Pakistan. As a counterbalance to U.S. power, Russia and China developed closer relations, particularly after the rise to power of nationalist Vladimir Putin in 2000. In 2001, the two countries signed a Treaty of Friendship and Cooperation. The EU, for its part, expanded during the decade from fifteen to twenty-seven member nations, which together constituted the world's largest economy. Also at the turn of the century, nonstate extreme Islamist security threats emerged, among them the Taliban, Hezbollah, the Iraqi insurgence against U.S. occupation, even Somali pirates. It was also a time of increased belligerence among authoritarian regimes such as Kim Jong Il's North Korea and Mahmoud Ahmadinejad's Iran.

As the hegemonic presence of the United States in the Americas continued to erode, China and Russia cultivated amicable relations and connections throughout the hemisphere, including military collaborations with Cuba and Venezuela. China also strengthened its relations with old and new allies and expanded its sphere of influence in Asia and the Middle East. Although China's military might grew immensely, the expansion of its influence, sometimes referred to as "China's peaceful rise," came to rest on "yuan diplomacy," a twenty-first-century version of "dollar diplomacy."

These international political realignments had parallels in the commercial and financial arenas. Paradoxically, after having won the Cold War, the economic and financial dominance of the United States began to slip away as a result of competition from the EU and a handful of so-called emerging economies, such as India, Brazil, and Indonesia. The U.S. economy also suffered from onerous foreign and domestic debts, the devaluation of the dollar, and dependence on expensive foreign oil. While the United States held to its position as the world's richest nation and single largest national economy, its manufacturing capacity continued to fall and its foreign debt grew heavier, making it vulnerable to foreign lenders, most saliently China, whose economy became the world's second largest in 2011.[3]

During these global political and economic realignments, Cuba pursued mutually beneficial alliances and trade relations with its Latin American neighbors, particularly Venezuela, Brazil, and Ecuador, and with China, Russia, Iran, Vietnam, and other nations in an attempt to climb out of the isolation and economic ruin it had suffered since the collapse of the Soviet Union and the Eastern Bloc. Cuba also sought to mitigate the impact of heightened U.S. hostility toward it during George W. Bush's presidency and growing pressures from the EU to improve its human rights record.

In the broader context of the Americas, Cuba's hemispheric integration reached its highest level perhaps since the establishment of the republic in 1902. By 2005, it had normalized diplomatic relations with all except two Latin American and Caribbean states and established trade relations with all of them. It had also established trade relations with the United States, which in 2000 began selling agricultural goods and medical supplies to Cuba.[4] By decade's end, the socialist island had diplomatic relations with all American nations except the United States. For the most part, relations with Latin America expanded; this became particularly evident with several countries that elected leftist or center-left presidents. First and furthest to the left was Chávez, who became president of Venezuela in 1999. Other left-leaning governments came to power in subsequent years: in Brazil and Argentina (2003), in Uruguay, (2005), in Bolivia (2006), in Chile (2006 and again in 2013), in Ecuador and Nicaragua (2007), in Paraguay (2008), and in Peru (2011). By contrast, Mexico, one of Cuba's friendliest neighbors since 1959, and Colombia moved in the opposite direction with the election of conservative, pro–United States administrations in 2000 and 1998, respectively.

Cuba's formal regional integration further advanced with a treaty with Venezuela in 2004 that served as the base for the future Alianza Bolivariana para los Pueblos de Nuestra América (Bolivarian Alliance for the Peoples of Our America, ALBA). The alliance's primary goal was to provide an alternative to the U.S.-led Free Trade Area of the Americas initiative. Keeping with its tradition of naming years, the Cuban government christened 2005 the Year of the Bolivarian Alternative for the Americas. When leftist Evo Morales was elected in 2006, Bolivia joined ALBA (figure 7.1). Other nations followed. By 2010, ALBA included five Latin American nations and three English-speaking Caribbean states. Significantly, in 2009 the OAS voted unanimously to invite Cuba back to its ranks, lifting the 1962 expulsion resolution. Cuba refused the invitation without any explanation other than the OAS's past record of alignment with Washington's policies.[5]

Since the beginning of the revolutionary process, Cuba had invested heavily throughout the Third World, providing generous support in the form of medical, technical, and educational aid to many nations near and far, from Ghana and Grenada to Peru and Palestine. Thousands of Cuban brigades built schools, hospitals, and water treatment plants and carried out innumerable development projects around the world and generations of students from every continent became doctors, dentists, and engineers

Figure 7.1. Presidents Hugo Chávez, Fidel Castro, and Evo Morales during an April 2006 meeting in Havana. Photograph by Javier Galeano. Courtesy of AP.

in Cuban universities free of charge. While the revolution had failed its own people in so many ways, it reaped its greatest successes abroad. Ironically, however, as Cuba went through its deepest crisis, it found almost no reciprocity for its decades-long internationalist generosity. Venezuela was the one notable exception.

Chávez's election in late 1998 marked the beginning of a new era for Cuba, and it soon became the island's biggest trading partner, lender, and benefactor as well as its staunchest political ally. Castro had befriended Chávez back in 1994 when Chávez's only claim to fame was having led a failed coup d'état in 1992 against the corrupt presidency of Carlos Andrés Pérez. After serving only two years in jail, a new president pardoned Chávez. Shortly after his release he paid the first of numerous visits to Cuba, where Castro received him with honors normally reserved for major world leaders.[6] After being elected in 1998, Chávez launched a far-reaching reformist agenda that he called the Bolivarian Revolution. These early reforms and Chávez's consolidation and centralization of power mirrored developments during Cuba's first years of revolution nearly half a century before. These included increased expenditures in the areas of health and education; the nationalization of various sectors of the economy, including telecommunications, utilities, banks, manufacturing and mining; agrarian reform; the establishment of an increasingly authoritarian government; and the expansion of militarism, media censorship, and human rights violations. Unlike his Cuban counterpart, Chávez first reached power through legitimate elections. He was re-elected in 2002 under the provisions of the new Constitution of 2000, he survived a 2004 recall referendum, and was reelected in 2006.[7]

Moved by his friendship and ideological affinities with Castro, his trenchant aversion toward the United States, and his desire to become Castro's heir as leader of Latin America's anti-imperialist, socialist, and internationalist movements, Chávez pursued strong political and economic bonds with Cuba. The first major step in that direction was the signing, in October 2000, of a cooperation accord whereby Venezuela agreed to sell discounted oil to Cuba under generous financing terms, while Cuba promised to deploy thousands of physicians, nurses, and other medical personnel to treat Venezuelans in impoverished and remote locations at no cost. The accord also stipulated that Cuba would provide a host of technical and educational services and products. These ranged from sugar-producing technology and vaccines to communications equipment and 3,000 sports trainers.[8]

The collaboration pact specified that Venezuela sell 53,000 barrels of crude oil and other fossil fuels every day at a preferential price, a portion of which Cuba had to pay in cash within ninety days and the rest in fifteen years at 2 percent interest, following a two-year grace period. The proportions of short- and long-term credit were set to be automatically adjusted according to the market price. If oil sold at $15 a barrel, for example, 95 percent had to be paid within ninety days and the remaining 5 percent in fifteen years; if oil prices reached $50, then 60 percent must be paid within three months and the balance in fifteen years.[9]

The agreement had immediate results. In 2001, Venezuela became Cuba's major trading partner. Meanwhile, an estimated 10,000 Cuban physicians served in Venezuela in 2003. By late 2007, 31,000 Cuban doctors and health workers and an additional 8,000 technicians and teachers were providing services throughout Venezuela. A 2001 amendment to the 2000 accord established that Venezuela would pay Cuba for those services. However, Cuba paid its professionals working in Venezuela only a small portion of what it charged; according to one estimate, their personal compensation amounted to only 18 percent of what Venezuela actually paid Cuba for their services. Toward the end of the decade, Cuba's

Table 4. Cuba's foreign trade, 2001–2011, in millions of Cuban pesos

Year	2001	2002	2003	2004	2005
Exports	1,622	1,221	1,688	2,332	2,159
Imports	4,851	4,118	4,673	5,615	7,604
Total trade	6,473	5,610	6,361	7,947	9,763
Trade balance	-3,229	-2,766	-2,985	-3,283	-5,445

Sources: Republic of Cuba, Oficina Nacional de Estadísticas (ONE), Anuario estadístico de Cuba (2006), table 7.4; ONE, Anuario estadístico de Cuba (2009), tables 8.3, 8.4, 8.5, and 8.6; ONE, Anuario estadístico de Cuba (2011), table 8.3; and Brenner, Jiménez, Kirk, and LeoGrande, A Contemporary Cuba Reader, 131.

dependence on Venezuela reached astronomical proportions, a whopping $10 billion worth of subsidies, credits, and aid.[10]

The Cuba-Venezuela political alliance served Chávez well. When a group of armed forces officers led a coup against him in April 2002, indignant Cuban officials maneuvered to bring him back to power. According to some sources, Castro personally directed over the phone the counter-coup that restored Chávez to power two days later.[11] Following the failed coup, relations between the two countries became even closer. Cuban intelligence agents played a larger role not only in protecting the increasingly authoritarian government of Chávez but also in helping it suppress its opposition. MININT chief Abelardo Colomé Ibarra and other officers traveled to Venezuela to establish intelligence and counterintelligence systems and create a Cuban-staffed personal guard for Chávez. A controversial provision, agreed upon in 2004, authorized Cuban agents to conduct criminal investigations and arrest Venezuelans suspected of political and other crimes.[12]

The 2004 treaty and subsequent accords raised oil and other fuel export levels to about 90,000 barrels daily and gave Cuba access to oil technology, an important concession given Cuba's rising domestic oil production and the discovery of substantial underwater deposits along its northern coast. The same treaty eliminated tariffs between the two nations and facilitated further agreements in the areas of communications, mining, agriculture, energy, and construction.[13] As a result, the volume of trade between the two nations skyrocketed, reaching $2.6 billion in 2006 and $8.3 billion in 2011. The vast majority of this trade consisted of oil imports, a significant percentage of which were financed at fifteen years. This represented a considerable subsidy to Cuba that was worth approximately $2.5 billion in 2008. In the process, Cuba accumulated a huge oil debt with Venezuela:

2006	2007	2008	2009	2010	2011
2,925	3,686	3,664	2,863	4,549	6,041
9,498	10,079	14,234	8,906	10,644	13,956
12,423	13,765	17,898	11,769	15,193	19,997
-6,573	-6,394	-10,570	-6,042	-17,200	-9,715

$144 million in 2002, $380 million in 2003, and $992 million in 2004. By mid-2009, its oil debt stood at $5 billion. In November 2010, Cuba and Venezuela agreed to extend the cooperation agreement they had made in 2000 for another decade.[14]

Canada, which never broke diplomatic or commercial relations with Cuba despite pressure from the United States to do so, remained one of the island's most important and dependable business and commercial partners. Throughout the first decade of the new century, Canada stood behind Spain as the nation with the largest number of joint ventures on the island. The lion's share of Canada-Cuba trade and business relations stemmed from agreements with Sherritt International, which included nickel and cobalt mining, communications, utilities, and oil and natural gas exploration and extraction. Between 2001 and 2011, Canada's position among Cuba's trading partners fluctuated between third and fifth, and Canada was, by far, the largest importer of Cuban products. Tourism became another major link between both nations. Since the early 1990s, Canada had been consistently and by substantial margins the source of the largest number of tourists. According to official statistics, one million Canadians visited Cuba in 2011, constituting around 30 percent of all tourist arrivals.[15]

China has become one of Cuba's most important allies, trade partners, and sources of credit. In its quest to establish and expand its economic presence and political influence in Latin America, China looked to Cuba and Venezuela more than any other countries. Not only did both countries share ideological affinities with communist China, they also offered vital and strategic products to satisfy the needs of China's expanding industrial economy: Cuban nickel and Venezuelan oil. Chinese investments in and trade with Cuba expanded throughout the century's first decade, following the signing of an Economic and Technical Cooperation Agreement during the 2001 visit of President Jiang Zemin. The agreement included a $400-million long-term trade credit at zero interest that sparked a boom in Cuba-China trade that reached a volume of $617 million in 2002.[16] In 2004, the Cuban government mandated that all state firms give priority to Venezuela and China over all other suppliers. Consequently, trade with China more than tripled between 2004 and 2006, when it reached close to $1.8 billion. In 2011, China was Cuba's second trading partner ($1.9 billion; 9.6 percent).[17]

Relations between China and Cuba go beyond sugar and rice and pesos and yuans. They include a political alliance and military collaboration. In the UN and other international forums, Cuba supports China's claims to Taiwan, while China defends Cuba from accusations of human rights abuses and supports its efforts to end the U.S. trade embargo. More disturbing to the United States was the construction of an electronic espionage center by the Chinese on Cuban soil and the continuing transfer of communications and intelligence-gathering technologies.[18]

Relations between Cuba and Russia have also become increasingly close. These have included modest trade credits and the expansion of trade. Major Cuban-Russian agreements in the second half of the decade included a $350 million credit to modernize Cuba's military and an oil exploration partnership that was signed in 2009. Still, at the end of the decade, Russia stood far below its 1989 level of dominance over Cuban trade and finances.[19]

Cuba has also benefited from expanding relations with Iran. After the election of Mahmoud Ahmadinejad in 2005, both nations became even closer allies. Cuba lobbied internationally to defend Iran's nuclear program and Iran reciprocated by extending Cuba's credit line to 200 million Euros in 2005 and further to 500 million in 2008.[20] While Cuba's trade partnership with Iran is small compared to those with other nations, it remains critical to the socialist island, particularly because Iran is a backup source for oil in case of any disruption of shipments from Venezuela, whose Bolivarian leader was diagnosed with cancer in 2011.

As Cuba grew closer to Venezuela, China, Vietnam, Russia and Iran, it further distanced itself from the United States and the EU. Cuba-U.S. relations during the first decade of the twenty-first century were a mix of continuity and change. The election of George W. Bush to the presidency in 2000 marked the beginning of a period of heightened acrimony. The U.S. State Department kept Cuba on its list of state sponsors of terrorism in spite of the lack of evidence to support that classification. Curiously, it removed both Libya and North Korea from that infamous list in 2006 and 2008, respectively. Cuban and U.S. delegates continued exchanging attacks in the UN by spearheading condemnatory resolutions against each other. Cuba, nonetheless, took surprisingly conciliatory steps when it categorically condemned Al-Qaeda's 9/11 attacks, temporarily allowed U.S. planes to fly through Cuban airspace, and remained relatively silent on the use of the Guantánamo Bay Naval Base as a detention center for Al-Qaeda and Taliban captives.[21]

The new century's most significant change in U.S.-Cuba relations has been the partial opening of trade since the passing of the Trade Sanctions Reform and Export Enhancement Act of 2000, which allows U.S. firms to sell pharmaceuticals, medical equipment, and agricultural products to Cuba. The act, however, did not allow Cuba to export any of its products to the United States.[22] At first the Cuban government refused to purchase U.S. goods because the new trade act required Cuba to prepay for its purchases in cash and included some humiliating restrictions. Vice-President Lage firmly stated that Cuba would not purchase "a single grain of rice or a single aspirin." Only in the aftermath of Hurricane Michelle in November 2001, which wrought havoc on the island's crops, did Cuba begin to purchase U.S. agricultural products such as rice, beans, poultry, and even lumber and paper.[23] The value of such U.S. exports increased over the next few years: $146 million in 2002, $259 million in 2003, and $404 million in 2004, at which time the United States became the fourth largest exporter to Cuba behind Venezuela, China, and Spain. After decreasing in 2005 and 2006, U.S. exports rebounded, reaching $711 million in 2008. In total, between 2001 and 2008, U.S. corporations sold Cuba $2.7 billion worth of goods. In 2009, however, the volume of exports decreased sharply to only $533 million and fell further to $363 million in 2011.[24]

To sum up, during the first decade of the twenty-first century, Cuba managed to stay afloat economically, if precariously so. The island nation took advantage of global political and economic realignments as it held on to some historical trading partnerships—with Canada and Spain, for example—and cultivated new commercial ties with Venezuela, China, and even the United States. American beans and other foodstuffs, Chinese tanks and other manufactures, Venezuelan oil and other fuels, and the Cuban diaspora's remittances were the four foreign economic lifelines that kept the Cuban economy from a complete collapse.

While beneficial, these new trade relations produced huge trade deficits that increased to $6.6 billion in 2006, when import values were triple the value of exports. By 2008, the trade deficit had risen to $11.5 billion.[25] The period also saw the ballooning of Cuba's foreign debt. According to a special EU report of 2010, Cuba carried a runaway debt of over $31 billion. Venezuela held over a third of that amount, followed by Spain and China, each of which was owed about $3.2 billion. Cuba is among the world's most heavily indebted nations; in 2011 its debt was equivalent to 125 percent of its GDP.[26]

The Lingering Little Cold War

In the twenty-first century, Cuba's relations with the United States have become increasingly complicated and have exposed the contradictions between the economic agendas of the United States, that nation's desire to push Cuba to liberalize its political system and improve its human rights record, and humanitarian concerns about the well-being of the Cuban people. The tension among these objectives produced policies regarding Cuba that have fluctuated throughout the first years of the century in response to changes in the political leadership of the United States.

In spite of the U.S.-Cuba trade act, Bush's administrations (2001–9) escalated the rhetoric and expanded sanctions against Cuba. In 2003, just thirteen months before the 2004 presidential elections, Bush made another gesture—more symbolic than effective—to increase pressure on Cuba. Pushed by Cuban American legislators, Bush created the Commission for Assistance to a Free Cuba. The commission's report recommended that the United States further restrict travel and remittances to Cuba, substantially increase funding for dissidents and opposition groups, and deter foreign investments with the explicit goal of bringing on "an expeditious end to the Castro dictatorship."[27] Within a few weeks, the Bush administration implemented most of those recommendations. As a result, legal travel from the United States to Cuba dropped 60 percent over the next twelve months.[28]

As discussed earlier, in the 2000 U.S. elections, the power of the South Florida Cuban vote had reached its peak. Demographic shifts since then changed what had been a virtually unanimous Republican preference among Cuban voters and prompted the gradual erosion of their electoral power relative to other Hispanic groups. On the one hand, by the turn of the century a second and third generation of Cuban Americans plus Mariel and *balsero* immigrants outnumbered Cubans who had arrived between

1959 and 1979. In 2004, 37 percent of the Cuban population had been born in the United States and only 30 percent of those who had been born in Cuba had arrived prior to 1980. Second- and third-generation Cuban Americans and more recent entrants have demonstrated a substantially lower tendency to vote Republican. On the other hand, the number of eligible Florida voters from Puerto Rico and other Latin American countries has grown at a faster rate than the Cuban and Cuban American electorate. Non-Cuban Hispanic voters in Florida, particularly Puerto Ricans, have a strong inclination to vote for Democratic candidates.[29]

The pluralization and generational differentiation of the Cuban electorate became even more evident in the 2004 and 2008 elections. In 2004, 78 percent of Cubans and Cuban Americans voted for Bush in his bid for reelection. However, pre-election polls demonstrate significant variations in this population when it is disaggregated by age and time of arrival to the United States: 92 percent of first-cohort immigrants stated that they would vote for Bush, while a much lower proportion of U.S.-born Cubans, 58 percent, expressed a preference for Bush. Among Mariel and post-Mariel immigrants, voter preferences split: 52 percent for Bush, 29 percent for Kerry.[30] Four years later, 35 percent of Miami-Dade's Cuban and Cuban American voters cast ballots for Democratic presidential candidate Barack Obama. This was a considerable increase over support for Kerry four years earlier. Even more telling is the fact that among those aged 29 or younger, 55 percent cast ballots for Obama in 2008.[31] Reflective of growing differences among generations and between more moderate and hard-line positions among Cubans and Cuban Americans were the founding in 2000 of the moderate anti-embargo organization Cuba Study Group; the 2001 split of CANF, then led by Jorge Mas Canosas's son, José Ramón Mas Santos; the ensuing formation of the more intransigent Cuban Liberty Council and its affiliated U.S.-Cuba PAC; and the creation of Raíces de Esperanza (Roots of Hope), composed of university students and young professionals, who, while denouncing civil rights abuses on the island, seek to cultivate common cultural bonds with their counterparts residing on the island.[32]

These demographic trends also had a profound impact on the Cuban diaspora and Cuban American positions on the embargo, restrictions on remittances, travel to Cuba, and the normalization of U.S.-Cuba relations. A 2008 poll conducted by FIU demonstrated that the growing proportion of recent immigrants—300,000 arrived between 1998 and 2008—and the increasing percentage of U.S.-born Cubans vis-à-vis older Cuban-born immigrants reversed the community's stance on various policy matters. The poll suggested that for the first time ever, a majority of Miami's Cuban and Cuban American population (55 percent) opposed the embargo and two-thirds favored ending restrictions on travel and remittances. While 68 percent of Cubans in the 65-and-over age group supported the embargo, 65 percent of those aged 18–44 opposed it.[33] Younger Cubans, second- and third-generation U.S.-born Cubans, and the *balsero* cohort have moderated and pluralized South Florida's political landscape. Exiled architect Raúl Rodríguez commented on this transformation prior to the 2008 election. Neither John McCain nor Obama "put on a guayabera or shouted, '*Viva Cuba libre*.'" "It may have taken 50 years," he added, "but that at least is no longer acceptable."[34]

The Obama administration that took office in January 2009 heralded a substantial break in ideology and foreign policy style with the Bush presidency, which had been characterized by arrogance, unilateralism, and military interventionism. Facing a deep economic recession, enormous domestic and international challenges, and obstructionist opposition from Republican legislators, however, Obama was not able to deliver substantial changes in U.S. policy toward Cuba. Instead, he made a few adjustments to policies about travel and remittances. When Republicans captured the U.S. House of Representatives in January 2011, they derailed pending legislation to allow all U.S. citizens to travel to Cuba. Since then, Cuban American members of congress Ileana Ros-Lehtinen, chair of the body's Committee on Foreign Affairs (2011–13), and Mario Díaz-Balart and David Rivera, fellow Republicans, presented aggressive bills to push back Obama's policy changes.[35]

During Obama's first term in office, the United States retained the most basic elements of its long-term Cuba policy: the Helms-Burton–enhanced trade embargo, the occupation of Guantánamo Bay Naval Base, broadcasts over Radio and TV Martí, and the "wet foot/dry foot" refugee policy. Much to Cuba's indignation, the administration also kept the island on its list of state sponsors of terrorism, and in January 2010, it included the island on a list of nations who posed a security risk to air travel along with thirteen other countries, all with majority Muslim populations.[36] Because Republican legislators rejected funding for the closing of the Taliban and Al-Qaeda detention center at Guantánamo and the transfer of its inmates to the United States, Obama was not able to keep his campaign promise of shutting down the notorious detention facility. He stated that the United

States would not return the naval base to Cuba as long as it served U.S. military purposes.[37]

Among the modest policy changes brought on during Obama's first presidential term were the lifting of Bush-era expanded restrictions on Cuban and Cuban American visits with family members and remittances. The Obama administration also allowed U.S. telecommunications companies to operate on the island and renewed migration negotiations with Cuba.[38] Because of less restrictive travel provisions, the number of family visits surged to over 350,000 in 2010. In January 2011, Obama eased travel restrictions for all U.S. citizens participating in humanitarian and cultural trips and for university study abroad groups. That year it also increased limits on money transfers and expanded the list of U.S. airports allowed to schedule flights to Cuba.[39]

The Domestic Economy

During the first decade of the twenty-first century, the Cuban economy went through several ups and downs but still failed to regain its pre–Special Period levels. During 2001–3, the economy slowed down, averaging a yearly GDP growth of 2.8 percent. It began to pick up steam in 2004 and experienced a robust average yearly growth rate of 10.2 percent between 2005 and 2007, largely spurred by generous injections of trade credits and loans from Venezuela, China, Iran, and a few other nations and deliveries of virtually free oil from Venezuela, since most of it was purchased through long-term financing. Beginning in 2007, the economy slowed again as it was pulled down by the great global recession that began that year. In 2008, the GDP jumped 4.1 percent; it grew by a negligible 1.4 percent in 2009 and 2010. In 2011, it grew by 2.7 percent.[40]

One of the few positive legacies of the Special Period was movement toward economic diversification. Whether willingly or forced by circumstances to do so, the government sought to establish a broader-based economy that included a handful of export products and a few services that would generate hard currency. Besides sugar, major revenue generators included nickel and cobalt; Cuba holds some of the world's largest deposits of these minerals. Other exports included cigars and other tobacco products, traditional, high-quality export items whose worldwide demand increased; biomedical and pharmaceutical products; fish and shellfish; new, nontraditional export items such as sea cucumbers and bullfrogs;

tourism; the delivery of medical services to Venezuela and foreign visitors in exchange for hard currency; and the continuing influx of remittances.[41] The profitability of the various economic sectors, however, ranged widely, from negative profitability in the case of sugar to marginal profitability in tourism, which generates only an estimated 20 percent net profit, to high profitability in the case of nickel, for which foreign, mostly Canadian, companies assume all investment risks while Cuba reaps half the profits.[42]

In 2002, the Cuban government made a concerted effort to phase out—"restructure" was the official term—the sugar industry. On April 10, 2002, the government announced that it would close half of its remaining *centrales*. The closings proceeded as scheduled, and sugar production was cut in half. In 2005, with only fifty-six mills operating, Castro wrote sugar's epitaph: "Sugar will never return to this country; it belongs to the time of slavery." The decades-old question—Will sugar destroy the country or will the country destroy sugar?—seemed to have been finally answered: they destroyed each other.[43] Production fell every year from 2002 to 2007, when the *zafra* reached only 1.2 million tons; that was the smallest harvest since 1908. Since then, production has fluctuated at about the same level.[44]

Eduardo Lamora's masterful documentary *Cuba: el arte de la espera* (2008) captures the physical and social decay that accompanied the closing of Central Guatemala (formerly Central Preston), a mill located within the municipal limits of Mayarí, Holguín Province. Built by the American-owned Nipe Bay Company almost a century earlier and acquired later by the United Fruit Company, the sugar mill was one of those closed by the government in 2002. Many of the town's social spaces went into ruin: the local cinema was in disrepair and had no one to project films; the bar-restaurant was still open, but according to an interviewee, it had nothing to offer; the Catholic church had burned down and the Protestant church had collapsed; and the mill's pier had also fallen apart, its surviving pillars piercing the bay water like two lines of rusty, mollusk-dotted periscopes (figure 7.2).[45]

Preston became a virtual ghost town. People of all ages loitered in the central plaza. Prematurely aged housewives and divorcees hit the streets to buy and sell black market products such as coffee, fish, rice; men of all hues reverted to the mangroves, the historic hiding places of their runaway slave ancestors, where they illegally caught crabs and fish on illegal boats whose makeshift engines ran on illegally acquired fuel; and

Figure 7.2. Workers dismantling rusted railroad sugarcane wagons at the Guatemala sugar mill, 2007. Still from Eduardo Lamora's documentary *Cuba: el arte de la espera*. Courtesy of Eduardo Lamora and ALBALENA Films.

twenty-first century maroons eluded gray- and blue-clad *rancheadores*, hopping on precarious rafts, hoping to reach the sprawling *palenque* that Miami had become.

Ironically, sugarcane, which had become a drag on the economy, could have perhaps alleviated some economic problems. Cuba cut down its sugar production at a time of low prices for raw sugar (7.88 U.S. cents per pound in 2002), but after that, the world price for sugar more than tripled to 34.78 U.S. cents (in the 1st quarter of 2011). With the benefit of hindsight, one could argue that Cuba would have fared better had it followed the Brazilian model of using the sweet tall grass to produce high-value ethanol instead of lower-value sugar: a single ton of sugarcane can be transformed into either 275.6 pounds of sugar or 22 gallons of ethanol. In 2007 prices, one gallon of ethanol was worth $2.30, while 12.53 pounds of sugar were worth only $1.45.[46] Cuba did not choose the ethanol path, however. Such a shift would have required a huge influx of investments that were not readily available at the time. Castro was also personally opposed to using crops to produce biofuels instead of food. This was a flawed rationale: sugar is not a foodstuff; it is a natural sweetener of little nutritional value. After almost fifty years at the helm of the revolution, Castro still acted as planter-in-chief, as if the island's remaining one million hectares of sugar-cane land were his personal domain. He would rather see the cane fields go up in flames or be overtaken by the insidious *marabú* weed than produce ethanol.[47]

There are signs, however, that Cuba may not be completely free from the centuries-old sugar trap. A spurt in world sugar prices since 2010 has sparked Cuban authorities to reenergize the sugar sector by expanding investment, exploring the use of sugarcane and its by-products as sources of energy, and modernizing sugar-making technology. In 2011, the British-owned Havana Energy company and the Cuban government began a pilot program at the Ciro Redondo sugar *central* to turn bagasse into energy. The hope is that the program can be expanded; it is believed to have the potential to provide between 40 and 50 percent of Cuba's energy needs. This plan, along with another that seeks to turn *marabú* bushes into energy, was formalized with a $50 million investment from the United Kingdom.[48]

Nonsugar agricultural products have not fared well. Already low production levels of essential foodstuffs decreased during the new century's first decade. Production levels were so low that by 2006 the island had to import 84 percent of its foodstuffs, a substantially higher proportion than in 1958, when, as a sugar island, Cuba produced 75 percent of the food consumed by its population. The growing dependence on imported food added to ever-increasing trade deficits. Total food purchases skyrocketed to $857 million in 2003 and then to $1.35 billion in 2008. As worldwide prices for foodstuffs shot up in the next few years, Cuba's total expenditures in food imports ranged between 1.5 and 2.0 billion dollars.[49]

Heralded by Cuban officials as the key to Cuba's economic recovery, tourism continued to play a prominent role. It experienced a temporary drop, however, following the worldwide decline in international travel in the aftermath of 9/11. In 2002, the number of tourist visits decreased for the first time since the industry reemerged in the late 1980s, falling short of 1.7 million. While the number of visitors jumped during the second half of the decade, tourism-derived revenues stagnated, a reflection of a sharp decline in per capita tourist expenditures. Hotel room occupancy rates also fell, remaining below 50 percent throughout the second half of the decade. In 2011, however, a record number of tourists, over 2.5 million, visited Cuba.[50]

Two sectors that have experienced expansion and growth are nickel and petroleum. Nickel became the most important export in 2000; in 2005, it earned Cuba $1 billon, and the following year it generated $1.3 billion. Nickel prices skyrocketed in 2007, doubling revenues, and nickel exports surpassed tourism as main revenue earner. This windfall was short-lived, however. Prices collapsed in 2008, in great measure due to increased production of nickel pig iron, a cheap substitute for nickel.[51] Aided by Venezuelan technology and know-how, Cuba explored for, extracted, and refined increasingly larger amounts of petroleum in the first decade of the century. By 2004 it was producing 75,000 barrels a day, enough to satisfy about half of the domestic need. However, production fell steadily over the next few years.[52]

The recent discovery of large underwater deposits of oil off the island's northwestern coast promised to reduce dependence on foreign sources. Estimates of these reserves vary from Cuba's official figure of 20 billion barrels to the U.S. Geological Service's statistic of 4.6 billion barrels.[53] Numerous foreign companies such as Sherritt International, Petróleos de Venezuela, Spain's Repsol, and other Norwegian, Indian, Malaysian, Russian, Vietnamese, even Angolan companies invested in deep water oil exploration and signed deals to share oil profits with Cuba. The Scarabeo 9 oil-drilling rig, which was made in China, owned by Italians, and operated by Spaniards, arrived in Havana in January 2012 and immediately began drilling for oil.[54] At the time, the Cuban government and experts around the world visualized an economic future in which the island could produce enough oil to satisfy all of its domestic needs and perhaps export its surplus to other nations.

Closed for Repairs

The combination of trade credits and loans from various trade partners, massive oil subsidies from Venezuela, and extraordinarily high international nickel prices gave some respite to the economy during 2005–7, which allowed the government to import more food, expand welfare payments, and modestly increase salaries and retiree pensions.[55] However, lingering structural problems such as decreasing productivity, growing budget and trade deficits, mounting indebtedness, and dependence on imported food continued to burden the economy, impeding real and sustained recovery. Several immediate factors, including three devastating hurricanes in 2008 (Gustave, Ike, and Paloma), which caused an estimated combined $10 billion worth of destruction; the negative impact of the global recession on tourism and the volume of remittances; and cuts in Venezuelan subsidies have pushed Cuba into a deep economic recession that rivals the collapse of 1993–94. Some have referred to this crisis as the

"Little Special Period." Perhaps more alarming is the EU's categorization of Cuba as "virtually insolvent since January 2009."[56]

Even during the period's best years, most people saw little if any improvement in their material circumstances. Salary statistics show that incomes never recovered to pre-Special Period levels. While median salaries rose steadily, real salaries remained virtually stagnant; in 2006 median salaries were only about a fourth of 1989 levels. The consumer price index jumped over eightfold between 1989 and 2006, then it dropped until 2009 and spiked again in 2011.[57] Food prices continued to rise, however, as dependence on imported food grew, ration book allocations decreased, and the state increased prices at hard-currency stores and supermarkets. As of 2007, *libreta* allocations cost an estimated 33 pesos per month but supplied enough food for only ten to fifteen days; consumers had to supplement their diet with more expensive food from *mercados* and/or the black market. However, the continuing flow of remittances, which were estimated to hover at around $1 billion in 2010, continued to supplement both income and food consumption for a segment of the population.[58]

Cubans also witnessed a sharp deterioration in the quality and extent of social services such as education, health care, housing, transportation, and recreation. The increasingly cash-strapped government cut back on social expenses, and many service providers, teachers, nurses, and custodial personnel in schools and hospitals left their jobs because of the surreally low salaries they earned. As seen earlier, Cuba deployed thousands of health professionals to Venezuela, along with vital medical equipment and supplies, thus reducing the availability and quality of health care for the Cuban people. The scarcity of essential equipment and supplies, much of which were *desviado* (stolen), also contributed to the erosion of social services: hospitals lacked basic cleaning equipment and supplies—alcohol and mops, for example; public phones fell into permanent disrepair; government exterminators sprayed adulterated formulas of insecticides that were not strong enough to kill dengue-carrying mosquitoes; and toilets and faucets at hospitals, libraries, bus stations, and other public places broke and there were no parts—or the will—to get them fixed. Even airplanes were missing essential parts—I once flew on a Soviet-made Cubana de Aviación plane and my seat belt had no buckle; I had no option other than to tie it around my waist in the fashion of a martial arts black belt.

Cubans commonly use the phrase "*no hay condiciones*" (conditions are inadequate) to refer to rundown, nonfunctioning facilities, be it a dilapidated neighborhood basketball court—with no rim, let alone a net—or a clinic where patients have to bring their own plaster to have a broken arm put in a cast. The use of the phrase "*no hay condiciones*" is itself a manifestation of popular mockery of stale official terminology, for example Marx's emphasis on certain "objective conditions" as preconditions for revolution.[59]

Nancy Alonso's *Closed for Repairs* (2003) is an enthralling collection of short stories that depicts both the dire and desperate conditions of society and the manifold ways Cubans confront or accommodate to quotidian material and existential challenges.[60] While Alonso's characters are fictional, they could very well be real men and women struggling to subsist. One character, simply referred to as "M," prepares for an excursion to search for a working public telephone from which to make a call. M. meticulously packs a backpack for the excursion with essential items: some food, water, Band-Aids, cigarettes, and tranquilizers. Shortly after embarking on the excursion, M. returns home to fetch a forgotten item: a rope to commit suicide in case "the call didn't get through on time." Another character, Berta, waits anxiously for the results of a gastrointestinal endoscopy. The results are positive: she still suffers from ulcers. She welcomes the news with jubilation. Oddly enough, she purposely smoked cigarettes and drank coffee in excess to exacerbate her ulcers, a condition that entitled her and other patients to rationed powdered milk. "Now she could have another year of breakfasts with milk. Problem solved." Ramón, an officious and well-intentioned ombudsman, is the protagonist of the book's title story. He expects an inspection visit from his supervisor but realizes that his own Department of Community Concerns lacks proper *condiciones*: his secretary was absent, the office phone worked only for incoming calls, and the building was structurally unsound. Avoiding the anticipated inspection, Ramón left the building, said to himself "Now let's see what happens," and hung up a sign that read "CLOSED FOR REPAIRS."[61]

Deteriorating conditions continued to push tens of thousands of Cubans, mostly young people, off the island. *Balsero* departures peaked in 2005 to their highest level since 1994 as desperate individuals jumped on board the most ingenious types of floating devices imaginable.[62] The most famous of these was engineered by *balsero* Luis Grass, who turned a 1951 Chevrolet pickup truck into a motorized raft in 2003 (figure 7.3). Intercepted at sea twice by the U.S. Coast Guard, Grass, his wife, and their five-year-old son finally made it to the United States in March 2005.[63] In the poem "Camionautas" (trucknauts) Cuban American poet Gabriel Bravo vividly describes Grass's first attempt: "In the photo, / he steers through

Figure 7.3. Luis Grass with his family and some friends on board a 1951 Chevrolet truck transformed into an amphibious motorized *balsa*. Photograph by U.S. Coast Guard.

the waves / atop oil drums. / The sharks confused / as the coastguard that circles / the makeshift truck-raft, /sputtering a trail of bubbles / from the axel-swapped propeller, / rather than a cloud of smoke."[64]

El Comandante in His Labyrinth

When the new millennium officially started in Cuba on January 1, 2001, Fidel Castro had been in power for forty-two years and was the world's third longest-lasting living ruler, surpassed only by King Bhumibol Adulyadej of Thailand and Queen Elizabeth of the United Kingdom. In spite of his age and the debilitating rigors of more than four intense decades as supreme leader of an embattled nation, 74-year-old Castro appeared to be in good health, exhibiting an extraordinary level of stamina unusual for septuagenarians. Later that year, however, his mind and body began to show signs of debility. While he was delivering a speech in Pinar del Río, Castro became embarrassingly incoherent. He had enormous difficulties enumerating the locations of the new super-hospitals he proposed to build. As he spoke, saliva visibly dribbled down his gray beard and he shuffled his notes out of order as visibly anxious dignitaries watched the spectacle unfold.[65]

Not ten days had elapsed when Castro had a fainting spell while addressing a crowd in the outskirts of Havana under the punishing summer solstice sun. Millions of Cubans who watched the speech on live TV witnessed Castro's first-ever public display of physical frailty. Later that day, millions saw a recovered Castro appear on TV in the company of his brother Raúl (who was 71) and Almeida (who was 75). All three wore distractingly profuse makeup intended to make them look younger and healthier. Castro assured the viewing public that he was in perfect health and even joked, "I was playing dead to see what kind of burial they would give me." Castro's health and mortality increasingly became the object of speculation and the source of rumors among Cubans on both sides of the Florida Straits.[66]

During the early years of the new century, Castro continued to focus on two primary matters, his political survival and the preservation of the communist regime, one of the five remaining (the others were China, Laos, North Korea, and Vietnam). To accomplish these goals, his government used a combination of strategies: enacting profound economic changes—as discussed earlier in this chapter—such as the diversification of the economy and trade partnerships; carrying out efforts to ameliorate the general population's poor living conditions, particularly in the area of nutrition; agitating for national causes, such as the quest for the release of five spies imprisoned in the United States, to stir up popular support; and unremitting repression against dissidents and a growing internal opposition.

Beginning in 2002, Cuba entered yet another pendular swing from the pragmatism of the Special Period to a renewed idealism—survivalist idealism—under the banner of what Castro called "The Battle of Ideas." This was a slogan he had coined and used during the Rectification of Errors period. This new shift was an ideological and policy reversal of a previous reversal of yet another reversal that had reversed the revolution's original idealistic course. It was codified in law by a 2002 amendment to the Constitution that prescribed that "socialism and the revolutionary political and social system in the Constitution . . . are irrevocable, and Cuba will never return to capitalism."[67]

This new round of idealism, however, was different from the previous idealist cycles, namely the "heroic idealism" of the 1960s and the much milder ideological and institutional idealism of the Rectification of Errors campaign. The new cycle, while constituting a partial retreat from the survivalist pragmatism of the Special Period, was even milder; rather than abandoning the existing market mechanisms, it sought to reduce and regulate them. Moreover, this new cycle was conflated with a national cause that became an official government obsession: the struggle to liberate the Cuban Five, five spies that had infiltrated several anti-Castro groups in Miami who were later convicted for espionage.[68]

The state curbed Special Period provisions used to stimulate individual entrepreneurship and joint ventures. It further limited self-employment, *paladares*, and bed-and-breakfast operations. Consequently, the ranks of the self-employed decreased from 160,000 in 1998 to 100,000 in 2003. So did the number of joint ventures, which fell to 342 in 2003. Half of all free trade zone businesses also closed in 2003.[69] Another major change was the banning of the U.S. dollar from circulation in 2004. It was replaced by the convertible peso, whose exchange value was artificially set at one convertible peso per 93 U.S. cents. Another set of counter reforms further centralized the economy, placing severe limitations on the operational autonomy that state firms had enjoyed for several years. Centralization became so extreme that in order for a state firm to issue any check larger than 5,000 pesos, it had to request the approval of the Central Bank of Cuba.[70]

Influenced by Raúl Castro's "beans-better-than-cannons" doctrine, the government paid increased attention to the delivery of food to the populace. As Cuba's domestic food production decreased, food imports such as Vietnamese rice and U.S. wheat skyrocketed, resulting in higher trade deficits and a bigger foreign debt.

In April 2005, amid increasing popular discontent, the state raised salaries slightly, from a monthly average of 282 pesos ($13) to 312 pesos ($15). Pensions also increased, as did the number of Cubans on the welfare rolls.[71] Earlier that year, when individual monthly rice rations amounted to about six pounds, Castro initiated a highly publicized program to provide the population with electric rice cookers and pressure cookers. The cookers were not free, however; they were actually expensive: $5.50 at a time when the average worker earned around $15 a month. Welfare recipients were entitled to receive these cooking instruments at no cost and others could purchase them in installments.[72]

When *balsero* child Elián González was in the custody of his Miami relatives, Castro took advantage of the unfortunate situation, turning it into a national cause to pump up anti-American sentiment, promote national unity, and spark popular mobilizations. After Elián returned to Cuba on June 28, 2000, the revolutionary leader embraced a new cause in pursuit of similar objectives: a massive campaign to seek the freedom of the Cuban Five.

Ten members of the suspected Cuban spy ring known as the Avispa (Wasp) network were apprehended in South Florida in September 1998 and sent to jail. While five of them collaborated with U.S. authorities and received lighter sentences, the other five, Gerardo Hernández, Antonio Guerrero, Ramón Labañino, Fernando González, and René González, were convicted in June 2001 and later sentenced to prison terms ranging from two life terms for ringleader Hernández to fifteen years for René González.[73]

Cuba embarked on a massive and unremitting national and international campaign for the release of the "Cuban Five." Posters, signs, and billboards with images of "*los cinco héroes*" became ubiquitous throughout the island, even in the lobbies of luxury hotels. Images of the jailed Cubans also appeared on most official websites. Notably, 2002, the year after the conviction and sentencing, was named the Year of the Heroes Imprisoned by the Empire. Indicative of the national obsession with the Cuban Five was the decision in 2004 to change the ritual slogan with which students start their school day from the historic pledge "*Seremos como el Che*" (We shall be like Che) to a lackluster slogan: "One. Two. Three. Four. Five. Thank you."[74]

In June 2009, the U.S. Supreme Court refused to hear an appeal of the case, but later that year the sentences of three of the Cuban Five were reduced. In October 2011, one of them, René González, finished his prison term and was released. However, a judge ruled that he would have to serve his three-year probation period in the United States. He was allowed to go to Cuba in May 2013.[75] The trial and treatment of the Cuban Five while in prison have been denounced by international human rights bodies such as the Working Group on Arbitrary Detentions of the UN Commission on Human Rights and Amnesty International.[76]

The shockingly lenient treatment of Luis Posada Carriles, who was convicted in Venezuela for the 1976 bombing of a Cuban civilian plane that killed all of its passengers, contrasts sharply with the heavy sentences the Cuban Five received. Posada Carriles escaped from captivity in 1985, reportedly with the help of CANF president Jorge Mas Canosa, and settled in El Salvador, where he became an operative for the United States in the Iran-Contra affair. He was subsequently implicated in the planning of several 1997 bombings in Havana, for which he was convicted in Panama in 2000. After his release through a presidential pardon four years later, he illegally entered the United States, where authorities arrested him for immigration violations and perjury. The U.S. government has since protected him from requests for extradition by Cuba and Venezuela. In April 2011, a Texas jury found 82-year-old Posada Carriles innocent of all charges. He relocated to Miami, where extremist Cubans view him as a hero.[77]

At the same time they were denouncing injustices committed against the "heroes imprisoned by the Empire," Cuban authorities continued to harass, repress, and imprison dissidents and members of the peaceful opposition, whom they routinely scorned as "mercenaries on the CIA's payroll." Among the main targets of repression were the supporters of the Varela Project, who in March 2001 relaunched efforts to collect over 10,000 signatures on a petition that sought a reform-seeking referendum.[78] In spite of the government's relentless intimidation campaign, Payá's MCL and numerous independent and opposition groups under the umbrella organization Todos Unidos collected 11,020 signatures and turned the petition in to the National Assembly as provided by the Constitution (figure 7.4).[79] Instead of acting on the Varela Project petition, the

Figure 7.4. Human rights leader Oswaldo Payá holds a document with signatures from supporters of the Varela Project. Photograph by José Goitía, 2005. Courtesy of AP.

National Assembly approved a government-orchestrated petition to declare untouchable the socialist character of the state as established by the Constitution.[80] Because of his leadership of the Varela Project, Payá's international stature grew and he received numerous international awards, including the prestigious Sakharov Prize for Freedom of Thought granted by the European Parliament.[81]

The various independent movements and opposition groups, nonetheless, did not always agree in terms of goals and strategies. These divisions were a partial response to successful government infiltration by agents who reached high leadership positions. Infiltrator Manuel David Orrio, for example, presided over the Federation of Cuban Journalists. A major rift became evident between Payá's MCL and rival opposition leaders who questioned the strategic value of the movement's signature-gathering project. The Partido Popular Joven Cuba (Young Cuba Popular Party), for example, stated that human rights were not matters to be settled through plebiscites. Marta Beatriz Roque and Óscar Elías Biscet González also opposed the Varela Project. On May 20, 2005, Roque and René Gómez Manzano convened a forum of over 100 opposition groups, which Payá criticized and refused to join.[82] One of the most divisive issues was which stance to take on the U.S. embargo. Some dissident leaders such as Roque, Bonne, and Gómez Manzano endorsed the embargo and Bush's hard-line policy, while others, such as Payá and Sánchez Santacruz, opposed the embargo, as apparently did the bulk of the population.[83]

One of the revolution's most far-reaching and controversial waves of repression happened between March 18 and 21, 2003, when state security agents apprehended seventy-five dissidents, independent journalists, and leaders of independent labor and professional organizations. Charged with the controversial gag law of 1999 or the even harsher Article 91 of the Penal Code, which prescribed punishments up to the death penalty for anyone "who in the interest of a foreign state, commits an act with the objective of damaging the independence or territorial integrity of the Cuban state," all seventy-five prisoners were expeditiously convicted and sentenced to between six and twenty-eight years in jail. The list of detainees included some well-known dissident leaders, among them Raúl Rivero, founder of Cuba Press; Roque, head of the Cuban Institute of Independent Economists; and Biscet González, president of the Lawton Human Rights Foundation.[84] Among those arrested was Ricardo González Alfonso, a courageous journalist from my old Havana neighborhood who had been routinely detained and harassed by authorities over the years. Assuming that his living room was bugged—which it likely was—when I first visited him in 1994, I spoke in a very low voice but he immediately assured me that this was his house and that he and his guests were free to speak their minds.[85]

Only two weeks after the arrest of the seventy-five dissidents, special forces operatives captured the *Baraguá* ferry, which had been hijacked by three men seeking to flee. Within a week, all three had been tried, convicted, and executed.[86] These two episodes, which came to be known as the Black Spring of 2003, elicited worldwide condemnation. Within a few weeks, the EU imposed diplomatic sanctions that included stopping the process of including Cuba among the beneficiaries of its Cotonou Agreement, a development assistance program and curtailing cultural and social diplomatic intercourse with Cuban officials. It also increased its interactions with dissidents. Spain, under the government of conservative prime minister José María Aznar, played a leading international role in denouncing Cuba's human rights violations and applying pressure for humane treatment for the seventy-five and other prisoners of conscience.[87] That same year, the Paris-based Reporters without Borders ranked Cuba second, after North Korea, on its annual list of worst violators of freedom of press. The organization characterized the trials of the seventy-five as "Stalinist." Amnesty International adopted the seventy-five as prisoners of conscience and demanded their immediate release.[88] In spite of continuing sanctions and international vigilance, in May 2005 authorities arrested 400 men, averaging 18 years of age, and charged them with crimes of disrespect for socialist morality and a juridical aberration called *peligrosidad predelictiva* (pre-criminal dangerousness). They received sentences of one to four years.[89]

The Interregnum

Castro turned 78 in 2004, surpassing the island's average life expectancy of 77 years.[90] A number of developments in 2004 and 2005 sparked a resurgence of interest and speculation about Castro's health and mortality. Two months after his 78th birthday, Castro tripped and fell after giving a speech in Santa Clara. He suffered serious injuries to his left knee and broke his right arm and underwent surgery that lasted over three hours. That same year, the CIA "diagnosed" Castro with Parkinson's disease. Amusingly, a few months earlier, Castro's personal head physician,

Eugenio Selman, had publicly stated that his patient could very well live to the ripe old age of 120 years.[91]

On July 26, 2006, Cuba's national holiday, Castro came close to death; while flying on an airplane from Holguín to Havana, he had a severe intestinal hemorrhage due to a rupture in his large intestine, the result of diverticulitis. Dr. Selman and a team of physicians performed emergency surgery. While the condition required a colostomy, Castro reportedly refused that course of action. The team of doctors acquiesced, proceeding instead to remove the affected segment of the large intestine and a segment of the rectum. The procedure failed and the Comandante developed peritonitis, requiring yet another emergency intervention and a colostomy. A third surgery became necessary in light of a gall bladder inflammation. Later that year, with an abdominal wound still oozing, Castro dismissed Dr. Selman and came under the care of world-renowned Spanish surgeon José Luis García Sabrido.[92]

Four days after the emergency surgeries, Castro issued a proclamation in which he yielded power provisionally to his brother and four other senior officials. He delegated to Raúl Castro the responsibilities of first secretary of the Central Committee of the PCC, commander-in-chief, and president of the Council of the State and Republic of Cuba. However, he retained his post as first secretary of the PCC. In the same document, Castro temporarily delegated some of his special functions to trusted Politburo members José Ramón Balaguer Cabrera, José Ramón Machado Ventura, Esteban Lazo, and Carlos Lage.[93] Long considered Cuba's third man, Lage also was given responsibility for major budget areas along with two other high-ranking officials. In spite of this, Lage did not become the de facto second man. Although no single individual was designated as Raúl Castro's second-in-command, there were several potential candidates among a handful of loyal, active, or retired military men, such as José Ramón Machado Ventura, José Ramón Fernández, Ulises Rosales del Toro, and Ramiro Valdés.[94]

To dispel mounting rumors that Castro had actually died, on August 13—his 80th birthday—the government released the first visual images of him since his surgeries, photographs of a bedridden Castro visiting with his brother and Chávez. The state-controlled media also showed videos of the occasion on national TV.[95] Due to his weak physical condition, Castro remained in seclusion, noticeably absent from major events such as the Havana-hosted NAM Summit in mid-September and commemorations of the revolution's forty-ninth anniversary (January 2008).[96] During this time, the government sporadically released pictures and short edited videos of the senior Castro.[97] While he was convalescing, Castro reached the Cubans and the world by writing a series of "reflections" for publication in *Granma*, and he has continued to do so. Rather than touch on domestic or policy matters, these reflections have mostly explored international topics and global themes such as climate change and the dangers of turning food crops into sources of biofuels. A large number of his reflections have targeted the United States.[98]

Raúl Castro's tenure as acting president was characterized by a more realistic and critical assessment of the economic system and its shortcomings. Some of the island's most renowned economists openly discussed the need to liberalize and decentralize the system, positions that clashed with the elder Castro's battle-of-ideas crusade. A longtime admirer of the Chinese reformist model, Raúl Castro favored market-oriented economic reforms while maintaining rigid, one-party political control. In his view, such reforms were critical to the regime's survival, especially in the area of food production and distribution. Increasing food production actually became a strategic priority for the state.[99]

Another area in which provisional president Raúl Castro demonstrated flexibility and willingness to negotiate was in Cuba-U.S. relations. In August and again in December 2006, he signaled his disposition to work with U.S. officials toward normalizing relations.[100] The Bush administration was not receptive.

Raúl Castro's Beans and Cannons Rule

On February 18, 2008, almost nineteen months since he began his illness-induced seclusion and only six days away from the presidential and vice-presidential elections, Fidel Castro made public his decision to step down permanently: "I will neither aspire to nor accept," he wrote, "the positions of President of the State Council and Commander in Chief." In choosing the timing of his resignation, Castro asserted one more time his resistance to cave in to any outside pressure; he actually confessed later that he would have resigned earlier but did not want to please the United States, "an adversary that had done everything possible to get rid of me."[101]

On the 24th, the National Assembly unanimously elected 76-year-old Raúl Castro president. On that occasion, delegates elected 77-year-old

Machado Ventura as first vice-president of the Council of State and Council of Ministers. Curiously, Machado Ventura, who also ran unopposed, received 600 of 609 possible votes. This absence of parliamentary unanimity reflected the dissatisfaction of some with the Castros' decision to favor man-on-horseback Machado Ventura over civilian Lage (who was 56), who incidentally was the only one out of five Council of State vice-presidents who was elected unanimously.[102]

Thus ended Fidel Castro's tenure as Cuba's supreme ruler. Had he remained president for a few more months, he would have presided over the fiftieth anniversary of the revolution and surpassed Brazil's King Dom Pedro II's record as the hemisphere's longest-lasting ruler (forty-nine years). Fidel Castro was so weak that he could not even attend the revolution's austere fiftieth anniversary celebrations. On that occasion, which coincided with one of the economy's lowest points, Raúl Castro exclaimed: "Today, the Revolution is stronger than ever." He went on to warn, however, that the coming years would not be easy and quoted his brother: "This Revolution can destroy itself, but they can never destroy us; we can destroy ourselves, and it would be our fault."[103]

The bulk of the text of Raúl Castro's inauguration speech was an homage to his brother, whom he mentioned by name seventeen times and quoted nine times. The tone of the speech bordered on sycophancy; it conveyed the message that he could not rule without his brother. Only one brief segment of the speech shed light on the new president's agenda: he referred to the existing "excess of prohibitions and regulations" and promised that "in the next few weeks we shall start removing the most simple of them."[104]

The Raúl Castro who assumed formal leadership of the revolution was not the same youthful, pony-tailed, fear-inspiring rebel who had fought to topple Batista half a century earlier. While he had always been in the shadow of Fidel Castro, over the decades he had amassed vast military and political experience. He had also shed the bad cop role that he had played during the rebellion and the first years of the revolution; actually, the brothers had years before exchanged the old good-cop/bad-cop roles. Cuba observers agreed that Raúl Castro had demonstrated a high degree of pragmatism and flexibility and had played the role of a reasonable Sancho Panza vis-à-vis his quixotic sibling. The younger Castro had also demonstrated formidable leadership and organizational skills and the capacity to listen, speak candidly about Cuba's problems, and accept constructive criticism.[105]

The selection of Machado Ventura as the revolution's second-in-command and first in the line of succession was indicative of Raúl Castro's determination to surround himself with trusted military officers, most of whom were hard-liners of the *sierra* generation, and his unwillingness to open top leadership positions to civilians and younger leaders. While he originally retained two of his brother's most loyal and accomplished civilian ministers, Lage and Roque, he was not close to them and perhaps even distrusted them.[106] Raúl Castro soon made significant changes to his cabinet, reshuffling the Council of Ministers, particularly its executive committee. He elevated one of his most trusted generals, newly elected vice-president of the Council of State Julio Casas Regueiro to head the FAR. When Casas Regueiro died at the age of 75 in 2011, Raúl Castro replaced him with another trusted septuagenarian general, Leopoldo Cintra Frías. In March 2009, he dismissed Lage from his position as secretary of the State Council of Ministers, replacing him with another man on horseback, General José Amado Ricardo Guerra.[107]

After he was purged, Lage ceased to be—if he ever fully was—the third man behind Raúl Castro and Machado Ventura. Several Cuba observers agreed that the hard-line Sierra Maestra veteran Ramiro Valdés then moved up to the third man position (figure 7.5). After falling out of grace with Raúl Castro in 1985, Valdés rejoined the cabinet in 2006 as minister of information technology and communications. He was reinstated in the PCC Politburo in 2008 and Raúl Castro elevated him to one of the vice-presidencies of the Council of Ministers in the spring of 2009.[108] The selection of Valdés illustrated Raúl Castro's willingness to put the bad blood behind them and his conciliatory approach; it was also a reflection of his recognition of the regime's growing vulnerability and the need for Valdés's expert leadership in the areas of intelligence, counterintelligence, and repression.

Despite the fact that he surrounded himself with hard-line communists and aging military men, Raúl Castro soon embraced pragmatic, selective reformism as his ruling strategy. The older Castro, with his charisma and larger-than-life presence, could get away with imposing additional rigors and suffering on the population, but the new ruler was expected to make concessions, particularly in the areas of economic reform, and to work toward the improvement of the material conditions of the people. Raúl Castro's rule has been one of beans and cannons; it is more sympathetic to the population's material needs but clings to repressive mechanisms to guarantee social control.

Figure 7.5. *Right to left*: Raúl Castro, José Ramón Machado Ventura, and Ramiro Valdés at July 26th celebration, 2009. Courtesy of AP.

Just a few weeks into his presidency, Raúl Castro announced a number of mild reforms, including an end to restrictions on the purchase of items such as CD players, computers, cell phones, and microwave ovens. He also ended odious rules that banned Cubans from staying in and even entering tourist hotels.[109] Given the generalized pauperization of the population, such products and services were beyond the means of the vast majority of Cubans, however. If it took more than a full month's average salary to buy a subsidized Chinese-made rice cooker, it would take years of income and saving to purchase a computer or pay for a weekend at a beach-front hotel. While this first round of reforms had more of a symbolic significance than a real impact on the lives of the average Cuban, new salary and pension increases provided some relief. It is important to note that Raúl Castro's salary scale reforms were not across-the-board raises but rather increases in salary caps and performance-based compensation schemes.[110]

One of Raúl Castro's most significant reforms has been the distribution of government land to cooperatives and individual farmers. Prompted by a sustained shrinkage of cultivated land acreage, falling levels of food crop production, and ever-increasing prices of imported food, the government began to distribute idle arable land to farmers' cooperatives in April 2008. Landmark legislation passed in July of that year extended land distribution to private farmers in the form of ten-year, renewable 33-acre land grants. These usufruct grants could not be sold or transferred and farmers had to sell a large proportion of what they produced to the state food distribution agency. By the end of 2009, the government had distributed nearly 1 million hectares of idle land to over 100,000 farmers. By September 2011, these numbers had increased to 1.8 million hectares for 146,000 farmers.[111]

Raúl Castro's most important and defining speech to date was the closing remarks he offered at the National Assembly's legislative session of July 11, 2008. On that occasion, he articulated a new vision and enumerated a new set of guiding principles, particularly pertaining to workers and their relation with the state and to the role of the state as a provider of free or subsidized goods and services. The speech heralded the most profound ideological shift in the history of the Cuban Revolution and a substantial redefinition of socialism. "Socialism," Raúl Castro remarked, "means social justice and equality, but equality of rights and opportunities, not of income." He also rejected Karl Marx's dictum for a communist society—"From each according to his ability, to each according to his needs"—in favor of the milder socialist principle of "to each according to his work." He went further, denouncing one of the revolution's most hallowed historical goals, egalitarianism, of which he said, "it is in itself a form of exploitation: exploitation of good workers by those who are less productive, or worse yet, lazy." Raúl Castro used the occasion to announce the elimination of unnecessary handouts and excessive subsidies.[112]

During the next few years, the government implemented numerous social and economic reforms that stemmed from the philosophical shift Raúl Castro outlined in his National Assembly speech. Among these were a renewed push to encourage private economic activities, such as food production, *paladares*, and private taxi services; reducing subsidized workplace meals; a phasing out of the rationing system and boarding schools in the countryside; the rationalization of the state bureaucracy; and the dismissal of 500,000 state employees, a massive layoff that was scheduled to begin on January 1, 2011. Because of internal protests and the fact that alternative sources of work were not made readily available, Raúl Castro postponed the layoffs, calling instead for a gradual implementation to be completed in 2015; a total of 140,000 state jobs were cut in 2011 alone.[113] During Raúl Castro's presidency, Fidel Castro's strong presence continued to be felt, regularly through his published *reflexiones*, sporadically through public appearances, and always in the minds of the people, for whom he remained the patriarch and ultimate symbol of the revolution. Between February 2008 and the end of 2009, the elder Castro published a total of 191 *reflexiones*.[114]

After four years of seclusion, Fidel Castro miraculously reappeared in public in July 2010. He was first seen on the 7th, when he paid a visit to the National Center for Scientific Research. Clad in a white track jacket, the former president looked frail and required assistance when walking. Later that month, he made another appearance, this time at the Center for Research on the World Economy to consult experts on how to create a new civilization in the aftermath of an impending nuclear war.[115] Fidel Castro had become obsessed with the possibility of global destruction stemming from a nuclear war initiated either in the Middle East or in the Korean Peninsula. Since June 2010, Fidel Castro had dedicated several of his published reflections to the subject of a coming nuclear holocaust. In his July 11 reflection he somberly wrote "Everything hangs by a thread."[116]

Twenty-First-Century *Mambises*

When Fidel Castro's guerrillas took power in January 1959, some contemporaries praised them by comparing them to the heroic *mambises*, nineteenth-century freedom fighters. Indignant about such comparisons, the last living *mambí* general, Enrique Loynaz del Castillo, blasted those misguided remarks.[117] Indeed, the battlefield feats of the Rebel Army paled in comparison with those of their *mambí* ancestors, who were known to charge toward firing Spanish troop formations half-naked, shoeless, and on occasion, armed only with their fists.

At the risk of making General Loynaz del Castillo turn in his grave, I have entitled this section "Twenty-First-Century *Mambises*." This section traces the emergence of new actors and modalities of peaceful yet forceful opposition to the government. Among these actors, las Damas de Blanco (Ladies in White) stands out, an organization of white-clad relatives of imprisoned dissidents seeking their release through peaceful demonstrations. Other notable actors include death-defying protesters such as Guillermo Fariñas and Orlando Zapata Tamayo, who have gone on extended hunger strikes; youthful bloggers, such as Yoani Sánchez, who openly denounce Cuba's economic and political shortcomings; opposition musicians such as rappers Los Aldeanos and the punk rock band Porno Para Ricardo, whose iconoclastic, often profane lyrics criticize social and political problems and even insult the Castros; outspoken university students such as Eliécer Ávila, a computer science student who in a town hall meeting of sorts courageously posed challenging questions to Ricardo Alarcón, the longtime president of the National Assembly; and gay, lesbian, and transgender activists such as Wendy Irepa, a transgender woman who was pressured to resign her job because of her ongoing relationship with a gay man who opposed the regime. It is remarkable that the segments of society that revolutionary leaders have long hailed as the greatest beneficiaries of the revolution, blacks like Zapata Tamayo and Biscet González and women like Sánchez and las Damas de Blanco, became the protagonists of the dissident and opposition movements. Cuba's youth also became a breeding ground for social activism and opposition, albeit at times marked by an apolitical, even nihilist orientation.[118]

Almost immediately after the March 2003 arrest of the seventy-five independent journalists, independent librarians and other dissidents, their mothers, wives, and other female relatives organized las Damas de Blanco with the goal of pressuring the government to set their loved ones free. They began to meet inside the Church of Santa Rita (patron saint of the impossible) in the Havana suburb of Miramar, and gradually they began testing the tolerance of authorities for outdoor demonstrations, first by marching around the church and later in highly visible locations such as the Plaza of the Revolution and the centric area of the city where L and 23rd Streets intersect. The government mobilized rapid response brigades to verbally and physically attack las Damas, while government-organized mobs insulted them and chanted slogans such as *"La calle es de Fidel"* (The streets belong to Fidel) and *"Pa' lo que sea Fidel"* (Count on us for whatever, Fidel). Undaunted, las Damas de Blanco continued to engage in peaceful public marches, proving that the streets no longer belong exclusively to the Castros. Their public protests, the first organized and successful opposition public demonstrations since 1960, raised international awareness about human rights abuses, and earned them the prestigious Sakharov Prize for Freedom of Thought in 2005. Following the release of their loved ones in 2011, they vowed to continue the struggle for the freedom of expression and other human rights. Their movement has expanded and has since become a national network.[119]

A handful of activists adopted the strategy of the hunger strike as a means to dramatize the plight of the island's dissidents and to bring international attention to human and civil rights abuses. Dissident Guillermo Fariñas, a psychologist and independent journalist who carried out his first hunger strike in 2003, has since embarked on over twenty such strikes in support of a variety of causes such as the freeing of incarcerated political prisoners and the opening of Internet access to the general population. Fellow dissident Orlando Zapata Tamayo, an imprisoned black bricklayer, began a hunger strike in early December 2009; he died eighty-five days later from malnutrition and pneumonia. Two days later, a jaundiced and chronically emaciated Fariñas began yet another hunger strike, accompanied by four fellow opposition activists seeking the freedom of dissidents in poor states of health. Fariñas's hunger strike lasted 134 days; he did not stop until July 8, when Raúl Castro announced the gradual liberation of fifty-two political prisoners. His sacrifices in the struggle for human rights earned Fariñas the Sakharov Prize for Freedom of Thought in 2010, the third time this honor was bestowed on Cuban dissidents in eight years.[120]

With the advent of new technologies and forms of mass communication, other critics of the regime have recently begun to use blogging, Twitter, and other types of social media to denounce government abuses and the social ills afflicting society. The government, however, has tight control over access to computers and the Internet. In 2004, it restricted access even further, limiting it to e-mail and the Cuban intranet; only a tiny percentage of the population has access to the broader cyberworld. Later in the decade, Internet control czar Ramiro Valdés further limited access to the Internet, which he dubbed the "wild colt of new technologies."[121] As of the end of 2011, Cuba had a lower per capita rate of access to the Internet—less than 3 percent—than that of the most impoverished countries of Latin America.[122] In the tradition of triangulation strategies, the government went to the length of creating a unit of 300 "cyber-soldiers" code-named Operación Verdad (Operation Truth) whose tasks included monitoring blog activities around the world, creating counter-blogs, acting as trolls (writing inflammatory comments or messages in social media), and even writing false and misleading information in Wikipedia articles and the like.[123]

Yoani Sánchez is Cuba's pioneer and most internationally renowned opposition blogger. Born in 1975 at the height of Cuba's Sovietization, she, like many children of her generation, was christened with a name that begins with the letter Y. Sánchez titled the blog she began in 2007 Generación Y. In spite of constant government harassment, attacks from Operación Verdad, cybersabotage, and a brief kidnapping and senseless beating in November 2009, Sánchez has persisted. Earlier in 2009, she adopted the new Twitter modality. Since then, Sánchez has received numerous recognitions and accolades for her journalistic work, including the Spanish Ortega y Gasset Journalism Award (2008) and the World Press Freedom Hero award from the International Press Institute (2010).[124]

By 2011, around twenty-five other bloggers were regularly reporting and commenting on conditions on the island, among them Laritza Diversent, a black Havana lawyer whose blog focuses on legal matters; Claudia Cadelo through the Octavo Cerco blog; and photographer/writer Orlando Luis Pardo Lazo, who runs the profusely illustrated Boring Home Utopics blog. That year, the government mobilized its own bloggers to mount counterattacks against the opposition.[125]

Protest music reached new levels of audacity and became a preferred medium for denouncing social problems and disparaging the revolutionary leadership. Cuban rap became the most prolific and widely disseminated genre of protest music; Los Aldeanos, Papá Humbertico, Anónimo Consejo, and Escuadrón Patriota are among its most popular performers. The ascendancy of Cuban rap, as argued by student of Cuban culture Sujatha Fernandes, responds to the growing marginalization and discrimination young black Cubans have endured since the 1990s, but it resonates with Cubans of all races. In one song, Anónimo Consejo criticized the discrimination Cubans endured while tourists enjoyed special privileges: "The official tells me, 'You can't go / there, much less leave here.' / In contrast, they treat tourists / differently. / People, is it possible that in my country / I don't count?" In their hit song "La naranja se picó" (2009), Los Aldeanos explicitly insulted the Castros, calling them "cuckolds" and "faggots."[126] The punk rock band Porno Para Ricardo, led by Gorki Águila, stands out as the period's most irreverently raw musical group. The band's emblems and CD covers desecrate some of the most hallowed symbols of the revolution. The band's emblem, for example, mocks the classic communist symbol, replacing the hammer with an erect penis. In August 2008, authorities arrested Águila and charged him with *peligrosidad predelictiva*. The charges were promptly reduced to a lesser offense and he was released after paying a nominal fine.[127]

The role of Cuba's youth is also significant. The 2008 incident mentioned above in which 21-year-old student Eliécer Ávila courageously and respectfully confronted 71-year-old National Assembly president Alarcón is worth recounting and viewing on YouTube. Some background on the duelers is in order. Ávila introduced himself as coming from the remote countryside town of Puerto Padre, Las Tunas Province, "surrounded by cane fields," as he put it. During the exchange, Alarcón for some reason said that he was descended from the old Camagüey's aristocracy. When given the microphone, Ávila asked several questions, among them why the average worker had to toil two or three days to be able to afford a toothbrush. Later he asked why Cubans "did not have viable possibilities of staying in hotels or traveling to places around the world?" He added, "I do not wish to die before seeing the place where El Che fell [in Bolivia]." As Ávila spoke, Alarcón listened patiently, his two hands propping up his forehead, while visibly anxious state officials paced nervously in the background. Infuriated, Alarcón began his response in a patronizing tone: "Perhaps because all of you are young, you will not believe this. . . ." and went on to explain that when he was young he could not afford to visit the Tropicana Nightclub or Varadero Beach. "That's the way it was back then [before 1959]," he said.[128]

Although repression of dissidents and opponents persisted during Raúl Castro's presidency, he recognized that the EU would not lift sanctions against Cuba or expand its assistance programs while Cuba held around 230 political prisoners, among them fifty-two of the seventy-five arrested in the Black Spring of 2003. He also recognized that freeing some of these prisoners would be a positive signal to the new Obama administration. Just four days after Castro took office in 2008, Cuba signed two international human rights agreements that the elder Castro had long opposed: the Covenant of Civil and Political Rights and the Covenant of Economic, Social and Cultural Rights. The following day, Raúl Castro began negotiations with Vatican officials for the release of a number of political prisoners.[129]

On July 7, 2010, over two years after the beginning of these discussions with the Vatican, a representative of the Catholic Church announced that Cuba had vowed to free fifty-two of the seventy-five dissidents and prisoners of conscience who remained in custody. On the 12th, the first seven were freed and were immediately flown to Spain as a condition for their release.[130] Among them was my acquaintance, 60-year-old Ricardo González Alfonso, who after enduring seven years of incarceration under horrible conditions was provided decent food, medical care, lodging, and clothing before being released. He told reporters: "It was as if they were trying to wash away in three days the whole seven years that they did not consider us real people." The state released thirty-four others by the end of the year, while another eleven remained in custody because they refused deportation to Spain. They were finally freed on March 23, 2011, and were allowed to remain on the island.[131] On December 23, 2011, in anticipation of Pope Benedict XVI's visit, the Cuban president announced the release of 2,900 common inmates, including women and elderly prisoners.[132]

While the regime released most of its longtime political prisoners, starting in 2011 it increased the number of detentions, beatings, and brief incarcerations of dissidents and opponents. Likewise, according to reports by the New York City–based Committee to Protect Journalists, in March and April of 2011, the government carried out at least fifty acts of repression, eleven of them violent, against independent journalists. According to the Cuban Commission on Human Rights and National Reconciliation (CCDHRN), the number of short-term political arrests doubled in 2011, when 4,123 such occurrences were recorded.[133] In August 2011, Amnesty International issued a report denouncing the harassment of, arrests of, and physical violence against members of las Damas de Blanco.[134]

Cuba in Transition?

The second half of the first decade of the twenty-first century lacked momentous events and dramatic changes—no wars, no government programs of epic proportions, not even a memorable guiding slogan or official year name—but it brought on many important changes.

The most significant of these was the gradual, peaceful, and successful transfer of power from one Castro to another. For decades, experts and non-experts had been speculating about possible transition scenarios. A legion of futurists produced mountains of books, reports, journal articles, and newspaper columns that offered prognostications about Cuba "after Fidel." Many forecasts equated Fidel Castro's passing with the end of the revolution and pointed to the possibility of a dreadful "bloodbath" scenario. The elder Castro, however, yielded power while still living, a political ending that did not fit the script of a dangerous and dramatic life. He was expected to die suddenly, with his boots on, ideally fighting off an apocalyptic Yankee invasion. Instead, he faded gradually from power. Fate denied him the martyrdom that he so fervently desired.

While the presidential succession was successful and uneventful, by the end of 2011, it had not translated into much change or rejuvenation in the top echelons of the party and the government. The line of succession behind Raúl Castro (who was now 79) consisted of General Machado Ventura (80) and "third man" General Valdés (79). The original *sierra* guerrilleros were still in full command.

Unlike Fidel Castro, whose leadership style was marked by stubbornness and whose policy decisions were shaped by impulsivity and an exaggerated sense of honor, Raúl Castro has demonstrated pragmatism, greater flexibility, and thoughtfulness. This was made patent by his willingness to engage the Church and the Spanish government in negotiations to free numerous prisoners of conscience; this was also a signal of his desire to engage the United States in dialogue to improve relations between the two nations.

For a moment, in 2009, factors lined up to create the most propitious juncture in half a century for a rapprochement between Havana, Washington, and Miami: a reformist, pragmatic new Cuban president, a progressive president in the United States, and an increasingly moderate exile population and leadership in South Florida. The alignment of these factors, however, failed to produce positive results.

Obama's first administration was unable to make any substantive concessions in sticking points that have long obstructed the normalization of bilateral relations, the embargo above all others.[135] A new major sticking point, the Alan Gross affair, became yet another obstacle. Gross, a U.S. citizen, worked for Development Alternatives, Inc., which received funding from the U.S. Department of State's USAID, an agency that supports development programs around the world. He was arrested in December 2009 while on a work-related visit to Cuba. He was accused of illegally importing highly regulated communications equipment. In March 2011, a Cuban court sentenced him to fifteen years, and two months later the Cuban Supreme Court upheld that decision. Gross has since suffered various health problems, including the loss of around 100 pounds. Gross's family, the U.S. government, Jewish organizations, and a number of NGOs have lobbied and pressured for his release to no avail. Cuba signaled a willingness to negotiate an exchange of Gross for the Cuban Five, but U.S. officials rejected the offer.[136]

Did Cuba begin a substantial process of socioeconomic transition in 2008? Raúl Castro did lay the foundations for a number of seemingly irreversible economic reforms in the direction of free enterprise and a market economy. He also redefined—updated, in his words—socialism by promising to reduce the state's social responsibilities and its role as the island's primary employer. Among the most salient transformations the regime spearheaded during 2008–11, a growing participation of individuals in profitable ventures stands out. By the end of 2011, 338,000 Cubans held self-employment licenses, over half of them granted since the beginning of that year. Some critics derided the reforms as superficial, leading only to what some dubbed an "economy of kiosks."[137]

8

▼

Rectify and Change . . . All That Should Be Rectified and Changed

Transitions, Elections, and Successions, 2011–2013

2011—Year Fifty-Three of the Revolution
2012—Year Fifty-Four of the Revolution
2013—Year Fifty-Five of the Revolution

In the ranks of this squadron I have enlisted
With a microphone in hand, from silence I've desisted
I know you have seen me . . . !!! Machine-gunning untruth
My words are bullets, which neither my mouth nor mind shoot
Los aldeanos, "El rap es guerra."

While history provides many useful tools for understanding contemporary realities, only hindsight and a longer-term perspective enable us to recognize fully the direction and lasting extent of contemporary change. From the late-2013 perspective from which I write, it is obvious that Cuba is undergoing profound, fast-paced changes, transitions, and transformations. As this manuscript morphs into a book, critical questions linger: Change to what? Change led by whom and for how long? And in partnership with which international players? Irreversible change? These questions notwithstanding, the pace and reach of change since the PCC Congress of April 2011 warrants a look at the 2011–13 period as a watershed. That is the rationale for combining these three years in a distinct, final chapter but still within the purview of this book's Part III: Survival. Whether 2011–13 is, indeed, a major turning point in the history of the Cuban Revolution and whether or not Cuba has begun to move beyond a state of survival, only time will tell.

This chapter examines the complex web of domestic and international continuities and changes impacting Cuba, its relations with the outside world, and its diaspora. It looks at demographic changes both on the island and among Cubans in the United States and relates them to changing political cultures on both sides of the Florida Straits. While Cuba's transformation process remains mostly driven by decisions made by its top political leadership, now, more than ever since the start of the revolution, dissidents and regular Cubans have a greater impact on government decisions and the way those decisions are implemented. The release of the last remaining political prisoners of the Black Spring of 2003 in 2011, the postponement of massive layoffs of government employees announced in 2010, and provisions that allow even the harshest critics of the regime to travel abroad since January 2013 are cases in point. Potentially most profoundly transformative is Raúl Castro's official announcement in February 2013 that he will step down from power in 2018, at which time he would be eighty-six, and his selection of 52-year-old civilian Miguel Díaz-Canel as first vice-president and second-in-command.

During his first five years at the helm of the revolution, Raúl Castro demonstrated that he had control of the government and the people and that his formula of gradualist reformism was a safe and sound strategy for preserving socialism while attempting to achieve economic growth through capitalist mechanisms (figure 8.1).

During those years, Cuba also made some modest progress in the area of human rights. Executions, for example, became a thing of the past, and the number of political prisoners dropped to historic lows. This was in large measure due to the valor and selflessness of a new generation of dissidents and opponents: bloggers, rappers, independent journalists, and perennial hunger strikers. That said, repression is alive and well, as is attested by hundreds of arrests of dissidents and members of the opposition for distributing anti-Castro leaflets, for expressing their views through blogs or on Twitter, or simply for attending José Payá's funeral. To follow on a phrase alluded to before: more and more Cubans have gone beyond playing with the chain; they are playing with the monkey itself.

Raúl Castro has rectified and changed what he believes "should be rectified and changed." He is applying a creolized Chinese formula of economic "rectification"—a term that now means exactly the opposite of what it meant in the late 1980s—while maintaining the regime's repressive, militarized, and authoritarian nature. One of his old and most benign

Figure 8.1. Billboard with Raúl Castro slogan: "We will preserve and develop social-ism," Havana, 2013. Courtesy of Reuters.

nicknames, el Chino, has now taken a completely new meaning. That said, to date, in contrast with China, where individual citizens and corpora-tions can establish direct business relations with foreign firms, hire large numbers of employees, and amass huge fortunes, Cuba maintains severe limitations on the size, hiring practices, and profits of private businesses. China had "produced" over one million millionaires and over one hundred billionaires by the end of 2012. Cuban entrepreneurs, meanwhile, con-tinue to run microbusiness and kiosks.[1]

The 2011–13 period has also been marked by parallel political changes in the two countries that have had the greatest impact on Cuba through-out the twenty-first century: its staunchest enemy, the United States, and its closest ally, Venezuela. In 2011, Republicans gained majority control of the U.S. House of Representatives and Cuban-born hard-liner Ileana Ros-Lehtinen became chair of the body's Committee on Foreign Affairs. Since then, House Republicans have pushed for stronger restrictions against Cuba and have thwarted Obama's efforts to expand people-to-people ex-changes between the two countries. Venezuela has also undergone po-litical changes, including the succession of the late Hugo Chávez by his hand-picked heir Nicolás Maduro in the spring of 2013.

Sixth PCC Congress and the *Lineamientos* of 2011

Since the PCC's First Congress in 1975, party leaders have convened sub-sequent congresses regularly, every five or six years, up until the Fifth Congress in 1997. Fourteen years elapsed, however, between the Fifth and Sixth Party Congresses, which Raúl Castro scheduled to coincide with the fiftieth anniversary of the Battle of Girón, on April 16–19, 2011. Raúl Castro announced the upcoming congress in November 2010, at which time he made public economic reform proposals for national discussion, the "Draft Guidelines (*lineamientos*) of Economic and Social Policy of the Party and the Revolution." The document was widely debated in a variety of forums, was slightly revised in the process, and was expanded to 311 *lineamientos* to be voted on in the scheduled Party Congress.[2]

With only minor modifications, PCC delegates unanimously approved the *lineamientos*, which included numerous economic reforms, among them plans for the legalization of home sales and purchases by Cuban citizens, the reduction of the state-employed labor force by one million workers, the expansion of usufruct land grants to cooperatives and individual farmers, the phasing out of food rationing, the expansion of foreign investments and self-employment, and the codification of a new taxation system. Raúl Castro selected former minister of the economy Marino Murillo to oversee the newly created Permanent Government Commission for Implementation and Development, responsible for carrying out the new reforms.[3]

The Sixth Congress also brought on a restructuring of the PCC and its power structure. This was the first PCC Congress under Raúl Castro's leadership, who now became the party's First Secretary, a post that Fidel Castro had not officially resigned from in 2006. Party delegates voted to reduce the Politburo from 24 to 15 members and the party's Central Committee from 150 to 115 members. The resulting new Politburo's composition actually strengthened the dominance of elderly leaders and the pre-dominance of men on horseback: the body's average age rose to 67, and it included seven generals aged 73 or older.[4] Nonetheless, aware of the need to eventually rejuvenate the party leadership, Raúl Castro proposed term limits for elected government officials: a maximum of two consecutive five-year terms, a proposal that ends his presidency in February 2018.[5]

Visibly absent from the Congress, the elder Castro appeared only in the closing session. Clad in a blue Fila athletic jacket, he walked with difficulty, holding on to an usher's arm. At the sight of him, the hall exploded in thunderous applause and rhythmic chants of "¡Fidel! Fidel!" Too frail to address the delegates, he later commented on the congress through one of his reflections. He was particularly interested in his brother's term limits proposition. "I like the idea," he said, closing his reflection with the announcement that he would soon start work on a book project that he hoped to finish "before the world ends."[6]

Several of the lineamientos-inspired reforms have already been implemented. In October 2011, the government legalized the sale and purchase of used cars by individuals and later extended those provisions to houses and apartments. In 2012, it expanded opportunities for individuals to join independent cooperatives that include a variety of services such as construction and transportation; and it increased the size of usufruct land grants from thirteen to sixty-seven acres.[7] As this book goes into production, the Raulista economic reform process—whether it is called "rectification" "updating," or "perfecting"—continues to move forward, too slowly for many, too quickly for others, particularly hard-line communists. Its results are not yet visible in economic ledgers or palpable to the vast majority of Cubans.

Five Key Elections within Six Months

In little over six months, between the fall of 2012 and the spring of 2013, five key elections took place, all with the potential to profoundly impact the course of the Cuban Revolution: one in Venezuela (October 2012), one in the United States (November 2012), two in Cuba (February 2013), and another in Venezuela (April 2013).

On June 30, 2011, Hugo Chávez appeared on TV and surprised Venezuelans by informing them that he had undergone two surgeries in Cuba to remove a cancerous tumor vaguely described as located in his pelvic area. Over the next few months, he received chemotherapy, also in Cuba. In October, his physicians gave him a clean bill of health. But on February 28, 2012, Chávez had to have another surgery to extract the recurring tumor and yet another one for the same reason later that year.[8]

Between surgeries and undergoing radiation treatment, Chávez won reelection to the presidency in October after telling voters that he was cured and promising that he would rule until 2031. Tellingly, his adversary, Henrique Capriles of the Justice First party, lost by eleven points, the smallest margin of victory for Chávez since his first election in 1998. He had run on a platform that promised to terminate all aid and subsidies to Cuba, which at the time, represented around 21 percent of the island's GDP.[9] The Venezuelan strongman died on March 5, 2013. At age 58, he was twenty-eight years younger than Fidel Castro, his beloved political mentor.

Less than a month after Chávez's reelection, Obama was reelected president of the United States, defeating Republican candidate Mitt Romney. Obama's reelection, and particularly his razor-thin victory in the heavily contested state of Florida, were indisputably the result of a high turnout of Latino voters—higher than that of any other U.S. ethnic or racial group—and overwhelming Latino support for Obama; an estimated 66–70 percent voted for him.[10]

Demographic trends that had become evident for over a decade transformed Florida's electorate. For one, in 2012 Hispanics constituted 13.1 percent of the state's registered voters. Moreover, because of the slower growth of the state's Cuban and Cuban American population compared to other Hispanic groups, particularly Puerto Ricans, whose numbers swelled from 482,027 in 2000 to 847,550 in 2010, Cubans no longer represented the majority of the state's Latino population. Actually, in 2010 they no longer constituted a majority even within Greater Miami's Hispanic population.[11] It is also worth noting that because of the high poverty rates among *balsero*-generation immigrants, the overall rate of poverty among Cubans and Cuban Americans in the United States came closer to that of immigrants from the Dominican Republic, El Salvador, and even Haiti.[12]

These demographic changes brought significant political reverberations. By 2008, more Hispanic Floridians were registered as Democrats than as Republicans. Major demographic transformations in the U.S. Cuban and Cuban American population translated into changing political attitudes and electoral behavior. The proportion of Republican-leaning first-cohort immigrants continues to decline, while the percentage of more Democrat-inclined second- and third-generation Cuban Americans and *balsero*-generation immigrants grows.

FIU's 2011 Cuba Poll reflected how the changing demographics were transforming the community's position on various Cuban issues. At the time of the poll, a slim majority of Cubans and Cuban Americans still supported the embargo, but 58 percent favored a dialogue between Cuba and the United States. Similarly, a considerable majority expressed support for unrestricted travel by Cubans to the island, the easing of limits on remittances, and the establishment of diplomatic relations with Cuba.

U.S.-born Cubans, 18- to 44-year-olds, and members of the *balsero* cohort expressed overwhelming support for those positions.[13]

Significantly, by 2011, the proportion of Cuban and Cuban American voters registered as Republican had fallen to approximately 56 percent. Most surprising of all, in 2012, Obama received more Cuban and Cuban American votes (49 percent) than Romney (47 percent). Trends had been moving in that direction, but no one anticipated that the tipping point would happen as early as 2012.[14]

Despite his victory, Obama continues to contend with obstructionist opposition in Congress that renders him unable to make significant changes in U.S.-Cuba relations. The United States has become the hemisphere's pariah because of its Cuba policy. Its isolation became painfully evident during the 2012 Inter-American Summit held in Cartagena, Colombia. On that occasion, thirty-three member nations supported Cuba's participation in future OAS Summits; only the United States and Canada opposed the proposition.[15]

Unlike the direct, albeit imperfect, elections carried out in the United States, Cuba's president and top leadership continue to be elected indirectly by the 612 members of the National Assembly, who are likewise not elected directly by the voters but are rather nominated by delegates serving in municipal assemblies as individual candidates, all from the PCC, who run unopposed. On February 3, 2013, voters ratified the full slate of party-approved delegates as well as the 1,269 members of provincial assemblies. The composition of the new National Assembly reflected a growing desire to rejuvenate and further diversify the body. The body's average age dropped substantially to 48 years, and 80 percent of its new members had been born after the start of the revolution. Nearly half of the delegates were women, and one transgender candidate, Adela Hernández, also joined the assembly.[16]

Three weeks later, the newly elected members of the National Assembly unanimously reelected Raúl Castro president, and to the surprise of many, selected as vice-president 52-year-old engineer Miguel Díaz-Canel, the former minister of higher education who had been a member of the PCC Politburo since 2003. Díaz-Canel replaced General Machado Ventura, twenty-nine years his senior. When Díaz-Canel was elected, President Castro stated that this was "a definitive step in the configuration of the future leadership of the nation through the gradual and orderly transfer of key roles to new generations." Ramiro Valdés, meanwhile, remained in place as the revolution's third man. Significantly, for the first time ever, a woman—actually two—were selected as vice-presidents, comptroller general Gladys Bejerano (66) and Mercedes López Acea, (48), head of Havana's PCC. The new members of the assembly also elected black politician Esteban Lazo (65) as the body's new president, replacing Ricardo Alarcón (79), who had held that position for two decades.[17]

Díaz-Canel's selection as second-in-command is significant on many counts, first because he is relatively young, and second because he is a civilian, the first to reach such a position since 1959. Also, despite the fact that he was a relatively obscure figure within the party and government hierarchy, those who know him speak well of his loyalty, pragmatism, effectiveness, and likeable character. He will not cast a shadow over Raúl Castro, historically the kiss of death for any rising leader, much less be a threat to the military brass. While he is constitutionally second-in-command, Díaz-Canel is not second in power. He lacks influence within the FAR, having served only the three obligatory years of military service.

The last of the five elections considered in this section took place in Venezuela, on April 14, 2013, only five weeks after Chávez's death. Despite having been anointed by Chávez as his successor, Vice-President Nicolás Maduro won the presidency by the slightest of margins: 50.72 of the votes against 48.99 for Henrique Capriles Radonski. The opposition challenged the results, but a recount of about half of the votes did not produce evidence of widespread fraud. The results, however, demonstrated the vulnerability and poor future prospects of Venezuela's ruling party.[18] Maduro's months in power have been characterized by erratic behavior and odd initiatives such as creating a new Vice-Ministry of Supreme Social Happiness, precisely at a time when Venezuela endured out-of-control inflation (over 50 percent in 2013) and its citizens suffered shortages of some of the most basic consumer goods, such as milk, rice, coffee, and toilet paper. Mounting scarcities, spiraling inflation, and the government's inability to stop a wave of violent crime sparked massive protests in early 2014. It is not likely that Venezuela will be able to continue subsidizing the Cuban economy as it faces severe economic challenges of its own that have drained the state's cash reserves. Observers are using the term "Cubanization of Venezuela," not because of ideological influence but in reference to the Bolivarian Republic's pauperization and increasingly dysfunctional economy.[19]

In sum, the five elections of 2012–13 had a significant impact on the island. Those in Venezuela and the United States assured the continuation of a status quo in terms of relations with Cuba. Chávez's victory over presidential contender Capriles in October 2012 and a second defeat for Capriles at the hands of Maduro six months later assured that Cuba's strongest ally and benefactor remained under the rule of the pro-Cuba United Socialist Party of Venezuela. Capriles denounced Maduro as a puppet of Castro's Cuba and had vowed to end all subsidies to the island.[20] Although the Cuban elections did not alter the reformist course of the revolution, they signaled the willingness of Raúl Castro to rejuvenate and further diversify the government and the PCC. This willingness, of course, is assuaged by the looming and inevitable demise of the guerrillero generation that reached power in 1959.

The Blog Heard around the World

In January 2013, the Cuban government relaxed travel restrictions, making it easier for Cubans on the island to travel abroad and for Cubans abroad to visit the island with fewer limitations. These significant changes were largely a response to the government's strategy to increase the flow of hard currency to the island: a retired septuagenarian, say, from Guanabacoa, can work long hours at a Hialeah factory over three months and bring back gifts and a few thousand dollars when he returns home. And even formerly hated defectors, such as U.S. Major League pitching star José Contreras, are warmly welcomed back and are able to contribute to their family's economy. But these changes are also the result of the trenchant transnationalism of hundreds of thousands of anonymous Cubans, in and out of the island, who for decades have treated the longest ninety miles as if they were the shortest.

One of the most significant ramifications of the relaxation of travel regulations has been the ability of Cuban dissidents and bloggers to spread their messages around the world. Salient examples of dissident travelers are Berta Soler, president of las Damas de Blanco; Rosa María Payá, who continues her crusade to find the truth behind her father's mysterious death in a car accident; and bloggers Orlando Luis Pardo Lazo and Yoani Sánchez, the latter indisputably the best-known Cuban dissident. Eliécer Ávila, who publicly confronted Alarcón back in 2008 about the right to travel, finally got his wish. He traveled to Sweden, arriving without a penny, he said. When an interviewer asked him whether he intended to stay there, he replied that he reserved the right to live anywhere in the world, "but at the moment Cuba is my life."[21]

Figure 8.2. Yoani Sánchez during her visit to Miami, April 2013. Photograph by Lynne Sladky, taken during Sánchez's interview at the Freedom Tower with Myriam Márquez of the *Miami Herald*. Courtesy of AP.

After having been previously denied a visa to leave Cuba more than ten times, on the Ides of March of 2013, Sánchez boarded a plane bound for New York City, where she began an 80-day tour that included the United States, Brazil, Mexico, the Netherlands, Spain, and a few other European countries. She spoke at the UN Headquarters and met with officials at the White House and members of the U.S. Congress, and spoke at Mexico's Senate and Miami's emotionally symbolic Freedom Tower, which was used during the 1960s to process hundreds of thousands of Cuban refugees (figure 8.2).

Dressed in the simple style of a 1960s folk singer, her black, waist-long mane cascading forward over her left shoulder, and an ever-present smile on her fair-skinned face, 37-year-old Sánchez spoke softly but strongly wherever she went, never losing her calm demeanor, even as some angry pro-Castro protestors booed and bombarded her with epithets and insults—"CIA agent," "mercenary," "traitor." In Brazil, a woman pulled her hair; in Mexico, another one interrupted her and showered her face with fake "CIA dollar bills." Undaunted by those disruptions, Sánchez carried on. Armed with a microphone and her impeccable mastery of the Spanish language, she conveyed information about the enduring repression and sordid realities of her communist homeland; expressed her desire for a free, unified Cuban nation; and emphasized the need to put an end to that "fossil from the Cold War [the U.S. trade embargo] that makes no sense."[22]

While repudiated and booed by some, Sánchez was welcomed and cheered by many more, nowhere more effusively than in Miami, where part of her family resides. In her Miami speaking engagements and interviews, she stressed the need for the many Cubas to unify and join a common cause for a democratic, independent, and prosperous fatherland. Her mere presence demonstrated the possibility of unity even among rival exile groups, who for decades have been divided by triangulation schemes—the embargo among them—conceived and manipulated from Washington, Havana, and Miami. As a *Miami Herald* editorial highlighted, Sánchez was admired and jointly welcomed by exile organizations as disparate as the 2056 Brigade (a Bay of Pigs veterans' association), composed of long-dismounted men on horseback; the hard-line pro-embargo Cuban Liberty Council; the right-of-center CANF, which supports the embargo but also the easing of restrictions on travel and remittances by Cubans in the United States; and the centrist Cuba Study Group, which opposes the embargo.[23]

While speaking at Miami's Freedom Tower, Sánchez shared an anecdote about an encounter with a German national, who upon learning that she was Cuban asked her whether she was from Fidel's Cuba or Miami's Cuba. With her characteristic wit, thoughtfulness, and respect even for the most absurd questions, Sánchez replied: "*Chico*, I am a José Martí Cuban."[24]

Conclusion

Rewinding the Threads in the Labyrinth

To find my way out of the labyrinth of the Cuban Revolution, I once again grab hold of the seven threads I unwound while trekking through its tortuous passages: "the pendular revolution," "the art of triangulation," "the revolution's third man," "the longest ninety miles," "an island on horseback," "the persistent plantation," and "many Cubas."

While making predictions about Cuba's future has proven to be a treacherous endeavor, best left to pundits and practitioners of more prophetic disciplines, the historian's perspective allows us to turn toward the future the same telescopes that we normally point to the past. In these concluding pages I discuss ways in which Cuba's history can provide tentative answers to key matters such as possible ideological shifts; the future of Cuba-U.S. relations; the possibilities for a civilian or combined civilian-military rule; the likelihood of the end of "the persistent plantation," both as economic anchor and a trope for Cuban society; and future relations among different cohorts of the Cuban diaspora.

The Pendular Revolution

Thus far, during the first thirteen years of the new millennium, the revolution has gone through two pendular swings: a partial ideological return to idealist visions (officially called "the battle of ideas") while Fidel Castro remained in power and later, a pragmatist swing led by Raúl Castro since 2007.

While the historical trajectory of the revolution has demonstrated that it is virtually impossible to forecast the next cycle or pendular shift, an inverted telescope makes it hard even to envision another shift. In the past, these ideological swings were directed, even if reluctantly, by Fidel Castro. His retirement from power marked the passing of the last of the "idealists"—those who were able to impose another swing toward idealism—and it is hard to conceive of Raúl Castro or anyone else leading another swing back to an idealist cycle. The ideologically fatigued population seems unlikely to reembrace ideological idealism anytime soon. Guevara's idealism will certainly be remembered, but no high priest is likely to resurrect his cult anytime soon.

The Art of Triangulation

Fidel Castro has vanished gradually and no longer has the power to apply the triangulation strategies he used so successfully throughout his life. During the struggle against Batista, he strategically pitted opposition organizations against one other and likewise pitted factions against each other within his own M-26-July. Once in power he pursued triangulation strategies to divide the various political and revolutionary organizations, He even created the ostensibly unifying ORI to eliminate two of its member organizations, the DR and the M-26-7. Once the PSP was the only standing political organization, he pitted its different factions against each other until only communist Fidelistas remained standing. Since then, he has pitted various communist factions against one another, be it idealists against pragmatists, civilians against the military, or reformists against hard-liners, and with the help of infiltrators has pitted dissidents against dissidents. Triangulation proved useful in the global context as well; he successfully pitted island residents against exiles, exiles against other exiles, nations against nations, and, incredibly, superpowers against other superpowers.

Fidel Castro's legacy of triangulation strategies has survived his rule and may have well become part of the island's political culture. Raúl Castro's regime has carried out triangulation strategies of its own but on a much smaller scale, creating counter-bloggers to battle independent bloggers and supporting pro-government rappers to counterbalance the acerbic criticism of independent rappers—nothing raising to the level of pitting Chairman Mao against Premier Khrushchev.

The Longest Ninety Miles

The combination of geographic proximity and fundamentally antagonistic social and cultural values that helps explain the acrimonious rift between Cuba and the United States also helps us understand the roles successive U.S. governments have played as they sought to sabotage, decapitate, isolate, "blockade," and otherwise annihilate the Cuban state and its economy. The combination also explains Cuba's trenchant defiance of U.S. designs through a buildup of its military, UN resolutions, propaganda, espionage, and even the downing of two Brothers to the Rescue planes in 1996. It is also a key to understanding the failure to achieve a rapprochement even under the most propitious of contexts—the Carter years and the ascendance of Obama to the presidency in 2009. The most vocal and visible leaders of the exile community have most certainly played a major role in lengthening the distance between the rebel island and its colossal neighbor to the North.

In spite of numerous positive signals from Raúl Castro's Cuba, Obama continues to contend with the increasingly conservative and bellicose positions of some members of Congress. For the time being, Obama lacks the congressional votes and political capital to shorten the proverbial ninety miles. The facts that Venezuela's ruling Chavista movement is gradually losing popular support and its economy began spiraling into ruin in 2013 and the U.S. electorate renewed Obama's mandate has opened a window of opportunity for the United States to improve relations with Cuba and exert a positive influence over the process of change.

"The long ninety miles" are likely to be shortened if and when the U.S. government stops its centuries-long treatment of Cubans as inferior, child-like, incapable of self-rule and undeserving of full sovereignty and territorial integrity. Whatever the outcome, Cuba and the United States will remain close neighbors and will have to contend with that inescapable reality.

One of the great ironies of the revolution is that despite all the headaches the Castro regimes have given to eleven U.S. presidents, from Eisenhower to Obama, they have delivered what the United States always wanted most: a socially and politically stable neighbor. This fact alone may help understand the mystery of the Castros' longevity in power.

In light of China's global rise and its growing economic and political influence throughout Latin America and the Caribbean, the intransigence

Figure C.1. Habaneros gaze at a Russian destroyer docked in the port of Havana, 2013. Courtesy of AP.

of the United States and its failure to engage Cuba in a dialogue toward a rapprochement may prove to be fatal mistakes, eerily reminiscent of the ones the Eisenhower-Nixon administration made in those crucial few weeks in 1959 between the rebel victory and Cuba's embrace of the Soviet Union as its new patron state. China's continuing ascendance as a global economic and military power is likely to enhance Chinese strategic interests in Cuba and will likely translate into a stronger China-Cuba alliance, perhaps similar to the one Cuba and the Soviet Union had for over three decades. For the foreseeable future, Cuba *"tiene un chino detrás"* (has a Chinese man behind), as a popular Cuban saying goes.

Symbolic of the major consequences of the Republican-dominated U.S. Congress's failure to support even the mildest of Obama's attempts to improve relations with Cuba was the early August 2013 arrival in Havana of three Russian warships, including the guided missile cruiser *Moskva* and the destroyer *Kulakov* (figure C.1). This friendly visit happened on the heels of the capture by Panamanian authorities of a North Korean vessel laden with antiquated Soviet-era Cuban weapons. The cargo, which violated the UN-imposed weapons embargo against North Korea, was sugarcoated—quite literally, as sacks of Cuban sugar covered the hidden weapons. In December 2013, Russia forgave Cuba $29 billion of the debt it had accumulated during the Soviet Era; that amount represented 90 percent of the total Cuba owed the Russians.[1]

The Revolution's Third Man

Between 1959 and 2013, Cuba has had six "third men," some of whom actually earned that position on the battlefields, like Guevara, and others who earned it behind desks. Some held that distinction de jure, as Ramiro Valdés has done since 2008, and those who served before 1976 were all de facto third men. Some were long lasting, Carlos Rafael Rodríguez being the most enduring, while Carlos Aldama was just a flash in the pan.

There have also been numerous pretenders and third men in waiting: Aníbal Escalante in the 1960s; Ricardo Alarcón during the 1970s; and two extraordinarily popular ones during the 1980s—one civilian, Roberto Robaina, the other, man on horseback Arnaldo Ochoa; and Fidel Castro's protégé Felipe Pérez Roque, among others, in the 1990s.

As demonstrated throughout this book, the ascension or demotion of Cuba's third men has been a reliable barometer of shifting ideological winds; they have signaled or confirmed new ideological shifts.

In February 2013, Raúl Castro selected Miguel Díaz-Canel as his constitutional successor. He was not a second man in waiting or even a third; actually he was not even in the radar of analysts around the world. He is not the strong, bigger-than-life leader that Cubans have become accustomed to following and obeying. That said, if his early public statements are any indication of the role he wishes to play, he seems poised to be the voice for a top-down loosening of rigid government control of education, the media, and information disseminated through social media. For example, he has said that the state's attempt to control electronic communications is "an almost impossible illusion. It makes no sense."[2] Curiously, third man Valdés has led efforts to curtail access to the Internet and various social media.

The Persistent Plantation

This thread proved most useful as I navigated in and out of the labyrinth of revolutionary Cuba. Fidel Castro, like many others before him, recognized the sugar socioeconomic complex as the primary reason for many of Cuba's ills. As discussed early in this book, after a failed attempt to rid Cuba of the sugar virus, the revolution relapsed back to it, first as a temporary generator of capital and later as the economy's long-term strategy.

The evil concomitants of the plantation that have been evident since the early 1600s have manifested themselves during the revolutionary era: concentration of land (sugar estates were not broken down but were turned into state-controlled latifundia); coerced forms of labor (the use of so-called volunteers and military conscripts and the establishment of forced labor camps); dependence on outside markets (the Soviet Union, Venezuela, and China); dependence on expensive, imported technology (Hungarian buses and Chinese trains); a reliance on imported food (Soviet grain, Vietnamese rice, and U.S. beans); ecological degradation; the formation of a sugar oligarchy that combined economic and political power (the revolutionary elite); and an authoritarian regime to maintain order, with the Castros as supreme planters and a string of replaceable overseers. "The persistent plantation" even generated its share of runaways who were marooned at the margins of society or settled in the fortified *palenque* that Miami has become.

Somewhat unexpectedly, in 2002, Fidel Castro ordered the gradual dismantling of the sugar industry. Nine years later, his brother shut down the Ministry of Sugar and replaced it with the state firm Azcuba, which in 2012 signed an agreement with a Brazilian corporation that allowed it to implement new technologies and to manage one of Azcuba's fifty-six plants. Brazil has since become the leading exporter of sugar to Cuba. A prosperous Brazil, meanwhile started "importing" doctors from an impoverished Cuba in mid-2013. By December, 5,400 Cuban doctors were practicing in Brazil, and Cuba was receiving around $4,300 per physician per month.[3]

In spite of these changes, the plantation's manifold curses continue to haunt Cuba long after most of its grinding mills have gone silent and the seductive aroma of molasses no longer permeates the countryside. Indeed, the echoes of authoritarian captains-general, aristocratic powdered wigs, colonial militia rifles, and cracking whips from a bygone era continue to haunt history's most splendid sugar island. This was vividly played out in the 2008 exchange between a descendant of great landowners, Ricardo Alarcón de Quesada, and a descendant of cane cutters, Eliécer Ávila. In the persistent counter-plantation tradition, Eliécer raised his microphone-shaped machete against Don Alarcón de Quesada. Five years later, Alarcón was forced out of the National Assembly and Ávila fulfilled his dream of traveling abroad. As long as the Cuban plantation persists, the counter-plantation will exist.

While the importance of sugar has subsided, Cuba remains one of only four nations ruled by communist parties; the other three (China, Laos, and Vietnam) have endured millennia of Oriental despotism. Arguably, the only vestiges of communism that they retain are repressive and authoritarian rule. Cuba appears to be moving that way. But with Cuba, one never really knows.

An Island on Horseback

Cuba's colonial heritage as a key military stronghold, its decades-long armed struggles for independence from Spain, the political-military caudilloism that characterized much of the first half of the twentieth century, and its revolutionary militarism since the late 1950s have produced and maintained a culture that venerates strong leaders and rule by military men. Since its independence from Spain in 1898, Cuba has been ruled by U.S. military occupation in 1898–1902, 1906–9, and 1912 and by home-grown dictators from 1928 to 1933 (Gerardo Machado), from 1934 to 1940 (Batista), from 1952 to 1958 (Batista again), from 1959 to 2007 (Fidel Castro), and since 2008 (Raúl Castro). That is eighty years of military or authoritarian rule out of 115 years for the period 1898–2013.

Up until 2013, when 52-year-old civilian and party loyalist Miguel Díaz-Canel became vice-president, Cuba's top three leaders, President Raúl Castro and Vice-Presidents José Ramón Machado Ventura, and Ramiro Valdés, were octogenarian, career military men who were leaders of the original rebel army. Raúl Castro, Valdés, and Fidel Castro are the last remaining survivors of the nucleus of guerrillas that landed in Oriente from the *Granma* in 1956.

At the moment, Raúl Castro appears to be the only one capable of maintaining unchallenged political control for an extended period of time. His leadership over the FAR provides strong assurances that the military will not move to depose him. There is too much at stake for Cuba's military brass and loyalty to Raúl Castro appears to offer the best guarantees of the preservation of the social and economic privileges of the highest-ranking military brass. Raúl Castro also offers the best possibility of a peaceful, gradual transition that is controlled from above and, by the same token, the best insurance against a chaotic, violent, and unpredictable transition.

All this said, Cuba is not doomed to eternal authoritarian rule by men on horseback. Other nations—Japan after World War II, Spain since 1975, and the Dominican Republic since 1978, to name but three—have demonstrated that sustained, democratic, civilian rule is possible following decades, if not centuries, of despotism and military rule.

A new breed of women and men are now galloping through Cuba and around the world, a Yoani Sanchez, for example, darting through Havana's brick-and-concrete *manigua* atop what Ramiro Valdés appropriately identified as the "wild colt of new technologies," and the rap band Los Aldeanos, brandishing tongues as sharp as Maceo's fabled saber was, machine-gunning untruths with words rather than bullets to the rallying cry "Rap Is War."

Many Cubas

The 1950s rebellion and the ensuing revolution drew much of their energy from differences and tensions between two Cubas: a predominantly white, more affluent Cuba and a multiracial, poorer Cuba. As discussed in this book, the revolution that strove to eradicate differences between the "two Cubas" succeeded at this task, in part, by pushing one of them away, toward exile in South Florida and beyond. Earlier cohorts of immigrants, generally speaking, have subordinated subsequent cohorts socially, thus recreating a highly hierarchical Cuba outside the island. Indeed, first-cohort exiles and their descendants constitute Cuban South Florida's upper, middle-upper, and middle classes; Mariel cohort exiles make up the middle and lower-middle class; and *balsero*-generation immigrants generally constitute the lower classes.

As demonstrated in previous chapters, the ideological and political-cultural distance between island Cuba and exile Cuba have increased over the decades. This has become painfully evident in Miami, where the values, ethics, and worldviews of recent immigrants clash with those of older waves of immigrants and their Cuban American descendants. Such class and cultural divides, as manifested among exile and émigré cohorts, would also hinder the reintegration of established Miami-based Cubans into island society if the opportunity for return migration were to arise.

There are rays of hope in the horizon, nonetheless, as is evidenced by the transnational character of the *balsero* cohort, whose members regularly ferry between the insula and the peninsula, and by conciliatory actions among Miami's exile groups, who set their differences aside to jointly welcome Yoani Sánchez in April 2013. At the Freedom Tower, she closed her speech with a call for all Cubans from all Cubas to unify: "In the Cuba that many of us dream about, there will be no need to clarify what kind of Cubans we are. We will be Cubans, plain and simple. Cubans. Period. Cubans."[4]

Epilogue

You Are My Friend

In 2001, my now-deceased father, Celestino Martínez Lindín, visited Cuba for the first time in almost fifty years. Among the hundreds of photographs that he took during that trip, one stands out as my favorite; it portrays a Cienfuegos Province *guajiro* family of modest means and their *bohío* home. The family graciously posed for my father. Before leaving, my father offered a $10 bill to the family son, who must have been around ten years old at the time. The boy's reply astonished my father: "No. I cannot accept this; you are my friend." A beautiful story behind a beautiful picture; it speaks of the resilience of long-held Cuban values—hospitality, friendliness, generosity, honor, and pride—and gives me a sliver of hope that in the future the two Cubas—the many Cubas—may become one again—one, arguably, for the first time.

Figure E.1. A *guajiro* family, Cienfuegos Province, 2001. Photograph by Celestino Martínez Lindín.

Notes

Introduction

1. Fidel Castro's speech to mark the twentieth anniversary of the proclamation of the socialist nature of the Cuban Revolution, April 16, 1981, Castro Speech Database, Latin American Network Information Center, University of Texas at Austin (hereafter cited as Castro Speech Database), http://lanic.utexas.edu/project/castro/db/1981/19810417.html, accessed May 15, 2013.

2. Emilio Morales, "2.6 Billion in Remittances in 2012," Havana Times Web site, http://www.havanatimes.org/?p=94444, accessed December 29, 2013.

3. Franqui, *Diary of the Cuban Revolution*, vii.

4. See, for example, Mesa-Lago, *Cuba in the 1970s*.

5. Amaro and Portes, "Una sociología del exilio"; Eckstein, "The Clash between Cuban Immigrant Cohorts," 130; Eckstein, *The Immigrant Divide*, 2–5, 89, 142; Alejandro Portes, "A Bifurcated Enclave: The Peculiar Evolution of the Cuban Immigrant Population in the Last Decades," keynote address, Cuban Research Institute, Florida International University, Ninth Conference on Cuban and Cuban-American Studies, May 23–25, 2013.

6. The first cohort included three genealogical generations (parents, children, and grandparents) who shared common sociopolitical values and beliefs. It was an immigrant group that was balanced in terms of gender. The latter two cohorts, by contrast, were dominated by young, single men.

7. Martínez-Fernández, "Trauma and Conflict."

8. Guerra y Sánchez, *Azúcar y población en las Antillas*; Ortiz, *Cuban Counterpoint*; Williams, *From Columbus to Castro*, 28–29.

Chapter 1. History Will Absolve Me

1. Francis L. McCarthy, "Historia de una revolución," *Bohemia*, March 30, 1952, 66–68; Desnoes, *La sierra y el llano*, 10–23.

2. Cuza Malé, "The Photogenic Ones," 64–65.

3. Anderson, *Che Guevara*, 345. Ameringer, *The Cuban Democratic Experience*, 177–78; Franqui, *Diary of the Cuban Revolution*, 503. Estimate of $90 million by the British ambassador to Cuba, cited in Paterson, *Contesting Castro*, 26.

4. For information on Batista's life until 1944, consult Argote-Freyre, *Fulgencio Batista*.

5. The new regime's top brass included longtime Batista loyalists Francisco Tabernilla Dolz, chairman of the Joint Chiefs of Staff; Rafael Salas Cañizares, chief of the National Police; and several other members of the interwoven Tabernilla and Cañizares clans. See Domínguez, "The Batista Regime in Cuba," 121; López Vilaboy, *Motivos y culpables de la destrucción de Cuba*, 273; García-Pérez, *Insurrection and Revolution*, 7–8.

6. García-Pérez, *Insurrection and Revolution*, 34; Dorschner and Fabricio, *The Winds of December*, 65–66; Bonachea and San Martín, *The Cuban Insurrection*, 31–34.

7. Ameringer, *The Cuban Democratic Experience*, 179; Karol, *Guerrillas in Power*, 126. Cuba was by far the world's largest producer of sugar; in 1953, it produced around 13 percent of the world's sugar, including cane and beet sugar.

8. The CTC's control over labor actions was limited. Workers struck often and burned cane fields in protest. García-Pérez, *Insurrection and Revolution*, 54–56, 67, 76; Bonachea and San Martín, *The Cuban Insurrection*, 56–60; Sims, "Cuban Labor and the Communist Party," 52–53; Sweig, *Inside the Cuban Revolution*, 123; Alexander, *History of Organized Labor*, 138, 151.

9. Paterson, *Contesting Castro*, 45; Schoultz, *That Little Infernal Republic*, 94. Photograph in Hart, *Aldabonazo*, between 238 and 239.

10. Franqui, *Diary of the Cuban Revolution*, 47; Oltuski, *Vida Clandestina*, 20; Llerena, *The Unsuspected Revolution*, 50–51.

11. Triple A leaders included Menelao Mora, Raúl Roa, Reynold García, César Lancís, and Faure Chomón. Morán Arce, *La revolución cubana*, 27; Bonachea and San Martín, *The Cuban Insurrection*, 15, 30.

12. Guerra, *Visions of Power in Cuba*, 53–54.

13. Argote-Freyre, *Fulgencio Batista*, 5–13; Ramonet and Castro, *Fidel Castro*, 48–49; Latell, *After Fidel*, 29; Pardo Llada, *Fidel y el "Che,"* 10–11.

14. De la Cova, *The Moncada Attack*, 7. Biographies of Fidel Castro abound. See, for example, Szulc, *Fidel*; and Quirk, *Fidel Castro*. See also Castro, "Comentarios de infancia y juventud"; Ramonet and Castro, *Fidel Castro*, 43–98; Latell, *After Fidel*, 36; and Symmes, *The Boys from Dolores*.

15. Bonachea and San Martín, *The Cuban Insurrection*, 13; Pardo Llada, *Fidel y el "Che,"* 35–38, 41; de la Cova, *The Moncada Attack*, 19, 26; "Memorandum for the Files," based on information provided by Manuel Márquez-Sterling y Domínguez, U.S. Embassy in Havana, January 2, 1958; Paul Wolf, "Gringos in the Revolution: North Americans in the Cuban Revolution," http://archive.is/51UOK, accessed November 21, 2013; Daniel M. Braddock, deputy chief of mission, "Biographic Information on Fidel Castro and Raúl Castro," confidential document dated July 28, 1960, in Wolf, "Gringos in the Revolution," http://archive.is/51UOK, accessed November 21, 2013. See also Latell, *After Fidel*, 116–17; Latell, *Castro's Secrets*, 44–46.

16. De la Cova, *The Moncada Attack*, 9; Symmes, *The Boys from Dolores*, 287.

17. Matthews, *Fidel Castro*, 173.

18. De la Cova, *The Moncada Attack*; *Veintiséis*; Castro, "Relato de Fidel," 41–47.

19. Franqui, *Diary of the Cuban Revolution*, 89; Ramonet and Castro, *Fidel Castro*, 132; Ruby Hart Phillips, "Fifty-Five Reported Killed in Cuban Rebellion," *New York Times*, July 27, 1953; de la Cova, *The Moncada Attack*, 37–38.

20. De la Cova, *The Moncada Attack*, 121–37; *Veintiséis*.

21. Franqui, *Diary of the Cuban Revolution*, 61; *Veintiséis*, 7–10, 70–71, 121; Karol, *Guerrillas in Power*, 134; Álvarez, *Frank País*, 37. De la Cova claims that only sixty-one rebels were killed and that reports of torture were exaggerated. See *The Moncada Attack*, 201, 173.

22. Castro, *History Will Absolve Me*, 83.

23. Sweig, *Inside the Cuban Revolution*, 22; Bonachea and San Martín, *The Cuban Insurrection*, 61.

24. Castro quoted in Franqui, *Diary of the Cuban Revolution*, 96; Llerena, *The Unsuspected Revolution*, 63; Castro's speech of August 15, 1953 in Castro, *Revolutionary Struggle*, 276.

25. The DR's top leadership included José Antonio Echeverría, René Anillo, Juan Pedro Carbó Serviá, Rolando Cubela, Faure Chomón, José Naranjo, Fructuoso Rodríguez, and Joe Westbrook. See Bonachea and San Martín, *The Cuban Insurrection*, 42–43; and Morán Arce, *La revolución cubana*, 35. In *Revolution and Reaction in Cuba*, Samuel Farber examines the historical connections between the 1930s revolutionary ferment and opposition to Batista during the 1950s.

26. Thomas, *The Cuban Revolution*, 90; Bonachea and San Martín, *The Cuban Insurrection*, 69–71.

27. Barquín, *Las luchas guerrilleras en Cuba*, 2:165–70; Lieutenant Colonel J. E. Treadway to Mr. Chapin, July 31, 1956, in Wolf, "Gringos in the Revolution," http://archive.is/51UOK, accessed November 21, 2013.

28. "Eleventh Body in a Mystery," *Life*, May 21, 1956, 55; López Vilaboy, *Motivos y culpables de la destrucción de Cuba*, 281; Military Intelligence Chief Carlos M. Cantillo to the minister of state, August 5, 1957, in Wolf, "Gringos in the Revolution," http://archive.is/51UOK, accessed November 21, 2013.

29. Bonachea and San Martín, *The Cuban Insurrection*, 73; memo from John L. Topping, Havana Embassy, to the U.S. Department of State on the assassination of Colonel Antonio Blanco Rico, November 2, 1956, in Wolf, "Gringos in the Revolution," http://archive.is/51UOK, accessed November 21, 2013. See also Llerena, *The Unsuspected Revolution*, 64; García-Pérez, *Insurrection and Revolution*, 26; and Franqui, *Diary of the Cuban Revolution*, 113.

30. There are several fine biographies of Guevara. See, for example, Castañeda, *Compañero*; Anderson, *Che Guevara*; Dosal, *Comandante Che*; Guevara, *Motorcycle Diaries*; Guevara, *Obras, 1957–1967*; and Guevara, *Reminiscences of the Cuban Revolutionary War*.

31. Pérez, "De Tuxpán a las Coloradas"; Bonachea and San Martín, *The Cuban Insurrection*, 78; Álvarez, *Frank País*, 104; Morán Arce, *La revolución cubana*, 48–49.

32. Bonachea and San Martín, *The Cuban Insurrection*, 79–83; Suárez, "The Cuban Revolution," 12; Dosal, *Comandante Che*, 16.

33. Pérez, "De Tuxpán a las Coloradas," 80; Franqui, *Camilo Cienfuegos*, 78.

34. "Cuba Wipes Out Invaders: Leader Is among 40 Dead," *New York Times*, December 3, 1956; Guevara, *Obras*, 1:197–207; Suárez, "The Cuban Revolution," 12; Franqui, *Cuba, la revolución*, 9; Franqui, *Cuba: el libro de los doce*.

35. Álvarez, *Frank País*, 171–76; Raúl Estrada Zamora, "Las Pascuas sangrientas," tiempo21 Web site, December 23, 2008, http://www.tiempo21.icrt.cu/lectura/

diciembre08/horrendo_crimen_pascuas_sangrientas_cuba_081223.htm,accessed November 12, 2013.

36. Morán Arce, *La revolución cubana*, 18; Macaulay, "The Cuban Rebel Army," 289.

37. Coltman, *The Real Fidel Castro*, 121.

38. For a fine discussion of this subject, see Sweig, *Inside the Cuban Revolution*.

39. Draper, *Castro's Revolution*, 171; Bonachea and San Martín, *The Cuban Insurrection*, 93, 161–62.

40. Guevara, "Combate en la Plata," 87–94; Franqui, *Diary of the Cuban Revolution*, 134.

41. See three *New York Times* articles by Herbert L. Matthews: "Cuban Rebel Is Visited in Hideout," February 24, 1957; "Old Order in Cuba Is Threatened by Forces of an Internal Revolt," February 26, 1957; and "Rebel Strength Gaining in Cuba, but Batista Has Upper Hand," February 25, 1957. See also DePalma, *The Man Who Invented Fidel*; and Morán Arce, *La revolución cubana*, 67. The *National Review* criticized the role of Matthews and the *New York Times* through an editorial cartoon of Castro with the caption "I got my job through the *New York Times*," which was the newspaper's slogan for the jobs section of its classified ads. See *National Review*, May 7, 1960, 289.

42. Letters País wrote to Fidel Castro exhibit a commanding rather than a requesting tone. See Suárez, "The Cuban Revolution," 15; Franqui, *Diary of the Cuban Revolution*, 186–87, 196–99, 202–10, 212–13; Farber, *The Origins of the Cuban Revolution Reconsidered*, 67; and Sweig, *Inside the Cuban Revolution*, 15–16.

43. Suárez, "The Cuban Revolution," 15; Álvarez, *Frank País*, 90.

44. Castro to Sánchez, July 5, 1957, in Franqui, *Diary of the Cuban Revolution*, 190–92.

45. Chomón, "El ataque al Palacio Presidencial," 97–136; Rodríguez Loeches, "El crimen de Humboldt 7," 139–55; Ruby Hart Phillips, "Cuba Recovering from Brief Rising," *New York Times*, March 15, 1957; Álvarez, *Frank País*, 110; Bonachea and San Martín, *The Cuban Insurrection*, 107; Guerra, *Visions of Power in Cuba*, 15.

46. Oltuski, *Vida Clandestina*, 164; Morán Arce, *La revolución cubana*, 197.

47. "Los mártires del Corynthia," *Revolución*, May 27, 1961; Morán Arce, *La revolución cubana*, 102–3; Bonachea and San Martín, *The Cuban Insurrection*, 134–37.

48. Sweig, *Inside the Cuban Revolution*, chapter 2; Franqui, *Diary of the Cuban Revolution*, 216–17.

49. País to Castro, July 26, 1957, in Franqui, *Diary of the Cuban Revolution*, 212–13; García-Pérez, *Insurrection and Revolution*, 90–91; Álvarez, *Frank País*, 1, 225–26, 238, 242.

50. In Franqui, *Diary of the Cuban Revolution*, see Castro to Sánchez, August 11 and 14, 1957, 220–21, 223; Ramos Latour to Castro, September 15, 1957, 229–31; Castro to M-26-7 leaders in Santiago, January 13, 1958, 279–80; Hart to Castro, October 16, 1957, 239–40; Hart to Sánchez, December 6, 1957, 262–64; and Castro to the National Directorate, December 14, 1957, 265–67. See also Morán Arce, *La revolución cubana*, 165, 172.

51. Farber, *The Origins of the Cuban Revolution Reconsidered*, 120; Sweig, *Inside the Cuban Revolution*, 64–65; Álvarez, *Principio y fin del mito fidelista*, 188–92; Castro to the Junta de Liberación Cubana, December 14, 1957, in Castro, *Revolutionary Struggle*, 351–63. In Franqui, *Diary of the Cuban Revolution*, see Ramos Latour to Guevara, December

19, 1957, 272–76; Ramos Latour to Castro, November 4 and 9, 1957, 244–47; Guevara to Ramos Latour, December 14, 1957, 268–70; Raúl Castro to Fidel Castro, November 20, 1957, 248–50.

52. Guevara to Ramos Latour, December 14, 1957, and Ramos Latour to Guevara, December 19, 1957, in Franqui, *Diary of the Cuban Revolution*, 268–70 and 272–76, respectively.

53. Ruiz, *Cuba*, 14; Karol, *Guerrillas in Power*, 139.

54. Andrew St. George, "Cuban Rebels," *Look*, February 4, 1958, 30; Castro, "Why We Fight," *Coronet*, February 1, 1958, in Castro, *Revolutionary Struggle*, 364–67, 369–71.

55. Ruby Hart Phillips, "Cuba Is Thriving on Dearer Sugar: Economic Expansion Goes on Despite Uprising," *New York Times*, January 8, 1958, 49; Domínguez, *Cuba*, 121.

56. Castro, *Revolutionary Struggle*, 367; Franqui, *Diary of the Cuban Revolution*, 261.

57. Paterson, *Contesting Castro*, 127; "Galería de asesinos," *Bohemia*, January 11, 1959, 152–58.

58. Schoultz, *That Little Infernal Republic*, 74–75; Llerena, *The Unsuspected Revolution*, 175; Barquín, *Las luchas guerrilleras en Cuba*, 2:530.

59. Pérez-Stable, *The Cuban Revolution*, 55; Draper, *Castro's Revolution*, 13; Morán Arce, *La revolución cubana*, 217–22.

60. Bonachea and San Martín, *The Cuban Insurrection*, 221–22; Buch Rodríguez, *Gobierno revolucionario cubano*, 17–21; Sweig, *Inside the Cuban Revolution*, 148–53; Guevara, *Obras*, 1:392–93.

61. Álvarez, *Frank País*, 261.

62. Guevara, *Obras*, 1:349; Macaulay, "The Cuban Rebel Army," 290.

63. Guevara, *Obras*, 1:348; Raúl Castro's report to Fidel Castro, April 20, 1958, in Desnoes, *La sierra y el llano*, 201–51; Franqui, *Diary of the Cuban Revolution*, 404; Franqui, *Retrato de familia con Fidel*, 24; Macaulay, "The Cuban Rebel Army"; Shayne, *The Revolution Question*, 120–21.

64. Macaulay, "The Cuban Rebel Army," 289.

65. Morán Arce, *La revolución cubana*, 111.

66. "Report on the Offensive: Part 1, August 18, 1958," in Castro, *Revolutionary Struggle*, 399–408.

67. Telegram of Ambassador Earl E. T. Smith to U.S. secretary of state, June 29, 1958, in Wolf, "Gringos in the Revolution," http://archive.is/51UOK, accessed November 21, 2013; Llerena, *The Unsuspected Revolution*, 246.

68. "Manifesto Broadcast by Rebel Radio on July 20, 1958," in Castro, *Revolutionary Struggle*, 386–89. This manifesto is also known as the Caracas Pact. See also Sweig, *Inside the Cuban Revolution*, 12; and Morán Arce, *La revolución cubana*, 270.

69. Oltuski, *Vida Clandestina*, 169; Guevara, *Obras*, 1:399–406; Morán Arce, *La revolución cubana*, 282.

70. Castañeda, *Compañero*, 126; Trento, *Castro and Cuba*, 27–28; Cushion, "The Most Expensive Port in the World," 10.

71. The first formal contacts between the M-26-7 and the PSP took place in late 1957, when communist leader Ursino Rojas traveled to the Sierra Maestra; Castañeda, *Compañero*, 116; Llerena, *The Unsuspected Revolution*, 201; Suárez, "The Cuban Revolution,"

18; Morán Arce, *La revolución cubana*, 272; Rodríguez quoted in Sims, "Cuban Labor and the Communist Party," 55. The assessment of the U.S. State Department was that communist infiltration had taken place but the extent of it could not be determined; Christian Herter to the State Department, January 1, 1959, in Wolf, "Gringos in the Revolution, http://archive.is/51UOK, accessed November 21, 2013.

72. Franqui, *Camilo Cienfuegos*, 90; Guevara, *Obras*, 1:28.

73. Franqui, *Camilo Cienfuegos*, 96–99; Dorschner and Fabricio, *The Winds of December*, 319–32; Macaulay, "The Cuban Rebel Army," 293.

74. Morley, "U.S. Imperial State in Cuba," 163–66; Schoultz, *That Little Infernal Republic*, 80; "Threat by Castro on Vote Explained," *New York Times*, October 15, 1958.

75. Paterson, *Contesting Castro*, 206–11; Smith, *The Fourth Floor*, 170; Blasier, "The Elimination of United States Influence," 48; Morán Arce, *La revolución cubana*, 294; Dorschner and Fabricio, *The Winds of December*, 159.

76. Ambassador Smith stated that on December 26 he had a meeting with Tabernilla, who offered to lead a transition military junta. Discussion between Arthur Gardner and Earl E. T. Smith (1960), in Smith, *What Happened in Cuba*, 275.

77. Smith, *The Fourth Floor*, 186; Dorschner and Fabricio, *The Winds of December*, 385, 395, 419; Raimundo, *Habla el Coronel Orlando Piedra*, 57.

78. Novas, *Everything You Need to Know about Latino History*, 182; Anderson, *Che Guevara*, 368.

79. Masud-Piloto, *With Open Arms*, 20; Pérez, *Cuba and the United States*, 219–20; Morley, "U.S. Imperial State in Cuba."

80. Marrero, *Cuba en la década de 1950*, 22, 36, 46. For an excellent assessment of the Cuban economy in the 1950s, see Baklanoff, "A Bountiful Legacy."

81. Marrero, *Cuba en la década de 1950*, 17; Gott, *Cuba*, 165; Conde, *Operation Pedro Pan*, 230–31; Guerra, *Visions of Power in Cuba*, 41–42; "Socio-Economic Conditions in Pre-Castro Cuba," *Cuba Facts* 43 (December 2008), http://ctp.iccas.miami.edu/FACTS_Web/Cuba%20Facts%20Issue%2043%20December.htm, accessed May 30, 2013.

82. Pérez, *On Becoming Cuban*, 451–58; Ibarra, *Prologue to Revolution*, 176; Llerena, *The Unsuspected Revolution*, 250; Franqui, *Camilo Cienfuegos*, 37.

83. Ameringer, *The Cuban Democratic Experience*, 169; María R. de Fontanills and Eduardo Fontanills, *Directorio social de La Habana, 1959*, 32–34, in "Government of Cuba, 1958," document 0221a, Cuban Information Archives Web site, http://cuban-exile.com/doc_201-225/doc0221a.html, accessed May 30, 2013.

84. Novas, *Everything You Need to Know about Latino History*, 183; Ubell, "High-Tech Medicine in the Caribbean," 1469; Guerra, *Visions of Power in Cuba*, 50.

85. U.S. Department of Agriculture, Office of Global Analysis, Foreign Agriculture Service, "Cuba's Food & Agriculture Situation Report," March 2008, http://www.fas.usda.gov/itp/cuba/cubasituation0308.pdf, accessed May 30, 2013; Domínguez, *Cuba*, 435; 1957 study by the Association of Catholic University Students quoted in Moreno, "From Traditional to Modern Values."

Chapter 2. Fatherland or Death!

1. Photograph in *Bohemia*, January 11, 1959, 147.

2. Thomas, *The Cuban Revolution*, 247–48; Castañeda, *Compañero*, 133; Barquín, *Las*

luchas guerrilleras en Cuba, 2:870–73; Dorschner and Fabricio, *The Winds of December*, 351, 365.

3. Franqui, *Retrato de familia con Fidel*, 22; Morán Arce, *La revolución cubana*, 300; Franqui, *Diary of the Cuban Revolution*, 504–5; Oltuski, *Vida Clandestina*, 250.

4. *Revolución*, January 7, 1959.

5. Fidel Castro's speech at Camp Columbia, Havana, January 8, 1959, in Cuban Government, Discursos e intervenciones del Comandante en Jefe Fidel Castro Ruz Presidente del Consejo de Estado de la República de Cuba, http://www.cuba.cu/gobierno/discursos/1959/esp/f080159e.html, accessed December 3, 2013; Guerra, *Visions of Power in Cuba*, 152–53; Valdés, "La Cachita y el Che." For actual footage of doves being pushed toward Castro, see "Entrada triunfal de Fidel Castro y Che Guevara a la Habana," http://www.youtube.com/watch?v=56Q8zXgR2HQ, accessed November 18, 2013.

6. Ramonet and Castro, *Fidel Castro*, 682n4.

7. Pérez, *Cuba: Between Reform and Revolution*, 240; Beruvides, *Cuba y su presidio político*, 74–75; Guerra, *Visions of Power in Cuba*, 48.

8. Organización de Estados Americanos, Comisión de Derechos Humanos, "La situación de los derechos humanos en Cuba," Séptimo informe, capítulo 7 (Derecho a la vida), October 4, 1983, http://www.cidh.oas.org/countryrep/Cuba83sp/indice.htm, accessed November 20, 2013; Fidel Castro's speech, October 26, 1959, in Castro, *Fidel Castro Speaks*, 70. The officially reported number of executions during the first half of 1959 was 550, a figure that does not include those killed under Raúl Castro's orders in Oriente. See various estimates in Anderson, *Che Guevara*, 376; Goldenberg, *The Cuban Revolution and Latin America*, 179; Castañeda, *Compañero*, 143; and Franqui, *Retrato de familia con Fidel*, 33.

9. The original cabinet members were Armando Hart (Education), Faustino Pérez (Recovery of Misappropriated Assets), Humberto Sorí Marín (Agriculture), Julio Martínez Páez (Health), Augusto R. Martínez Sánchez (Defense), Luis Orlando Rodríguez (Government), Raúl Cepero Bonilla (Commerce), Manuel Fernández García (Labor), Rufo López-Fresquet (Finance), Ángel Fernández Rodríguez (Justice), Enrique Oltuski (Communications), Julio Camacho Aguilera (Transportation), Osvaldo Dorticós Torrado (Revolutionary Laws), and Luis M. Buch Rodríguez (secretary of the presidency and Council of Ministers). Also holding cabinet-level appointments were Felipe Pazos Roque and Regino Boti, who became president of the National Bank and chair of the National Economic Council, respectively. Buch Rodríguez, *Gobierno revolucionario cubano*, 52–58; Anderson, *Che Guevara*, 341; Draper, *Castro's Revolution*, 43.

10. Dorticós had been a member of the PSP and at one point had served as personal secretary to Juan Marinello. Interestingly, he had also benefited from a generous sinecure from Batista. Goldenberg, *The Cuban Revolution and Latin America*, 188; Bonachea and San Martín, *The Cuban Insurrection*, 150.

11. Deputy Chief of the U.S. Mission in Havana Daniel Bradcock commented that the cabinet was "basically friendly toward the United States and oriented against communism"; Benjamin, *The United States and the Origins of the Cuban Revolution*, 169. Cabinet member Faustino Pérez was a *Granma* veteran but did not belong to Castro's inner circle.

12. Ramonet and Castro, *Fidel Castro*, 223; Szulc, *Fidel*, 463, 472–73.

13. Portell Vilá, *Nueva historia de la República de Cuba*, 756; López-Fresquet, *My Fourteen Months with Castro*, 45; Guerra, *Visions of Power in Cuba*, 60. The new cabinet members were Raúl Roa (State); Moncada veteran Pedro Miret Prieto (Agriculture); Miret Prieto's wife, Raquel Pérez González (Social Welfare); José Naranjo Morales (Government); and Serafín Ruiz Zárate (Health). See "Foreign News: Cuba, Cabinet Split," *Time*, June 22, 1959, 30, http://www.time.com/time/magazine/article/0,9171,937785-1,00.html, accessed May 30, 2013.

14. Castro quoted in Franqui, *Camilo Cienfuegos*, 116.

15. Arboleya, *The Cuban Counterrevolution*, 43.

16. "Abolidos los partidos políticos," *Revolución*, January 7, 1959; Domínguez, *Cuba*, 144, 201; Thomas, *The Cuban Revolution*, 303; "Discurso pronunciado por el comandante Fidel Castro Ruz, primer ministro del gobierno revolucionario, con motivo de conmemorarse el primer aniversario de la huelga del 9 de abril, en la Alameda de Paula, el 9 de abril de 1959" (Castro's speech, April 9, 1959, in commemoration of the first anniversary of the strike of April 1958), http://www.cuba.cu/gobierno/discursos/1959/esp/f090459e.html, accessed December 3, 2013; Pérez-Stable, *The Cuban Revolution*, 77; Speech by Fidel Castro at Havana May Day Celebrations, May 1, 1961, Castro Speech Database,http://lanic.utexas.edu/project/castro/db/1961/19610502.html, accessed November 20, 2013; Thomas, *The Cuban Revolution*, 301–2.

17. Goldenberg, *The Cuban Revolution and Latin America*, 211.

18. López-Fresquet, *My Fourteen Months with Castro*, 97; Pérez, *Cuba: Between Reform and Revolution*, 242.

19. Republic of Cuba, "Ley de reforma urbana de 14 de octubre de 1960," http://www.juridicas.unam.mx/publica/librev/rev/indercom/cont/41/leg/leg8.pdf, accessed December 3, 2013.

20. Dorticós Torrado, *Exposición y divulgación de le Ley de Reforma Agraria*, 3; Núñez Jiménez, *La ley de Reforma Agraria*; and Guerra, *Visions of Power in Cuba*, 60.

21. López-Fresquet, *My Fourteen Months with Castro*, 171–72; Asociación Nacional de Hacendados de Cuba, "Un mensaje de los hombres de la zafra a los gobernantes de la Revolución," *Bohemia*, March 1, 1959, 53–54.

22. Pérez, *Cuba: Between Reform and Revolution*, 245; Núñez Jiménez, *Informe al pueblo en el segundo aniversario de la reforma agraria*, 3–5.

23. Mesa-Lago, "Economic Policies and Growth," 282–83; Amaro and Mesa-Lago, "Inequality and Classes," 359.

24. The CIA director was Allen Dulles, former president of the United Fruit Company. His brother, Secretary of State John Foster Dulles, had previously served as corporate lawyer for the company. Most astonishingly, former CIA director Walter Bedell Smith, at the time undersecretary of state and a United Fruit Company board member, became the company's president following the coup against Arbenz; see Gleijeses, *Shattered Hope*, 235; and interview with Allen Ginsberg, November 8, 1996, in "Make Love, Not War (The Sixties)," *Cold War*, CNN series, episode 13.

25. Castro quoted in "Cuba: Vengeful Visionary," *Time*, January 26, 1959, 40; Farber, *The Origins of the Cuban Revolution Reconsidered*, 79; Arboleya, *The Cuban Counterrevolution*, 4; Szulc, *Fidel*, 480–81.

26. López-Fresquet, *My Fourteen Months with Castro*, 169; Duncan, "Cuba-U.S. Relations and Political Conditions in Cuba," 220; Pérez, *On Becoming Cuban*, 490; Jacobs, "Meeting the Neighbors"; "Memo of Conversation between Vice President Nixon and Fidel Castro," attached to confidential letter from Frank J. Devine to Roy R. Rubottom, April 29, 1959, Latin American Studies Web site, http://www.latinamericanstudies. org/embassy/R25-Nixon-4-29-1959.pdf, accessed November 25, 2013; Memorandum of a Conference between President Eisenhower and the acting U.S. Secretary of State, Augusta, Georgia, April 18, 1959, in U.S. Department of State, *Foreign Relations of the United States, 1958–1960*, vol. 6, *Cuba*, Document 286, available at the Web site of the U.S. Department of State, Office of the Historian, http://history.state.gov/historicaldocuments/frus1958-60v06/d286, accessed November 30, 2013; Nixon quoted in Thomas, *The Cuban Revolution*, 430; "Richard M. Nixon's Memorandum on Meeting with Fidel Castro, April 19, 1959," in Pfeiffer, "Official History of the Bay of Pigs Operation," vol. 3, appendix F.

27. López-Fresquet, *My Fourteen Months with Castro*, 106; Matthews, *Fidel Castro*, 161; Baklanoff, "International Economic Relations," 258–59; Goldenberg, *The Cuban Revolution and Latin America*, 181–82.

28. Jacobs, "Meeting the Neighbors"; Fursenko and Naftali, *"One Hell of a Gamble."*

29. Domínguez, *To Make a World Safe for Revolution*, 23; Latell, *After Fidel*, 7; CIA, "Biographic Register on Che Guevara," August 1964, Office of Central Reference, CIA, http://archive.is/2cQ6B, accessed December 3, 2013; George, *The Cuban Intervention in Angola*, 17–18.

30. Betancourt, "Exporting Revolution to Latin America," 108; "Discurso pronunciado por el comandante Fidel Castro Ruz, primer ministro del gobierno revolucionario, en conmemoración del vii aniversario del 26 de julio, en Las Mercedes, estribaciones de la Sierra Maestra, el 26 de julio de 1960," http://cuba.cu/gobierno/discursos/1960/esp/ f260760e.html, accessed April 20, 2014.

31. "Cuba Nationalizes Yule: Santa Claus Is Banned," *New York Times*, October 8, 1959; *Bohemia*, January 1, 1961, 113.

32. Franqui, *Retrato de familia con Fidel*, 80–81; Portell Vilá, *Nueva historia de la República de Cuba*, 758–59; Quirk, *Fidel Castro*, 249–51; Guerra, *Visions of Power in Cuba*, 68–69, 73–74.

33. Raúl Castro quoted in Franqui, *Retrato de familia con Fidel*, 324; Latell, *After Fidel*, 11; Pfeiffer, "Official History of the Bay of Pigs Operation," 3:43.

34. Open letter of Pedro Luis Díaz Lanz, October 21, 1959, Latin American Studies Web site, http://www.latinamericanstudies.org/cuba/diaz-lanz.pdf, accessed January 14, 2014; Guerra, *Visions of Power in Cuba*, 85. On communists in the military, see Despatch from the U.S. Embassy in Cuba to the Department of State, April 14, 1959, in *Foreign Relations of the United States, 1958–1960*, vol. 6, *Cuba*, Document 278, available at the Web site of the U.S. Department of State, Office of the Historian, http://history. state.gov/historicaldocuments/frus1958-60v06/d278, accessed November 30, 2013.

35. Matos to Castro, October 19, 1959, in Matos, *Cómo llegó la noche*, 575–76, 343–47; Franqui, *Camilo Cienfuegos*, 154, 168, 176–88; Fidel Castro's speech, October 26, 1959, in Castro, *Fidel Castro Speaks*, 70.

36. Guerra, *Visions of Power in Cuba*, 89; Portell Vilá, *Nueva historia de la República de Cuba*, 766, 769–70; "Castro no ordenó muerte de Cienfuegos, dice autor," *El Miami*

Herald, July 27, 1981; "Fidel mató a Camilo, dice Huber Matos," *El Miami Herald*, June 1, 1981.

37. The previous minister of defense, Martínez Sánchez, who had been Raúl Castro's secretary, was reassigned to head the Ministry of Labor. On the sixth, minister of government Luis Orlando Rodríguez was replaced by José A. Naranjo. Key within that ministry was comandante Ramiro Valdés, formerly Guevara's second-in-command. López-Fresquet, a moderate who was actually considered the cabinet's most conservative member, wished to resign but remained as head of the Ministry of Finance until March 1960. Matthews, *Fidel Castro*, 172; Franqui, *Retrato de familia con Fidel*, 109.

38. The old-guard faction also included Blas Roca Calderío, Juan Marinello, and César Escalante. Among the other younger Fidelistas were Leonel Soto-Prieto and Ramón Calcines. Portell Vilá, *Nueva historia de la República de Cuba*, 807; Suárez, *Cuba*, 59, 99, 114.

39. Daniel M. Braddock, "Political Conditions in Cuba," despatch from the Cuban Embassy in Havana to the Department of State, February 25, 1959, Latin American Studies Web site, http://www.latinamericanstudies.org/cuba/cuba2-25-59.htm, accessed November 30, 2013; González, *The Secret Fidel Castro*, 207–8.

40. *Coletilla* quoted in Portell Vilá, *Nueva historia de la República de Cuba*, 752. See also Thomas, *The Cuban Revolution*, 483–85; Goldenberg, *The Cuban Revolution and Latin America*, 180; Llerena, *The Unsuspected Revolution*, 255–56; Suárez, *Cuba*, 230. *Hoy* and *Revolución* merged in 1965, becoming *Granma*, the official organ of the Cuban Communist Party.

41. Goldenberg, *The Cuban Revolution and Latin America*, 205; García, *Havana USA*, 28; Bunck, *Fidel Castro and the Quest for a Revolutionary Culture in Cuba*, 34.

42. Amaro and Mesa-Lago, "Inequality and Classes," 359.

43. Farber, *The Origins of the Cuban Revolution Reconsidered*, 122; Welch, *Response to Revolution*, 6.

44. Before the revolution, 73 percent of the population identified itself as Catholic, but only 25 percent actually practiced the faith. Gómez Treto, *La Iglesia Católica*, 22.

45. Ibid., 35–37, 43–44; "Carta abierta del episcopado al Primer Ministro Dr. Castro, diciembre 4, 1960," http://www.radiomambi.com/iglesia/Carta_Episcopado.html, accessed December 3, 2013; Kirk, *Between God and the Party*, 80–86; Azicri, *Cuba Today and Tomorrow*, 252; Ramos, *Protestantism and Revolution in Cuba*, 68; Guerra, *Visions of Power in Cuba*, 148; de la Fuente, *A Nation for All*, 291–92.

46. Fidel Castro's speech, March 26, 1962, in García Luis, *Cuban Revolution Reader*, 113–21; Suárez, *Cuba*, 148; Thomas, *The Cuban Revolution*, 598–99.

47. Gus Russo and Stephen Molton, "The Sordid History of Cuba's Spy Apparatus," appendix to Russo and Molton, *Brothers in Arms*, Document 0451, Cuba Information Archives Web site, http://cuban-exile.com/doc_451-475/doc0451.html, accessed December 3, 2013. Estimates of political prisoners in López Vilaboy, *Motivos y culpables de la destrucción de Cuba*, 430; Pérez, *Cuba: Between Reform and Revolution*, 252; Anderson, *Che Guevara*, 376; Goldenberg, *The Cuban Revolution and Latin America*, 179. See also Farber, *Cuba since the Revolution*, 222.

48. Speech by Fidel Castro at Havana May Day Celebrations, May 1, 1961, Castro Speech Database, http://lanic.utexas.edu/project/castro/db/1961/19610502.html, accessed December 3, 2013.

49. Domínguez, *Cuba since the Revolution*, 208–9; Bunck, *Fidel Castro and the Quest for a Revolutionary Culture in Cuba*, 92–95; Randall, *Cuban Women Now*, 291–305.

50. Domínguez, *Cuba*, 208–9; Fagen, Brody, and O'Leary, *Cubans in Exile*, 81.

51. Domínguez, *Cuba*, 209.

52. Guevara, *Obras*, 2:132–37; Yafee, *Che Guevara*, 204–5.

53. Bernardo, *The Theory of Moral Incentives in Cuba*, 57; Bunck, *Fidel Castro and the Quest for a Revolutionary Culture in Cuba*, 130; Córdova, *El trabajador cubano*, 98; Liss, *Roots of Revolution*, 166–67.

54. Guevara quoted in Bunck, *Fidel Castro and the Quest for a Revolutionary Culture in Cuba*, 133; Castañeda, *Compañero*, 178, 186.

55. Archibald R. M. Ritter used the term "sucrophobic tradition"; Ritter, *The Economic Development of Revolutionary Cuba*, 129. See also Guevara, *Obras*, 1:411.

56. Guerra y Sánchez, *Azúcar y población en las Antillas*; Ortiz, *Cuban Counterpoint*, 52–54, 61–64.

57. Mesa-Lago, *The Economy of Socialist Cuba*, 17; Ritter, *The Economic Development of Revolutionary Cuba*, 134–35; Pérez-López, *Economics of Cuban Sugar*, 12.

58. Echevarría, "Cuba and the International Sugar Market," 369; Zimbalist and Eckstein, "Patterns of Cuban Development," 8–9; and Turits, "Trade, Debt, and the Cuban Economy," 167.

59. Castañeda, *Compañero*, 213; Paulston, "Education," 386; Bunck, *Fidel Castro and the Quest for a Revolutionary Culture in Cuba*, 94–96.

60. Bunck, *Fidel Castro and the Quest for a Revolutionary Culture in Cuba*, 95; Smith and Padula, *Sex and Revolution*, 37–42; U.S. State Department, "White Paper on Cuba," April 1961, in Smith, *What Happened in Cuba*, 312–26; Randall, *Cuban Women Now*, 13–15.

61. Over half of the alphabetizers had only a primary education; Armando Hart, report on the success of the Alphabetization Campaign, Havana, December 22, 1961, in García Luis, *Cuban Revolution Reader*, 83–87. See also Valdés, "The Radical Transformation of Cuban Education," 426–29; Dahlman, "The Nation-Wide System of Learning in Cuba," 43; Republic of Cuba, Gobierno Revolucionario, Ministerio de Educación, Comisión Nacional de Alfabetización, *¡Venceremos!*; Republic of Cuba, Ejército de Alfabetizadores Brigadas Conrado Benítez, *Cumpliremos!*; Republic of Cuba, Gobierno Revolucionario, Ministerio de Educación, Comisión Nacional de Alfabetización, *Alfabeticemos*.

62. Feinsilver, *Healing the Masses*, 31–32; Mesa-Lago, *The Economy of Socialist Cuba*, 41; Leyva [pseud.], "Health and Revolution in Cuba," 478–79, 490.

63. Luzón, "Housing in Socialist Cuba"; Scarpaci, Segre, and Coyula, *Havana*, 134–35.

64. Matas, "Theater and Cinematography," 432–38; Benedetti, "Present Status of Cuban Culture," 500–26; Liss, *Roots of Revolution*, 154; Espinosa and Llópiz, *Cine cubano*; Stermer, *The Art of Revolution*; Cushing, *¡Revolución!* See also *El maná*, directed by Jesús de Armas (Havana: Instituto Cubano del Arte e Industrias Cinematográficos, 1960), four-minute animated cartoon; and *La prensa seria*, directed by Jesús de Armas (Havana: Instituto Cubano del Arte e Industrias Cinematográficos, 1960), short animated cartoon.

65. Casal, "Literature and Society," 456; Liss, *Roots of Revolution*, 154–55; Franqui, *Retrato de familia con Fidel*, 130, 202, 265. See also Luis, *Lunes de Revolución*.

66. Matas, "Theater and Cinematography," 439; Martínez Marún, *Historia de Cuba (Sexto Grado)*, 327. See also *P.M.*, directed by Alberto Cabrera Infante and Orlando Jiménez-Leal (Havana, 1961), documentary film.

67. Fidel Castro, "Address to Intellectuals," June 30, 1961, in García Luis, *Cuban Revolution Reader*, 76–82; Padilla, *Self-Portrait of the Other*, 52–55; Casal, "Literature and Society," 459.

68. Franqui, *Retrato de familia con Fidel*, 282–84; Franqui, *Cuba, la revolución*, 260.

69. Blasier, *The Hovering Giant*, 190–92.

70. Thomas, *The Cuban Revolution*, 491; Kornbluh, *Bay of Pigs Declassified*, 269; Fidel Castro's speech at the funeral of the victims of the March 4 ship explosion in Havana, March 5, 1960, Castro Speech Database, http://lanic.utexas.edu/project/castro/db/1960/19600307-1.html, accessed May 30, 2013.

71. Casey, *Che's Afterlife*.

72. Pfeiffer, "Official History of the Bay of Pigs Operation," 3:64–65, 72.

73. Pérez-López, *Economics of Cuban Sugar*, 136–37; Pavlov, *Soviet-Cuban Alliance*, 8; Goldenberg, *The Cuban Revolution and Latin America*, 259; Gott, *Cuba*, 184; Cheng, "Sino-Cuban Relations during the Early Years of the Castro Regime," 94–95; Castañeda, *Compañero*, 183.

74. Welch, *Response to Revolution*, 50; Thomas, *The Cuban Revolution*, 511; Karol, *Guerrillas in Power*, 574; Franqui, *Cuba, la revolución*, 261.

75. Guevara quoted in Draper, *Castro's Revolution*, 81. For the nationalization decree, see García Luis, *Cuban Revolution Reader*, 41–44. See also Domínguez, *Cuba*, 146–47; Ritter, *The Economic Development of Revolutionary Cuba*, 74.

76. *Revolución*, January 7, 1959.

77. Pérez, *Cuba: Between Reform and Revolution*, 247–48; Yafee, *Che Guevara*, 102; Blasier, "The Elimination of United States Influence," 71–72; "U.S. Breaks Diplomatic Ties with Cuba and Advises Americans to Leave Island," *New York Times*, January 4, 1961.

78. Pérez-López, *Economics of Cuban Sugar*, 138; Cheng, "Sino-Cuban Relations during the Early Years of the Castro Regime," 93–94.

79. Pérez-López, "Cuba's Balance of Payments Statistics," 141; Pérez, *Cuba: Between Reform and Revolution*, 249. By 1961, the Cuban government had nationalized 37 percent of agriculture, 85 percent of industry, 92 percent of transportation, and 100 percent of banking and wholesale and foreign trade; Pérez-López, *Cuba's Second Economy*, 36.

80. Fagen, Brody, and O'Leary, *Cubans in Exile*, 63; García, *Havana USA*, 13.

81. Fagen, Brody, and O'Leary, *Cubans in Exile*, 19, 23.

82. Pérez, *Cuba: Between Reform and Revolution*, 261; Yafee, *Che Guevara*, 100.

83. García, *Dreaming in Cuban*, 70–72.

84. Personal communication with Juan Valdés, July 15, 2010, Washington, D.C.

85. Torres, *In the Land of Mirrors*, 73.

86. "Health Aspects of the Cuban Refugee Problem," 147, 158, 170.

87. See Triay, *Fleeing Castro*; Conde, *Operation Pedro Pan*; and Eire, *Waiting for Snow in Havana*.

88. Conde, *Operation Pedro Pan*, 101–13.

89. Masud-Piloto, *With Open Arms*, 67.

90. Arboleya, *The Cuban Counterrevolution*, 4, 41–42; Fursenko and Naftali, "*One Hell of a Gamble*," 64.

91. Arboleya, *The Cuban Counterrevolution*, 71; U.S. Central Intelligence Agency, "Cuban Counter Revolutionary Handbook," October 10, 1962, Cuban Information Archives Web site, http://cuban-exile.com/doc_351-375/doc0370.html, accessed December 3, 2013.

92. Arboleya, *The Cuban Counterrevolution*, 77; Draper, *Castro's Revolution*, 70.

93. Arboleya, *The Cuban Counterrevolution*, 115; Molina, *Diario de Girón*, 70; Franqui, *Retrato de familia con Fidel*, 227; Beruvides, *Cuba y su presidio político*, 119.

94. For a brief discussion of U.S. historiography on the Bay of Pigs, see Kornbluh, *Bay of Pigs Declassified*, 4–5. CIA deputy director Richard Bissell was in charge of the Bay of Pigs project. Agents Grayston Lynch and William Robertson assumed direct command of the troops. Agent E. Howard Hunt was involved in the planning of the invasion. Schoultz, *That Little Infernal Republic*, 192–200.

95. Johnson, *The Bay of Pigs*, 206–7; Karol, *Guerrillas in Power*, 17; Draper, *Castro's Revolution*, 92. The brigade's battalion commanders were Alejandro del Valle (1), Hugo Sueiro (2), Noelio Montero (3), Valentín Bacallao (4), Ricardo Montero (5), and Francisco Montiel (6). Castro and Fernández, *Playa Girón*, 101–2.

96. Portell Vilá, *Nueva historia de la República de Cuba*, 788.

97. Schlesinger, *A Thousand Days*, 243; Arboleya, *The Cuban Counterrevolution*, 89; Matthews, *Fidel Castro*, 214; Schoultz, *That Little Infernal Republic*, 180; Johnson, *The Bay of Pigs*, 121; Pino Machado, *La Batalla de Girón*, 76. Quote from "[CIA] Inspector General's Survey of the Cuban Operation, October, 1961," in Kornbluh, *Bay of Pigs Declassified*, 74.

98. Bissell, *Reflections of a Cold Warrior*, 183; Kornbluh, *Bay of Pigs Declassified*, 303.

99. Kornbluh, *Bay of Pigs Declassified*, 37, 301; Welch, *Response to Revolution*, 77.

100. Kornbluh, *Bay of Pigs Declassified*, 3; Gott, *Cuba*, 194; Pino Machado, *La Batalla de Girón*, 67.

101. Ramón Barreras Ferrán, "Los del 339 resistieron hasta la llegada de refuerzos," *Granma*, April 17, 2001, Latin American Studies Web site, http://www.latinamericanstudies.org/bay-of-pigs/batallon-339.htm, accessed November 30, 2013; Franqui, *Retrato de familia con Fidel*, 247; Castro and Fernández, *Playa Girón*, 111.

102. Wyden, *Bay of Pigs*, 235–36.

103. Johnson, *The Bay of Pigs*, 93; Pino Machado, *La Batalla de Girón*, 9, 35, 39; Schoultz, *That Little Infernal Republic*, 166–67. Khrushchev's letter of April 18, 1961, is reproduced in Seymour Topping, "Premier Is Grim: Bids U.S. Halt Attack; Thousands Storm Moscow Embassy," *New York Times*, April 19, 1961.

104. Johnson, *The Bay of Pigs*, 135. Ulises Carbó's firsthand account of the battle is in the memo of Lieutenant Frank Kappel to Dade County sheriff Thomas J. Kelly, May 29, 1961, Dade County OCB file no. 153-D, Cuban Information Archives Web site, http://cuban-exile.com/doc_026-050/doc0041.html, accessed December 3, 2013.

105. Johnson, *The Bay of Pigs*, 160–61, 167.

106. Ibid., 179, 328–31; Molina, *Diario de Girón*, 130; Portell Vilá, *Nueva historia de la República de Cuba*, 791; "Memorias," lyrics by Carlos Varela, *Monedas al aire*, 1993, CD.

107. Welch, *Response to Revolution*, 88,

108. Fidel Castro's speech on the Popular University program, April 23, 1961, Castro Speech Database,http://www1.lanic.utexas.edu/project/castro/db/1961/19610423. html, accessed December 3, 2013; Matthews, *Fidel Castro*, 188; "A Communist Cuba," *New York Times*, December 4, 1961.

109. *Bohemia*, February 19, 1961, 14, 61, 113.

110. Fidel Castro's speech at Havana May Day celebrations, May 1, 1961, Castro Speech Database, http://www1.lanic.utexas.edu/project/castro/db/1961/19610502. html, accessed May 30, 2013; Jover Marimón, "The Church," 404–5; Gómez Treto, *La Iglesia Católica*, 48; Portell Vilá, *Nueva historia de la República de Cuba*, 774.

111. Fourteen countries, including the United States, voted in favor; Cuba, as expected, voted against; and Mexico, Brazil, Argentina, Chile, Bolivia, and Ecuador abstained. Welch, *Response to Revolution*, 97.

112. Secret memos of Richard Goodwin to John F. Kennedy, August 22 and November 1, 1961, Bay of Pigs, National Security Archive, http://www.gwu.edu/~nsarchiv/ bayofpigs/19610822.pdf and http://www.gwu.edu/~nsarchiv/bayofpigs/19611101.pdf, respectively, accessed December 30, 2013.

113. George Crile III, "The Riddle of AM LASH," *Washington Post,* May 2, 1976, http://www.latinamericanstudies.org/belligerence/amlash.htm. "Ideas in Support of Project [Mongoose]," memo from Brigadier General William H. Craig to Brigadier General Edward G. Lansdale, February 2, 1962, in Chang and Kornbluh, *The Cuban Missile Crisis*, 53–61.

114. Latell, *Castro's Secrets*, 2–3, 13.

115. "Justification for U.S. Military Intervention in Cuba," memo of L. L. Lemnitzer, chairman of Joint Chiefs of Staff, to the secretary of defense, March 13, 1962, National Security Archives, http://www.gwu.edu/~nsarchiv/news/20010430/doc1.pdf, accessed December 3, 2013.

116. Executive order by John F. Kennedy for the imposition of a trade embargo, February 3, 1962, in García Luis, *Cuban Revolution Reader*, 98; Matthews, *Fidel Castro*, 238.

117. Castañeda, *Compañero*, 228; Benítez-Rojo, *The Repeating Island*, 10.

118. Detzer, *The Brink*, 237, 243–47.

119. Juan O. Tamayo, "A Nuclear Secret in '62 Cuba Crisis," *Miami Herald*, May 3, 1998.

120. Franqui, *Retrato de familia con Fidel*, 408; Castañeda, *Compañero*, 229; Matthews, *Fidel Castro*, 234.

121. Goldenberg, *The Cuban Revolution and Latin America*, 279.

122. Echevarría, "Cuba," 369; Mesa-Lago, "Economic Policies and Growth," 288–89.

123. Guevara, *Obras*, 2:142.

124. Benjamin, Collins, and Scott, *No Free Lunch*, 23; Mesa-Lago, "Economic Policies and Growth," 291.

125. Cabrera Infante, "Salieron las amas de casa," 397; Franqui, *Retrato de familia con Fidel*, 289.

126. Karol, *Guerrillas in Power*, 586; Pérez-Stable, *The Cuban Revolution*, 85–86.

127. Molina, *Diario de Girón*, 118.

128. *Memorias del subdesarrollo*, directed by Tomás Gutiérrez Alea (Havana: Instituto Cubano del Arte e Industrias Cinematográficos, 1968).

Chapter 3. The Ten Million Will Happen

1. Mesa-Lago, *The Economy of Socialist Cuba*, 17. Agricultural production index based on 100 for 1959. See Brunner, *Cuban Sugar Policy from 1963 to 1970*, 33; and Pérez-López, *Economics of Cuban Sugar*, 142.

2. Ritter, *The Economic Development of Revolutionary Cuba*, 157; Baklanoff, "International Economic Relations," 266.

3. Guevara quoted in Goldenberg, *The Cuban Revolution and Latin America*, 279.

4. Dumont, *Is Cuba Socialist?*, 321.

5. Halperin, *The Rise and Decline of Castro*, 213–19; see also *Viva Kuba!*

6. Pérez-López, *Economics of Cuban Sugar*, 142–43; Brunner, *Cuban Sugar Policy from 1963 to 1970*, 55; Baklanoff, "International Economic Relations," 268–69; Pérez-López, "Cuban-Soviet Sugar Trade," 127.

7. Halperin, *The Rise and Decline of Castro*, 313–14; Domínguez, *To Make a World Safe for Revolution*, 64; Pérez-López, *Economics of Cuban Sugar*, 126, 162; Baklanoff, "International Economic Relations," 260–61.

8. Cheng, "Sino-Cuban Relations during the Early Years of the Castro Regime," 94.

9. Mesa-Lago, "Economic Policies and Growth," 302; Pérez-López, *Economics of Cuban Sugar*, 40–41; George, *The Cuban Intervention in Angola*, 19.

10. Goldenberg, *The Cuban Revolution and Latin America*, 281; Tozian, *Fidel's Cuba*, 60. Castro quoted in Roca, *Cuban Economic Policy and Ideology*, 12.

11. Mesa-Lago, "Economic Policies and Growth," 288–89.

12. Castañeda, *Compañero*, 259; Franqui, *Cuba, la revolución*, 281.

13. Amaro and Mesa-Lago, "Inequality and Classes," 359; Goldenberg, *The Cuban Revolution and Latin America*, 268; Pérez-López, *Cuba's Second Economy*, 36.

14. Mesa-Lago, *Cuba in the 1970s*, 9, 57; Liss, *Roots of Revolution*, 166; Anderson, *Che Guevara*, 426.

15. Mesa-Lago, *Cuba in the 1970s*, 9, 57.

16. Guevara, *El socialismo y el hombre en Cuba*.

17. Anderson, *Che Guevara*, 468; Cheng, *Creating the New Man*, 241. On the Great Debate, see Yafee, *Che Guevara*, chapter 3.

18. Mesa-Lago, *Cuba in the 1970s*, 6; Castañeda, *Compañero*, 286; CIA, "Biographic Register on Che Guevara," August 1964, Office of Central Reference, CIA, http://archive.is/2cQ6B, accessed December 3, 2013. Guevara quoted in Karol, *Guerrillas in Power*, 304.

19. "Current and Past Revolutionary Leaders," in Horowitz and Suchlicki, *Cuban Communism*, 876–92; Mesa-Lago, "Historia y evaluación," 515.

20. García Luis, *Cuban Revolution Reader*, 113–21; Suárez, "Leadership, Ideology, and Political Party," 148; Thomas, *The Cuban Revolution*, 598–99.

21. Pérez-López, *Economics of Cuban Sugar*, appendix 5, 255–58; Baklanoff, "International Economic Relations," 260–61.

22. Ritter, *The Economic Development of Revolutionary Cuba*, 210; LeoGrande, "Cuban Dependency," 27; Mesa-Lago, *Cuba in the 1970s*, 18; Duncan, *The Soviet Union and Cuba*, 101.

23. Gleijeses, "Cuba's First Venture in Africa," 165, 177, 189; George, *The Cuban Intervention in Angola*, 21.

24. Pan-American Union, "Final Act of the Ninth Meeting of Consultation of Ministers of Foreign Affairs," Washington, D.C., July 21–26, 1964, http://www.oas.org/columbus/docs/mfa9eng.pdf, accessed December 3, 2013. See also Castañeda, *Compañero*, 241, 254, and four *New York Times* articles: "Arms Cache in Venezuela Called Foreign Origin," November 7, 1963; "O.A.S. Official Says Weapons in Venezuela Had Cuban Insignias," December 14, 1963; "Venezuela, in O.A.S.[,] Accuses Castro of Plot," January 4, 1964; and Tad Szulc, "O.A.S., by 15 to 4 Votes Sanctions against Cuba," July 26, 1964.

25. See original and edited version of photograph on the cover of Franqui, *Retrato de familia con Fidel*.

26. Anderson, *Che Guevara*, 488–89, 518–19; Gleijeses, "Cuba's First Venture in Africa," 187–88.

27. Pardo Llada, *Fidel y el "Che,"* 191; Franqui, *Cuba, la revolución*, 311; George, *The Cuban Intervention in Angola*, 22; Ryan, *The Fall of Che Guevara*, 26.

28. Mwakikagile, *Nyerere and Africa*, 183; LeoGrande, *Cuba's Policy in Africa*, 9–10; Castañeda, *Compañero*, 300; Ratliff, "Cuban Military Policy in Sub-Saharan Africa," 33; George, *The Cuban Intervention in Angola*, 11–12.

29. Pan-American Union, "Final Act of the Ninth Meeting of Consultation of Ministers of Foreign Affairs," Washington, D.C., July 21–26, 1964; Szulc, "O.A.S., by 15 to 4[,] Votes Sanctions against Cuba."

30. Lyndon Johnson, "Published Text of Speech on the Dominican Republic Intervention, May 2, 1965," http://millercenter.org/president/speeches/detail/4033, accessed December 28, 2013.

31. Fidel Castro's speech calling for vast program of economic aid to Latin America, May 2, 1959, Castro Speech Database, http://lanic.utexas.edu/project/castro/db/1959/19590505-2.html, accessed December 3, 2013.

32. "Preliminary Formulations of the Alliance for Progress," address by President Kennedy at a White House reception for Latin American diplomats and members of Congress, March 13, 1961, Fordham University Internet Modern History Sourcebook, http://www.fordham.edu/halsall/mod/1961kennedy-afp1.html, accessed June 1, 2013.

33. United States Central Intelligence Agency, Board of National Estimates, "Bolsheviks and Heroes: The USSR and Cuba," special memorandum by Sherman Kent, November 21, 1967, in National Security Archive, http://www.gwu.edu/~nsarchiv/NSAEBB/NSAEBB67/gleijeses8.pdf, accessed December 3, 2013; González, "Relationship with the Soviet Union," 84.

34. Castañeda, *Compañero*, 377–79; Campello, "The Cuban Communist Party's Anti-Castro Activities," http://campello.tripod.com/castro.html, accessed December 3, 2013.

35. See Gosse, *Where the Boys Are*.

36. Cheng, "Sino-Cuban Relations during the Early Years of the Castro Regime," 104–5; Low, *The Sino-Soviet Dispute*, 260.

37. Cheng, "Sino-Cuban Relations during the Early Years of the Castro Regime," 110–12; Karol, *Guerrillas in Power*, 304–5; Castañeda, *Compañero*, 285–86; Halperin, *Return to Havana*, 50.

38. Karol, *Guerrillas in Power*, 298, 323; Anderson, *Che Guevara*, 544; Yafee, *Che Guevara*, 50.

39. Guevara gave Castro his letter of resignation on April 1, 1966, and Castro read it publicly six months later. See García Luis, *Cuban Revolution Reader*, 146–48; Anderson, *Che Guevara*, 534, 539–40, 545, 549, 591.

40. Ryan, *The Fall of Che Guevara*, 32; Castañeda, *Compañero*, 303–4.

41. Klepak, *Cuba's Military*, 44; Ernesto Guevara's Message to the 1966 Tricontinental Conference, in Guevara, *Che Guevara Presente*, 367–79; Anderson, *Che Guevara*, 620.

42. Guevara, *The Bolivian Diary of Ernesto Che Guevara*; Anderson, *Che Guevara*, 591.

43. Castañeda, *Compañero*, 373; Inti Peredo, "My Campaign with Che," in Guevara, *The Bolivian Diary of Ernesto Che Guevara*, 356.

44. Castañeda, *Compañero*, 377–79; Campello, "The Cuban Communist Party's Anti-Castro Activities"; Latell, *Castro's Secrets*, 120.

45. "Current and Past Revolutionary Leaders," in Horowitz and Suchlicki, *Cuban Communism*, 876–92; Mesa-Lago, "Historia y evaluación," 515.

46. LeoGrande, "Party Development in Revolutionary Cuba," 162; Mesa-Lago, *Cuba in the 1970s*, 71.

47. The Politburo members in 1965 were Fidel Castro, Raúl Castro, Juan Almeida, Sergio del Valle Jiménez, Osvaldo Dorticós Torrado, Guillermo García Frías, Armando Hart, and Ramiro Valdés. The Secretariat included Fidel Castro, Raúl Castro, Faure Chomón, Osvaldo Dorticós Torrado, Blas Roca, and Carlos Rafael Rodríguez. See Suárez, "Leadership, Ideology, and Political Party," 12; and del Águila, *Cuba*, 68.

48. Ryan, *The Fall of Che Guevara*, 33; Mesa-Lago, "Present and Future of the Revolution," 515; Fernández, "Historical Background," 13–14.

49. Significantly, the two highest-ranking women in government were Castro's intimate friend Celia Sánchez (secretary to the presidency) and Raúl Castro's wife, Vilma Espín (president, FMC). See Moreno, "From Traditional to Modern Values," 482; and Smith and Padula, *Sex and Revolution*, 32.

50. Clytus, *Black Man in Red Cuba*, 24; Amaro and Mesa-Lago, "Inequality and Classes," 350–51; de la Fuente, *A Nation for All*, 276–79, 310–11.

51. Kapcia, *Cuba in Revolution*, 131.

52. Goldenberg, *The Cuban Revolution and Latin America*, 279; Franqui, *Retrato de familia con Fidel*, 227; Fuentes, *Condenados del Condado*, 15; Beruvides, *Cuba y su presidio político*, 119. On forced resettlements, see Escobar Ramírez, *Memorias del horror*.

53. Domínguez, *To Make a World Safe for Revolution*, 73–74; González, "Relationship with the Soviet Union," 94.

54. CIA, Board of National Estimates, "Bolsheviks and Heroes"; Duncan, *The Soviet Union and Cuba*, 73; González, "Relationship with the Soviet Union," 93; Karol, *Guerrillas in Power*, 392.

55. Domínguez, *To Make a World Safe for Revolution*, 72–74; González, "Relationship with the Soviet Union," 93; "Informe al Comité Central del Partido Comunista de Cuba (Sobre las actividades de la "microfacción")," *Punto Final* (Santiago de Chile) 48 (supplement) (February 16, 1968), http://www.pf-memoriahistorica.org/PDFs/1968/PF_048_doc2.pdf, accessed December 3, 2013.

56. Karol, *Guerrillas in Power*, 507, 586; Domínguez, *To Make a World Safe for Revolution*, 73–79.

57. Guevara's essay on the "New Man" was first published in the Uruguayan newspaper *Marcha* in March 1965; the following month, it appeared in Cuba in *Verde Olivo* under the title "El socialismo y el hombre en Cuba." See Guevara, *El socialismo y el hombre en Cuba*.

58. Brundenius, "Measuring Income Distribution," 36; Bernardo, *The Theory of Moral Incentives in Cuba*, 58, 69–71; Córdova, *El trabajador cubano*, 159; Ritter, *The Economic Development of Revolutionary Cuba*, 263; Zimbalist, "Incentives and Planning in Cuba," 67.

59. Mesa-Lago, "Economic Policies and Growth," 291; Dumont, *Is Cuba Socialist?*, 63; Zimbalist and Eckstein, "Patterns of Cuban Development," 16; Pérez-López, *Cuba's Second Economy*, 46.

60. Mesa-Lago, "Economic Policies and Growth," 324; Pérez-López, *Economics of Cuban Sugar*, 13, 41.

61. Feinsilver, *Healing the Masses*, 32, 36; Luis, *Culture and Customs of Cuba*, 41.

62. Mesa-Lago, *The Economy of Socialist Cuba*, 41; Santana, "The Cuban Health Care System," 117; Domínguez, *Cuba*, 185.

63. Dahlman, "The Nation-Wide System of Learning in Cuba," 70–80; Amaro and Mesa-Lago, "Inequality and Classes," 345; Paulston, "Education," 387, 392; Bunck, *Fidel Castro and the Quest for a Revolutionary Culture in Cuba*, 39–43.

64. Brundenius, "Development Strategies and Basic Human Needs," 113; Scarpaci, Segre, and Coyula, *Havana*, 202.

65. Scarpaci, Segre, and Coyula, *Havana*, 218–20; see also Curry-Machado, "Surviving the 'Cuban Nightmare,'" 4–7.

66. Fidel Castro's speech, March 13, 1968, in Castro, *Fidel Castro Speaks*, 303, 308.

67. Karol, *Guerrillas in Power*, 442; Mesa-Lago, "Economic Policies and Growth," 283; Espina Prieto, "Cambios," 113.

68. Pérez, *Cuba: Between Reform and Revolution*, 265–66; Casal, "Literature and Society," 459; Eckstein, *Back from the Future*, 25.

69. Cabrera Infante, "Mordidas del caimán barbudo," and "Pax cubana," both in Cabrera Infante, *Mea Cuba*, 108, 432; Farber, *Cuba since the Revolution*, 209–11; Gutiérrez Agramonte, "Una nueva técnica," 79–86. See also *Conducta Impropia*, directed by Néstor Almendros and Orlando Jiménez-Leal (Barcelona: Editorial Egales, 1984), documentary film.

70. Farber, *Cuba since the Revolution*, 173; Gómez Treto, *La Iglesia Católica*, 61.

71. Following confrontations of earlier years, the Catholic Church accepted its subordination to the state and pursued a conciliatory strategy; Jover Marimón, "The Church," 405; Kirk, *Between God and the Party*, 117.

72. Cabrera Infante, "Prisioneros de la Isla del Diablo," in Cabrera Infante, *Mea Cuba*, 255; Franqui, *Cuba, la revolución*, 364.

73. Howe, *Transgression and Conformity*, 41, 7; Lumsden, *Machos, Maricones, and Gays*, 71; Cabrera Infante, "La confundida lengua del poeta," in Cabrera Infante, *Mea Cuba*, 47; Bejel, *Gay Cuban Nation*, 101; Guerra, *Visions of Power in Cuba*, 274.

74. Eteocles speaking in Arrufat, *Los siete contra Tebas*, 75, my translation.

75. Padilla, *Fuera del juego*, 43–44, my translation. See also Editors of *La Habana Elegante*, "En mi jardín (no) pastan los héroes," http://www.habanaelegante.com/Spring2001/Barco.html, accessed May 30, 2013; and Padilla, *Self-Portrait of the Other*.

76. "Declaración de la UNEAC acerca de los premios otorgados a Heberto Padilla en Poesía y Antón Arrufat en Teatro (November 15, 1968)," in Padilla, *Fuera del juego*, 115–21.

77. See interviews with Antón Arrufat and Pablo Armando Fernández in Kirk and Padura Fuentes, *Culture and the Cuban Revolution*, 17–38, 78–92.

78. J. M. Cohen, introduction to *Sent off the Field: A Selection from the Poetry of Heberto Padilla*, in Editors of *La Habana Elegante*, "En mi jardín (no) pastan los héroes."

79. Mesa-Lago, *Cuba in the 1970s*, 106–12; Matas, "Theater and Cinematography," 44; Benedetti, "Present Status of Cuban Culture," 500–26; Stermer, *The Art of Revolution*; Benmayor, "The 'Nueva Trova'"; Segal, "Dance and Diplomacy," 30–32.

80. Photograph in Jenkins, *Havana in My Heart*, 106.

81. Desnoes, "Epílogo para intelectuales," 551–52. For a fine discussion of nueva trova, see Moore, *Music and Revolution*, 135–69; and Fernandes, *Cuba Represent!*, 51.

82. Arboleya, *The Cuban Counterrevolution*, 137; Latell, *Castro's Secrets*, 103.

83. Díaz-Briquets and Pérez, "Cuba," 26; Mesa-Lago, *The Economy of Socialist Cuba*, 43.

84. Fidel Castro's speech at the Plaza of the Revolution, September 28, 1965, Discursos e intervenciones del Comandante en Jefe Fidel Castro Ruz, Presidente del Consejo de Estado de la República de Cuba, http://www.cuba.cu/gobierno/discursos/1965/esp/f280965e.html, accessed December 3, 2013; Masud-Piloto, *With Open Arms*, 57; Bender, "Cuban Exiles," 273; Gott, *Cuba*, 213; Antón and Hernández, *Cubans in America*, 168.

85. U.S. Public Law 89-732, November 6, 1966, http://uscode.house.gov/statutes/1966/1966-089-0732.pdf.

86. Sources provide conflicting data about the number of exiles who left via the airlift. Bender, "Cuban Exiles," 272, says 277,242; García, *Havana USA*, 43, says 297,000; and Portes and Stepick, *City on the Edge*, 104, says 340,000.

87. García, *Havana USA*, 43.

88. "Table 9, Cuban Origin Persons in Selected States by Rank: 1980 and 1970," in U.S. Department of Commerce, Bureau of the Census, *Current Population Survey: Annual Demographic File, 1985*, 13; Torres, *In the Land of Mirrors*, 81; Díaz-Briquets and Pérez, "Cuba," 1–43; Esteve, *El exilio cubano en Puerto Rico*, 26; Gutiérrez, *The Columbia History of Latinos in the United States since 1960*, 172.

89. U.S. Central Intelligence Agency, "Cuban Counter Revolutionary Handbook," October 10, 1962, Cuban Information Archives Web site, http://cuban-exile.com/doc_351-375/doc0370.html, accessed December 3, 2013.

90. Torres, *In the Land of Mirrors*, 85; William Montalbano and Clarence Jones, "Exile Terrorist Bombers: Who Are They?" *Miami Herald*, September 10, 1968, Latin American Studies Web site, http://www.latinamericanstudies.org/belligerence/bombers.htm, accessed December 3, 2013; "Blasted Freighter off Puerto Rico, Cuban Power Says," *Miami Herald*, September 14, 1968, Latin American Studies Web site, http://www.latinamericanstudies.org/belligerence/blasted-freighter.htm, accessed December 3, 2013; "Criminal Index File of Orlando Bosch Ávila," *Granma*, October 19, 1980, Cuban Information Archives Web site, http://cuban-exile.com/doc_051-075/doc0057.html, accessed December 3, 2013; County Manager's Office, Dade County, Florida, "Cuban Exile Organizations Hard-Line: 1970s," Cuban Information Archives Web site, http://

cuban-exile.com/doc_001-025/doc0014.html, accessed December 3, 2013; Memo of John E. McHugh, FBI SA, to SAC Miami on the subject of Cuba, July 18, 1966, National Security Archive, http://www.gwu.edu/~nsarchiv/NSAEBB/NSAEBB153/19660718.pdf, accessed December 3, 2013; FBI cable, July 13, 1965, Representación Cubana en el Exilio, National Security Archive, http://www.gwu.edu/~nsarchiv/NSAEBB/NSAEBB153/19650713.pdf, accessed December 3, 2013.

91. Fidel Castro's speech, March 13, 1968, in Castro, *Fidel Castro Speaks*, 275; Fidel Castro, "Report to the People on the Progress of the Sugar Harvest," *Granma Weekly Review*, February 9, 1970, quoted in Mesa-Lago, "Economic Policies and Growth," 304; Karol, *Guerrillas in Power*, 408, 418.

92. Ritter, *The Economic Development of Revolutionary Cuba*, 167, 183–87.

93. "Informe al Comité Central del Partido Comunista de Cuba."

94. Mesa-Lago, "Economic Policies and Growth," 302; U.S. Information Agency, *Cuba Annual Report* (1988), 368; Scarpaci, Segre, and Coyula, *Havana*, 141. Castro's televised speech is available in "The Yankee Years," part 1 of *Crisis in Central America*, written and produced by Judith Vecchione, aired on PBS program *Frontline* on April 9, 1985.

95. Brundenius, "Development and Prospects of Capital Goods Production in Revolutionary Cuba," 99.

96. Mesa-Lago, "Economic Policies and Growth," 291; Dumont, *Is Cuba Socialist?*, 63; Zimbalist and Eckstein, "Patterns of Cuban Development," 16; Pérez-López, *Cuba's Second Economy*, 46.

97. Brundenius, "Development Strategies and Basic Human Needs," 113; "Table 2.5," in Pérez-López, *Cuba's Second Economy*, 45. In 1965, the FAO recommended seventy-one grams of protein per capita; in 1957, the recommendation was 3,200 calories for adult males and 2,300 for adult women. See Périssé, "Energy and Requirements"; Togores González, "Ingresos monetarios," 205. The level in 1959 was 2,500 calories for rural dwellers, not counting sugar; Gordon, "The Nurtiture of Cubans," 8, 11.

98. Thirty percent of the children of Alquizar, Havana, were malnourished; in Caiguanabo, Pinar del Río, the statistic was 48 percent; Mesa-Lago, "Economic Policies and Growth," 288–89; Dumont, *Is Cuba Socialist?*, 76; Ritter, *The Economic Development of Revolutionary Cuba*, 188–91.

99. Domínguez, *Cuba*, 453; Mesa-Lago, "Economic Policies and Growth," 301.

100. Ritter, *The Economic Development of Revolutionary Cuba*, 195; Karol, *Guerrillas in Power*, 485, 439.

101. Scarpaci, Segre, and Coyula, *Havana*, 140.

102. *Coffea Arábiga*, directed by Nicolás Guillén Landrián (Havana: Instituto Cubano del Arte e Industrias Cinematográficos, 1968), http://www.youtube.com/watch?v=em-2nq9aopU, accessed December 29, 2013. See also Guerra, *Visions of Power in Cuba*, 348, 274.

103. Mesa-Lago, "Present and Future of the Revolution," 507; Zimbalist and Eckstein, "Patterns of Cuban Development," 11; Brundenius, "Measuring Income Distribution," 33.

104. Roca, *Cuban Economic Policy and Ideology*, 19; Pérez-López, *Economics of Cuban Sugar*, 59.

105. Moreno, "From Traditional to Modern Values," 480–82, 490; Nazzari, "The

Woman Question in Cuba," 254; *Granma* article dated August 8, 1969, cited in Bunck, *Fidel Castro and the Quest for a Revolutionary Culture in Cuba*, 103; Prieto, "Cuban Women in the U.S. Labor Force," 74.

106. Portes, Clark, and Bach, "The New Wave," 17; Bunck, *Fidel Castro and the Quest for a Revolutionary Culture in Cuba*, 146; Guerra, *Visions of Power in Cuba*, 310–11.

107. Bunck, *Fidel Castro and the Quest for a Revolutionary Culture in Cuba*, 149; Karol, *Guerrillas in Power*, 582.

108. Last stanza of song "Cuba Va" (1970) by Milanés, Nicola, and Rodríguez, my translation

109. Fidel Castro's speech on the occasion of the merging of the National Institute for Water Resources with the National Agricultural Development Department, May 27, 1969, Castro Speech Database, http://www1.lanic.utexas.edu/project/castro/db/1969/19690527.html, accessed December 3, 2013.

110. The length of the 1970 *zafra* has been calculated by different scholars. I have selected numbers produced by Pérez-López as "effective *zafra* days." See Pérez-López, *Economics of Cuban Sugar*, 49; Deere, Rojas, and Vila, *Güines, Santo Domingo, Majibacoa*, 65; Roca, *Cuban Economic Policy and Ideology*, 12; Mesa-Lago, "Economic Policies and Growth," 304.

111. Pérez, *Cuba: Between Reform and Revolution*, 260; Roca, *Cuban Economic Policy and Ideology*, 18; Ritter, *The Economic Development of Revolutionary Cuba*, 293–94; Dumont, *Is Cuba Socialist?*, 92; Pérez-López, *Economics of Cuban Sugar*, 59; Randall, *Cuban Women Now*, 80.

112. Mesa-Lago, "Economic Policies and Growth," 305; Escobar Ramírez, *Memorias del horror*, 36; Randall, *Cuban Women Now*, 80.

113. Roca, *Cuban Economic Policy and Ideology*, 7; Brunner, *Cuban Sugar Policy from 1963 to 1970*, 66.

114. Brunner, *Cuban Sugar Policy from 1963 to 1970*, 82–83.

115. Codina Jiménez, "Worker Incentives in Cuba," 133; Eckstein, *Back from the Future*, 40; Ritter, *The Economic Development of Revolutionary Cuba*, 181; Pérez-Stable, "Cuban Women and the Struggle for 'Conciencia,'" 51–72; Mesa-Lago, "Economic Policies and Growth," 321; Guerra, *Visions of Power in Cuba*, 316.

116. Halperin, *The Rise and Decline of Castro*, 239–40; Pérez-López, *Economics of Cuban Sugar*, 63–65, 68; Roca, *Cuban Economic Policy and Ideology*, 51–57; Brundenius, "Development and Prospects of Capital Goods Production in Revolutionary Cuba," 107–8.

117. Arenas, *Before Night Falls*, 133.

118. Roca, *Cuban Economic Policy and Ideology*, 15, 20–22, 27; Ritter, *The Economic Development of Revolutionary Cuba*, 181; Brunner, *Cuban Sugar Policy from 1963 to 1970*, 82–83; Dumont, *Is Cuba Socialist?*, 74.

119. Fidel Castro's speech on the seventeenth anniversary of the Moncada assault, July 26, 1970, Castro Speech Database, http://www1.lanic.utexas.edu/project/castro/db/1970/19700726.html, accessed December 3, 2013.

120. Karol, *Guerrillas in Power*, 346; Luzón, "Housing in Socialist Cuba," 74; Benjamin, Collins, and Scott, *No Free Lunch*, 23; Fidel Castro's speech, March 13, 1968, in Castro, *Fidel Castro Speaks*, 264.

121. LeoGrande, "Cuban Dependency," 9–10.

122. Brundenius, "Development and Prospects of Capital Goods Production in Revolutionary Cuba," 100; Zimbalist and Eckstein, "Patterns of Cuban Development," 9.

123. LeoGrande, "Cuban Dependency," 19; Mesa-Lago, *Cuba in the 1970s*, 18.

124. LeoGrande, "Cuban Dependency," 5–7, 8–10; Baklanoff, "International Economic Relations," 261–62.

125. LeoGrande, "Cuban Dependency," 9–15.

126. Pérez-Stable, *The Cuban Revolution*, 120.

Chapter 4. We Must Turn the Setback into Victory

1. Fidel Castro's speech reporting on the May 1970 sugar harvest, May 20, 1970, Castro Speech Database, http://www1.lanic.utexas.edu/project/castro/db/1970/19700521 .html, accessed June 3, 2013; Fidel Castro's speech inaugurating the new town of Doce y Medio near Bayamo, Oriente Province, May 31, 1970, Castro Speech Database, http:// lanic.utexas.edu/project/castro/db/1970/19700531.html, accessed December 3, 2013; and Fidel Castro's speech on the seventeenth anniversary of the Moncada assault, July 26, 1970, Castro Speech Database, http://www1.lanic.utexas.edu/project/castro/ db/1970/19700726.html, accessed December 3, 2013.

2. See, for example, Fidel Castro's speech on the grounds of the former Moncada Barracks in Santiago de Cuba, July 26, 1973, Castro Speech Database, http://lanic. utexas.edu/project/castro/db/1973/19730727.html, accessed June 3, 2013; and Fidel Castro's speech at the closing ceremony of the 13th Congress of the Central Organization of Cuban Workers, November 15, 1973, Castro Speech Database, http://lanic. utexas.edu/project/castro/db/1973/19731116.html, accessed December 3, 2013.

3. Mesa-Lago, *Cuba in the 1970s*, 45; Zimbalist, "Incentives and Planning in Cuba," 71.

4. Mesa-Lago, *Cuba in the 1970s*, 45–46; Zimbalist, "Incentives and Planning in Cuba," 75.

5. Zimbalist and Brundenius, *The Cuban Economy*, 134–35; Zimbalist, "Incentives and Planning in Cuba," 76–77, 80–81.

6. Zimbalist, "Incentives and Planning in Cuba," 70; Córdova, *El trabajador cubano*, 81; Bunck, *Fidel Castro and the Quest for a Revolutionary Culture in Cuba*, 155, 158.

7. Mesa-Lago, *Cuba in the 1970s*, 42; Nazzari, "The Woman Question in Cuba," 258.

8. CIA, *Cuban Economy*, 16; Benjamin, Collins, and Scott, *No Free Lunch*, 49.

9. Zimbalist, "Incentives and Planning in Cuba," 84.

10. Del Águila, *Cuba*, 99–100; Mesa-Lago, "The Economic Effects on Cuba of the Downfall of Socialism in the USSR and Eastern Europe," 133; Zimbalist, "Incentives and Planning in Cuba," 72–73.

11. Pérez-López, *Cuba's Second Economy*, 36, 93; Mesa-Lago, "Cuba's Economic Policies and Strategies for Confronting the Crisis," 201; Eckstein, *Back from the Future*, 47.

12. Mesa-Lago, "Cuba's Economic Counter-Reform," 107–8; Benjamin, Collins, and Scott, *No Free Lunch*, 61; Pérez-López, *Cuba's Second Economy*, 86.

13. Pérez-López, *Cuba's Second Economy*, 61; *Se Permuta*, directed by Juan Carlos Tabío (Havana: Instituto Cubano del Arte e Industrias Cinematográficos, 1984).

14. Benjamin, Collins, and Scott, *No Free Lunch*, 43, 75; Zimbalist, "Incentives and Planning in Cuba," 74; Pérez-López, *Cuba's Second Economy*, 108.

15. Nazzari, "The Woman Question in Cuba," 260; Pérez-Stable, "Cuban Women and the Struggle for 'Conciencia,'" 60–64; Smith and Padula, *Sex and Revolution*, 101; Zimbalist and Eckstein, "Patterns of Cuban Development," 16.

16. Mesa-Lago, "The Economic Effects on Cuba of the Downfall of Socialism in the USSR and Eastern Europe," 177.

17. Domínguez, *To Make a World Safe for Revolution*, 82; LeoGrande, "Cuban Dependency," 20; Pérez-López, *Economics of Cuban Sugar*, 140–44; Pérez-López, "Cuban-Soviet Sugar Trade," 123, 129.

18. Mesa-Lago, "The Economic Effects on Cuba of the Downfall of Socialism in the USSR and Eastern Europe," 149; Thomas O. Enders, "Cuban Support for Terrorism and Insurgency in the Western Hemisphere: March 12, 1982," 3, U.S. Departmment of State, Bureau of Public Affairs, Office of Public Communication, Editorial Division, Washington, D.C.

19. Mesa-Lago, "The Economic Effects on Cuba of the Downfall of Socialism in the USSR and Eastern Europe," 148–49; Shearman, "Gorbachev and the Restructuring of Soviet-Cuban Relations," 71–73.

20. Price information from Pérez-López, *Economics of Cuban Sugar*, 126, 140. See also Domínguez, *To Make a World Safe for Revolution*, 83.

21. Domínguez, *To Make a World Safe for Revolution*, 85, 207; Pavlov, *Soviet-Cuban Alliance*, 77.

22. Zimbalist and Brundenius, *The Cuban Economy*, 89–97. In 1975–79, investments in agriculture amounted to 2,553 million pesos and investments in industry reached 4,393 million pesos, a 1 to 1.7 ratio. In 1980–84, the respective amounts were 3,851 and 5,907, a ratio of 1 to 1.5. Mesa-Lago, *Cuba in the 1970s*, 58–60; Ubell, "High-Tech Medicine in the Caribbean," 1469; Brundenius, "Development and Prospects of Capital Goods Production in Revolutionary Cuba," 103.

23. Zimbalist and Eckstein, "Patterns of Cuban Development," 17; CIA, *Cuban Economy*, 3; Pérez-López, *Economics of Cuban Sugar*, 43; Halperin, *Return to Havana*, 103.

24. Sugar-derived revenues increased at an even greater rate, from $657 million in 1971 to $1,032 million in 1973, then tripling to $3,201 million in 1975; CIA, *Cuban Economy*, 29.

25. In 1975–80, economic growth figures were 3.2 percent for Cuba and 2.6 percent for Latin America. During the first half of the 1980s, the economies of Latin America contracted at a yearly rate of -1.8 percent, while the economy of Cuba grew at a rate of 6.8 percent per annum. Zimbalist and Brundenius, *The Cuban Economy*, 165; Eckstein, *Back from the Future*, 51; Mesa-Lago, "On Rectifying Errors of a Courteous Dissenter," 101.

26. Pérez-López, *Economics of Cuban Sugar*, 128; Zimbalist and Eckstein, "Patterns of Cuban Development," 18; Feuer, "The Performance of the Cuban Sugar Industry," 79; Mesa-Lago, *Cuba in the 1970s*, 18; Mesa-Lago, "Cuba's Economic Counter-Reform," 138.

27. Joe Contreras, "The Name Games of Cuban Athletes," *Newsweek International*, August 25, 2008, 35; Guerra, "Redefining Revolution in Cuba," 179.

28. Duncan, *The Soviet Union and Cuba*, 102, 108; Pérez-Stable, "Cuban Women and the Struggle for 'Conciencia,'" 55; Fermoselle, *The Evolution of the Cuban Military*, 341; Mesa-Lago, *Cuba in the 1970s*, 71; United States Central Intelligence Agency, Directorate of Intelligence, "Directory of Officials of the Republic of Cuba: A Reference Aid,"

Directorate of Intelligence, Springfield, Va., 1985; Rudolph, *Cuba*, 246; Córdova, *El trabajador cubano*, 41.

29. LeoGrande, "The Communist Party of Cuba since the First Congress," 174; Suchlicki, *Cuba*, 185.

30. Preamble and articles 1, 4, and 5 of the Constitution of 1976, Political Database of the Americas Web site, http://pdba.georgetown.edu/Constitutions/Cuba/cuba1976.html, accessed November 19, 2013; Sznajder and Roniger, "Política en la Cuba contemporánea," 162–63; de la Cuesta, "The Cuban Socialist Constitution."

31. Baloyra, "Cuba," 523–24; Suchlicki, *Cuba*, 188.

32. De la Cuesta, "The Cuban Socialist Constitution," 21.

33. Domínguez, *Cuba*, 247; de la Cuesta, "The Cuban Socialist Constitution," 26.

34. Roman, *People's Power*, 74; Suchlicki, *Cuba*, 186; Domínguez, *Cuba*, 244–47.

35. Articles 72 and 93–95 of the Constitution of 1976.

36. Articles 122, 128, and 72 of the Constitution of 1976.

37. Articles 44, 46, 49–51, 52–54, and 61 of the Constitution of 1976.

38. United States Central Intelligence Agency, National Foreign Assessment Center, "Directory of the Cuban Government and Mass Organizations: A Reference Guide," National Foreign Assessment Center, Washington, D.C., 1978; article 91 of the Cuban Constitution of 1976.

39. Santana, "The Cuban Health Care System," 122; Pérez-Stable, "Cuban Women and the Struggle for 'Conciencia,'" 55; de la Fuente, *A Nation for All*, 311.

40. Nora Frómeta Silva, Minister of Light Industry (1970–80); Asela de los Santos Tamayo, Vice-Minister of Education (1973–84); Irma Sánchez Valdés, Minister of the State Committee for Technical and Material Supplies (1976–85). See also Santana, "The Cuban Health Care System," 122.

41. Guerra, *Visions of Power in Cuba*, 27; Farber, *Cuba since the Revolution*, 192; Bunck, *Fidel Castro and the Quest for a Revolutionary Culture in Cuba*, 110–11; "Table 828, Farms—Number, Acreage, and Value by Tenure of Principal Operator and Type of Organization: 2002 and 2007," *Statistical Abstract of Latin America* 35 (1999): 209; "Abortion and Population Stagnation," *CubaNews*, February 1998, 10; Mirta Rodríguez Calderón and Armando Zambrana, "Ojo al divorcio en Cuba," *Bohemia*, November 2, 1980, 11–15.

42. Camnitzer, *New Art of Cuba*, 128; Luis, *Culture and Customs of Cuba*, 66; Moore, *Music and Revolution*, 104.

43. See Padilla's account of his imprisonment and forced confession in *Self-Portrait of the Other*, 133–66. See also Padilla, *Fuera del juego*. Letter to Fidel Castro, May 20, 1971, published in the daily newspaper *Madrid* (May 21, 1971), reproduced in Padilla, *Fuera del juego*, 160–61. See also Del Águila, *Cuba*, 157.

44. Artaraz, *Cuba and Western Intellectuals since 1959*, 129–32; Álvarez García and González Núñez, *¿Intelectuales vs. Revolución?*, 56, 116; Redruello, "Algunas reflexiones," 84–89.

45. Argüelles and Rich, "Homosexuality, Homophobia, and Revolution," 697; Mesa-Lago, *Cuba in the 1970s*, 105; Ubell, "High-Tech Medicine in the Caribbean," 1470.

46. *Fresa y chocolate*, directed by Tomás Gutiérrez Alea and Juan Carlos Tabío (Havana: Instituto Cubano del Arte e Industrias Cinematográficos, 1992). The screenplay is by Senel Paz, based on his short story "El lobo, el bosque y el hombre nuevo" (1990).

47. Bunck, *Fidel Castro and the Quest for a Revolutionary Culture in Cuba*, 76; Córdova, *El trabajador cubano*, 197.

48. Inter-American Commission on Human Rights, OAS, "Six[th] Report on the Situation of Political Prisoners in Cuba," chapter II, https://www.cidh.oas.org/countryrep/Cuba79eng/chap.2.htm, accessed November 30, 2013; Walters and Castro, "An Interview with Fidel Castro," 49.

49. Rivero Caro, "Prólogo" to "Antecedentes del movimiento de derechos humanos," Siglo XXI, Cuban Committee for Human Rights, http://www.sigloxxi.org/Anexos-libro/anex-00.htm, accessed December 3, 2013.

50. Resolution 2/82, Case 2300, Armando Valladares (Cuba), March 8, 1982, Inter-American Human Rights Commission, Inter-American Human Rights Database, Washington College of Law, http://www.wcl.american.edu/humright/digest/sp1981/282.cfm, accessed May 30, 2013; Valladares, *Against All Hope*.

51. Kirk, *Between God and the Party*, 128–46; Ramos, *Protestantism and Revolution in Cuba*, 78. See also Castro and Beto, *Fidel y la religión*.

52. Skoug, *Cuba as a Model and a Challenge*, 1.

53. Fermoselle, *The Evolution of a Cuban Military*, 298, 495; Duncan, *The Soviet Union and Cuba*, 101; del Águila, "The Changing Character of Cuba's Armed Forces," 30.

54. Fermoselle, *The Evolution of a Cuban Military*, 495, 328; Baloyra, "Cuba," 647; CIA, *World Factbook 1985*, 10, 30, 56; Rudolph, *Cuba*, 247; Fernández, "Historical Background," 15.

55. LeoGrande, *Cuba's Policy in Africa*, 12; "800 tanquistas cubanos pelearon en Siria en 1974 contra Israel: por primera vez hace la revelación el *Granma*," *Diario de las Américas*, October 23, 1998, Latin American Studies Web site, http://www.latinamericanstudies.org/cuba/tanquistas.htm, accessed December 3, 2013; ICCAS, "Castro and Terrorism: A Chronology," *Focus on Cuba* 57 (July 29, 2004), http://ctp.iccas.miami.edu/FOCUS_Web/Issue57.htm, accessed December 3, 2013.

56. Fernández, *Cuba's Foreign Policy in the Middle East*, 86.

57. Marta Rojas, "Carlota, la rebelde" and "Carlota: luchadora lukumí/yoruba para la liberación, masacrada en Matanzas, Cuba, en 1844," both at AfroCubaWeb, http://www.afrocubaweb.com/carlota.htm, accessed December 26, 2013; Manuel Moreno Fraginals, "Manuel de Angola," 172–78, in Moreno Fraginals, *La historia como arma*; George, *Cuban Intervention in Angola*, 148.

58. Valenta, "Comment: The Soviet-Cuban Alliance in Africa and Future Prospects in the Third World," 37; George, *The Cuban Intervention in Angola*, 148; Gleijeses, "Moscow's Proxy?"; Domínguez, *To Make a World Safe for Revolution*, 153; LeoGrande, *Cuba's Policy in Africa*, 16–19; María Julia Mayoral, "Nace la Operación Carlota," *Granma*, October 1, 2005, Latin American Studies Web site, http://www.latinamericanstudies.org/cuba/carlota.htm, accessed December 3, 2013.

59. LeoGrande, *Cuba's Policy in Africa*, 38; Duncan, *The Soviet Union and Cuba*, 134; Gleijeses, "Moscow's Proxy?," 109–10.

60. Gleijeses, "Moscow's Proxy?," 131–38; Oppenheimer, *Castro's Final Hour*, 84–85.

61. Landau, "History Absolved Him," 42.

62. Ramonet and Castro, *Fidel Castro*, 298.

63. Halperin, *Return to Havana*, 110.

64. Del Águila, *Cuba*, 129; Gioia Minuti, "Piero Gleijeses: A Truly Special Italian,"

Granma International, August 19, 2004, Latin American Studies Web site, http://www.latinamericanstudies.org/cuba/piero.htm, accessed December 3, 2013.

65. Farber, *Cuba since the Revolution*, 114–16.

66. Duncan, *The Soviet Union and Cuba*, 88–97; Mesa-Lago, *Cuba in the 1970s*, 162; Domínguez, *To Make a World Safe for Revolution*, 225; "Cold War Prompted Decades of Severed Relations," *CubaNews*, February 1998, 2.

67. Valenta, "Comment: The Soviet-Cuban Alliance in Africa and Future Prospects in the Third World," 40; Latell, *After Fidel*, 202.

68. Domínguez, *To Make a World Safe for Revolution*, 171–72; Zimbalist and Brundenius, *The Cuban Economy*, 153.

69. Hunt and Risch, *Warrior: Frank Sturgis*, 296; Waldron, *Watergate: The Hidden History*; "Bernard Barker Dies at 92; Watergate Burglar Was a CIA Operative," *Los Angeles Times*, June 6, 2009.

70. Barberia, "Remittances," Rosemarie Rogers Working Paper no. 15, Inter-University Committee on International Migration, September 2002, http://web.mit.edu/cis/www/migration/pubs/rrwp/15_barberia.html, accessed December 3, 2013, 2, 7.

71. Del Águila, *Cuba*, 129.

72. Ramonet and Castro, *Fidel Castro*, 263; Latell, *Castro's Secrets*, 118.

73. Domínguez, *To Make a World Safe for Revolution*, 176–77; Valenta, "Comment: The Soviet-Cuban Alliance in Africa and Future Prospects in the Third World," 42; Prevost, "Cuba," 126–28.

74. Prevost, "Cuba," 129–30; Duncan, *The Soviet Union and Cuba*, 165; Fermoselle, *The Evolution of a Cuban Military*, 411–12; Alan Riding, "Salvador Rebels: Five-Sided Alliance Searching for New, Moderate Image," *New York Times*, March 18, 1982; U.S. Department of State, "Cuban Support for Terrorism," 1.

75. Cotman, *The Gorrión Tree*, 73, 79, 89, 114.

76. Del Águila, *Cuba*, 130; Richard Halloran, "Marines Will Conduct Maneuvers and Fire Artillery in Guantanamo," *New York Times*, October 3, 1979; A. O. Sulzberger Jr., "1,800 Marines Land at Guantánamo in Show of U.S. Might," *New York Times*, October 18, 1979.

77. Sullivan, "Cuba: U.S. Restrictions on Travel and Remittances," 3; Schoultz, *That Little Infernal Republic*, 3.

78. Cotman, *The Gorrión Tree*, 221; Fermoselle, *The Evolution of a Cuban Military*, 325, 441–42; John Hoyt Williams, "Cuba: Havana's Military Machine," *The Atlantic*, August 1998, http://www.theatlantic.com/magazine/archive/1988/08/cuba-havana-apos-s-military-machine/5932, accessed December 3, 2013.

79. See various documents reproduced in "Luis Posada Carriles: The Declassified Record," at the National Security Archive Web site, http://www2.gwu.edu/~nsarchiv/NSAEBB/NSAEBB153/, accessed December 28, 2013.

80. Antón and Hernández, *Cubans in America*, 184; Portes, Clark, and Bach, "The New Wave," 3.

81. Portes and Stepick, *City on the Edge*, 20; Metropolitan Dade County, Dade County Public Schools, and the Florida Department of Health and Rehabilitative Services, "The Cuban Refugee in 1979: A Rebuttal," http://cuban-exile.com/doc_026-050/doc0030.html, accessed December 3, 2013. Comparative data from "Table 9, Cuban

Origin Persons in Selected States by Rank: 1980 and 1970," in U.S. Department of Commerce, Bureau of the Census, *Current Population Survey, 1985*, 13.

82. *El Súper*, directed by León Ichaso and Orlando Jiménez-Leal (New York: Max Mambrú Films, 1979); Suárez, *Going Under*, 154–55; García, *Dreaming in Cuban*, 25–26, 57–58.

83. Levine and Asís, *Cuban Miami*, 64–77; Madeline Baró Díaz, "Cuban Institutions Live in Exile," *South Florida Sun-Sentinel*, January 22, 2005, Latin American Studies Web site, http://latinamericanstudies.org/exile/institutions.htm, accessed December 3, 2013; Web site of the Asociación de Antiguos Empleados de El Encanto, http://www.tiendaselencantodecuba.com/main.html, accessed December 3, 2013.

84. Portes, "A Bifurcated Enclave."

85. U.S. Census Bureau, *1977 Survey of Minority-Owned Business Enterprises*, 58; Olson and Olson, *Cuban Americans*, 77.

86. Levine and Asís, *Cuban Miami*, 103.

87. The number of Cubans who were eligible to vote in 1970 was negligible. In Puerto Rico, for example, there were 21,905 nonnaturalized Cuban residents and only 1,718 naturalized residents. William R. Armlong, "Se 'cubaniza' la política en Dade," *El Miami Herald*, July 12, 1981; Esteve, *El exilio cubano en Puerto Rico*, 26.

88. García, *Havana USA*, 146.

89. Eckstein, "Cuban Émigrés and the American Dream," 298.

90. FBI report on Omega 7, October 9, 1993, Cuban Information Archives Web site, http://cuban-exile.com/doc_001-025/doc0011.html, accessed December 3, 2013; appendix 2, "Omega 7 Incidents," http://cuban-exile.com/doc_001-025/doc0013.html, accessed December 3, 2013.

91. "Cuban Exile Organizations, Hard-Line: 1970s," Cuban Information Archives Web site, http://cuban-exile.com/doc_001-025/doc0014.html, accessed December 3, 2013; "The Posada File: Part II," National Security Archive, http://www.gwu.edu/~nsarchiv/NSAEBB/NSAEBB157/index.htm, accessed December 3, 2013.

92. Arboleya, *The Cuban Counterrevolution*, 224–25; Fernández, "From Little Havana to Washington, D.C.," 115–34; García, *Havana USA*, 153–54.

93. Masud-Piloto, *With Open Arms*, 73. See also Grupo Areíto, *Contra viento y marea*.

94. García, *Havana USA*, 47.

95. Ojito, *Finding Mañana*, 45, 48, 51; Levine, *Secret Missions to Cuba*.

96. See entire list of travelers in "Lista de los que participan," *El Miami Herald*, November 21, 1978; "Lista de los dialogantes," *El Miami Herald*, December 9, 1978; and Helga Silva, "Cuba Selects Exile Leaders for 'Dialogue,'" *Miami News*, November 6, 1978, all at Latin American Studies Web site, http://www.latinamericanstudies.org/dialogue/dialogue-leaders.htm, accessed December 3, 2013.

97. Ojito, *Finding Mañana*, 55, 63; Olson and Olson, *Cuban Americans*, 79.

98. Ojito, *Finding Mañana*, 63; Masud-Piloto, *With Open Arms*, 77.

99. García, *Havana USA*, 71.

100. Ojito, *Finding Mañana*, 8, 106, 117; Portes and Stepick, *City on the Edge*, 18.

101. Ojito, *Finding Mañana*, 131–32; Fernández, *Cuba and the Politics of Passion*, 78, 87.

102. Portes and Stepick, *City on the Edge*, 21; Don Bohning, "Turbas atacan a expresos en Cuba," *El Miami Herald*, May 3, 1980.

103. Carter quoted in Masud-Piloto, *With Open Arms*, 83; Portes and Stepick, *City on the Edge*, 25–26.

104. I use the word *marielito* sparingly as a neutral term.

105. García, *Havana USA*, 68; Antón and Hernández, *Cubans in America*, 208; Fernández, *Cuba and the Politics of Passion*, 83, 92; Ackerman, "The Balsero Phenomenon," 175–80.

106. For a useful definition of socialization in the Cuban context, see Fernández, *Cuba and the Politics of Passion*, 86.

107. Ackerman, "The Balsero Phenomenon," 181; Pedraza, "*Los Marielitos* of 1980," 89, 91; Peterson, "Work Attitudes of Mariel Boatlift Refugees," 7; Portes, Clark, and Manning, "After Mariel," 45–49; Antón and Hernández, *Cubans in America*, 208; Silvia M. Unzueta, "The Mariel Exodus: A Year in Retrospective," Cuban Information Archives Web site, http://www.cuban-exile.com/doc_026-050/doc0033.html, accessed December 3, 2013; Gastón A. Fernández, "Race, Gender, and Class in the Persistence of the Mariel Stigma Twenty Years after the Exodus from Cuba," 79, 84.

108. García, *Havana USA*, 64; Duany, "Cuban Communities in the United States," 81; Glenn Garvin, "Story's Fallout Was Felt for Decades," *Miami Herald*, April 3, 2005, Latin American Studies Web site, http://www.latinamericanstudies.org/mariel/fallout.htm, accessed December 26, 2013; Elaine De Valle, "Mariel: New Leaders Were Forged in Heat of Mariel Crisis," *Miami Herald*, April 4, 2005, Latin American Studies Web site, http://www.latinamericanstudies.org/mariel/forged.htm, accessed December 3, 2013.

109. Torres, *In the Land of Mirrors*, 113; Bertot, "Postmodernidad y la Generación del Mariel."

110. "Carter Promises," *Time*, May 19, 1980; Gay Nemeti, "Mariel Chronology," Latin American Studies Web site, http://www.latinamericanstudies.org/mariel/mariel-chronology.htm, accessed December 3, 2013.

111. Unzueta, "The Mariel Exodus."

112. Llanes, *Cuban Americans*, 178; Fernández, *The Mariel Exodus*, 48–49; Azicri, *Cuba Today and Tomorrow*, 184.

113. Nemeti, "Mariel Chronology"; Masud-Piloto, *With Open Arms*, 94.

114. Portes and Stepick, *City on the Edge*, 31; Duany, "Cuban Communities in the United States," 81; Liz Balmaseda, "Marielito . . . no es mala palabra," *El Miami Herald*, November 1, 1981.

115. Fernández, "Race, Gender, and Class"; Eckstein and Barberia, "Cuban Americans and Their Transnational Ties," 268; Portes and Stepick, *City on the Edge*, 33; Portes, Clark, and Manning, "After Mariel," 55; Zita Arocha and Alfonso Chardy, "Exiliados radicados rechazan al nuevo éxodo, afirman," *El Miami Herald*, August 23, 1980; Portes, "A Bifurcated Enclave."

116. Arenas, *Before Night Falls*, 301–2; Brett Sokol, "Requiem for a True Original," *Miami NewTimes News*, December 14, 2000, http://www.miaminewtimes.com/2000-12-14/news/requiem-for-a-true-original/, accessed December 3, 2013.

Chapter 5. Now We Are Going to Build Socialism

1. Fidel Castro's speech to mark the thirtieth anniversary of his first speech [in Havana] after the revolution's victory, January 8, 1989, Castro Speech Database, http://lanic.utexas.edu/project/castro/db/1989/19890109.html, accessed December 3, 2013.

2. See, for example, Gunn, "Will Castro Fall?"; Montaner, "Castro's Last Stand"; Oppenheimer, *Castro's Final Hour*; Alfred Padula, "Is Cuba Next?," *Times of the Americas*, November 29, 1989; William Safire, "Castro's Last Stand," *New York Review*, February 19, 1990; and Tad Szulc, "Can Castro Last?" *New York Times Magazine*, May 31, 1990, 12–15.

3. Echevarría, "Fla. Sugar King Pepe Fanjul Dreams of Post-Castro Cuba," *CubaNews*, December 1, 2007, http://www.thefreelibrary.com/Fla.+sugar+king+Pepe+Fanjul+dreams+of+post-Castro+Cuba.-a0171812516, accessed January 24, 2014; Carreño, "Action Plan for the Reconstruction of the Cuban Sugar Industry"; Doreen Hemlock, "What Businesses Are Doing in Puerto Rico," *CubaNews*, April 1994, 9.

4. Eckstein, "The Rectification of Errors"; Mesa-Lago, "Cuba's Economic Counter-Reform"; Mesa-Lago, "On Rectifying Errors of a Courteous Dissenter."

5. Shearman, "Gorbachev and the Restructuring of Soviet-Cuban Relations," 71–73.

6. Torres, *In the Land of Mirrors*, 119; Zimbalist and Brundenius, *The Cuban Economy*, 155; Schoultz, *That Little Infernal Republic*, 399.

7. Zimbalist and Brundenius, *The Cuban Economy*, 155; Oppenheimer, *Castro's Final Hour*, 25.

8. Schoultz, *That Little Infernal Republic*, 440–45; Franklin, *Cuba and the United States*, 271–72, 284.

9. Mesa-Lago, "The Economic Effects on Cuba of the Downfall of Socialism in the USSR and Eastern Europe," 147; Azicri, *Cuba Today and Tomorrow*, 21; Blasier, "Soviet-Cuban Partnership," 88.

10. Erickson, "Cuba, China, Venezuela," 414; Franklin, *Cuba and the United States*, 325.

11. Azicri, *Cuba Today and Tomorrow*, 229.

12. Pérez-López, *Cuba's Second Economy*, 124–26; Mesa-Lago, "The Economic Effects on Cuba of the Downfall of Socialism in the USSR and Eastern Europe," 161; Canler, "The Miracle of the Cuban Economy," 64.

13. Mesa-Lago, "The Economic Effects on Cuba of the Downfall of Socialism in the USSR and Eastern Europe," 143–44; Pérez-López, *Economics of Cuban Sugar*, 162; Azicri, *Cuba Today and Tomorrow*, 34; "Yearly Average Crude Prices: 1977 to Present," Illinois Oil and Gas Association Web site, http://www.ioga.com/PDF_Files/oilpricechart.pdf, accessed December 30, 2013.

14. Pérez-López, *Cuba's Second Economy*, 123; Canler, "The Miracle of the Cuban Economy," 64; Mesa-Lago, "Cuba's Economic Counter-Reform," 118; Mesa-Lago, "On Rectifying Errors of a Courteous Dissenter," 90.

15. Mesa-Lago, "The Economic Effects on Cuba of the Downfall of Socialism in the USSR and Eastern Europe," 146, 161, 65; Vice-President Carlos Lage's televised speech on challenges to the Cuban economy, November 6, 1992, in García Luis, *Cuban Revolution Reader*, 277; Pavlov, *Soviet-Cuban Alliance*, 242; Mesa-Lago, "Cuba's Economic Counter-Reform," 124.

16. Mesa-Lago, "The Economic Effects on Cuba of the Downfall of Socialism in the USSR and Eastern Europe," 185; Mesa-Lago, "On Rectifying Errors of a Courteous Dissenter," 89–90.

17. Domínguez, *To Make a World Safe for Revolution*, 90; Eckstein, "The Rectification of Errors," 73; Pollitt, "Sugar, 'Dependency' and the Cuban Revolution," 25.

18. Fidel Castro's speech at the Continental Dialogue on the Foreign Debt held at Havana's Palace of Conventions, August 4, 1985, Castro Speech Database, http://www1.lanic.utexas.edu/project/castro/db/1985/19850804.html, accessed December 3, 2013; Mesa-Lago, *Economía y bienestar social en Cuba*, 28; Canler, "The Miracle of the Cuban Economy," 65; Stubbs, *Cuba: The Test of Time*, 115–16.

19. Domínguez, "The Political Impact on Cuba of the Reform and Collapse of Communist Regimes," 112, 121; LeoGrande, "The Cuban Nation's Single Party," 55; Ramonet and Castro, *Fidel Castro*, 585–86; Mesa-Lago, "Cuba's Economic Counter-Reform," 131; Pavlov, *Soviet-Cuban Alliance*, 111–12, 121.

20. Castro quoted in *Granma*, December 27, 1986; Pérez-López, *Cuba's Second Economy*, 122; Ramonet and Castro, *Fidel Castro*, 585; Azicri, *Cuba Today and Tomorrow*, 49; Domínguez, "The Political Impact on Cuba of the Reform and Collapse of Communist Regimes," 105; Fidel Castro's speech on the twenty-fifth anniversary of the victory at Giron, April 19, 1986, http://www.cuba.cu/gobierno/discursos/1986/esp/f190486e.html, accessed December 3, 2013; Fernández, *Cuba and the Politics of Passion*, 97, 106.

21. Fidel Castro's speech during final session of the deferred Third Communist Party of Cuba Congress at Havana's Palace of Conventions, December 2, 1986, Castro Speech Database,http://www1.lanic.utexas.edu/project/castro/db/1986/19861202-1.html, accessed December 3, 2013; Guevara quoted in Domínguez, "The Political Impact on Cuba of the Reform and Collapse of Communist Regimes," 119. See also Bunck, *Fidel Castro and the Quest for a Revolutionary Culture in Cuba*, 64; and Stubbs, *Cuba: The Test of Time*, 72.

22. Fidel Castro's speech at the second national meeting of agricultural production cooperatives, May 18, 1986, http://www.cuba.cu/gobierno/discursos/1986/esp/f180586e.html, accessed December 3, 2013; Eckstein, *Back from the Future*, 63.

23. Mesa-Lago, "Cuba's Economic Counter-Reform," 106; Pérez-López, *Cuba's Second Economy*, 122; Fidel Castro's speech at rally in Artemisa, Havana province, to mark the 34th anniversary of the assault on the Moncada Barracks, July 26, 1987, Castro Speech Database,http://www1.lanic.utexas.edu/project/castro/db/1987/19870726.html, accessed December 3, 2013; Eckstein, "Rectification of Errors," 69–70.

24. Fidel Castro's speech during final session of the deferred Third Communist Party of Cuba Congress at Havana's Palace of Conventions, December 2, 1986.

25. Córdova, *El trabajador cubano*, 164; Mesa-Lago, "The Economic Effects on Cuba of the Downfall of Socialism in the USSR and Eastern Europe," 177; Pérez-López, *Cuba's Second Economy*, 123.

26. Stubbs, *Cuba: The Test of Time*, 3.

27. Pérez-Stable, *The Cuban Revolution*, 157; LeoGrande, *The Cuban Communist Party and Electoral Politics*, 11; LeoGrande, "The Cuban Nation's Single Party," 52; Mesa-Lago, "The Economic Effects on Cuba of the Downfall of Socialism in the USSR and Eastern Europe," 135; del Águila, *Cuba*, 99–101.

28. Fermoselle, *The Evolution of a Cuban Military*, 338, 341; U.S. Information Agency, *Cuba Annual Report* (1987), 127–30; Kapcia, "The Cuban Revolution in Crisis," 187.

29. Rachel Ehrenfeld, "Castro Is Shocked! to Find Drug-Dealing Comrades," *Wall Street Journal*, June 23, 1989; Oppenheimer, *Castro's Final Hour*, 130–64.

30. "Investigación al General de División Arnaldo Ochoa Sánchez," *Granma*, June 22, 1989, 1; Oppenheimer, *Castro's Final Hour*, 41–43.

31. *8-A*, directed by Orlando Jiménez-Leal (Los Angeles: Meridian Video, 1992), documentary film.

32. U.S. Information Agency, *Cuba Annual Report* (1989), 286–318; Oppenheimer, *Castro's Final Hour*, 19; Cuban American National Foundation, *Aftermath of a Purge*, 1–7; Mujal-León and Buzón, "Exceptionalism and Beyond," 406; Latell, *Castro's Secrets*, 38.

33. Raúl Castro quoted in Cuban American National Foundation, "Aftermath of a Purge," 5; Oppenheimer, *Castro's Final Hour*, 93; Latell, *After Fidel*, 207, 211; Fidel Castro quoted in Jiménez-Leal, *8-A*, 76.

34. Pérez-Stable, "The Invisible Crisis," 28; Amuchástegui, "Cuba's Armed Forces," 109–14.

35. Economist Intelligence Unit, *Country Report: Cuba, Dominican Republic, Haiti, Puerto Rico (1990)*, 13; Eckstein, *Back from the Future*, 115; LeoGrande, "Cuban Communist Party," 14–18; Economist Intelligence Unit, *Country Report: Cuba, Dominican Republic, Haiti, Puerto Rico (1991)*, 14–15; Azicri, *Cuba Today and Tomorrow*, 105–7, 253.

36. Aguirre, "Social Control in Cuba," 83; Prevost "Cuba," 350.

Chapter 6. Socialism or Death!

1. Castro coined the slogan on January 2, 1989; see speech given at the Carlos Manuel de Céspedes Park in Santiago de Cuba during the ceremony marking the 30th anniversary of the Cuban Revolution, Castro Speech Database, http://lanic.utexas.edu/project/castro/db/1989/19890102.html, accessed December 3, 2013; Mesa-Lago, "Historia y evaluación," 537.

2. Mesa-Lago, *Economía y bienestar social en Cuba*; 32; Dye, "Cuba and Origins of the US Sugar Quota," 194; Fernández, *Adrift*, 4; Halperin, *Return to Cuba*, 179; Alonso and Lago, "A First Approximation Model of the Balance of Payments, Output, Employment and Foreign Aid Requirements of a Democratic Cuba."

3. Mesa-Lago, *Economía y bienestar social en Cuba*, 32; del Águila, *Cuba*, 102; Sánchez, "Cuba: An Unreliable Producer of Sugar," 260; Nicolás Rivero, "More Trouble with Sugar," *CubaNews*, August 1994, 2; Gott, *Cuba*, 288; Sinclair and Thompson, "Going against the Grain," 157.

4. Mesa-Lago, *Economía y bienestar social en Cuba*, 32; "Facts and Stats," *CubaNews*, January 1996, 3; Economist Intelligence Unit, *Cuba Country Report 1st Quarter 2000*, 5.

5. Klepak, *Cuba's Military*, 95–96.

6. Mesa-Lago, "The Economic Effects on Cuba of the Downfall of Socialism in the USSR and Eastern Europe," 161; Ferriol Muruaga, "La seguridad alimentaria en Cuba," 86; Curry-Machado, "Surviving the 'Cuban Nightmare,'" 11; Armando H. Portela, "Food Shortages Damage Nutrition, Health," *CubaNews*, March 1998, 10; Prout, "Jail-House Rock," 423–36.

7. Álvarez, "Rationed Products and Something Else," 308; Pérez-López, *Cuba's Second Economy*, 138.

8. "Rationing, Shortages Define Cuban Dilemma," *CubaNews*, October 1996, 9; Álvarez, "Rationed Products and Something Else," 309; "Comparative Dollar Prices of Some Items in Havana, Paris, Toronto and Miami," *CubaNews*, October 1993, 4.

9. Pérez-López, *Cuba's Second Economy*, 128–30; Álvarez, "Rationed Products and Something Else," 311.

10. Michael Molinski, "Ante la crisis, todo se recicla y reusa en Cuba," *El Nuevo Día* (San Juan), August 7, 1990, 22.

11. Álvarez, "Rationed Products and Something Else," 308; Álvaro García Uriarte and Alberto Ortega, interviewed by William Shurtleff, "Recent History of Soy in Cuba," January 1996, Soyinfo Center Web site, http://www.soyinfocenter.com/HSS/recent-history-of-soy-in-cuba.php, accessed December 3, 2013.

12. Villapol, *Comida al minuto*, 32.

13. MacDonald, *A Developmental Analysis of Cuba's Health Care System since 1959*, xiv, 261; "Epidemic Neuropathy—Cuba, 1991–1994," *Morbidity and Mortality Weekly Report* 43, no. 10 (March 18, 1994): 183, 189–92; Mesa-Lago, *Economía y bienestar social en Cuba*, 58–59; Luis, *Culture and Customs of Cuba*, 42; Armando H. Portela, "Infant Mortality," *CubaNews*, February 1997, 5; "Shortages Lead to Decline in Surgery, Intensive Care," *CubaNews*, May 1997, 9; Armando H. Portela, "Cuba's Health System: Tested in Hard Times," *CubaNews*, November 1994, 11; "Senior Citizens," and "Low Weight at Birth," both in *CubaNews*, March 1998, 10.

14. García, "Urban Transportation in Cuba"; Mesa-Lago, The Economic Effects on Cuba of the Downfall of Socialism in the USSR and Eastern Europe," 16; Pérez-López, *Cuba's Second Economy*, 140.

15. Eckstein, "Dollarization and Its Discontents in the Post-Soviet Era," 325; Álvarez García and González Núñez, *¿Intelectuales vs. Revolución?*, 30; Guerra, "Redefining Revolution in Cuba," 176–77.

16. Republic of Cuba, Instituto Nacional de la Vivienda, *40 años de la vivienda en Cuba*, 13; "Scarcity, Desperation Define Cuba Housing," *Miami Herald*, January 3, 2000; Eric Driggs, "Deteriorating Living Conditions in Cuba," *Focus on Cuba* 59 (October 14, 2004), http://ctp.iccas.miami.edu/FOCUS_Web/spn/Issue59SPANISH.htm, accessed November 7, 2013.

17. Skaine, *The Cuban Family*, 24, 63; Farber, *Cuba since the Revolution*, 209.

18. "Socio-Economic Conditions in Pre-Castro Cuba"; Eckstein, "Dollarization and Its Discontents," 325; John Suárez, compiler, "Cuba Facts," Directorio Democrático Cubano Web site, http://www.directorio.org/cubafacts/index.php, accessed December 3, 2013. According to the United Nations Development Programme, in 1995 Cuba's 96 percent literacy rate was equaled or surpassed by that of the Bahamas (98 percent), Guyana (98 percent), Trinidad and Tobago (98 percent), Barbados (97 percent), Uruguay (97 percent), and Argentina (96 percent); United Nations Development Project, *Human Development Report, 1998*, 23, 127–29.

19. Life expectancy rates at birth among Latin American and Caribbean nations (top ten, 1995): Costa Rica (76.6), Barbados (76), Cuba (75.7), Chile (75.1), Antigua-Barbuda (75), Belize (74.2), Jamaica (74.1), Panama (73.4), the Bahamas (73.2), Trinidad and Tobago (73.1); *Human Development Report, 1998*, 127–29.

20. Ibid.

21. Mesa-Lago, *Economía y bienestar social en Cuba*, 33; Fidel Castro's speech during the extraordinary session of the National Assembly of the People's Government, February 20, 1990, Castro Speech Database, http://lanic.utexas.edu/project/castro/db/1990/19900220-3.html, accessed December 3, 2013.

22. LeoGrande, "The Cuban Nation's Single Party," 55.

23. Álvarez García and González Núñez, *¿Intelectuales vs. Revolución?*, 23; Fuentes, "Cuentapropismo o cuentapriapismo."

24. Aguirre, "Social Control in Cuba," 88; Azicri, *Cuba Today and Tomorrow*, 147; Cuba Unemployment Rates 1995–2000, TheGlobalEconomy.com, http://www.theglobaleconomy.com/Cuba/indicator-SL.UEM.TOTL.ZS/, accessed December 3, 2013.

25. Zimbalist, "Whither the Cuban Economy?," 22; Pérez-López, *Cuba's Second Economy*, 166–68; Azicri, *Cuba Today and Tomorrow*, 146, 150–51; Fuentes, "Cuentapropismo o cuentapriapismo," 345; "Law 73: Personal Taxes, Corporate Taxes and More," *CubaNews*, March 1998, 7.

26. Barberia, "Remittances to Cuba," 11.

27. LeoGrande, "Cuban Communist Party," 19.

28. Azicri, *Cuba Today and Tomorrow*, 143–44; Sinclair and Thompson, "Going against the Grain," 159.

29. On *paladares*, see "'Paladares' Legalized," *CubaNews*, July 1995, 5; Scarpaci, "Emerging Food and *Paladar* Market in Havana"; and Henken, "'Vale Todo' (Anything Goes)."

30. Mesa-Lago, *Economía y bienestar social en Cuba*, 83.

31. Eckstein, "Dollarization and Its Discontents," 320; "New Currency Moves Aim to Strengthen Peso," *CubaNews*, October 1995, 2; Álvarez, "Rationed Products and Something Else," 310.

32. Ritter, "Canadian-Cuban Economic Relations," 257–59.

33. Pérez-López, "Foreign Investment in Cuba."

34. Azicri, *Cuba Today and Tomorrow*, 153–54; "Funcionan en Cuba más de 400 asociaciones mixtas con capital extranjero," *Granma Internacional*, November 23, 2001.

35. Casanova Montero and Monreal González, "Cuba's External Economic Constraints," 94; Espino, "Tourism in Cuba," 55; Halperin, *Return to Cuba*, 24–25.

36. Jorge Pérez-López, excerpt of ASCE 1991 presentation, http://lanic.utexas.edu/la/cb/cuba/asce/cuba1/panel.html, accessed February 3, 2011; Espino, "Tourism in Cuba," 54; "Castro Cites Tourism as Engine of Economy," *CubaNews*, June 1997, 10.

37. Peters, *International Tourism*, 3; "Castro Cites Tourism as Engine of Economy," 10.

38. Suárez, "Cuba Facts"; Feinsilver, "Cuba as a 'World Medical Power,'" 20; Feinsilver, *Healing the Masses*, 124, 142–43; Scarpaci, Segre, and Coyula, *Havana*, 297.

39. "Bombing Victim," *CubaNews*, September 1997, 1–2; Ann Louise Bardach and Larry Rother, "Key Cuba Foe Claims Exiles' Backing," *New York Times*, July 12, 1998; Anita Snow, "U.S. Probes 1997 Cuba Hotel Bombings," *Washington Post*, May 10, 2007.

40. Mastrapa, "Soldiers and Businessmen," 431 and passim; Pérez-López, *Cuba's Second Economy*, 157; Klepak, *Cuba's Military*, 82–86; Pollitt, "The Rise and Fall of the Cuban Sugar Economy," 330.

41. LeoGrande, "The Cuban Nation's Single Party," 56; Mastrapa, "Soldiers and Businessmen," 408; Klepak, *Cuba's Military*, 61.

42. Azicri, *Cuba Today and Tomorrow*, 214.

43. "CEPAL Report on Cuban Economy," *CubaNews*, February 1998, 12; Pérez-López, "The Cuban Economy in an Unending Special Period," 508.

44. Mesa-Lago, *Economía y bienestar social en Cuba*, 36, 44.

45. Economic Commission for Latin America and the Caribbean, "Latin America and the Caribbean: Total External Debt, 1980–2006," http://www.eclac.org/colombia/noticias/documentosdetrabajo/9/35249/EstEco2246-03-_07-G-ES.pdf, accessed December 3, 2013; "Cuba Debt Trading at US$.22 Per U.S. Dollar," Economic Eye on Cuba Web site, August 17–23, 1998, http://www.cubatrade.org/eyeonz7.html, accessed December 3, 2013.

46. Azicri, *Cuba Today and Tomorrow*, 139.

47. Speech by Fidel Castro at the Close of the Fifth Congress of the Communist Party of Cuba, October 10, 1997, http://www.cuba.cu/gobierno/discursos/1997/esp/f101097e.html, accessed December 3, 2013; Zimbalist, "Whither the Cuban Economy?," 22; Henken, "'Vale Todo,'" 348.

48. Domingo Amuchástegui, "Congress Continues Trend toward Younger Leaders"; "Eight Politburo Members Demoted to Central Committee"; "The New Politburo," all in *CubaNews*, November 1997, 8–9. Politburo members' biographies in http://archive.is/J1Q3Z, accessed November 19, 2013.

49. The text of the Torricelli Act, also known as the Cuban Democracy Act of 1992, is available at http://www.treasury.gov/resource-center/sanctions/Documents/cda.pdf, accessed December 3, 2013.

50. Tom Fiedler, "Clinton Backs Torricelli Bill: 'I Like It,' He Tells Cuban Exiles," *Miami Herald*, April 24, 1992; Christopher Marquis, "Bush Gives Support to Cuba Bill," *Miami Herald*, May 6, 1992.

51. Hoffman, "The Helms-Burton Law and Its Consequences for Cuba, the United States and Europe."

52. H.R. 927, Cuban Liberty and Democratic Solidarity Act of 1996 (Helms-Burton Act), http://www.gpo.gov/fdsys/pkg/PLAW-104publ114/html/PLAW-104publ114.htm, accessed November 19, 2013.

53. Ana Radelat, "Administration Critiques GOP Cuba Proposals," *CubaNews*, April 1995, 6; Ana Radelat, "Helms-Burton Hits a Snag," *CubaNews*, July 1995, 8.

54. Transcriptions of flight recordings available at the Hermanos al Rescate/Brothers to the Rescue Web site, http://www.hermanos.org, accessed June 1, 2013.

55. "Resolution Adopted by the Council of the International Civil Aviation Organization at the Twentieth Meeting of Its 148th Session on 27 June 1996," http://www.shootdownvictims.org/documents/ICAOReport.pdf, accessed November 19, 2013.

56. Perl, "Whither Helms-Burton?; "'Exploratory Contracts' Reported between ITT, STET," *CubaNews*, May 1997, 7; "STET-ITT Deal May Set Pattern for Others," *CubaNews*, August 1997, 5; Ana Radelat, "Helms-Burton Sanctions Hit Israeli Group in Cuba," *CubaNews*, December 1997, 2. See also "The Helms-Burton Effect"; Sally Hughes, "Cemex Withdraws as Mexico Protests"; Sallie Hughes, "Mexican Firms Claim They Should Be Exempt," all in *CubaNews*, June 1996, 1, 6.

57. "UN Censures Cuba," *CubaNews*, May 1996, 6; Bárbara González, "Cuba, the U.N. Human Rights Commission and the OAS Race," Council on Hemispheric Affairs Web

site, May 2, 2005, http://www.coha.org/cuba-the-un-human-rights-commission-and-the-oas-race, accessed December 3, 2013.

58. Domingo Amuchástegui, "Anger over Helms Bill," *CubaNews*, May 1995, 10; "Allies Still Annoyed," *CubaNews*, August 1996, 5; Azicri, *Cuba Today and Tomorrow*, 226.

59. "Common Position of 2 December 1996 Defined by the Council on the Basis of Article J.2 of the Treaty on European Union, on Cuba, 96/697/CFSP," http://eurlex.europa.eu/LexUriServ/LexUriServ.do?uri=CELEX:31996E0697:EN:HTML, accessed December 3, 2013; Fernando Ravsberg, "La UE prepara el terreno para cambiar su política hacia Cuba," Público.es Web site, January 3, 2013, http://www.publico.es/448337/la-ue-prepara-el-terreno-para-cambiar-su-politica-hacia-cuba, accessed December 3, 2013.

60. Douglass Norvell, "Cuban Income Figures Do Not Reflect Subsidies," *CubaNews*, February 1999, 10.

61. Zimbalist, "Whither the Cuban Economy?," 26.

62. Blue, "The Erosion of Racial Equality in the Context of Cuba's Dual Economy," 35–68; Curry-Machado, "Surviving the 'Cuban Nightmare,'" 16; Eckstein, "Dollarization and Its Discontents," 323; Zimbalist, "Incentives and Planning in Cuba," 75.

63. Zimbalist, "Whither the Cuban Economy?," 13; Safa, "Women and Household Change in the Special Period," 222.

64. De la Fuente, *A Nation for All*, 319–20; estimates by Sarah Blue and Claus Brundenius cited in Safa, "Women and Household Change in the Special Period," 217–18, 222; Eckstein, "Dollarization and Its Discontents," 185.

65. Farber, *Cuba since the Revolution*, 204–7; "Cuba—Self-Employed," Indexmundi.com, http://www.indexmundi.com/facts/cuba/self-employed, accessed December 3, 2013.

66. "Authorities Stop Havana Immigration by Enforcing Decree on Movement," *CubaNews*, November 1998, 11; de la Fuente, *A Nation for All*, 327–28; Eckstein, "Dollarization and Its Discontents," 323.

67. Jorge I. Domínguez, presentation in panel discussion, "The Current Economic Situation in Cuba" (abstract), *Cuba in Transition* 1 (1991), http://www.ascecuba.org/publications/proceedings/volume1/panel.asp, accessed December 3, 2013.

68. William Booth, "Cubans Capture 2 Speedboats Waiting for Refugees," *Washington Post*, July 5, 1993; Christopher Marquis and David Hancock, "U.S. Rips Cuba's 'Extreme Cruelty': Protests 3 Killings Near Base," *Miami Herald*, July 7, 1993.

69. Utset, "Creating Citizens"; "El Partido Pro Derechos Humanos en Cuba," *Diario de las Américas*, July 4, 1995, http://www.sigloxxi.org/fisura/braga-38.htm, accessed December 3, 2013.

70. Democracia Participativa, "Bosquejo biográfico de Oswaldo Payá Sardiñas," http://democraciaparticipativa.net/documentos/MinibiogrPaya.htm, accessed December 3, 2013; Torres, *In the Land of Mirrors*, 149.

71. Grupo de Trabajo y Apoyo a Concilio Cubano, "Concilio Cubano," http://www2.fiu.edu/~fcf/concilio.html, accessed December 3, 2013; "Lista actualizada de organizaciones firmantes del Foro Concilio Cubano, 15 de Agosto de 1996," Cubanet Web site, http://www.cubanet.org/CNews/y96/sep96/doc2.html, accessed December 3, 2013; Concilio Cubano, "Official Statement by Concilio Cubano Concerning the Event

Scheduled for February 24, 1996," http://www2.fiu.edu/~fcf/state.html, accessed December, 2013; Domínguez, *Democratic Politics in Latin America and the Caribbean*, 183; Democracia Participativa, "Bosquejo biográfico de Oswaldo Payá Sardiñas."

72. Gershman and Gutiérrez, "Ferment in Civil Society," 38–39.

73. "Proyecto Varela," January 22, 1998, Movimiento Cristiano de Liberación Web site, http://www.oswaldopaya.org/es/proyecto-varela/, accessed December 3, 2013; Economist Intelligence Unit, *Country Report: Cuba, May 2001*, 12.

74. Democracia Participativa, "Bosquejo biográfico de Oswaldo Payá Sardiñas"; Economist Intelligence Unit, *Country Report: Cuba, Dominican Republic, Haiti, Puerto Rico (1993)*, 10–11; Azicri, *Cuba Today and Tomorrow*, 116–17; del Águila, *Cuba*, 168.

75. "La Patria es de todos," Cubanet Web site, http://www.cubanet.org/CNews/y97/jul97/07adoc1.htm, accessed December 3, 2013; "Proyecto el Partido de la unidad, la democracia y los derechos humanos que defendemos," *Granma*, May 27, 1997.

76. Economist Intelligence Unit, *Country Profile: Cuba 1993–94*, 6; Domínguez, "The Political Impact on Cuba of the Reform and Collapse of Communist Regimes," 124; Aguirre, "Social Control in Cuba," 78–79.

77. Torres, *In the Land of Mirrors*, 20; Democracia Participativa, "Bosquejo biográfico de Oswaldo Payá Sardiñas."

78. U.S. Department of State, "Human Rights in Cuba: An Update," *US Department of State Bulletin*, April 1989, http://archive.org/stream/departmentofstatb89unit/departmentofstatb89unit_djvu.txt, accessed December 3, 2013.

79. "Ley 88 de Protección de la Independencia Nacional y la Economía de Cuba," February 16, 1999, Cubanet Web site, http://cubanet.org/ref/dis/021699.htm, accessed December 3, 2013; Mesa-Lago, *Economía y bienestar social en Cuba*, 38.

80. Utset, "Creating Citizens"; U.S. Department of State, "Human Rights in Cuba"; Inter-American Commission on Human Rights, Organization of American States, "Human Rights in Cuba: An Update," chapter IV of Annual Report on Human Rights, 1988–1989, OEA/Ser.L/V/II.76, Doc. 10, 18 September 1989, http://www.cidh.oas.org/annualrep/88.89eng/chap.4.htm, accessed November 7, 2013.

81. Examples of international human rights awards received by dissidents: Sánchez Santacruz, French Human Rights Award (1996); Payá, Homo Homini Award (1999); Cruz Varela, Premio Libertad de la Internacional Liberal (1992); Raúl Rivero, Reporters Sans Frontiers—Fondation de France (1997); and Sebastián Arcos Bergnes, Human Rights Award by the Spanish-Cuban Foundation (1997).

82. Pastoral letter "El amor todo lo espera," message of the Conference of Catholic Bishops of Cuba, September 1993, my translation, http://www.cubaencuentro.com/revista/documentos/carta-pastoral-el-amor-todo-lo-espera-117949, accessed December 3, 2013; "Church Lashes Out," *CubaNews*, October 1993, 8.

83. Both quotes from the welcome ceremony address of Pope John Paul II, Havana, January 21, 1998, http://www.vatican.va/holy_father/john_paul_ii/speeches/1998/january/documents/hf_jp-ii_spe_19980121_lahavana-arrival_en.html, accessed December 3, 2013. See also Pedraza, "The Impact of Pope John Paul II's Visit to Cuba."

84. Azicri, *Cuba Today and Tomorrow*, 96–99; Mario Vicent, "Subsistir en Cuba," *Revista Domingo* supplement, *El Nuevo Día* (San Juan), June 8, 2003, 10–12.

85. Pérez-López, *Cuba's Second Economy*, 114; Fernández, *Cuba and the Politics of Passion*, 97.

86. "Flores nocturnas," song by Silvio Rodríguez, my translation; Andrei Coderscu, "Picking the Flowers of the Revolution," *New York Times Magazine*, February 1, 1998, 32–35; Miguel Barnet, "Hijo de obrero," translated and reproduced in Howe, *Transgression and Conformity*, 173–74.

87. Ileana Fuentes, "Prostitutas o jineteras?," *Encuentro en la Red*, December 5, 2003, http://arch1.cubaencuentro.com/sociedad/20031205/1ab3098438cd926bdebc dc2da1137971/2.html, accessed December 3, 2013; Azicri, *Cuba Today and Tomorrow*, 81. See also Fusco, "Hustling for Dollars," 139–59; "HIV/AIDS 1997 Update," *CubaNews*, February 1998, 9; Molyneaux, "State, Gender, and Institutional Change," 309–10.

88. Scott, *Weapons of the Weak*, xvi–xvii and passim; Fernández, *Cuba and the Politics of Passion*, 29, 97–98.

89. Pérez, *To Die in Cuba*, especially 352–61.

90. Guerra, "Redefining Revolution in Cuba," 182–86; Aguirre, "Social Control in Cuba," 71–72; Fernández, *Cuba and the Politics of Passion*, 30–31; Cabrera, *Refranes de negros viejos*.

91. Guerra, "Redefining Revolution in Cuba," 180–81; Pérez-López, *Cuba's Second Economy*, 79; Fernández, *Cuba and the Politics of Passion*, 109.

92. Hernández-Reguant, "Multicubanidad," 78.

93. Meer, "Preemptive Nostalgia," 100; "Prieto Replaces Hart as Culture Minister," *CubaNews*, March 1997, 12; Fernandes, *Cuba Represent!* 46, 142, 151.

94. Redruello, "Algunas reflexiones," 82–99; Kirk and Padura Fuentes, *Culture and the Cuban Revolution*, 163, 172–73; Padura Fuentes, "Living and Creating in Cuba," 351; Chanan, *Cuban Cinema*, 362; Fernandes, *Cuba Represent!*, 49–50.

95. Padura Fuentes, "Living and Creating in Cuba," 352; Kirk and Padura Fuentes, *Culture and the Cuban Revolution*, 184; Torres, *In the Land of Mirrors*, 139; Álvarez García and González Núñez, *¿Intelectuales vs. Revolución?* appendix 4, 173–83; Sánchez, *Havana Real*, 57.

96. Fernandes, *Cuba Represent!*, 140–42; Orlando Luis Pardo Lazo, "Fecaliteratura," *Penúltimos Días*, March 16, 2009, http://www.penultimosdias.com/2009/03/16/fe-caliteratura/ accessed December 3, 2013; "Angel Delgado: The Famous Performance," [September 2008], YouTube video, http://www.youtube.com/watch?v=wzQsX564HTg, accessed December 3, 2013.

97. Chanan, *Cuban Cinema*, 360; Camnitzer, *New Art of Cuba*, 258.

98. Fiedler, "Clinton Backs Torricelli Bill."

99. Jorge Mas Canosa quoted in Moreno and Warren, "The Conservative Enclave Revisited," 176.

100. Curry-Machado, "Surviving the 'Cuban Nightmare,'" 19; Henken, "Balseros in Alabama," 413; Fernández, *Adrift*, 192; Torres, *In the Land of Mirrors*, 132.

101. Fernández, *Adrift*, 62–63.

102. Ackerman, "The Balsero Phenomenon," 173.

103. Fernández, *Adrift*, 20–22, 31–33; Curry-Machado, "Surviving," 2; William Booth, "Cubans Capture Two Speedboats Waiting for Refugees," *Washington Post*, July 5, 1993; Christopher Marquis and David Hancock, "U.S. Rips Cuba's 'Extreme Cruelty,' Protests Three Killings Near Base," *Miami Herald*, July 7, 1993.

104. Gershman and Gutiérrez, "Ferment in Civil Society," 37; Domingo Amuchástegui, "Rioting on the Malecón: Castro's Response," *CubaNews*, September 1994, 9;

Fernández, *Adrift*, 45; Aguirre, "Social Control in Cuba," 81; de la Fuente and Glasco, "Are Blacks 'Getting out of Control'?" 53.

105. Fernández, *Adrift*, 81; Ramonet and Castro, *Fidel Castro*, 587; Prevost, "Cuba," 349; Wasem, "Cuban Migration to the United States: Policy and Trends," Congressional Research Service report, Congressional Research Service, Washington, D.C., June 2, 2009, 2–4.

106. Eric Schmitt, "Cuban Refugees Riot in Panama," *New York Times*, December 9, 1994, http://www.nytimes.com/1994/12/09/world/cuban-refugees-riot-in-panama.html, accessed December 27, 2013.

107. Jefferson Morley, "What Is the 'Wet-Foot, Dry-Foot' Policy?" *Washington Post*, July 27, 2007.

108. Moreno and Warren, "Pragmatism and Strategic Realignment in the 1996 Election," 211–12, 218–19, 223, 228; "Recent Cuban-American Voting Patterns," *Cuba Facts* 57 (November 2011), http://ctp.iccas.miami.edu/FACTS_Web/Cuba%20Facts%20Issue%2057.htm, accessed November 7, 2013.

109. Cuban Research Institute, Florida International University, "The Cuban Diaspora in the 21st Century," July 2011, 50, 62, Cuban Research Institute, Florida International University, http://casgroup.fiu.edu/news/docs/2554/1331179294_Cuban_Diaspora_in_the_21st_Century.pdf, accessed December 3, 2013.

110. Barberia, "Remittances to Cuba," 30; "Flights, Remittances Get Official Green Light Again," *CubaNews*, June 1998, 8; Sullivan, "Cuba: U.S. Restrictions on Travel and Remittances," 3–4; Emilio Morales, "Cuba: $2.6 Billion in Remittances in 2012," Havana Times Web site, June 11, 2013, http://www.havanatimes.org/?p=94444, accessed December 30, 2013.

111. Fernández, *Adrift*, 233.

112. Rick Bragg, "Tug of War over Cuban Boy in Miami Is Escalating Again," *New York Times*, March 24, 2000; Katharine Q. Seelye, "Gore Supporting Residency Status for Cuban Child," *New York Times*, March 31, 2000; Guerra, "Elián González and the 'Real Cuba' of Miami," 1–25.

113. Ramonet and Castro, *Fidel Castro*, 589.

114. "Recent Cuban-American Voting Patterns"; Abby Goodnough, "Hispanic Vote in Florida: Neither a Bloc nor a Lock," *New York Times*, October 17, 2004.

115. U.S. Department of Commerce, Bureau of the Census, "The Hispanic Population: Census 2000 Brief," May 2001, http://www.census.gov/prod/2001pubs/c2kbr01-3.pdf, accessed December 3, 2013; Fabiola Santiago, "Separated Yet Together, Exiles Span Many Lands," *Miami Herald*, December 29, 1998; Díaz-Briquets, "Cuban Global Emigration at the Turn of the Century."

116. Fuentes, "Cuentapropismo o cuentapriapismo," 342; Eckstein and Barberia, "Cuban Americans and Their Transnational Ties," 269; Díaz-Briquets, "Cuban Global Emigration," 403–4; Ackerman, "The Balsero Phenomenon," 175, 179–81, 185.

117. Portes, "A Bifurcated Enclave."

118. Eckstein, "Cuban Émigrés and the American Dream," 301–5.

119. Fernández, "Race, Gender, and Class," 84–85.

120. Luisa Yánez, "Balseros Documentary Nominated," *Miami Herald*, January 28, 2004; *Balseros*, directed by Carles Bosch and Josep Maria Domènech (Barcelona: Bausan Films and Buenavida Producciones S.L., 2002).

121. Lydia Guzmán, "Hace sándwiches en vez de salvar vidas," *El Nuevo Día* (Orlando), December 15, 2005.

122. William Kleinknecht, "Journalists at Risk," *American Journalism Review*, December 1999, http://www.ajr.org/Article.asp?id=766, accessed December 3, 2013; Torres, *In the Land of Mirrors*, 140; Howe, *Transgression and Conformity*, 49.

123. "Bay of Pigs Vets Expel 2," *Orlando Sentinel*, April 10, 2001.

124. Myreya Navarro, "Miami's Generations of Exiles Side by Side, Yet Worlds Apart," *New York Times*, February 11, 1999.

125. According to a 2004 study by the University of Miami's Institute for Cuban and Cuban-American Studies, 82 percent of recently arrived Cubans held a good or average opinion of Cuba's educational system and 96 percent said that they would not change it, and 81 percent had a good or average opinion of the medical system and 94 percent said they would not change it. The respondents' opinion of other aspects of Cuba such as the political system and its leaders were overwhelmingly negative. Gómez and Rothe, *Value Orientations and Opinions of Recently Arrived Cubans in Miami*, 31. Quote from Echevarría, "Fla. Sugar King Pepe Fanjul Dreams of a Post-Castro Cuba."

Chapter 7. This Revolution Can Destroy Itself

1. Cheng, "Sino-Cuban Relations during the Early Years of the Castro Regime," 112.

2. [Central Intelligence Agency], [Director of National Intelligence] Open Source Center, "Cuban Leadership Overview, April 2009," http://www.fas.org/irp/world/cuba/overview.pdf, accessed December 3, 2013.

3. Justin McCurry and Julia Kollewe, "China Overtakes Japan as World's Second Largest Economy," *The Guardian*, February 13, 2011, http://www.guardian.co.uk/business/2011/feb/14/china-second-largest-economy, accessed November 7, 2013.

4. Republic of Cuba, Oficina Nacional de Estadísticas, *Anuario estadístico de Cuba (2009)*, table 8.4.

5. Romero, "South-South Cooperation between Venezuela and Cuba"; Leslie Clark and Frances Robles, "OAS Cuba Move Touches Off Outcry," *Miami Herald*, June 4, 2009; "Declaration of the Revolutionary Government," Republic of Cuba, Ministry of Foreign Relations Web site, http://anterior.cubaminrex.cu/English/Statements/Articulos/StatementsGovernment/2009/09-06-08.html, accessed November 19, 2013.

6. Gustavo Coronel, "Hugo Chávez: The New Sugar Daddy," Vcrisis Web site, August 14, 2005, Vcrisis.com. http://www.vcrisis.com/?content=letters/200508141043, accessed December 3, 2013; Coronel, "When Oil Lubricates Fascism," 477; Brian Latell, "The Castro Brothers and Hugo Chávez," *Latell Report*, October 2006, http://ctp.iccas.miami.edu/Latell_Web/10The%20Latell%20Report%20October%202006.htm, accessed December 3, 2013.

7. See election and referenda results on the Electoral Geography 2.0 Web site, http://www.electoralgeography.com/new/en/category/countries/v/venezuela, accessed December 3, 2013.

8. "Convenio Integral de Cooperación entre la República de Cuba y la República Bolivariana de Venezuela," October 2000, http://www.mpdc.es/index.php?option=com_mtree&task=viewlink&link_id=528&Itemid=66, accessed November 19, 2013; Romero, "South-South Cooperation between Venezuela and Cuba," 108–10.

9. "Convenio Integral"; Romero, "South-South Cooperation between Venezuela and Cuba," 108; "Cuba, Venezuela Sign Oil Deal," Associated Press, October 30, 2000, Latin American Studies Web site, http://www.latinamericanstudies.org/venezuela/oil-deal. htm, accessed December 3, 2013.

10. Pérez-López, "Cuba's International Trade," 49; "How Venezuela Subsidizes the Castro Regime," *Cuba Facts* 10 (April 2005), http://ctp.iccas.miami.edu/FACTS_Web/ Cuba%20Facts%20Issue%2010%20April%202005.htm, accessed December 3, 2013; Romero, "South-South Cooperation between Venezuela and Cuba," 110.

11. Eugenio Yánez, "Cuba-Venezuela: Interdependence and Influence," Cuba-Venezuela Project Web site, September 2007, 2, http://www6.miami.edu/iccas/Docs/September-2007.pdf, accessed December 3, 2013; Erikson, *The Cuba Wars*, 259.

12. Yánez, "Cuba-Venezuela," 2–4; Coronel, "Hugo Chávez," 480; Ramonet and Castro, *Fidel Castro*, 597.

13. Coronel, "Hugo Chávez," 478; Romero, "South-South Cooperation between Venezuela and Cuba," 108; Jorge Piñón, "Venezuelan Oil Subsidies to Cuba Surpassed $3 Billion in 2006," *Cuba Facts* 34 (August 2007), http://ctp.iccas.miami.edu/FACTS_Web/ Cuba%20Facts%20Issue%2034%20August2007.htm, accessed December 3, 2013.

14. Romero, "South-South Collaboration," 109–10; "Castro's Venezuelan Bonanza," *Focus on Cuba* 54 (April 20, 2004), http://ctp.iccas.miami.edu/FOCUS_Web/Issue54. htm, accessed December 3, 2013; Hans Salas-Del Valle, "Cuba's Debt Crisis: Foreign Debt, Unemployment, and Migration," *Focus on Cuba* 174 (August 9, 2011), http:// ctp.iccas.miami.edu/FOCUS_Web/Issue147.htm, accessed December 3, 2013; "Speech Given by General of the Army Raúl Castro Ruz . . . in the Event Commemorating the 10th Anniversary of the Cuba-Venezuela Integral Cooperation Agreement," Havana, November 8, 2010, *Granma Internacional*, November 9, 2010, http://www.granma.cu/ ingles/cuba-i/9noviembre-45R-discurso.html, accessed December 3, 2013; Republic of Cuba, Oficina Nacional de Estadísticas, *Anuario estadístico de Cuba (2011)*, table 8.4.

15. Azicri, *Cuba Today and Tomorrow*, 154; Pérez-López, "Foreign Investment in Cuba," 109; Scarpaci, Segre, and Coyula, *Havana*, 292; "Tourism in Cuba: Selected Statistics," *Cuba Facts* 14 (June 2005), http://ctp.iccas.miami.edu/FACTS_Web/Cuba%20 Facts%20Issue%2014%20June%202005.htm, accessed December 3, 2013; Republic of Cuba, Oficina Nacional de Estadísticas, *Anuario estadístico de Cuba (2010)*; Republic of Cuba, Oficina Nacional de Estadísticas, *Anuario estadístico de Cuba (2011)*; European Commission, Directorate-General for Trade, "European Union, Trade in Goods with Cuba," *DG Trade Statistics*, June 8, 2011, http://trade.ec.europa.eu/doclib/docs/2006/ september/tradoc_122460.pdf, accessed December 3, 2013.

16. Yinghong Cheng, "Beijing and Havana: Political Fraternity and Economic Patronage," *China Brief*, April 30, 2009, http://www.jamestown.org/single/?no_cache=1&tx_ ttnews%5Btt_news%5D=34921, accessed December 3, 2013; Erikson, "The Future of American Business with Cuba," 697; Erikson, "Cuba, China, Venezuela: New Developments," 414–15.

17. Mark Frank, "Cuba's Trade Booms with China and Venezuela," Reuters, February 26, 2007, http://uk.reuters.com/article/2007/02/26/cuba-trade-idUKN263061132 0070226, accessed December 3, 2013; Republic of Cuba, Oficina Nacional de Estadísticas, *Anuario estadístico de Cuba (2011)*, tables 8.4. 8.5, and 8.6; European Union, "Bilateral Trade and Trade with the World: Cuba."

18. Great Britain, Parliament, House of Commons, Foreign Affairs Committee, *East Asia: Seventh Report of Session 2005–06*, 2:210–15; Suchlicki, "El desafío de Cuba y Venezuela," 2; Jaime Suchlicki, "Those Men in Havana Are Now Chinese," *Wall Street Journal*, July 30, 2009; Jennifer Hernández, "Chinese Technology Companies in Cuba," *Focus on Cuba* 186 (March 13, 2013), http://ctp.iccas.miami.edu/FOCUS_Web/Issue186. htm, accessed December 3, 2013.

19. John Otis, "As Inflation Soars, Venezuela's Leader Opts for Drastic Steps," December 10, 2013, NPR blog, http://www.npr.org/blogs/parallels/2013/12/11/248222305/as-inflation-soars-venezuelas-leader-opts-for-drastic-steps, accessed December 28, 2013; Suchlicki, "El desafío de Cuba y Venezuela," 2; Evgenij Haperskij, "Cuba—Russia Now and Then," Council of Hemispheric Affairs Web site, February 24, 2010, http://www.coha.org/cuba-russia-now-and-then, accessed December 3, 2013; Republic of Cuba, Oficina Nacional de Estadísticas, *Anuario estadístico de Cuba (2009)*, table 8.4; European Union, "Bilateral Trade and Trade with the World: Cuba."

20. John Hughes, "Latin America's Leftist Regimes Get Cozy with Iran," *Christian Science Monitor*, February 15, 2006; Suchlicki, "El desafío de Cuba y Venezuela," 2.

21. Anya K. Landau and Wayne S. Smith, "Cuba on the Terrorist List: In Defense of the Nation or Domestic Political Calculation?," *International Policy Report*, November 2002, 5, http://www.ciponline.org/images/uploads/publications/CubaontheTerroristList.pdf, accessed December 3, 2013; Erikson, *The Cuba Wars*, 194; Latell, *After Fidel*, 246.

22. "Trade Sanctions Reform and Export Enhancement Act of 2000," http://www.treasury.gov/resource-center/sanctions/Programs/Pages/tsra.aspx, accessed November 27, 2013.

23. Carlos Lage quoted by Tim Johnson in "U.S. Farmers Elated over Cuba Trade," *Miami Herald*, November 16, 2001.

24. Erikson, "The Future of American Business with Cuba," 698; Pablo Bachelet, "U.S. Trade Limits with Cuba Stay," *Miami Herald*, July 28, 2007; U.S. Census Bureau, Foreign Trade Statistics, "Trade in Goods with Cuba," U.S. Census Bureau Web site, www.census.gov/foreign-trade/balance/c2390.html, accessed November 19, 2013; Republic of Cuba, Oficina Nacional de Estadísticas, *Anuario estadístico de Cuba (2009)*, table 8.6; Republic of Cuba, Oficina Nacional de Estadísticas, *Anuario estadístico de Cuba (2011)*, table 8.6; Marc Frank, "U.S. Food Sales to Cuba Fell by 30 Percent from January through November Compared with the Same Period in 2009," Reuters, January 14, 2011, http://www.reuters.com/article/2011/01/14/us-cuba-usa-idUSTRE70D5H520110114?feedType=RSS&feedName=domesticNews, accessed December 3, 2013; Sullivan, "Cuba: Issues for the 112th Congress," 44.

25. Marc Frank, "Cuba's Current Account Back in the Red in 2006," Reuters, July 27, 2007, http://uk.reuters.com/article/idUKN2733358620070727, accessed December 3, 2013; European Union, "Republic of Cuba—European Union Country Strategy Paper and National Indicative Programme for the Period 2011–2013," March 24, 2010, http://ec.europa.eu/development/icenter/repository/scanned_cu_csp10_en.pdf, accessed December 3, 2013; Economic Commission for Latin America and the Caribbean, "Cuba," 113–14; Republic of Cuba, Oficina Nacional de Estadísticas, *Anuario estadístico de Cuba (2011)*, table 8.3.

26. European Union, "Republic of Cuba," 88–89; "Castro's Legacy: Cuba's Foreign Debt," *Cuba Facts* 29 (March 2007), http://ctp.iccas.miami.edu/FACTS_Web/Cuba%20 Facts%20Issue%2029%20March%202007.htm, accessed December 3, 2013; "Cuban Foreign Debt Per Capita in Comparative Context," *Cuba Facts* 48 (August 2009), http:// ctp.iccas.miami.edu/FACTS_Web/Cuba%20Facts%20Issue%2048%20August.htm, accessed November 19, 2013; Salas-Del Valle, "Cuba's Debt Crisis."

27. Commission for Assistance to a Free Cuba, Report to the President, May 2004, http://babungroup.com/currentevents/COMMISSION%20FREE%20CUBA%20RE-PORT.pdf, accessed November 19, 2013; Commission for Assistance to a Free Cuba, Report to the President, July 2006, International Security Relations Web site, http:// www.isn.ethz.ch/About-Us/Staff/Detail/?lng=en&id=20756 accessed November 19, 2013.

28. Sullivan, "Cuba: U.S. Restrictions on Travel and Remittances," 6; Paolo Spadoni, "Family Ties Could Defy Cuba Travel Rules," *Orlando Sentinel*, February 6, 2006, http:// www.orlandosentinel.com/news/opinion/orl-edpcuba06020606feb06,0,3860896. story?coll=orl-opinion-headlines, accessed June 5, 2013.

29. Henken, "Balseros in Alabama," 411–13; Pew Hispanic Center, "Cubans in the United States," August 25, 2006, 3; Martínez-Fernández, "La diáspora en la frontera," 44–47; "Non-Cuban Latinos May Tip Florida Vote," *Newsweek*, September 29, 2008, http://www.newsweek.com/2008/09/29/a-new-latino-mix.html, accessed December 3, 2013; Paper presented at the Hispanic Heritage of Florida Conference, Tampa, 2012, http://scholarcommons.usf.edu/las_hhfc/, accessed April 20, 2014.

30. "Recent Cuban-American Voting Patterns," *Cuba Facts* 57 (November 2011); Bendixen and Associates, "New Democratic Network Hispanic Project" (2004 poll), 15, http://bendixenandamandi.com/wp-content/uploads/2010/08/NDN-Survey-of-Hispanic-Voters-in-4-states-2004.pdf, accessed November 26, 2013.

31. "Recent Cuban-American Voting Patterns"; Roger Cohen, "The End of the End of the Revolution," *New York Times Magazine*, December 5, 2008, http://www.nytimes. com/2008/12/07/magazine/07cuba-t.html?pagewanted=1&_r=1, accessed December 3, 2013; Marifeli Pérez-Stable; "Open Travel, Remittances Best Course for Cuba," *Miami Herald*, November 20, 2008.

32. Eckstein, "How Cubans Transformed Florida Politics."

33. Institute for Public Opinion Research, Florida International University and The Brookings Institution Cuba Study Group, "2008 Cuba/US Transition Poll," 12, http:// www2.fiu.edu/~ipor/cuba-t/Cuba-T.pdf, accessed December 3, 2013; Institute for Public Opinion Research, Florida International University, "2007 FIU Cuba Poll: Tabulation of Questions," http://www2.fiu.edu/~ipor/cuba8/pollresults.html, accessed December 3, 2013; David Rieff, "Will Little Havana Go Blue?" *The Times Magazine*, July 13, 2008.

34. Rieff, "Will Little Havana Go Blue?"

35. "Reaching Out to the Cuban People," White House press release, January 14, 2011, http://www.whitehouse.gov/the-press-office/2011/01/14/reaching-out-cuban-people, accessed June 5, 2013; Lesley Clark, "Obama to Ease Travel Restrictions to Cuba, Allow More U.S. Cash to Island," *Miami Herald*, January 14, 2011 Free Republic Web site, http://www.freerepublic.com/focus/f-news/2657119/posts, accessed November 26, 2013; Matthew Aho, "Cuba Travel Restrictions in the Spotlight in Brooklyn and

Beyond," *Americas Quarterly* blog, July 5, 2011, http://www.americasquarterly.org/node/2631, accessed December 3, 2013.

36. Michael Collins, "Arrest of Alleged American Spy in Cuba Further Sets Back U.S.-Cuba Relations," *Reuters*, January 14, 2010, http://coreysviews.wordpress.com/2010/01/16/arrest-of-alleged-american-spy-in-cuba-further-sets-back-u-s-cuba-relations/, accessed December 3, 2013.

37. Jeremy Herb, "Obama Promise to Close Guantánamo Prison Unfulfilled," *The Hill*, January 11, 2012, http://thehill.com/homenews/administration/203727-obama-promise-to-close-prison-at-guantanamo-still-unfulfilled, accessed June 5, 2013; Barack Obama, "Presidential Memorandum—Continuation of Authorities under the Trading with the Enemy Act," September 2, 2010, http://www.whitehouse.gov/the-press-office/2010/09/02/presidential-memorandum-continuation-authorities-under-trading-with-enem, accessed December 3, 2013; Carol Rosenberg, "How Congress Helped Thwart Obama's Plan to Close Guantánamo," *Miami Herald*, January 22, 2011, http://www.miamiherald.com/2011/01/22/2029364/how-congress-thwarted-obamas-closing.html, accessed December 3, 2013.

38. Sullivan, "Cuba: Issues for the 112th Congress," 3.

39. For a list of Obama's Cuba policy reforms, see Listing of All Recent Articles about Cuba, *Federal Register*, https://www.federalregister.gov/topics/cuba, accessed December 3, 2013. See also Sullivan, "Cuba: Issues for the 112th Congress," 39; "Cuba Allows More Charter Flights from the US; 350.000 Visited the Island in 2010," MercoPress, July 30, 2011, http://en.mercopress.com/2011/07/30/cuba-allows-more-charter-flights-from-the-us-350.000-visited-the-island-in-2010, accessed December 3, 2013; Sullivan, "Cuba: U.S. Restrictions on Travel and Remittances"; European Union, "Republic of Cuba," 18.

40. "Cuba Economic Indicators," TheGlobalEconomy.com, http://www.theglobaleconomy.com/Cuba/GDP_constant_dollars/, accessed January 14, 2014; "Cuba's Trade Booms with China and Venezuela"; Erikson, "Cuba, China, Venezuela," 414–15; Republic of Cuba, Oficina Nacional de Estadísticas, *Anuario estadístico de Cuba (2006)*, table 4.3; Republic of Cuba, Oficina Nacional de Estadísticas, *Panorama social y económico de Cuba (2010)*; Economic Commission for Latin America and the Caribbean, "Cuba," 113; Economic Commission for Latin America and the Caribbean, "Latin America and the Caribbean," 3; "Cuba Sees Economy Growing 3.1 pct in 2012, below Forecast," Reuters, December 3, 2012, http://www.reuters.com/article/2012/12/03/cuba-economy-idUSL1E8N353U20121203, accessed December, 2013; Sullivan, "Cuba: Issues for the 112th Congress," 20.

41. "2005 Cuba Trade Profile," *Cuba Facts* 25 (October 2006), http://ctp.iccas.miami.edu/FACTS_Web/Cuba%20Facts%20Issue%2025%20OCTOBER%202006.htm, accessed December, 2013.

42. Patrick Michael Rucker, "Sour Times for Cuba's Once-Thriving Sugar Industry," *Christian Science Monitor*, December 26, 2002, http://www.csmonitor.com/2002/1226/p07s01-woam.html, accessed December 3, 2013; Paolo Spadoni, "Tracking the Embargo: Restrictions Show Little Effect," *Cuba Trade and Investment News*, November 2005; Paolo Spadoni, "Tourism's Challenges: Low Spending, High Cost," *Cuba Trade and Investment News*, June 2006; Ramonet and Castro, *Fidel Castro*, 524; Sánchez, "Cuba y el etanol," 200.

43. Pablo Alfonso, "Menos azúcar y más pobreza," *El Nuevo Herald*, March 20, 2005; Castro quoted in Patricia Grogg, "Sugar: Former Lifeblood of Cuban Economy Reduced to Mere Trickle," Inter Press Service News Agency, January 11, 2006, http://havana-journal.com/business/entry/sugar_former_lifeblood_of_cuban_economy_reduced_to_mere_trickle/, accessed December 3, 2013.

44. Peters, *Cutting Losses*; Patricia Grogg, "Sugarcane—Source of Renewable Energy, But Not Ethanol," Inter Press Service News Agency, June 1, 2007, http://www.ipsnews.net/2007/06/cuba-sugarcane-source-of-renewable-energy-but-not-ethanol/, accessed January 14, 2014; Alfonso, "Menos azúcar"; Ramonet and Castro, *Fidel Castro*, 524; Rucker, "Sour Times"; "Cuban Sugar Crop Worst in a Century; Brazilian Investors Could Take over Industry," MercoPress, May 8, 2010, http://en.mercopress.com/2010/05/08/cuban-sugar-crop-worst-in-a-century-brazilian-investors-could-take-over-industry, accessed June 5, 2013; Peter Orsi, "Cuba Reports Sugar Production to Be Akin to 2010," Associated Press, April 6, 2011, http://www.deseretnews.com/article/700125001/Cuba-reports-sugar-production-to-be-akin-to-2010.html, accessed November 19, 2013; Sullivan, "Cuba: Issues for the 112th Congress," 20; Álvares, "The Current Restructuring of Cuba's Sugar Agribusiness."

45. *Cuba: el arte de la espera*, directed by Eduardo Lamora (Paris: Injam Productions, 2008).

46. Sánchez, "Cuba y el etanol," 202; U.S. Department of Agriculture, Economic Research Service, "Table 3a, World Raw Sugar Price," Excel table, http://www.ers.usda.gov/data-products/sugar-and-sweeteners-yearbook-tables.aspx#.UtUtxJ5dWSo, accessed December 30, 2013.

47. Grogg, "Sugarcane." Information on hectares (2004) from Álvarez, "Evaluating the Performance of Cuba's Sugarcane Basic Units of Cooperative Production during Their First Decade."

48. "UK Firm Signs Cuban Renewable Energy Deal," BBC News, January 17, 2011, http://www.bbc.co.uk/news/uk-scotland-scotland-business-12204109, accessed December 3, 2013.

49. Percentage changes based on comparison between 2003 and 2008; production data from Mario A. González-Corzo, "The End of Rationing in Cuba: Motivations and Socioeconomic Impact," *Focus on Cuba* 116 (November 9, 2009), http://ctp.iccas.miami.edu/FOCUS_Web/Issue116.htm, accessed June 5, 2013. See also Mesa-Lago, "Historia y evaluación," 536; Marrero, *Cuba en la década de 1950*, 22; and "Cuba Admits Food Imports Bill Is Up 25% and 'Miracles Are Running Out,'" MercoPress, April 16, 2011, http://en.mercopress.com/2011/04/16/cuba-admits-food-imports-bill-is-up-25-and-miracles-are-running-out, accessed December 3, 2013.

50. Mesa-Lago, *Economía y bienestar social en Cuba*, 50–51; Philip Brenner, "Cuba in 2012," Cuba Central News Blast, December 30, 2011, http://www.democracyinamericas.org/blog-post/cuba-central-new-years-news-blast-special-edition-cuba-in-2012/, accessed December 3, 2013.

51. Farber, *Cuba since the Revolution*, 90; Marc Franks, "Cuba Says Nickel Production Picks up after Floods," Reuters, November 12, 2007, http://www.reuters.com/article/2007/11/12/metals-cuba-nickel-idUSN1245924020071112, accessed December 3, 2013; Archibald Ritter, "Bad News for Cuba's Nickel Industry and Sherritt," The Cuban Economy Web site, June 28, 2010, http://thecubaneconomy.com/articles/2010/06/

bad-news-for-cuba%E2%80%99s-nickel-industry-and-sherritt/, accessed December 3, 2013; Requirements for U.S. Citizens to Enter Cuba, http://www.traveldocs.com/index.php?page=cuba, accessed January 14, 2014; "Sherritt Earnings Drop in Q 1," CubaStandard.com, http://www.cubastandard.com/2012/04/25/sherritt-earnings-drop-in-q1/, accessed December 3, 2013.

52. Jorge R. Piñón, "Cuba's Energy Crisis: Part III," *Focus on Cuba* 72 (January 25, 2006), http://ctp.iccas.miami.edu/FOCUS_Web/Issue72.htm, accessed December 3, 2013; Wilfredo Cancio Isla, "More Imported Sugar on Cuba's Plate," *Miami Herald*, June 6, 2007; Cuban oil production chart, Index Mundi Web site, http://www.indexmundi.com/g/g.aspx?c=cu&v=88, accessed December 3, 2013.

53. Piñón, "Venezuelan Oil"; European Union, "Republic of Cuba," 10.

54. European Union, "Republic of Cuba," 10; "Cuba, Vietnam Sign Energy Agreement," *Washington Post*, June 1, 2007, http://www.washingtonpost.com/wp-dyn/content/article/2007/06/01/AR2007060102321.html, accessed February 11, 2014; Jane Bussey, "Cuba Oil Boom May Complicate U.S. Embargo," *Miami Herald*, March 2, 2007; "RPT-Cuba Offshore Oil Rig Delayed Til Mid-Summer," Reuters, January 8, 2011, http://af.reuters.com/article/energyOilNews/idAFN0723371820110108, accessed December 3, 2013; Jeff Franks, "Chinese-Built Oil Rig Setting Sail for Cuban Waters," Reuters, August 26, 2011, http://af.reuters.com/article/energyOilNews/idAFN1E77P03U20110826?sp=true, accessed December 3, 2013; "Cuba's Oil Prospects: The Other Way Out," *The Economist*, November 19, 2011, http://www.economist.com/blogs/americasview/2010/11/cubas_oil_prospects, accessed December 3, 2013; Paula López-Gamundi, "Cuban Oil Demands Washington's Attention," *Council on Hemispheric Affairs*, June 22, 2011, http://cohaforum.wordpress.com/2011/06/22/cuban-oil-demands-washington%E2%80%99s-attention/, accessed November 23, 2013.

55. Ritter, "Survival Strategies and Economic Illegalities in Cuba," 352.

56. European Union, "Republic of Cuba," 11; confidential cable of Jonathan D. Farrar, chief of the U.S. Interests Section Office, Havana, June 9, 2009, reproduced at Along the Malecón Weblog, http://alongthemalecon.blogspot.com/2010/12/2009-cable-cuban-economy-stronger-than.html, accessed December 3, 2013.

57. Salary information from Pavel Vidal Alejandro, "La inflación y el salario real," February 2007, http://www.nodo50.org/cubasigloXXI/economia/vidal_300607.pdf, accessed December 3, 2013; inflation statistics from "Inflation Rate (Consumer Prices): Cuba," Index Mundi, http://www.indexmundi.com/g/g.aspx?c=cu&v=71, accessed December 3, 2013.

58. Anita Snow, "Reporter to Spend Month on Cuban Rations," *Washington Post*, May 31, 2007, http://www.washingtonpost.com/wp-dyn/content/article/2007/05/31/AR2007053101446.html, accessed December 3, 2013; Mauricio Vicent, "Ante el drama de más restricciones," *Nuevo Día* (San Juan), May 19, 2004; European Union, "Republic of Cuba," 10; Fernando Ravsberg, "Remittances to Cuba: With 28 Cents," *Havana Times*, November 18, 2010, http://www.havanatimes.org/?p=33170, accessed December 3, 2013; Morales, "Cuba: $2.6 Billion in Remittances in 2012."

59. Sandra Domínguez Ayala, "La salud cubana en estado crítico," La Visita Miami Web site, August 17, 2006, http://www.lavisitamiami.com/comentarios/La%20salud%20cubana%20estado%20critico.htm, accessed December 3, 2013; Caridad Caballero Batista, "Falta de higiene en hospital de Holguín," Agencia Holguín Press, May 7, 2007, http://cuba.blogspot.com/2007/05/falta-de-higiene-en-hospital-de-holgun.

html, accessed December 3, 2013; "Cuban Healthcare," confidential cable of Michael E. Parmly, chief of the U.S. Interests Section Office, Havana, January 31, 2008, reproduced in "Cable de EE UU que denuncia el mal funcionamiento de la sanidad cubana," WikiLeaked document reproduced at *El País International*, http://www.elpais.com/articulo/internacional/Cable/EE/UU/denuncia/mal/funcionamiento/sanidad/cubana/elpepuint/20110131elpepuint_16/Tes, accessed December 3, 2013; Sánchez, *Havana Real*, 22.

60. *Closed for Repairs* was originally published in Spanish in 2002.

61. "The Excursion," 3; "The Test," 22; "Closed for Repairs," 89, all in Alonso, *Closed for Repairs*.

62. Daniel de Vise and Elaine de Valle, "'Rafters' Desperate Journeys Reshaped the Exile Experience," *Miami Herald*, August 22, 2004; Oscar Corral, "Migration from Cuba to U.S. Grew in 2005," *Orlando Sentinel*, January 2, 2006.

63. "Truck-Sailing Cubans Finally Reach U.S.," *NBC News*, March 22, 2005, http://www.msnbc.msn.com/id/7267457/ns/us_news/, accessed December 3, 2013.

64. Excerpts from Gabriel Bravo, "Camionautas," *The Cypress Dome* 19 (2008): 138.

65. Fragments of Castro's speech as broadcast by Chanel 51, Telemundo, Miami, in "Fidel Castro—Comienzo del final de 'El Coma-Andante,'" YouTube video, http://www.youtube.com/watch?v=6OX3YHMoQyY&feature=related, accessed December 3, 2013.

66. "Castro Appears to Faint at Podium," *New York Times*, June 23, 2001, Latin American Studies Web site, http://www.latinamericanstudies.org/fidel/castro-faints.htm, accessed December 3, 2013.

67. Cuban Constitution of 1976, chapter 1, article 3; Mark P. Sullivan and Maureen Taft-Morales, "Cuba: Issues for the 107th Congress," 1, updated August 30, 2002, http://fpc.state.gov/documents/organization/13406.pdf, accessed December 3, 2013.

68. Font, "Cuba and Castro," 46–50; Yafee, *Che Guevara*, 266.

69. Henken, "'Vale Todo,'" 347–48; Pérez-López, "Foreign Investment in Cuba," 107.

70. Mesa-Lago, "Historia y evaluación," 529; Yafee, *Che Guevara*, 268.

71. "Aumenta salario mínimo en más del doble," *Granma Internacional*, April 22, 2005, http://www.granma.cu/nacionales1.html, accessed November 26, 2013.

72. Alfonso, "Menos azúcar"; Myriam Márquez, "Diplomacia de ollas," *El Sentinel*, March 19–25, 2005.

73. Erikson, *The Cuba Wars*, 16; Sullivan, "Cuba: Issues for the 112th Congress," 75.

74. Manuel Roig-Franzia, "Cubans Jailed in U.S. as Spies Are Hailed at Home as Heroes," *Washington Post*, June 3, 2006, http://www.washingtonpost.com/wp-dyn/content/article/2006/06/02/AR2006060201780.html, accessed December 3, 2013; Guerra, "Redefining Revolution in Cuba," 173–74.

75. Erikson, *The Cuba Wars*, 16; Michael Collins, "Latest Chapter in the Case of the Cuban Five: U.S. Justice as a Political Weapon," North American Congress on Latin America Web site, October 18, 2009, https://nacla.org/node/6166, accessed December 3, 2013; Jay Weaver, "First of the 'Cuban Five' Spies Set to Be Released from Prison on Friday," *Miami Herald*, October 1, 2011, Cuba, National Committee to Free the Cuban Five Web site, http://www.freethefive.org/updates/USMedia/USMReneMH100111.htm, accessed November 19, 2013; Sullivan, "Cuba: Issues for the 112th Congress," 64; Portia Siegelbaum, "Cuban Spy Back in Havana: No Grudge against U.S.," *CBS News*,

May 8, 2013, http://www.cbsnews.com/8301-202_162-57583546/cuban-spy-back-in-havana-no-grudge-against-u.s/, accessed December 3, 2013.

76. "UN Recommendations Regarding US Custody of Cuban Five," *Havana Journal*, May 27, 2005, http://havanajournal.com/politics/entry/un_recommendations_regarding_us_custody_of_cuban_five/, accessed December 3, 2013; Amnesty International, "USA: The Case of the Cuban Five," http://www.amnesty.org/en/library/info/AMR51/093/2010, accessed December 3, 2013.

77. Farber, *Cuba since the Revolution*, 19. For numerous declassified CIA and FBI documents on Posada Carriles, see "Luis Posada Carriles: Declassified Record," Electronic Briefing Book No. 153, National Security Archive, http://www.gwu.edu/~nsarchiv/NSAEBB/NSAEBB153/, accessed December 3, 2013.

78. Economist Intelligence Unit, *Country Report: Cuba, May 2001*, 12.

79. Democracia Participativa, "Bosquejo biográfico de Oswaldo Payá Sardiñas," http://democraciaparticipativa.net/documentos/MinibiogrPaya.htm, accessed June 1, 2013.

80. "Castro: Sign Up and Declare Cuba's System 'Untouchable,'" *Miami Herald*, June 14, 2002.

81. Democracia Participativa, "Bosquejo biográfico de Oswaldo Payá Sardiñas"; Sullivan, "Cuba: Issues for the 112th Congress," 76.

82. Partido Popular Joven Cuba, "¿Por qué no firmamos el Proyecto Varela?" Cubanet Web site, August 2001, http://www.cubanet.org/ref/dis/05130201.htm, accessed June 6, 2013; Patricia Grogg, "Cuba: Duelling Dissidents Clash over Conference," Inter Press Service, March 3, 2005, http://www.ipsnews.net/2005/03/cuba-duelling-dissidents-clash-over-conference/, accessed December 31, 2013.

83. Pablo Bachelet, "Castro Foes Testify, Support the U.S.," *Miami Herald*, March 4, 2005; Gómez and Rothe, *Value Orientations and Opinions of Recently Arrived Cubans in Miami*, 54.

84. See list of detainees with biographical information and length of sentence in Amnesty International, "Cuba: One Year Too Many: Prisoners of Conscience from the March 2003 Crackdown," March 16, 2004, http://www.amnesty.org/en/library/info/AMR25/005/2004, accessed December 3, 2013. See also Amnesty International, "Cuba: Newly Declared Prisoners of Conscience," January 29, 2004, http://www.amnesty.org/en/library/asset/AMR25/002/2004/en/308bf23e-d648-11dd-ab95-a13b602c0642/amr250022004en.html, accessed December 3, 2013.

85. Ibid., accessed December 3, 2013.

86. The three executed men were Lorenzo Enrique Copello Castillo (age 31), Bárbaro Leodán Sevilla García (age 22), and Jorge Luis Martínez Isaac (age 40). Amnesty International, "Cuba: Executions Mark an Unjustifiable Erosion in Human Rights," press release, April 14, 2003, http://www.amnesty.org/en/library/asset/AMR25/014/2003/en/f5100290-fad8-11dd-b531-99d31a1e99e4/amr250142003en.pdf, accessed December 3, 2013.

87. Tzivelis, "The European Union's Foreign Policy towards Cuba."

88. "Reporters without Borders Condemns Stalinist Trials as Independent Journalists Are Handed Down Jail Sentences," Reporters without Borders Web site, April 7, 2003, http://en.rsf.org/cuba-reporters-without-borders-condemns-07-04-2003,06107.html,

accessed December 3, 2013; European Union Parliament, Resolución del Parlamento Europeo sobre Cuba, November 17, 2004, http://eurlex.europa.eu/LexUriServ/LexUriServ.do?uri=OJ:C:2005:201E:0083:0084:ES:PDF, accessed December 3, 2013; Ramonet and Castro, *Fidel Castro*, 601.

89. Amnesty International, "Cuba: Executions Mark an Unjustifiable Erosion in Human Rights." See legislation on *criminalidad predelictiva* in Penal Code, Title XI, http://www.lwob.org/Pages/ImageAttachment.aspx?KJRdbueokj4YIZOGoCH%2FJZTmRZDoGlHHFkouTRn5xrE%2BrltMlAcg4HInHCwNXx6IrWAUTdPYz1LqsFPEJysXNQR3p7F8UNUm90Csjxs4H0U%3D, accessed November 19, 2013.

90. In 2004, Cuba ranked fifty-third among 225 nations and eleventh within the Americas, surpassed by Canada, the Cayman Islands, Aruba, Martinique, the U.S. Virgin Islands, Guadeloupe, Bermuda, Puerto Rico, and the United States. See "Rank Order: Life Expectancy at Birth," in CIA, *The World Factbook* (2004), http://www.travlang.com/factbook/rankorder/2102rank.html, accessed December 3, 2013.

91. Pablo Bachelet and Frances Robles, "Castro Has Parkinson's Disease, CIA Has Concluded," *Miami Herald*, November 16, 2005; Ramonet and Castro, *Fidel Castro*, 598.

92. Oriol Güel and Ana Alfageme, "Una cadena de actuaciones médicas fallidas agravó el estado de Castro," *El País*, January 16, 2007; "How Believable Is a Fidel Castro Comeback?" confidential cable of Michael E. Parmly, head of the U.S. Interests Section office, Havana, March 16, 2007, reproduced in "Cable sobre la crisis de Castro en pleno vuelo," WikiLeaked document reproduced at *El País International*, December 15, 2010, http://www.elpais.com/articulo/internacional/Cable/crisis/Castro/pleno/vuelo/elpepuint/20101215elpepuint_22/Tes, accessed December 3, 2013; Mauricio Vicent, "El ex presidente se da de alta," *El País*, August 8, 2010, http://www.elpais.com/articulo/internacional/ex/presidente/da/alta/elpepiint/20100808elpepiint_2/Tes, accessed December 3, 2013.

93. Fidel Castro, proclamation to the Cuban People, July 31, 2006, http://www.cubahora.cu/index.php?tpl=dossiers/discursos/share-tpls/ver-not.tpl.html&newsid_obj_id=1014262, accessed December 3, 2013.

94. Brian Latell, "The Third Man," *Latell Report*, September 2006, http://ctp.iccas.miami.edu/Latell_Web/7The%20Latell%20Report%20September%202006.htm, accessed December 3, 2013; Anita Snow, "Cuba's Military Men Loyal to Raul Castro," *Washington Post*, August 8, 2006.

95. Saul Landau, "Cuba Misunderestimated," Foreign Policy in Focus Web site, August 24, 2006, http://www.fpif.org/articles/cuba_misunderestimated, accessed December 3, 2013. For Castro's first post-surgery video, see "Primer video de Castro desde operación," YouTube video, www.youtube.com/watch?v=vVDeiPoTQXA&feature=related, accessed December 3, 2013.

96. Parmly, "How Believable?" in "Cable sobre la crisis de Castro en pleno vuelo"; "The Speculation on Fidel Castro's Health," secret cable of Jonathan Farrar, chief of U.S. Interests Section office in Havana, January 14, 2009, WikiLeaked document reproduced at "Secret Cable: Fidel Castro's Death Won't Spark Riots or Migration," Along the Malecón Web site, December 16, 2010, http://alongthemalecon.blogspot.com/2010/12/secret-cable-fidel-castros-death-wont.html, accessed December 3, 2013; María Argelia Vizcaíno, "Las irreflexiones de un fantasma," part 2, http://www.maria

argeliavizcaino.com/e-Irreflexiones_de_un_fantasma.html, accessed December 3, 2013.

97. "Video de Fidel que demuestra su mejora" (video demonstrating the extent of Fidel Castro's recovery shortly after surgery), YouTube video, www.youtube.com/watch ?v=soJr9L6Cdj4&feature=related, accessed December 3, 2013; interview with Fidel Castro, June 2007, Daily motion Web site, http://www.dailymotion.com/video/ x26m0a_fidelcastroentrevistajunio2007recup_news, accessed June 6, 2013; "Cuba, Encuentro entre Hugo Chávez, Raúl y Fidel Castro," video of Fidel Castro's June 17, 2008, meeting with his brother and Hugo Chávez, YouTube video, www.youtube.com/ watch?v=P18WaWYkFb8&feature=related, accessed December 3, 2013.

98. Monthly Review offers an online collection of Castro's reflections; see "Reflections of Fidel," http://monthlyreview.org/castro/, accessed December 3, 2013. See also Brian Latell, "Fidel's Reflections," *Latell Report*, May 2007, http://ctp.iccas.miami.edu/ Latell_Web/5The%20Latell%20Report%20May2007.htm, accessed February 3, 2011.

99. Marc Frank, "Cuba Debates Economic Path Ahead under Raul Castro," Reuters, February 7, 2007, http://www.reuters.com/article/idUSN0727964120070207, accessed December 3, 2013.

100. "Raul Castro Says Cuba Open to Normalized Relations with U.S.," *USA Today*, August 19, 2006.

101. "Fidel Castro's Resignation Letter," February 18, 2008, CNN.com, http://articles.cnn.com/2008-02-19/world/castro.letter_1_health-condition-state-council-dear-compatriots?_s=PM:WORLD, accessed December 3, 2013.

102. "Miembros del Consejo de Estado," and "Elegido Raúl Castro Presidente de los Consejos de Estado y de Ministros," both in *Granma*, February 25, 2008.

103. Fidel Castro's speech at the commemoration of the 60th anniversary of his admission to University of Havana, November 17, 2005, http://www.cuba.cu/gobierno/ discursos/2005/ing/f171105i.html, accessed December 3, 2013; Raúl Castro's speech on the 50th Anniversary of the Revolution, January 1, 2009, Havana Journal, http:// havanajournal.com/politics/entry/text-of-speech-by-president-raul-castro-on-50th-anniversary-of-the-revoluti/, accessed December 3, 2013.

104. "Cuba: Pres. Raul Castro's Speech at the National Assembly of People's Power, Havana," February 24, 2008, HCVANNALYSIS Web site, http://hcvanalysis.wordpress. com/2008/02/24/cuba-pres-raul-castro-speech-at-the-national-assembly-of-peoples-power-havana/, accessed December 4, 2013.

105. Latell, "Raul Castro," 56.

106. Jaime Suchlicki, "It's Party Time," *Focus on Cuba* 93 (March 3, 2008), http://ctp. iccas.miami.edu/FOCUS_Web/Issue93.htm, accessed December 3, 2013; Latell, "Raúl Castro," 60.

107. Will Weissert, "Raul Castro Ousts Top Cubans Loyal to Fidel Castro," *New York Daily News*, March 2, 2009, http://www.nydailynews.com/latino/raul-castro-ousts-top-cubans-loyal-fidel-article-1.367991, accessed November 15, 2013; Mauricio Vicent's article from *El País*, June 28, 2009, translated and printed as "Why Cuba Purged 3 Top Officials," *Miami Herald*, June 29, 2009, http://www.miamiherald. com/2009/06/29/1119251/why-cuba-purged-3-top-officials.html, accessed December 3, 2013; Sullivan, "Cuba: Issues for the 112th Congress," 7.

108. Brian Latell, "The Emergence of Ramiro Valdés," *Latell Report*, February 2010, http://ctp.iccas.miami.edu/Latell_Web/The%20Latell%20ReportFebruary2010.htm, accessed December 3, 2013; Rui Ferreira, "Primer cambio en el gobierno cubano," *Nuevo Herald*, September 1, 2006.

109. Jeff Franks, "Cubans Buy First Computers in Latest Change," Reuters, May 2, 2008, http://uk.reuters.com/article/idUKN0229508020080502, accessed December 3, 2013; Will Weissert, "Raul Castro: Cubans Can Have Cell Phones," Associated Press, March 28, 2008, http://www.huffingtonpost.com/2008/03/28/raul-castro-cubans-can-ha_n_94000.html, accessed December 3, 2013; Marc Frank, "Cubans Allowed to Stay at Tourist Hotels," Reuters, March 31, 2008, http://www.reuters.com/article/idUSN2815132920080331, accessed December 3, 2013.

110. Will Weissert, "After Fifty Years, Cuba Finally Realizing That Marx Was Wrong," *Havana Journal*, June 11, 2008, http://havanajournal.com/business/entry/after-50-years-cuba-finally-starting-to-realize-that-karl-marx-was-wrong/, accessed December 3, 2013; Brian Latell, "Fidel Looms Large," *Latell Report*, July–August 2008, http://ctp.iccas.miami.edu/Latell_Web/The%20Latell%20ReportJuly-August2008.htm, accessed December 3, 2013.

111. Pujol, "The Cuban Economy as Seen by Economists within the Island and Other Observers"; Cuba Lends Farmers Unused State Land," MSNBC, April 1, 2009, http://www.msnbc.msn.com/id/23907266/ns/world_news-americas/, accessed December 3, 2013; Carlos Batista, "Cuba to Put More Farm Land in Private Hands," Agence France-Presse, July 18, 2008, http://afp.google.com/article/ALeqM5h0TOWlkmA5_9HQRzp AmplPf2xlZQ, accessed December 3, 2013; Farber, *Cuba since the Revolution*, 63–66; Fernando Ravsberg, "Cuba habla de lo bueno y lo malo de su reforma agraria," BBC Mundo, September 27, 2011, http://www.bbc.co.uk/mundo/noticias/2011/09/110927_cuba_entrevista_minagri_az.shtml, accessed December 3, 2013.

112. Raúl Castro's speech to the National Assembly, July 11, 2008, CubaEncuentro Web site, http://www.cubaencuentro.com/documentos/texto-completo-del-discurso-de-raul-castro-ante-la-asamblea-nacional-del-poder-popular-96879, accessed December 3, 2013.

113. How Might Cuba Enter Another Special Period?," confidential cable by Jonathan Farrar, chief of the Cuba Interests Section office, Havana, June 9, 2009, WikiLeaked document reproduced in "2009 Cable: Cuban Economy Stronger Than in the 1990s," Along the Malecón Web site, December 19, 2010, http://alongthemalecon.blogspot.com/2010/12/2009-cable-cuban-economy-stronger-than.html, accessed December 3, 2013; González-Corzo, "The End of Rationing in Cuba"; Rory Carroll, "Cuba Cuts Subsidy for Toiletries," *The Guardian*, December 31, 2010, http://www.guardian.co.uk/world/2010/dec/31/cuba-cuts-toiletries-subsidy, accessed December 3, 2013; Jeff Franks, "Cash-Strapped Cuba Moves Ahead with Job Cuts," Reuters, January 4, 2011, http://www.reuters.com/article/2011/01/04/us-cuba-reform-layoffs-idUSTRE7034 VU20110104, accessed December 3, 2013; Marc Frank, "Chronology: Raul Castro's Road to Reform in Cuba," Reuters, April 13, 2011, http://www.reuters.com/article/2011/04/13/us-cuba-reform-chronology-idUSTRE73C70C20110413, accessed December 3, 2013; Sánchez, *Havana Real*, 147.

114. Renato Pérez, "Fidel: I Don't Like Recent Reforms," *Miami Herald*, April 16,

2008; Brian Latell, "Raul a Year Later," *Latell Report*, February 2009, http://ctp.iccas.miami.edu/Latell_Web/The%20Latell%20ReportFebruary2009.htm, accessed December 3, 2013; Brian Latell, "Fidel Redux," *Latell Report*, January 2010, http://ctp.iccas.miami.edu/Latell_Web/The%20Latell%20ReportJanuary2010.htm, accessed December 3, 2013; Shasta Darlington, "Fidel Castro Praises Brother Raul's Leadership," CNN World, November 18, 2010, http://www.cnn.com/2010/WORLD/americas/11/18/cuba.castro/index.html?section=cnn_latest, accessed December 3, 2013. For the entire texts of all of Fidel Castro's *reflexiones*, see "Reflections of Fidel."

115. Jeff Franks, "Fidel Castro Makes First Appearance in Four Years," Reuters, July 10, 2010, http://www.reuters.com/article/idUSTRE66921920100711, accessed December 3, 2013; Jeff Franks, "Cuba Frees Prisoners, But Fidel Steals Spotlight," July 13, 2010, http://www.reuters.com/article/idUSTRE66D0DE20100714, accessed December 3, 2013.

116. Brian Latell, "Fidel's Challenge," *Latell Report*, Summer 2010, http://ctp.iccas.miami.edu/Latell_Web/The%20Latell%20ReportSummer2010.htm, accessed December 3, 2013.

117. "Alto a la guataquería," *Bohemia*, February 8, 1959, 70.

118. Juan O. Tamayo, "Jailed Cuban Activist Orlando Zapata Tamayo Dies on Hunger Strike," *Miami Herald*, February 22, 2010, reproduced in The New Centrist Web site, http://newcentrist.wordpress.com/2010/02/23/jailed-cuban-activist-orlando-zapata-tamayo-dies-on-hunger-strike/, accessed December 3, 2013; Erikson, *The Cuba Wars*, 277–78; Brian Latell, "Cuba's Unquiet Youth," *Latell Report*, March 2008, http://ctp.iccas.miami.edu/Latell_Web/The%20Latell%20ReportMarch2008.htm, accessed December 3, 2013; "2006 Cable: U.S. Official Vowed to Help Anti-Castro Youth," confidential cable from Michael E. Parmly, chief of the U.S. Interests Section, Havana, November 27, 2006, WikiLeaked document, Along the Malecón Web site, http://alongthemalecon.blogspot.com/2010/12/2006-cable-us-official-vowed-to-help.html, accessed December 28, 2013; Gershman and Gutiérrez, "Ferment in Civil Society," 42–43; Juan O. Tamayo, "Transgender Activist Resigns after Clash with Castro Daughter," *Miami Herald*, July 10, 2011.

119. García Freyre, "De la iglesia a la plaza," 284–92; Erikson, *The Cuba Wars*, 71; Ramonet and Castro, *Fidel Castro*, 602; "Damas de Blanco seguirán en pie de lucha," *Nuevo Herald*, March 27, 2011, http://www.elnuevoherald.com/2011/03/27/911024/damas-de-blanco-seguiran-en-pie.html, accessed December 3, 2013; Sánchez, *Havana Real*, 178–80, 218; Sullivan, "Cuba: Issues for the 112th Congress," 10–11.

120. Ángel Tomás González, "Cuba es un anacronismo totalitario," *El Mundo* (Madrid) October 22, 2010; Tamayo, "Jailed Cuban Activist Orlando Zapata Tamayo Dies on Hunger Strike"; Juan O. Tamayo, "Cinco disidentes inician huelga de hambre en Cuba," *Nuevo Herald*, February 27, 2010; "Cuban Activist Ends Hunger Strike," *New York Times*, July 8, 2010, http://www.nytimes.com/2010/07/09/world/americas/09cuba.html, accessed December 3, 2013. More recently, in January 2012, yet another prisoner of conscience, Wilmar Villar Mendoza, died in state custody while staging a hunger strike; Jeff Franks, "Jailed Cuba Dissident Dies in Hunger Strike," Reuters, January 30, 2012, http://www.reuters.com/article/2012/01/20/us-cuba-dissident-death-idUSTRE80J0C020120120, accessed December 3, 2013.

121. "Taming the 'Wild Colt': Internet and Control in Cuba," *Cuba Facts* 30 (March 2007), http://ctp.iccas.miami.edu/FACTS_Web/Cuba%20Facts%20Issue%2030%20March%202007.htm, accessed December 3, 2013; Carlos Lauría and María Salazar Ferro, "Special Report: Chronicling Cuba, Bloggers Offer Fresh Hope," Committee to Protect Journalists Web site, September 10, 2009, http://www.cpj.org/reports/2009/09/cuban-bloggers-offer-fresh-hope.php, accessed December 3, 2013.

122. "Taming the 'Wild Colt'"; Andrés Oppenheimer, "After 50 Years, Cuba Has Little to Show," *Miami Herald*, December 14, 2008, http://www.miamiherald.com/2008/12/12/v-fullstory/810847/after-50-years-cuba-has-little.html, accessed December 3, 2013; Ramonet and Castro, *Fidel Castro*, 592; Farber, *Cuba since the Revolution*, 69; Nick Miroff, "In Cuba, Dial-Up Internet Is a Luxury," *NPR News*, December 14, 2011, http://www.npr.org/2011/12/14/143721874/in-cuba-dial-up-internet-is-a-luxury, accessed December 3, 2013; Sánchez, *Havana Real*, 65–66.

123. "Operación Verdad," Yoani Sánchez interview with former Operación Verdad cyber-soldier Eliécer Ávila, February 11, 2013, YouTube video, http://www.youtube.com/watch?v=bYbgwMwJa-0, accessed December 3, 2013.

124. Lauría and Salazar Ferro, "Chronicling Cuba"; "Cuba Tightens Restrictions on Bloggers," *Wall Street Journal*, December 5, 2008, http://online.wsj.com/article/SB122843846791581591.html, accessed December 3, 2013; Henken, "Desde Cuba con Yoani Sánchez: animando al periodismo ciudadano digital y desafiando a la violencia verbal"; Yoani Sánchez, "A Gangland Style Kidnapping," Generacion Y blog, November 7, 2009, http://www.desdecuba.com/generationy/?p=1123, accessed December 3, 2013; David Luhnow, "Beating Rattles Cuban Bloggers," *Wall Street Journal*, November 12, 2009; Sánchez's blogs in Sánchez, *Havana Real*.

125. Erik Maza, "Top Ten Cuban Bloggers You Don't Know," April 14, 2010, *Miami New Times Blogs*, http://blogs.miaminewtimes.com/riptide/2010/04/top_ten_cuban_bloggers_you_hav.php, accessed December 3, 2013; "Category Archives: Las Leyes de Laritza," Desde la Habana blog, http://www.desdelahabana.net/?cat=8, accessed December 3, 2013; Octavo Cerco blog, http://octavocercoen.blogspot.com/, accessed June 7, 2013; Lunes de Post-Revolución (Orlando Luis Pardo Lazo's blog), http://orlandoluispardolazo.blogspot.com/, accessed December 3, 2013.

126. Fernandes, *Cuba Represent!*, 90, 102; "Los Aldeanos—La naranja se picó," YouTube video, http://www.youtube.com/watch?v=X_tF_f6e5V0, accessed December 3, 2013.

127. Porno Para Ricardo Web site, http://www.pornopararicardo.org/#, accessed December 3, 2013; Sánchez, *Havana Real*, xi.

128. For footage of the exchange between Ávila and Alarcón, see "Alarcon enfrenta cuestionamientos de estudiantes BBC," YouTube video, http://www.youtube.com/watch?v=X_nMQD2xwJs; and "Eliecer Avila vs Ricardo Alarcon Cuba II," YouTube video, http://www.youtube.com/watch?v=v16o17eu1tQ, both accessed December 3, 2013.

129. Edith M. Lederer, "Cuba Signs Human Rights Treaties at UN," February 28, 2008, *NBC News*, http://www.nbcnews.com/id/23397572/, accessed December 3, 2013.

130. Franks, "Cuba Frees Prisoners, But Fidel Steals Spotlight"; Sara Nawaz,

"Cuba Pledges to Release Political Prisoners," Council on Hemispheric Affairs Web site, July 8, 2010, http://www.coha.org/coha-staff-memorandum-cuba-pledges-to-release-political-prisoners/, accessed December 3, 2013; Larry Birns, "Response to Washington Post Editorial, 'Cuba's Gesture,'" Council on Hemispheric Affairs Web site, July 19, 2010, http://www.coha.org/response-to-washington-post-editorial-%E2%80%9Ccuba%E2%80%99s-gesture%E2%80%9D/, accessed December 3, 2013; "Freed Cuban Dissidents Arrive in Spain," *BBC News*, July 13, 2010, http://www.bbc.co.uk/news/10595296, accessed December 3, 2013; Wilfredo Cancio Isla, "¿Dónde están ahora los 75?," October 16, 2010, Cafefuerte Web site, http://cafefuerte.com/cuba/cpolitica/507-donde-estan-ahora-los-75/ accessed December 30, 2013.

131. Juan O. Tamayo, "Cuba Briefly Delays Release of 13 Political Prisoners," *Miami Herald*, November 11, 2010, http://www.cubaverdad.net/weblog/2010/11/cuba-briefly-delays-release-of-13-political-prisoners/, accessed November 20, 2013; "Cuba Frees Political Prisoner Who Refused Exile Deal," *BBC News*, November 14, 2010, http://www.bbc.co.uk/news/world-latin-america-11752157, accessed December 3, 2013; "Damas de Blanco seguirán en pie de lucha."

132. Raúl Castro Speech, December 23, 2011, *Granma*, December 24, 2011.

133. Sullivan, "Cuba: Issues for the 112th Congress," 9–11; Comisión Cubana de Derechos Humanos y Reconciliación Nacional, "Cuba: algunos actos de represión política durante septiembre de 2012, http://www.procubalibre.org/informes/pdf/COMISION_Sept_2012.pdf, accessed December 3, 2013; "Political Detentions Surged in Cuba in 2012," Agence France-Presse, http://www.rawstory.com/rs/2013/01/03/political-detentions-surged-in-cuba-in-2012/, accessed November 20, 2013.

134. Manuel Guerra Pérez, "Las Damas de Blanco siguen caminando por los presos políticos cubanos," Desde mi isla blog, April 14, 2011, http://manuelguerraperez.blogspot.com/2011/04/las-damas-de-blanco-siguen-caminando.html, accessed December 3, 2013; Andrea González, "Cuba Commutes Death Sentence against U.S. Man," *HuffPost World*, December 28, 2010, http://www.huffingtonpost.com/2010/12/29/cuba-commutes-death-sente_n_802475.html, accessed December 3, 2013; "Cuba: Stop Imprisoning Peaceful Dissidents: Six Sentenced in Summary Trials for Exercising Basic Rights," Human Rights Watch Web site, http://www.hrw.org/en/news/2011/06/01/cuba-stop-imprisoning-peaceful-dissidents, accessed December 3, 2013; Karen Phillips, "After the Black Spring, Cuba's New Repression," Committee to Protect Journalists Web site, July 6, 2011, http://www.cpj.org/reports/2011/07/after-the-black-spring-cubas-new-repression.php, accessed December 3, 2013; "Cuban 'Ladies in White' Targeted with Arrest and Intimidation," Amnesty International News, August 22, 2011, http://www.amnesty.org/en/news-and-updates/cuba%E2%80%99s-%E2%80%98ladies-white%E2%80%99-targeted-arbitrary-arrest-and-intimidation-2011-08-22, accessed December 3, 2013.

135. Fidel Castro, "Fidel Is Dying," October 21, 2012, Reflections of Fidel, Monthly Review Web site, http://monthlyreview.org/castro/2012/10/22/fidel-castro-is-dying-by-fidel-castro/, accessed December 3, 2013.

136. "Cuba Jails US Internet Project Worker Alan Gross," *BBC News*, March 12, 2011, http://www.bbc.co.uk/news/world-latin-america-12724632, accessed December 3, 2013; "NY Rabbi Meets with Jailed American in Cuba," *CBS News*, March 6, 2012, http://

www.cbsnews.com/8301-202_162-57391978/ny-rabbi-meets-with-jailed-american-in-cuba/, accessed December 3, 2013; Sullivan, "Cuba: Issues for the 112th Congress," 36–37; Juan O. Tamayo, "Secretary of State: No Swap of Cuban Spies for Alan Gross," *Miami Herald*, April 4, 2013, http://www.miamiherald.com/2013/04/18/3352048/secretary-of-state-no-swap-of.html, accessed December 13, 2013.

137. Ivette Fernández Sosa, "Trabajadores por cuenta propia sobrepasan las 300,000 personas," *Granma*, May 21, 2011; Brenner, "Cuba in 2012."

Chapter 8. Rectify and Change . . . All That Should Be Rectified and Changed

1. Frederik Balfour, "China's Millionaires Leap Past 1 Million on Growth, Savings," Bloomberg.com, June 1, 2011, http://www.bloomberg.com/news/2011-05-31/chinas-millionaires-jump-past-one-million-on-savings-growth.html, accessed November 8, 2013.

2. See original guidelines at PCC, "Lineamientos de la política económica y social," http://www.granma.cubaweb.cu/secciones/6to-congreso-pcc/Folleto%20Lineamientos%20VI%20Cong.pdf, accessed December 3, 2013.

3. Rosa Tania Valdés, "Cuba Economy Minister, Replaced to Focus on Reform," Reuters, March 25, 2011, http://www.reuters.com/article/2/011/0326/us-cuba-economy-minister-idUSTRE72P0B920110326, accessed November 8, 2013; Sullivan, "Cuba: Issues for the 112th Congress," 7, 23.

4. Pedro Roig, "Cuba's Politburo Threatened by Senility," *Miami Herald*, April 26, 2011; Marifeli Pérez-Stable, "Cuban Congress an 'Indictment of Past 50 Years,'" *Miami Herald*, April 20, 2011, http://www.cubaverdad.net/weblog/2011/04/cuban-congress-an-indictment-of-past-50-years/, accessed November 20, 2013.

5. Randal C. Archibold, "Cuban Leader Proposes Term Limits in Sign of New Era," April 16, 2011, *New York Times*, http://www.nytimes.com/2011/04/17/world/americas/17cuba.html, accessed December 3, 2012.

6. Fidel Castro, "My Absence from the Central Committee," *Granma Internacional*, April 19, 2011, http://en.cubadebate.cu/reflections-fidel/2011/04/19/my-absence-from-central-committee/, accessed November 20, 2013.

7. Leticia Martínez Hernández and Yaima Puig Meneses, "Celebrada reunión de Consejo de Ministros," *Granma Internacional*, May 17, 2011, http://granma.cu/espanol/cuba/17mayo-celebrada.html, accessed December 4, 2013; Juan O. Tamayo, "Cuban Plans to Lift Remaining Restriction against Hiring Non-Relatives," *Miami Herald*, May 17, 2011, http://cubarights.blogspot.com/2011/05/cuban-plans-to-lift-remaining.html, accessed November 20, 2013; Shasta Darlington, "Cuba Further Eases Limits on Private Businesses," CNN World, May 18, 2011, http://edition.cnn.com/2011/WORLD/americas/05/17/cuba.private.businesses/, accessed December 3, 2013; Ivette Fernández Sosa, "Trabajadores por cuenta propia sobrepasan las 300,000 personas," *Granma*, May 21, 2011; Sullivan, "Cuba: Issues for the 112th Congress," 25; Philip Brenner, "Cuba in 2012," Center for Democracy in the Americas Web site, December 30, 2011, http://www.democracyinamericas.org/blog-post/cuba-central-new-years-news-blast-special-edition-cuba-in-2012/, accessed November 28, 2013.

8. "Chronology: Hugo Chavez's Losing Battle against Cancer," Reuters, March 5, 2013, http://www.reuters.com/article/2013/03/05/us-venezuela-chavez-chronology-idUSBRE9241AB20130305, accessed December 31, 2013.

9. "Hugo Chávez, 1954–2013: fin de una era," special supplement on Hugo Chávez, *Nuevo Día* (San Juan), March 6, 2013.

10. Tom File, "The Diversifying Electorate—Voting Rates by Race and Hispanic Origin in 2012 (and Other Recent Elections)," *Current Population Survey*, May 2013, http://www.census.gov/prod/2013pubs/p20-568.pdf, accessed December 3, 2013.

11. "Voter Registration Statistics for Latinos in Florida," Pew Research Center, January 27, 2012, http://www.pewresearch.org/daily-number/voter-registration-statistics-for-latinos-in-florida/, accessed December 3, 2013; U.S. Bureau of the Census, "Florida, 2000," August 2002, http://www.census.gov/prod/2002pubs/c2kprof00-fl.pdf, accessed December 3, 2013.

12. "Voter Registration Statistics for Latinos in Florida," Pew Research Center, January 27, 2012, http://www.pewresearch.org/daily-number/voter-registration-statistics-for-latinos-in-florida/, accessed November 8, 2013; Portes, "A Bifurcated Enclave."

13. Cuba Research Institute, Florida International University, "2011 Cuba Poll," http://cri.fiu.edu/research/cuba-poll/2011-cuba-poll.pdf, accessed November 8, 2013.

14. Mark Hugo López and Paul Taylor, "Latino Voters in the 2012 Election," Pew Research Hispanic Trends Project Web site, November 7, 2012, http://www.pewhispanic.org/2012/11/07/latino-voters-in-the-2012-election/, accessed November 8, 2013; Cuba Research Institute, Florida International University, "2011 Cuba Poll," 21; Grenier, "The Cuban American Transition?" Bildner Center for Western Hemispheric Studies Web site, http://web.gc.cuny.edu/dept/bildn/events/2011.11.21.shtml, accessed December 3, 2013.

15. Peter Harkin, "A Consequential Summit?" April 12, 2012, Inter-American Dialogue Web site, http://www.thedialogue.org/page.cfm?pageID=32&pubID=2939, accessed November 8, 2013; Roman Surver, "Looking Back on the Cuba Distraction at Cartagena and the Failure of the U.S.' Latin America Policy," Council on Hemispheric Affairs Web site, April 24, 2012, http://www.coha.org/looking-back-on-the-cuba-distraction-at-cartagena-and-the-failure-of-the-u-s-latin-america-policy/, accessed November 8, 2013.

16. Juan O. Tamayo, "Cuba Begins Transition to a New Generation of Leaders," *Miami Herald*, February 24, 2013; Marc Frank, "Cuban Leader Raul Castro Announces He Will Retire in 2018," Reuters, February 24, 2013, http://www.reuters.com/article/2013/02/24/us-cuba-castro-idUSBRE91N0HB20130224, accessed December 3, 2013.

17. Sarah Rainsford, "Miguel Diaz-Canel: The Man Tipped to Lead Cuba," *BBC News*, April 8, 2013, http://www.bbc.co.uk/news/world-latin-america-22066591?utml, accessed December 3, 2013; Frank, "Cuban Leader Raul Castro Announces He Will Retire in 2018"; Tamayo, "Cuba Begins Transition to a New Generation of Leaders."

18. "Elections in Venezuela," Electoral Geography 2.0 Web site, http://www.electoralgeography.com/new/en/category/countries/v/venezuela, accessed December 3, 2013.

19. John Otis, "As Inflation Soars, Venezuela's Leader Opts for Drastic Steps," December 10, 2013, NPR blog, http://www.npr.org/blogs/parallels/2013/12/11/248222305/as-inflation-soars-venezuelas-leader-opts-for-drastic-steps, accessed December 28, 2013.

20. Brian Ellsworth, "Venezuela's Capriles Vows to End Cuba Giveaways," Reuters, March 18, 2013, http://www.reuters.com/article/2013/03/18/venezuela-election-idUSL1N0CA6L120130318, accessed December 3, 2013.

21. "Eliécer Ávila en entrevista desde Suecia," February 2013, YouTube video, http://www.youtube.com/watch?feature=endscreen&v=IsT_CbavzBQ&NR=1, accessed November 8, 2013.

22. Mauricio Torres, "Una protesta 'empaña' la visita de Yoani Sánchez al Senado mexicano," March 12, 2013, CNN México, http://mexico.cnn.com/nacional/2013/03/12/una-protesta-empana-la-visita-de-yoani-sanchez-al-senado-mexicano, accessed November 8, 2013; "Yoani Sánchez on Why It's Time to End the Embargo," Foreign Policy Web site, March 19, 2013, http://blog.foreignpolicy.com/posts/2013/03/19/yoani_sanchez_on_why_its_time_to_end_the_embargo, November 8, 2013; Marco Sibaja, "Cuba's Dissident Blogger Yoani Arrives in Brazil," February 13, 2013, The Guardian, http://www.guardian.co.uk/world/feedarticle/10665207, accessed November 8, 2103.

23. "Winds of Change: Our Opinion: Cuban Blogger Yoani Sánchez's Visit Has Brought Together Miami Exiles of All Political Stripes, Generations," Miami Herald, April 4, 2013, http://www.miamiherald.com/2013/04/04/3324039/winds-of-change.html, November 8, 2013.

24. "Yoani Sánchez Speaks at Freedom Tower in Miami," April 1, 2013, YouTube video, http://www.youtube.com/watch?v=zytHDGg1WjY, accessed November 8, 2013.

Conclusion

1. Marc Frank, "Exclusive: Russia Signs Deal to Forgive $29 Billion of Cuba's Soviet-Era Debt—Diplomats," Reuters, December 8, 2013, http://www.reuters.com/article/2013/12/09/us-cuba-russia-debt-idUSBRE9B813P20131209, accessed December 29, 2013.

2. "Cuban VP Says Controlling the News Is an Illusion," May 6, 2013, Latin American Herald Tribune, http://www.laht.com/article.asp?ArticleId=771473&CategoryId=14510, November 8, 2013.

3. Ramos Nallely, "The Harvest in Cuba Short of Its Goals Written," ZafraNet Web site, April 10, 2012, http://www.zafranet.com/2012/04/la-zafra-en-cuba-lejos-de-cumplir-sus-objetivos/?lang=en, accessed November 8, 2013; "Brazil in Talks to Hire 6,000 Cuban Doctors," BBC News, May 6, 2013, http://www.bbc.co.uk/news/world-latin-america-22429101, accessed November 8, 2013; Anthony Boadle, "Cuban Doctors Tend to Brazil's Poor, Giving Rousseff a Boost," Reuters, December 1, 2013, http://www.reuters.com/article/2013/12/01/us-brazil-doctors-cuba-idUSBRE9B005720131201, accessed December 31, 2013.

4. "Yoani Sanchez Speaks at Freedom Tower in Miami," YouTube video of Yoani Sánchez speech and interview by Myriam Márquez, April 1, 2013, http://www.youtube.com/watch?v=zytHDGg1WjY, accessed December 30, 2013.

Bibliography

Ackerman, Holly. "The Balsero Phenomenon, 1991–1994." *Cuban Studies* 26 (1996): 169–200.

Aguirre, Benigno. "Social Control in Cuba." *Latin American Politics and Society* 44, no. 2 (2002): 67–98.

Alexander, Robert J. *A History of Organized Labor in Cuba*. Westport, Conn.: Praeger, 2002.

Alonso, José F., and Armando M. Lago. "A First Approximation Model of the Balance of Payments, Output, Employment and Foreign Aid Requirements of a Democratic Cuba." *Cuba in Transition* 3 (1993). http://www.ascecuba.org/publications/proceedings/volume3/alonslag1.asp. Accessed January 14, 2014.

Alonso, Nancy. *Closed for Repairs*. Willimantic, Conn.: Curbstone Press, 2007.

Álvarez, José. "The Current Restructuring of Cuba's Sugar Agribusiness." Food and Resource Economics Department, Florida Cooperative Extension Service, Institute of Food and Agricultural Sciences, University of Florida, Gainesville. http://edis.ifas.ufl.edu/pdffiles/FE/FE47200.pdf. Accessed December 28, 2013.

———. "Evaluating the Performance of Cuba's Sugarcane Basic Units of Cooperative Production during Their First Decade." Department of Food and Resource Economics, Florida Cooperative Extension Service, Institute of Food and Agricultural Services Extension, University of Florida, Gainesville, June 2005. http://edis.ifas.ufl.edu/pdffiles/FE/FE56200.pdf. Accessed November 7, 2013.

———. *Frank País y la Revolución Cubana*. Denver, Colo.: Outskirts, 2009.

———. *Principio y fin del mito fidelista*. Victoria, B.C.: Trafford, 2008.

———. "Rationed Products and Something Else: Food Availability and Distribution in 2000 Cuba." *Cuba in Transition* 11 (2001): 305–22.

Álvarez García, Alberto F., and Gerardo González Núñez. *¿Intelectuales vs. Revolución?: el caso del Centro de Estudios sobre América, CEA*. Montreal: Ediciones Arte D.T., 2001.

Amaro, Nelson, and Alejandro Portes. "Una sociología del exilio: situación de los grupos cubanos en Estados Unidos." *Aportes* 23 (January 1972): 7–24.

Amaro, Nelson, and Carmelo Mesa-Lago. "Inequality and Classes." In *Revolutionary Change in Cuba*, ed. Carmelo Mesa-Lago, 341–74. Pittsburgh: University of Pittsburgh Press, 1971.

Ameringer, Charles D. *The Cuban Democratic Experience: The Auténtico Years, 1944–1952*. Gainesville: University Press of Florida, 2000.

Amnesty International. *USA: The Case of the Cuban Five*. London: Amnesty International Publications, 2010.

Amuchástegui, Domingo. "Cuba's Armed Forces: Power and Reforms." *Cuba in Transition* 9 (1999): 109–14.

Anderson, Jon Lee. *Che Guevara: una vida revolucionaria*. Barcelona: Emecé, 1997.

Antón, Alex, and Roger E. Hernández. *Cubans in America: A Vibrant History of a People in Exile*. New York: Kensington, 2003.

Arboleya, Jesús. *The Cuban Counterrevolution*. Athens: Ohio University Center for International Studies, 2000.

Arenas, Reinaldo. *Before Night Falls*. New York: Viking, 1993.

Argote-Freyre, Frank. *Fulgencio Batista: From Revolutionary to Strongman*. New Brunswick, N.J.: Rutgers University Press, 2006.

Argüelles, Lourdes, and B. Ruby Rich. "Homosexuality, Homophobia, and Revolution: Notes toward an Understanding of the Cuban Lesbian and Gay Male Experience, Part I." *Signs* 9, no. 4 (1984): 683–99.

Arrufat, Antón. *Los siete contra Tebas*. Havana: Unión, 1968.

Artaraz, Kepa. *Cuba and Western Intellectuals since 1959*. New York: Palgrave Macmillan, 2009.

Arzuaga, Javier. *Cuba, 1959: La galera de la muerte*. Miami: Editorial Carta de Cuba, 2006.

Azicri, Max. *Cuba Today and Tomorrow: Reinventing Socialism*. Gainesville: University Press of Florida, 2000.

Baklanoff, Eric N. "A Bountiful Legacy: U.S. Investments and Diversification in Cuba during the 1950s." *Cuba in Transition* 19 (2009): 325–35.

———. "International Economic Relations." In *Revolutionary Change in Cuba*, ed. Carmelo Mesa-Lago, 251–76. Pittsburgh: University of Pittsburgh Press, 1971.

Baloyra, Enrique A. "Cuba." In *Latin America and Caribbean Contemporary Record*, vol. 1, *1981–1982*, ed. Jack W. Hopkins, Edward F. Lowenthal, James M. Malloy, and Eduardo Gamarra, 522–39. New York: Holmes and Meier, 1983.

Barberia, Lorena. "Remittances to Cuba: An Evaluation of US Government Policy Measures." Working Paper no. 15, Inter-University Committee on International Migration, September 2002. http://web.mit.edu/cis/www/migration/pubs/rrwp/15_remittances.pdf. Accessed December 30, 2013.

Bardach, Ann Louise. *Cuba Confidential: Love and Vengeance in Miami and Havana*. New York: Random House, 2002.

Barquín, Ramón. *Las luchas guerrilleras en Cuba: de la colonia a la Sierra Maestra*. 2 vols. Madrid: Editorial Playor, 1975.

Bejel, Emilio. *Gay Cuban Nation*. Chicago: University of Chicago Press, 2001.

Bender, Lynn Darrell. "Cuban Exiles: An Analytical Sketch." *Journal of Latin American Studies* 5, no. 2 (1973): 271–78.

Benedetti, Mario. "Present Status of Cuban Culture." In *Cuba in Revolution*, ed. Rolando E. Bonachea and Nelson P. Valdés, 500–526. New York: Anchor, 1972.

Benítez-Rojo, Antonio. *The Repeating Island: The Caribbean and the Postmodern Perspective*. Durham, N.C.: Duke University Press, 1992.

Benjamin, Jules R. *The United States and the Origins of the Cuban Revolution: An Empire of Liberty in an Age of Liberation*. Princeton, N.J.: Princeton University Press, 1990.

Benjamin, Medea, Joseph Collins, and Michael Scott. *No Free Lunch: Food and Revolution in Cuba Today*. San Francisco: Institute for Food and Development Policy, 1984.

Benmayor, Rina. "La 'Nueva Trova': New Cuban Song." *Latin American Music Review/ Revista de Música Latinoamericana* 2, no. 1 (1981): 11–44.

Bernardo, Robert M. *The Theory of Moral Incentives in Cuba*. Tuscaloosa: University of Alabama Press, 1971.

Bertot, Lillian D. "Postmodernidad y la Generación del Mariel." Cuban American National Foundation Cuba Paper Series, no. 17, n.d.

Beruvides, Esteban M. *Cuba y su presidio político*. Coral Gables, Fla.: 12th Avenue Graphics, 1994.

Betancourt, Ernesto F. "Exporting Revolution to Latin America." In *Revolutionary Change in Cuba*, ed. Carmelo Mesa-Lago, 105–26. Pittsburgh: University of Pittsburgh Press, 1971.

Bissell, Richard M. *Reflections of a Cold Warrior from Yalta to the Bay of Pigs*. New Haven, Conn.: Yale University Press, 1996.

Blasier, Cole. "The Elimination of United States Influence." In *Revolutionary Change in Cuba*, ed. Carmelo Mesa-Lago, 59–97. Pittsburgh: University of Pittsburgh Press, 1971.

———. *The Hovering Giant: U.S. Responses to Revolutionary Change in Latin America*. 2nd ed. Pittsburgh: University of Pittsburgh Press, 1989.

Blue, Sarah A. "The Erosion of Racial Equality in the Context of Cuba's Dual Economy." *Latin American Politics & Society* 49, no. 3 (2007): 35–68.

Blum, Denise F. *Cuban Youth and Revolutionary Values: Educating the New Socialist Citizen*. Austin: University of Texas Press, 2011.

Bonachea, Ramón L., and Marta San Martín. *The Cuban Insurrection, 1952–1958*. New Brunswick, N.J.: Transaction, 1974.

Brenner, Philip, Marguerite Rose Jiménez, John M. Kirk, and William LeoGrande, ed. *A Contemporary Cuba Reader: Reinventing Revolution*. Lanham, Md.: Rowman and Littlefield, 2008.

Brundenius, Claes. "Development and Prospects of Capital Goods Production in Revolutionary Cuba." In *Cuba's Socialist Economy toward the 1990s*, ed. Andrew Zimbalist, 97–114. Boulder, Colo.: Lynne Rienner, 1987.

———. "Development Strategies and Basic Human Needs." In *The Cuba Reader: The Making of a Revolutionary Society*, ed. Phillip Brenner, William M. LeoGrande, Donna Rich, and Daniel Siegel, 108–23. New York: Grove, 1989.

———. "Measuring Income Distribution in Pre- and Post-Revolutionary Cuba." *Cuban Studies* 9, no. 2 (1970): 29–44.

Brunner, Heinrich. *Cuban Sugar Policy from 1963 to 1970*. Pittsburgh: University of Pittsburgh Press, 1977.

Buch Rodríguez, Luis M. *Gobierno revolucionario cubano: génesis y primeros pasos*. Havana: Editorial de Ciencias Sociales, 1999.

Bunck, Julie Marie. *Fidel Castro and the Quest for a Revolutionary Culture in Cuba*. University Park: Pennsylvania State University Press, 1994.

Büntig, Aldo J. "The Church in Cuba." In *Religion in Cuba Today: A New Church in a New Society*, ed. Alice L. Hageman and Philip E. Wheaton, 95–128. New York: Association Press, 1971.

Cabrera, Lydia. *Refranes de negros viejos. Recogidos por Lydia Cabrera.* Miami: Ediciones C.R.: 1970.

Cabrera Infante, Guillermo. *Mea Cuba.* Madrid: Grupo Santillana de Ediciones, 1999.

———. "Salieron las amas de casa." In *Dispositivos de la flor: Cuba, literatura desde la Revolución*, ed. Edmundo Desnoes and William Luis, 397–98. New York: Ediciones del Norte, 1981.

Camnitzer, Luis. *New Art of Cuba.* Austin: University of Texas Press, 2003.

Canler, Ed. "The Miracle of the Cuban Economy in the 1990s." *Cuba in Transition* 11 (2001): 64–69.

Carlson, Lori Marie, and Oscar Hijuelos, ed. *Burnt Sugar/Caña Quemada: Contemporary Cuban Poetry in English and Spanish.* New York: Free Press, 2006.

Carreño, Pablo A. "Action Plan for the Reconstruction of the Cuban Sugar Industry." *Cuba in Transition* 12 (2002): 431–34.

Casal, Lourdes. "Literature and Society." In *Revolutionary Change in Cuba*, ed. Carmelo Mesa-Lago, 447–69. Pittsburgh: University of Pittsburgh Press, 1971.

Casanova Montero, Alfonso, and Pedro Monreal González. "Cuba's External Economic Constraints in the 1980s." In *Cuba after Thirty Years*, ed. Richard Gillespie, 84–98. London: Frank Cass, 1990.

Casey, Michael J. *Che's Afterlife: The Legacy of an Image.* New York: Vintage, 2009.

Castañeda, Jorge G. *Compañero: The Life and Death of Che Guevara.* New York: Knopf, 1997.

Castro, Fidel. "Comentarios de infancia y juventud." In *Los dispositivos de la flor: Cuba, literatura desde la Revolución*, ed. Edmundo Desnoes and William Luis, 65–76. New York: Ediciones del Norte, 1981.

———. *Fidel Castro Speaks.* Ed. Martin Kenner and James F. Petras. New York: Grove Press, 1969.

———. *History Will Absolve Me.* Havana: Guairas Book Institute, 1967.

———. "Relato de Fidel." In *La sierra y el llano*, ed. Edmundo Desnoes, 41–47. Havana: Casa de las Américas, 1961.

———. *Revolutionary Struggle, 1947–1958.* Ed. Rolando E. Bonachea and Nelson P. Valdés. Cambridge, Mass.: MIT Press, 1974.

Castro, Fidel, and Frei Beto. *Fidel y la religión.* Havana: Oficina de Publicaciones del Consejo de Estado, 1985.

Castro, Fidel, and José Ramón Fernández. *Playa Girón: Washington's First Military Defeat in the Americas.* New York: Pathfinder, 2001.

Central Intelligence Agency (CIA). *The Cuban Economy: A Statistical Review.* Washington, D.C.: CIA, Directorate of Intelligence, 1989.

Chanan, Michael. *Cuban Cinema.* 2nd ed. Minneapolis: University of Minnesota Press, 2004.

———. "Cuban Cinema." In *A Contemporary Cuba Reader: Reinventing Revolution*, ed. Philip Brenner, Marguerite Rose Jiménez, John M. Kirk, and William LeoGrande, 360–64. Lanham, Md.: Rowman and Littlefield, 2008.

Chang, Laurence, and Peter Kornbluh, ed. *The Cuban Missile Crisis: A National Security Archives Documents Reader*. New York: New Press, 1992.

Cheng, Yinghong. *Creating the New Man: From Enlightenment Ideals to Socialist Realities*. Honolulu: University of Hawai'i Press, 2009.

———. "Sino-Cuban Relations during the Early Years of the Castro Regime, 1959–1966." *Journal of Cold War Studies* 9, no. 3 (2007): 78–114.

Chomón, Faure. "El ataque al Palacio Presidencial, 13 de marzo de 1957." In *La sierra y el llano*, ed. Edmundo Desnoes, 97–136. Havana: Casa de las Américas, 1961.

Chomsky, Aviva. *A History of the Cuban Revolution*. Chichester, West Sussex: Wiley-Blackwell, 2011.

Clytus, John, with Jane Ricker. *Black Man in Red Cuba*. Coral Gables, Fla.: University of Miami Press, 1970.

Codina Jiménez, Alexis. "Worker Incentives in Cuba." In *Cuba's Socialist Economy toward the 1990s*, ed. Andrew Zimbalist, 129–40. Boulder, Colo.: Lynne Rienner, 1987.

Collins, Joseph, and Medea Benjamin. "Cuba's Food Distribution System." In *Cuba: Twenty-Five Years of Revolution, 1959–1984*, ed. Sandor Halebsky and John M. Kirk, 63–78. New York: Praeger, 1985.

Coltman, Leycester. *The Real Fidel Castro*. New Haven, Conn.: Yale University Press, 2003.

Combs, Jack Beckham. *The Cubans*. Santa Fe, N.M.: Documentary Photography Press, 2010.

Conde, Yvonne M. *Operation Pedro Pan: The Untold Exodus of 14,048 Cuban Children*. New York: Routledge, 1999.

Córdova, Efrén. *El trabajador cubano*. Miami: Ediciones Universal, 1990.

Coronel, Gustavo. "When Oil Lubricates Fascism: The Venezuelan-Cuban Connection." *Cuba in Transition* 15 (2005): 477–80.

Cotman, John Walton. *The Gorrión Tree: Cuba and the Grenada Revolution*. New York: Peter Lang, 1993.

Cuban American National Foundation. *Aftermath of a Purge*. Cuban Update Special Report. Washington, D.C.: CANF, n.d.

Curry-Machado, Jonathan. "Surviving the 'Cuban Nightmare': Securing Stability in the Face of Crisis in Cuba (1989–2004)." Working paper 64, Crisis States Research Centre, London School of Economics, June 2005.

Cushing, Lincoln. *¡Revolución!: Cuban Poster Art*. San Francisco: Chronicle, 2003.

Cushion, Steve. "The Most Expensive Port in the World: Dock Workers and the Cuban Revolution, 1948–1959." Paper presented at the 34th annual meeting of the Society for Caribbean Studies. http://www.caribbeanstudies.org.uk/papers/2010/Cushion_2010.pdf. Accessed May 30, 2013.

Cuza Malé, Belkis. "The Photogenic Ones." In *Burnt Sugar/Caña Quemada: Contemporary Cuban Poetry in English and Spanish*, ed. Lori Marie Carlson and Oscar Hijuelos, 64–65. New York: Free Press, 2006.

Dahlman, Carl J. "The Nation-Wide System of Learning in Cuba." Discussion paper no. 38, Research Program in Economic Development, Woodrow Wilson School, Princeton University, Princeton, N.J., 1973.

Debray, Régis. *Revolution in the Revolution?* New York: Grove Press, 1967.

Deere, Carmen Diana, Niurka Pérez Rojas, and Cary Torres Vila. *Güines, Santo Domingo, Majibacoa: sobre sus historias agrarias*. Havana: Editorial de Ciencias Sociales, 1998.

Deere, Carmen Diana, Ernel Gonzáles, Niurka Pérez, and Gustavo Rodríguez. "Household Incomes in Cuban Agriculture: A Comparison of the State, Co-operative and Peasant Sectors." *Development and Change* 26, no. 2 (1995): 209–34.

De la Cova, Antonio Rafael. *The Moncada Attack: Birth of the Cuban Revolution*. Columbia: University of South Carolina Press, 2007.

De la Cuesta, Leonel-Antonio. "The Cuban Socialist Constitution: Its Originality and Role in Institutionalization." *Cuban Studies* 6, no. 2 (1976): 15–30.

De la Fuente, Alejandro. *A Nation for All: Race, Inequality, and Politics in Twentieth-Century Cuba*. Chapel Hill: University of North Carolina Press, 2001.

De la Fuente, Alejandro, and Laurence Glasco. "Are Blacks 'Getting Out of Control'?: Racial Attitudes, Revolution, and Political Transformation in Cuba." In *Toward a New Cuba? Legacies of a Revolution*, ed. Miguel Ángel Centeno and Mauricio Font, 53–71. Boulder, Colo.: Lynne Rienner, 1997.

Del Águila, Juan M. "The Changing Character of Cuba's Armed Forces." In *The Cuban Armed Forces: Status and Outlook*, ed. Jaime Suchlicki, 27–59. Miami: Institute of Interamerican Studies, 1989.

———. *Cuba: Dilemmas of a Revolution*. 3rd ed. Boulder, Colo.: Westview, 1994.

DePalma, Anthony. *The Man Who Invented Fidel: Castro, Cuba, and Herbert L. Matthews of the "New York Times."* New York: Public Affairs, 2006.

Desnoes, Edmundo. "Epílogo para intelectuales." In *Dispositivos de la flor: Cuba, literatura desde la Revolución*, ed. Edmundo Desnoes and William Luis, 533–52. New York: Ediciones del Norte, 1981.

———, ed. *La sierra y el llano*. Havana: Casa de las Américas, 1961.

Detzer, David. *The Brink: The Cuban Missile Crisis, 1962*. New York: Thomas Y. Crowell, 1979.

Díaz, Jesús. *The Initials of the Earth*. Durham, N.C.: Duke University Press, 2006.

Díaz-Briquets, Sergio, and Lisandro Pérez. "Cuba: The Demography of Revolution." *Population Bulletin* 36, no. 1 (1981): 1–43.

Díaz-Versón, Salvador. "When Castro Became a Communist: The Impact on U.S.-Cuba Policy." Occasional Paper Series 1, no. 1, Institute for U.S.-Cuba Relations, Coral Gables, Fla., 1997.

Domínguez, Jorge I. "The Batista Regime in Cuba." In *Sultanistic Regimes*, ed. H. E. Chehabi and Juan J. Linz, 113–31. Baltimore, Md.: Johns Hopkins University Press, 1998.

———. *Cuba: Order and Revolution*. Cambridge, Mass.: Belknap, 1978.

———. "The Cuban Armed Forces, the Party and Society in Wartime and during Rectification (1986–1988)." *Journal of Communist Studies* 5, no. 4 (1989): 45–62.

———. *Democratic Politics in Latin America and the Caribbean*. Baltimore, Md.: Johns Hopkins University Press, 1998.

———. "The Political Impact on Cuba of the Reform and Collapse of Communist Regimes." In *Cuba after the Cold War*, ed. Carmelo Mesa-Lago, 99–132. Pittsburgh: University of Pittsburgh Press, 1993.

———. *To Make a World Safe for Revolution: Cuba's Foreign Policy*. Cambridge, Mass.: Harvard University Press, 1989.

Domínguez, Jorge I., and Rafael Hernández, ed. *U.S.-Cuban Relations in the 1990s*. Boulder, Colo.: Westview Press, 1989.

Dorschner, John, and Roberto Fabricio. *The Winds of December*. New York: Coward, McCann and Geoghegan, 1980.

Dorticós Torrado, Osvaldo. *Exposición y divulgación de la Ley de Reforma Agraria*. Havana: Capitolio Nacional, 1959.

Dosal, Paul J. Comandante *Che: Guerrilla Soldier, Commander, and Strategist, 1956–1967*. State Park: Pennsylvania State University Press, 2003.

Draper, Theodore. *Castro's Revolution: Myths and Realities*. New York: Praeger, 1962.

Duany, Jorge. "Cuban Communities in the United States: Migration Waves, Settlement Patterns and Socio-Economic Diversity." *Pouvoirs dans la Caraibe* 11 (1999): 69–103.

Dumont, René. *Is Cuba Socialist?* New York: Viking, 1974.

Duncan, W. Raymond. "Cuba-U.S. Relations and Political Contradictions in Cuba." In *Conflict and Change in Cuba*, ed. Enrique A. Baloyra and James A. Morris, 215–41. Albuquerque: University of New Mexico Press, 1993.

———. *The Soviet Union and Cuba: Interests and Influence*. Praeger: New York, 1985.

Dunn, Gordon E., and Staff, U.S. Weather Bureau Office, Miami. "The Hurricane Season of 1963." *Monthly Weather Review* 92, no. 3 (1964): 128–38.

Dye, Alan D. "Cuba and Origins of the US Sugar Quota." *Revista de Indias* 65, no. 233 (2005): 193–218.

Echevarría, Oscar A. "Cuba and the International Sugar Market." *Cuba in Transition* 5 (1995): 363–73.

Eckstein, Susan Eva. *Back from the Future: Cuba under Castro*. 2nd ed. New York: Routledge, 2003.

———. "Cuban Émigrés and the American Dream." *Political Science and Politics* 4, no. 2 (2006): 297–307.

———. "Dollarization and Its Discontents in the Post-Soviet Era." In *A Contemporary Cuba Reader: Reinventing Revolution*, ed. Philip Brenner, Marguerite Rose Jiménez, John M. Kirk, and William LeoGrande, 179–92. Lanham, Md.: Rowman and Littlefield, 2008.

———. "The Clash between Cuban Immigrant Cohorts: Power, Policy, and Transnational Ties." In *Cuba Today: Continuity and Change since the "Periodo Especial,"* ed. Mauricio Font. New York: Bildner Center of CUNY, 2004.

———. *The Immigrant Divide: How Cuban Americans Changed the U.S. and Their Homeland*. New York: Routledge, 2009.

———. "The Rectification of Errors or the Errors of Rectification Process in Cuba?" *Cuban Studies* 20 (1990): 67–85.

Eckstein, Susan Eva, and Lorena Barberia. "Cuban Americans and Their Transnational Ties." In *A Contemporary Cuba Reader: Reinventing Revolution*, ed. Philip Brenner, Marguerite Rose Jiménez, John M. Kirk, and William LeoGrande, 267–74. Lanham, Md.: Rowman and Littlefield, 2008.

Economic Commission for Latin America and the Caribbean. "Cuba." In *Preliminary Overview of the Economies of Latin America and the Caribbean, 2010*, 113–14. New York: ECLAC, 2011.

———. "Latin America and the Caribbean: Total Gross Domestic Product." *CEPAL News* 31, no. 12 (2011): 3.

Economist Intelligence Unit. *Cuba Country Report 1st Quarter 2000*. London: Economist Intelligence Unit, 2000.

———. *Country Profile: Cuba 1993–94*. London: Economist Intelligence Unit, 1994.

———. *Country Report: Cuba, Dominican Republic, Haiti, Puerto Rico (1990)*. London: Economist Intelligence Unit, 1990.

———. *Country Report: Cuba, Dominican Republic, Haiti, Puerto Rico (1991)*. London: Economist Intelligence Unit, 1991.

———. *Country Report: Cuba, Dominican Republic, Haiti, Puerto Rico (1993)*. London: Economist Intelligence Unit, 1993.

———. *Country Report: Cuba, May 2001*. London: Economist Intelligence Unit, 2001.

Eire, Carlos. *Waiting for Snow in Havana*. New York: Free Press, 2003.

Erikson, Daniel. "Cuba, China, Venezuela: New Developments." *Cuba in Transition* 15 (2005): 410–18.

———. *The Cuba Wars: Fidel Castro, the United States, and the Next Revolution*. New York: Bloomsbury Press, 2008.

———. "The Future of American Business with Cuba: Realities, Risks, and Rewards." *Transnational Law and Contemporary Problems* 14, no. 691 (2004): 691–717.

Escobar Ramírez, Abel. *Memorias del horror: los pueblos cautivos del Escambray*. Miami: Editorial Carta de Cuba, 2006.

Espina Prieto, Mayra P. "Cambios estructurales desde los noventa y nuevos temas de estudio de la sociedad cubana." In *Cambios en la sociedad cubana desde los noventa*, ed. Joseph S. Tulchin, Lilian Bobea, Marya P. Espina Prieto, and Rafael Hernández, 109–36. Washington, D.C.: Woodrow Wilson International Center for Scholars, 2005.

Espino, María Dolores. "Tourism in Cuba: A Development Strategy for the 1990s?" *Cuban Studies* 23 (1993): 49–69.

Espinosa, Belkis, and Jorge Luis Llópiz, ed. *Cine cubano: 30 años de revolución*. Havana: Centro de Promoción y Estudio del Cine "Saúl Yelín," 1989.

Esteve, Himilce. *El exilio cubano en Puerto Rico: su impacto político-social, 1959–1983*. San Juan: Editorial Raíces, 1984.

Fagen, Richard R. *The Transformation of Political Culture in Cuba*. Stanford, Calif.: Stanford University Press, 1969.

Fagen, Richard R., Richard M. Brody, and Thomas J. O'Leary. *Cubans in Exile: Disaffection and Revolution*. Stanford, Calif.: Stanford University Press, 1968.

Farber, Samuel. *Cuba since the Revolution of 1959: A Critical Assessment*. Chicago: Haymarket Books, 2011.

———. *The Origins of the Cuban Revolution Reconsidered*. Chapel Hill: University of North Carolina Press, 2006.

———. *Revolution and Reaction in Cuba, 1933–1960: A Political Sociology from Machado to Castro*. Middletown, Conn.: Wesleyan University Press, 1976.

Feinsilver, Julie Margot. "Cuba as a 'World Medical Power': The Politics of Symbolism." *Latin American Research Review* 24, no. 2 (1989): 1–34.

————. *Healing the Masses: Cuban Health Politics at Home and Abroad.* Berkeley: University of California Press, 1993.

Fermoselle, Rafael. *The Evolution of the Cuban Military: 1492–1986.* Miami: Ediciones Universal, 1987.

Fernandes, Sujatha. *Cuba Represent! Cuban Arts, State Power, and the Making of New Revolutionary Cultures.* Durham, N.C.: Duke University Press, 2006.

Fernández, Alfredo A. *Adrift: The Cuban Raft People.* Houston: Arte Público Press, 2000.

Fernández, Damián J. *Cuba and the Politics of Passion.* Austin: University of Texas Press, 2000.

————. *Cuba's Foreign Policy in the Middle East.* Boulder, Colo.: Westview, 1988.

————. "From Little Havana to Washington, D.C.: Cuban-Americans and U.S. Foreign Policy." In *Ethnic Groups and U.S. Foreign Policy*, ed. Mohammed E. Ahrari, 115–34. Westport, Conn.: Greenwood, 1987.

————. "Historical Background: Achievements, Failures, and Prospects." In *The Cuban Military under Castro*, ed. Jaime Suchlicki, 1–26. Miami: Research Institute for Cuban Studies, 1989.

————. "The New Cuban American Politics: Passion, Affection, Dollars, and the Emergence of MiHavana." In *Fifty Years of Revolution: Perspectives on Cuba, the United States, and the World*, ed. Soraya M. Castro Mariño and Ronald W. Pruessen, 333–45. Gainesville: University Press of Florida, 2012.

————, ed. *Cuban Studies since the Revolution.* Gainesville: University Press of Florida, 1992.

Fernández, Gastón A. *The Mariel Exodus: Twenty Years Later.* Miami: Ediciones Universal, 2002.

————. "Race, Gender, and Class in the Persistence of the Mariel Stigma Twenty Years after the Exodus from Cuba." *Cuba in Transition* 14 (2004): 78–88. http://www.ascecuba.org/publications/proceedings/volume14/pdfs/fernandez.pdf.

Ferriol Muruaga, Ángela. "La seguridad alimentaria en Cuba." In *Cuba crisis, ajuste y situación social (1990–1996)*, ed. Ángela Ferriol Muruaga et al., 76–114. Havana: Editorial de Ciencias Sociales, 1998.

Feuer, Carl Henry. "The Performance of the Cuban Sugar Industry, 1981–1985." In *Cuba's Socialist Economy toward the 1990s*, ed. Andrew Zimbalist, 69–83. Boulder, Colo.: Lynne Rienner, 1987.

File, Tom. "The Diversifying Electorate—Voting Rates by Race and Hispanic Origin in 2012 (and Other Recent Elections)," U.S. Census Bureau Current Population Report, May 2013. http://www.census.gov/prod/2013pubs/p20-568.pdf.

Fitzgerald, Frank T. *The Cuban Revolution in Crisis: From Managing Socialism to Managing Survival.* New York: Monthly Review Press, 1994.

Font, Mauricio. "Cuba and Castro: Beyond the 'Battle of Ideas.'" In *Changing Cuba/Changing World*, ed. Mauricio Font, 46–50. New York: The Bildner Center of the City University of New York, 2008.

Fraginals, Manuel Moreno. *La historia como arma.* Barcelona, Editorial Crítica, 1983.

Franklin, Jane. *Cuba and the United States: A Chronological History.* Melbourne: Ocean Press, 1997.

Franqui, Carlos. *Camilo Cienfuegos.* Bogotá: Planeta, 2001.

———. *Cuba: el libro de los doce*. 2nd ed. Mexico City: Serie Popular Era, 1970.

———. *Cuba, la revolución: ¿mito o realidad?* Barcelona: Ediciones Península, 2006.

———. *Diary of the Cuban Revolution*. New York: Viking, 1980.

———. *Retrato de familia con Fidel*. Barcelona: Seix Barral, 1981.

Freyre, Laura García. "De la iglesia a la plaza: las Damas de Blanco y la lucha por el espacio público en La Habana." *Cuba in Transition* 18 (2008): 284–92.

Fuentes, Ileana. "Cuentapropismo o cuentapriapismo: retos y consideraciones sobre género, auto-empleo y privatización." *Cuba in Transition* 18 (2008): 341–48.

Fuentes, Norberto. *Condenados del Condado*. Barcelona: Seix Barral, Biblioteca Breve, 2000.

Fursenko, Alexandr, and Timothy J. Naftali. *"One Hell of a Gamble": Khrushchev, Castro, and Kennedy, 1958–1964*. New York: Norton, 1997.

Fusco, Coco. "Hustling for Dollars." In *Imported: A Reading Seminar*, ed. Rainer Ganahl, 139–59. New York: Semiotext(e), 1998.

García, Cristina. *Dreaming in Cuban*. New York: Knopf, 1992.

García, María Cristina. *Havana USA: Cuban Exiles and Cuban Americans in South Florida, 1959–1994*. Berkeley: University of California Press, 1996.

García, Mario G. "Urban Transportation in Cuba, Past, Present and Future: What Can We Learn from the U.S. Experience?" *Cuba in Transition* 4 (1994). http://www.asce-cuba.org/publications/proceedings/volume4/garcia.asp.

García Luis, Julio, ed. *Cuban Revolution Reader*. Melbourne: Ocean Press, 2001.

García-Pérez, Gladys Marel. *Insurrection and Revolution: Armed Struggle in Cuba, 1952–1959*. Boulder, Colo.: Lynne Rienner, 1998.

George, Edward. *The Cuban Intervention in Angola, 1965–1991: From Che Guevara to Cuito Cuanavale*. London: Frank Cass, 2005.

Gershman, Carl, and Orlando Gutiérrez. "Ferment in Civil Society." *Journal of Democracy* 20, no. 1 (2009): 36–54.

Geyer, Georgie Anne. *Guerrilla Prince: The Untold Story of Fidel Castro*. Boston: Little, Brown and Company, 1991.

Gleijeses, Piero. "Cuba's First Venture in Africa: Algeria, 1961–1965." *Journal of Latin American Studies* 28, no. 1 (1996): 159–95.

———. *Conflicting Missions: Havana, Washington, and Africa, 1959–1976*. Chapel Hill: University of North Carolina Press, 2002.

———. "Moscow's Proxy? Cuba and Africa, 1975–1988." *Journal of Cold War Studies* 8, no. 2 (2006): 98–102.

———. *Shattered Hope: The Guatemalan Revolution and the United States, 1944–1954*. Princeton, N.J.: Princeton University Press, 1992.

Goldenberg, Boris. *The Cuban Revolution and Latin America*. New York: Praeger, 1965.

Gómez, Andy S., and Eugenio M. Rothe. *Value Orientations and Opinions of Recently Arrived Cubans in Miami*. Miami: Institute for Cuban and Cuban-American Studies, University of Miami, 2004.

Gómez Treto, Raúl. *La Iglesia Católica durante la construcción del socialismo en Cuba*. Matanzas, Cuba: CEHILA, 1988.

González, Edward. "The Party Congress and Poder Popular." *Cuban Studies* 6, nos. 1 and 2 (1976): 1–14.

———. "Relationship with the Soviet Union." In *Revolutionary Change in Cuba*, ed. Carmelo Mesa-Lago, 81–104. Pittsburgh: University of Pittsburgh Press, 1971.

González, Servando. *The Secret Fidel Castro: Deconstructing the Symbol*. Oakland, Calif.: InteliBooks, 2002.

Gordon, Antonio M., Jr. "The Nurtiture of Cubans: Historical Perspective and Nutritional Analysis." *Cuban Studies* 13, no. 2 (1983): 1–34.

Gosse, Van. *Where the Boys Are: Cuba, Cold War America, and the Making of a New Left*. Chicago: Haymarket Books, 1996.

Gott, Richard. *Cuba: A New History*. New Haven, Conn.: Yale University Press, 2004.

Great Britain, Parliament, House of Commons, Foreign Affairs Committee. *East Asia: Seventh Report of Session 2005–06*. Vol. 2. London: Stationary Office, 2006.

Grenier, Guillermo J. "The Cuban American Transition?: How Becoming More Cuban Is Helping Miami Become More American." Presentation at the Bildner Center, Graduate Center, City University of New York, November 25, 2011. http://web.gc.cuny.edu/dept/bildn/events/2011.11.21.shtml.

Grupo Areíto. *Contra viento y marea*. Havana: Casa de las Américas, 1978.

Guerra, Lillian. "Elián González and the 'Real Cuba' of Miami: Visions of Identity, Exceptionality and Divinity." *Cuban Studies* 38 (2007): 1–25.

———. Redefining Revolution in Cuba: Creative Expression and Cultural Conflict in the Special Period. In *Cuba: contrapuntos de cultura, historia y sociedad*, ed. Francisco A. Scarano and Margarita Zamora, 173–204. San Juan: Ediciones Callejón, 2007.

———.*Visions of Power in Cuba: Revolution, Redemption, and Resistance, 1959–1971*. Chapel Hill: University of North Carolina Press, 2012.

Guerra y Sánchez, Ramiro. *Azúcar y población en las Antillas*. Havana: Cultural, S.A., 1927.

Guerra, Sergio, and Alejo Maldonado. *Historia de la Revolución Cubana*. Navarra, Spain: Txalaparta, 2009.

Guevara, Ernesto. *The Bolivian Diary of Ernesto Che Guevara*. Ed. Mary-Alice Waters. New York: Pathfinder, 1994.

———. *Che Guevara Presente*. Ed. María del Carmen Ariet García and David Deutschmann. Melbourne: Ocean Press, 2004.

———. "Combate en la Plata." In *La sierra y el llano*, ed. Edmundo Desnoes, 87–94. Havana: Casa las Américas, 1961.

———. *Guerrilla Warfare*. Lincoln: University of Nebraska Press, 1985.

———. *Motorcycle Diaries: Notes on a Latin American Journey*. Melbourne: Ocean Press, 2003.

———. *Obras, 1957–1967*. 2 vols. Havana: Casa de las Américas, 1970.

———. *Reminiscences of the Cuban Revolutionary War*. New York: Monthly Review Press, 1969.

———. *El socialismo y el hombre en Cuba*. Melbourne: Ocean Sur, 2007.

Gunn, Gillian. "Will Castro Fall?" *Foreign Policy* 79 (1990): 132–50.

Gutiérrez, David Gregory, ed. *The Columbia History of Latinos in the United States since 1960*. New York: Columbia University Press, 2004.

Gutiérrez, Pedro Juan. *El Rey de La Habana*. Barcelona: Editorial Anagrama, 1999.

———. *Trilogía sucia de La Habana*. Barcelona: Editorial Anagrama, 1998.

Gutiérrez Agramonte, Eduardo. "Una nueva técnica de conducterapia en el tratamiento de la homosexualidad." *Revista Cubana de Medicina* 1, no. 1 (1962): 79–86.

Halebsky, Sandor, and John M. Kirk, ed. *Cuba: Twenty-Five Years of Revolution, 1959–1984.* New York: Praeger, 1985.

Halebsky, Sandor, and John M. Kirk, ed., with the assistance of Rafael Hernández. *Transformation and Struggle: Cuba Faces the 1990s.* New York: Praeger, 1990.

Halebsky, Sandor, and John M. Kirk, eds., with Carollee Bengelsdorf, Richard L. Harris, Jean Stubbs, and Andrew Zimbalist. *Cuba in Transition: Crisis and Transformation.* Boulder, Colo.: Westview Press, 1992.

Halperin, Maurice. *Return to Havana: The Decline of Cuba under Castro.* Nashville, Tenn.: Vanderbilt University Press, 1994.

———. *The Rise and Decline of Castro: An Essay in Contemporary History.* Berkeley: University of California Press, 1972.

Hart, Armando. *Aldabonazo: Inside the Cuban Revolutionary Underground, 1952–1958.* New York: Pathfinder, 2004.

"Health Aspects of the Cuban Refugee Problem." *Florida Health Notes* 5, no. 7 (1961): 147–70.

Henken, Ted. "Balseros in Alabama: Refugee Resettlement Experiences and the Divided Fates of Cuban Rafters in the New South." *Cuba in Transition* 16 (2006): 408–17.

———. "Desde Cuba con Yoani Sánchez: animando al periodismo ciudadano digital y desafiando a la violencia verbal." *Cuba in Transition* 18 (2008): 83–95.

———. "'Vale Todo' (Anything Goes): Cuba's Paladares." *Cuba in Transition* 12 (2002): 344–53.

———. "Vale Todo: In Cuba's *Paladares* Everything Is Prohibited but Anything Goes." In *A Contemporary Cuba Reader: Reinventing Revolution*, ed. Philip Brenner, Marguerite Rose Jiménez, John M. Kirk, and William LeoGrande, 168–78. Lanham, Md.: Rowman and Littlefield, 2008.

Hernández-Reguant, Ariana. "Multicubanidad." In *Cuba in the Special Period: Culture and Ideology in the 1990s*, ed. Ariana Hernández-Reguant, 68–88. New York: Palgrave Macmillan, 2009.

Hoffman, Bert. "The Helms-Burton Law and Its Consequences for Cuba, the United States and Europe." Paper presented at the 21st International Congress of the Latin American Studies Association, Chicago, September 1998.

Horowitz, Irving Louis, and Jaime Suchlicki, ed. *Cuban Communism, 1959–2003.* 10th ed. New Brunswick, N.J.: Transaction, 2001.

Howe, Linda S. *Transgression and Conformity: Cuban Writers and Artists after the Revolution.* Madison: University of Wisconsin Press, 2004.

Hunt, Jim, and Bob Risch. *Warrior: Frank Sturgis—the CIA's #1 Assassin-Spy Who Nearly Killed Castro but Was Ambushed by Watergate.* New York: Tom Doherty Associates, 2011.

Ibarra, Jorge. *Prologue to Revolution: Cuba, 1898–1958.* Boulder, Colo.: Lynne Rienner, 1998.

Jacobs, Matt. "Meeting the Neighbors: Fidel Castro's April 1959 Trip to the United States." Paper presented at the Cuba Futures International Symposium, Bildner Center, New York City, April 2011.

Jenkins, Gareth, ed. *Havana in My Heart: Seventy-Five Years of Cuban Photography*. Chicago: Chicago Review Press, 2002.

Jiménez-Leal, Orlando. *8-A: la realidad invisible*. Miami: Ediciones Universal, 1997.

Johnson, Haynes. *The Bay of Pigs: The Leaders' Story of Brigade 2506*. New York: Norton, 1964.

Jover Marimón, Mateo. "The Church." In *Revolutionary Change in Cuba*, ed. Carmelo Mesa-Lago, 399–426. Pittsburgh: University of Pittsburgh Press, 1971.

Kapcia, Antoni. *Cuba: Island of Dreams*. Oxford: Berg, 2000.

———. *Cuba in Revolution: A History since the Fifties*. London: Reaktion Books, 2008.

———. "The Cuban Revolution in Crisis." In *Latin America and the Caribbean: Prospects for Democracy*, ed. William Gutteridge, 179–206. Aldershot, UK: Ashgate, 1997.

Karol, K. S. *Guerrillas in Power: The Course of the Cuban Revolution*. New York: Hill and Wang, 1970.

Kirk, John M. *Between God and the Party: Religion and Politics in Revolutionary Cuba*. Tampa: University of South Florida Press, 1989.

Kirk, John M., and Leonardo Padura Fuentes, ed. *Culture and the Cuban Revolution: Conversations in Havana*. Gainesville: University Press of Florida, 2001.

Kleinknecht, William. "Journalists at Risk." *American Journalism Review* (December 1999). http://www.ajr.org/Article.asp?id=766.

Klepak, Hal. *Cuba's Military, 1990–2005: Revolutionary Soldiers during Counter-Revolutionary Times*. New York: Palgrave MacMillan, 2005.

Kornbluh, Peter, ed. *Bay of Pigs Declassified: The Secret CIA Report on the Invasion of Cuba*. New York: New Press, 1998.

Landau, Anya K., and Wayne S. Smith. "Cuba on the Terrorist List." *International Policy Report* (2002): 1–10. http://www.ciponline.org/images/uploads/publications/Cuba-ontheTerroristList.pdf.

Landau, Saul. "July 26: History Absolved Him; Now What?" In *A Contemporary Cuba Reader: Reinventing Revolution*, ed. Philip Brenner, Marguerite Rose Jiménez, John M. Kirk, and William LeoGrande, 41–44. Lanham, Md.: Rowman and Littlefield, 2008.

Latell, Brian. *After Fidel: The Inside Story of Castro's Regime and Cuba's Next Leader*. New York: Palgrave Macmillan, 2005.

———. *Castro's Secrets: The CIA and Cuba's Intelligence Machine*. New York: Palgrave Macmillan, 2012.

———. "Raul Castro: Confronting Fidel's Legacy in Cuba." *The Washington Quarterly* 30, no. 3 (2007): 53–65.

LeoGrande, William M. "The Communist Party of Cuba since the First Congress." In *Communist Politics: A Reader*, ed. Stephen White and Daniel N. Nelson, 173–91. New York: New York University Press, 1986.

———. *The Cuban Communist Party and Electoral Politics: Adaptation, Succession, and Transition*. Miami: Institute for Cuban and Cuban-American Studies, Miami University, 2002.

———. "Cuban Dependency: A Comparison of Pre-Revolutionary and Post-Revolutionary International Economic Relations." *Cuban Studies* 9, no. 2 (1979): 1–28.

———. "The Cuban Nation's Single Party." In *A Contemporary Cuba Reader: Reinventing*

Revolution, ed. Philip Brenner, Marguerite Rose Jiménez, John M. Kirk, and William LeoGrande, 50–62. Lanham, Md.: Rowman and Littlefield, 2008.

———. *Cuba's Policy in Africa, 1959–1980.* Berkeley, Calif.: Institute of International Studies, 1980.

———. "Party Development in Revolutionary Cuba." In *The Cuba Reader: The Making of a Revolutionary Society*, ed. Phillip Brenner, William M. LeoGrande, Donna Rich, and Daniel Siegel, 156–72. New York: Grove, 1989.

Levine, Robert M. *Secret Missions to Cuba: Fidel Castro, Bernardo Benes, and Cuban Miami.* New York: Palgrave, 2001.

Levine, Robert M., and Moisés Asís. *Cuban Miami.* New Brunswick, N.J.: Rutgers University Press, 2000.

Leyva, Ricardo [pseud]. "Health and Revolution in Cuba." In *Cuba in Revolution*, ed. Rolando E. Bonachea and Nelson P. Valdés, 456–96. New York: Anchor, 1972.

Liss, Sheldon B. *Roots of Revolution: Radical Thought in Cuba.* Lincoln: University of Nebraska Press, 1987.

Llanes, José. *Cuban Americans: Masters of Survival.* Cambridge, Mass.: Abt Books, 1982.

Llerena, Mario. *The Unsuspected Revolution: The Birth and Rise of Castroism.* Ithaca, N.Y.: Cornell University Press, 1978.

López-Fresquet, Rufo. *My Fourteen Months with Castro.* Cleveland: World Publishing, 1966.

López Vilaboy, José. *Motivos y culpables de la destrucción de Cuba.* San Juan: Editora de Libros Puerto Rico, 1973.

Low, Alfred D. *The Sino-Soviet Dispute: An Analysis of the Polemics.* Cranbury, N.J.: Associated University Presses, 1976.

Luis, William. *Culture and Customs of Cuba.* Westport, Conn.: Greenwood, 2001.

———. *Lunes de Revolución: literatura y cultura en los primeros años de la Revolución Cubana.* Madrid: Verbum, 2003.

Lumsden, Ian. *Machos, Maricones, and Gays: Cuba and Homosexuality.* Philadelphia: Temple University Press, 1996.

Luzón, José L. "Housing in Socialist Cuba: An Analysis Using Cuban Censuses of Population and Housing." *Cuban Studies* 18 (1988): 65–93.

Macaulay, Neil. "The Cuban Rebel Army: A Numerical Survey." *Hispanic American Historical Review* 58, no. 2 (1978): 284–95.

MacDonald, Theodore H. *A Developmental Analysis of Cuba's Health Care System Since 1959.* Lewiston, N.Y.: Edwin Mellen Press, 1999.

Márquez-Sterling, Manuel. *Cuba 1952–1959: The True Story of Castro's Rise to Power.* Wintergreen, Va.: Kleiopatria Digital Press, 2009.

Marrero, Leví. *Cuba en la década de 1950: un país en desarollo.* San Juan: Carta de Cuba, 2005.

Martínez-Fernández, Luis. "Trauma and Conflict: New Perspectives on Cuban Exile and Emigration to South Florida since 1959." *Ibero-Americana Pragensia* Supplementum 31 (2012): 93–106.

———. La diáspora en la frontera: retos y oportunidades para el estudio del Orlando puertorriqueño. *Centro Journal* 22, no. 1 (Spring 2010): 32–55.

Martínez Marún, Victoria. *Historia de Cuba (Sexto Grado)*. Havana: Instituto Cubano del Libro. 1973.

Mastrapa, Armando F., III. "Soldiers and Businessmen: The FAR during the Special Period." *Cuba in Transition* 10 (2000): 428–32.

Masud-Piloto, Félix Roberto. *With Open Arms: Cuban Migration to the United States*. Totowa, N.J.: Rowman and Littlefield, 1988.

Matas, Julio. "Theater and Cinematography." In *Revolutionary Change in Cuba*, ed. Carmelo Mesa-Lago, 427–45. Pittsburgh: University of Pittsburgh Press, 1971.

Matos, Huber. *Cómo llegó la noche*. Barcelona. Tusquets Editores, 2002.

Matthews, Herbert L. *Fidel Castro*. New York: Simon and Schuster, 1970.

Meer, Laurie Frederik. "Preemptive Nostalgia and *La Batalla* for Cuban Identity: Option Zero Theater." In *Cuba in the Special Period: Culture and Ideology in the 1990s*, ed. Ariana Hernández-Reguant, 89–104. New York: Palgrave Macmillan, 2009.

Menton, Seymour. *Prose Fiction of the Cuban Revolution*. Austin: University of Texas Press, 1975.

Mesa-Lago, Carmelo. *Cuba in the 1970s: Pragmatism and Institutionalization*. Albuquerque: University of New Mexico Press, 1978.

———. "Cuba's Economic Counter-Reform (Rectificación): Causes, Policies and Effects." In *Cuba after Thirty Years: Rectification and the Revolution*, ed. Richard Gillespie, 98–139. London: Frank Cass, 1990.

———. "Cuba's Economic Policies and Strategies for Confronting the Crisis." In *Cuba after the Cold War*, ed. Carmelo Mesa-Lago, 197–258. Pittsburgh: University of Pittsburgh Press, 1993.

———. *Economía y bienestar social en Cuba a comienzos del siglo XXI*. Madrid: Editorial Colibrí, 2003.

———. "The Economic Effects on Cuba of the Downfall of Socialism in the USSR and Eastern Europe." In *Cuba after the Cold War*, ed. Carmelo Mesa-Lago, 133–96. Pittsburgh: University of Pittsburgh Press, 1993.

———. "Economic Policies and Growth." In *Revolutionary Change in Cuba*, ed. Carmelo Mesa-Lago, 277–338. Pittsburgh: University of Pittsburgh Press, 1971.

———. *The Economy of Socialist Cuba*. Albuquerque: University of New Mexico Press, 1981.

———. "Historia y evaluación de medio siglo de políticas económico-sociales en Cuba socialista." In *Historia de Cuba*, ed. Consuelo Naranjo Orovio, 507–37. Madrid: Editorial Doce Calles, 2009.

———. "On Rectifying Errors of a Courteous Dissenter." *Cuban Studies* 20 (1990): 87–110.

———. "Present and Future of the Revolution." In *Revolutionary Change in Cuba*, ed. Carmelo Mesa-Lago, 501–28. Pittsburgh: University of Pittsburgh Press, 1971.

Mesa-Lago, Carmelo, and June S. Belkin, ed. *Cuba in Africa*. Pittsburgh: University of Pittsburgh Press, 1982.

Mesa-Lago, Carmelo, and Jorge Pérez-López. *Cuba's Aborted Reform: Socioeconomic Effects, International Comparisons, and Transition*. Gainesville: University of Florida Press, 2005.

Molina, Gabriel. *Diario de Girón*. Havana: Editora Política, 1983.

Molyneux, Maxine. "State, Gender and Institutional Change: The Federación de Mujeres Cubanas." In *Hidden Histories of Gender in Latin America*, ed. Elizabeth Dore and Maxine Molyneux, 291–321, Durham, N.C.: Duke University Press, 2000.

Montaner, Carlos Alberto. "Castro's Last Stand." *Journal of Democracy* 1, no. 3 (1990): 71–80.

———. *Viaje al corazón de Cuba*. Barcelona: Plaza & Janés, 1999.

Moore, Robin D. *Music and Revolution: Cultural Change in Socialist Cuba*. Berkeley: University of California Press/Chicago: Center for Black Music Research of Columbia College, 2006.

Morales, Waltraud Q. "La era después de Fidel: el futuro de las relaciones entre Cuba y EUA." *Military Review* (2007): 2–15.

Morán Arce, Lucas. *La revolución Cubana: una versión rebelde*. Ponce, P.R.: Imprenta Universitaria, Universidad Católica, 1980.

Morejón, Nancy. "Mujer Negra." *Casa de las Américas* 88 (1975). In *Transgression and Conformity: Cuban Writers and Artists after the Revolution*, ed. Linda S. Howe, 129–31. Madison: University of Wisconsin Press, 2004.

Moreno, Dario, and Christopher Warren. "The Conservative Enclave Revisited: Cuban Americans in Florida." In *Ethnic Ironies: Latino Politics in the 1992 Elections*, ed. Rodolfo O. de la Garza and Louis DeSipio. Boulder, Colo.: Westview Press, 1996.

———. "Pragmatism and Strategic Realignment in the 1996 Election: Florida's Cuban Americans." In *Awash in the Mainstream: Latino Politics in the 1996 Election*, ed. Rodolfo O. de la Garza and Louis DeSipio, 211–37. Boulder, Colo.: Westview Press, 1999.

Moreno, José A. "From Traditional to Modern Values." In *Revolutionary Change in Cuba*, ed. Carmelo Mesa-Lago, 471–97. Pittsburgh: University of Pittsburgh Press, 1971.

Moreno Fraginals, Manuel. "Manuel de Angola." In *La historia como arma*, ed. Manuel Moreno Fraginals, 172–78. Barcelona, Editorial Crítica, 1983.

Morley, Morris H. "U.S. Imperial State in Cuba, 1952–1958: Policymaking and Capitalist Interest." *Journal of Latin American Studies* 14, no. 1 (May 1982): 143–70.

Moses, Catherine. *Real Life in Castro's Cuba*. Wilmington, Del.: Scholarly Resources, 2000.

Mujal-León, Eusebio, and Lorena Buzón. "Exceptionalism and Beyond: Civil-Military Relations in Cuba, 1986–2008." *Cuba in Transition* 18 (2008): 402–16.

Mwakikagile, Godfrey. *Nyerere and Africa: End of an Era*. Pretoria, South Africa: New Africa Press, 2010.

Nazzari, Muriel. "The 'Woman Question' in Cuba: An Analysis of Material Constraints on Its Solution." *Signs* 9, no. 2 (1983): 246–63.

Novas, Himilce. *Everything You Need to Know about Latino History*. New York: Plume, 2008.

Núñez Jiménez, Antonio. *Informe al pueblo en el segundo aniversario de la reforma agraria*. Havana: Imprenta del INRA, 1961.

———. *La ley de Reforma Agraria en su aplicación*. Havana: Capitolio Nacional, 1959.

Ojito, Mirta. *Finding Mañana: A Memoir of a Cuban Exodus*. New York: Penguin Books, 2005.

Olson, James Stuart, and Judith E. Olson. *Cuban Americans: From Trauma to Triumph.* New York: Twayne Publishers, 1995.

Oltuski, Enrique. *Vida Clandestina: My Life in the Cuban Revolution.* New York: Wiley, 2002.

Oppenheimer, Andrés. *Castro's Final Hour: An Eyewitness Account of the Disintegration of Castro's Cuba.* New York: Touchstone, 1993.

Ortiz, Fernando. *Cuban Counterpoint: Tobacco and Sugar.* Durham, N.C.: Duke University Press, 1995.

Padilla, Heberto. *Fuera del juego: edicion conmemorativa, 1968–1998.* Miami: Ediciones Universal, 1998.

———. *Self-Portrait of the Other.* New York: Farrar, Straus and Giroux, 1990.

Padura Fuentes, Leonardo. "Living and Creating in Cuba: Risks and Challenges." In *A Contemporary Cuba Reader: Reinventing Revolution,* ed. Philip Brenner, Marguerite Rose Jiménez, John M. Kirk, and William LeoGrande, 348–54. Lanham, Md.: Rowman and Littlefield, 2008.

Pardo Llada, José. *Fidel y el "Che."* Barcelona: Esplugues de Llobregat, 1988.

Paterson, Thomas G. *Contesting Castro: The United States and the Triumph of the Cuban Revolution.* New York: Oxford University Press, 1994.

Paulston, Rolland G. "Education." In *Revolutionary Change in Cuba,* ed. Carmelo Mesa-Lago, 375–97. Pittsburgh: University of Pittsburgh Press, 1971.

Pavlov, Yuri I. *Soviet-Cuban Alliance, 1959–1991.* Coral Gables, Fla.: North-South Center Press, University of Miami, 1996.

Pedraza, Silvia. "The Impact of Pope John Paul II's Visit to Cuba." *Cuba in Transition* 8 (1998): 482–85.

———. "*Los Marielitos* of 1980: Race, Class, Gender, and Sexuality." *Cuba in Transition* 14 (2004): 89–102.

———. *Political Dissatisfaction in Cuba's Revolution and Exodus.* New York: Cambridge University Press, 2007.

Peredo, Inti. "My Campaign with Che." In Ernesto Guevara, *The Bolivian Diary of Ernesto Che Guevara,* ed. Mary-Alice Waters, 322–408. New York: Pathfinder, 1994.

Pérez, Faustino. "De Tuxpán a las Coloradas." In *La sierra y el llano,* ed. Edmundo Desnoes, 73–80. Havana: Casa de las Américas, 1961.

Pérez, Lisandro. "The 1990s: Cuban Miami at the Crossroads." *Cuban Studies* 20 (1990): 3–9.

Pérez, Louis A., Jr. *Cuba and the United States: Ties of Singular Intimacy.* Athens: University of Georgia Press, 1990.

———. *Cuba: Between Reform and Revolution.* 4th ed. New York: Oxford University Press, 2011.

———. *On Becoming Cuban: Identity, Nationality, and Culture.* Chapel Hill: University of North Carolina Press, 1999.

———. *To Die in Cuba: Suicide and Society.* Chapel Hill: University of North Carolina Press, 2005.

Pérez-López, Jorge F. "The Cuban Economy in an Unending Special Period." *Cuba in Transition* 12 (2002): 507–21.

———. "Cuba's Balance of Payments Statistics." *Cuba in Transition* 10 (2000): 136–44.

http://www.ascecuba.org/publications/proceedings/volume10/pdfs/perezlopez. pdf.

———. "Cuban-Soviet Sugar Trade: Price and Subsidy Issues." *Bulletin of Latin American Research* 7, no. 1 (1988): 123–47.

———. "Cuba's International Trade: Becoming More Invisible." *Cuba in Transition* 18 (2008): 144–53.

———. *Cuba's Second Economy: From Behind the Scenes to Center Stage.* New Brunswick, N.J.: Transaction, 1995.

———. *Economics of Cuban Sugar.* Pittsburgh: University of Pittsburgh Press, 1991.

———. "Foreign Investment in Cuba: An Inventory." *Cuba in Transition* 14 (2004): 103–15.

Pérez-Stable, Marifeli. *The Cuban Revolution: Origins, Course, and Legacy.* 2nd ed. New York: Oxford University Press, 1999.

———. "Cuban Women and the Struggle for 'Conciencia.'" *Cuban Studies* 17 (1987): 51–72.

———. "The Invisible Crisis: The Exhaustion of Politics in 1990s Cuba." In *Toward a New Cuba: Legacies of a Revolution*, ed. Miguel Ángel Centeno and Mauricio Font, 25–38. Boulder, Colo.: Lynne Rienner, 1997.

———. "Reflections on Political Possibilities: Cuba's Peaceful Transition That Wasn't (1954–1958)." Occasional paper series 1, Cuban Research Institute, Florida International University, September 1998. http://marifeliperez-stable.com/wp-content/19980900-fiu-cuban-research-institute-cubas-peaceful-transition-that-wasnt.pdf.

Périssé, J. "Energy and Protein Requirements: Past Work and Future Prospects and the International Level." Paper presented at the International Colloquium CENECA, Paris, March 1981. FAO/WHO/UNU EPR/81/INF.1 September 1981. http://www.fao.org/DOCREP/MEETING/004/M2995E/M2995E00.HTM.

Perl, Shoshana. "Wither Helms-Burton?: A Retrospective on the 10th Year Anniversary." Miami European Union Center, Jean Monnet/Robert Schuman Paper Series vol. 6, no. 5 (February 2006), http://aei.pitt.edu/8171/1/perlfinal.pdf.

Peters, Philip. *Cutting Losses: Cuba Downsizes Its Sugar Industry.* Arlington, Va.: Lexington Institute, 2003.

———. *International Tourism: The New Engine of Cuba's Economy.* Arlington, Va.: Lexington Institute, 2002.

Peterson, Mark F. "Work Attitudes of Mariel Boatlift Refugees." *Cuban Studies* 14, no. 2 (1984): 1–19.

Pfeiffer, Jack B. "Official History of the Bay of Pigs Operation." Vol. 3, "Evolution of CIA's Anti-Castro Policies, 1959–January 1961." CIA, Langley, Va., 1979. http://www.gwu.edu/~nsarchiv/NSAEBB/NSAEBB353/bop-vol3.pdf.

Pino Machado, Quintín. *La Batalla de Girón: razones de una victoria.* Havana: Editorial de Ciencias Sociales, 1983.

Pollitt, Brian H. "The Rise and Fall of the Cuban Sugar Economy." *Journal of Latin American Studies* 36, no. 2 (2004): 319–48.

———. "Sugar, 'Dependency' and the Cuban Revolution." Occasional Paper 43, University of Glasgow, Latin American Studies, 1985.

Portell Vilá, Herminio. *Nueva historia de la República de Cuba*. Miami: La Moderna Poesia, 1986.

Portes, Alejandro. "A Bifurcated Enclave: The Peculiar Evolution of the Cuban Immigrant Population in the Last Decades." Paper presented at the 9th conference of the Cuban Research Institute, Florida International University, Miami, May 2013.

Portes, Alejandro, Juan M. Clark, and Robert L. Bach. "The New Wave: A Statistical Profile of Recent Cuban Exiles to the United States." *Cuban Studies* 7 (1977): 1–32.

Portes, Alejandro, Juan M. Clark, and Robert Manning. "After Mariel: A Survey of the Resettlement Experiences of 1980 Cuban Refugees in Miami." *Cuban Studies* 15, no. 2 (1985): 35–59.

Portes, Alejandro, and Alex Stepick. *City on the Edge: The Transformation of Miami*. Berkeley: University of California Press, 1993.

Prevost, Gary. "Cuba." In *Politics in Latin America: The Power Game*, ed. Harry E. Vanden and Gary Prevost, 325–56. New York: Oxford University Press 2002.

———. "Cuba and Nicaragua: A Special Relationship?" *Latin American Perspectives* 17 (1990): 120–37.

Prieto, Yolanda. "Cuban Women in the U.S. Labor Force: Perspectives on the Nature of the Change." *Cuban Studies* 17 (1987): 73–91.

Prout, Ryan. "Jail-House Rock: Cuba, AIDS, and the Incorporation of Dissent in Bengt Norborg's *Socialism or Death*." *Bulletin of Latin American Studies* 18, no. 4 (1999): 23–36.

Pujol, Joaquín P. "The Cuban Economy as Seen by Economists within the Island and Other Observers." *Cuba in Transition* 20 (2010): 1–16.

Purcell, Susan Kaufman, and David J. Rothkopf, ed. *Cuba: The Contours of Change*. Boulder, Colo.: Lynne Rienner, 2000.

Quirk, Robert E. *Fidel Castro*. New York: Norton, 1993.

Raimundo, Daniel Efraín. *Habla el Coronel Orlando Piedra*. Miami: Ediciones Universal, 1994.

Ramonet, Ignacio, and Fidel Castro. *Fidel Castro: biografía a dos voces*. Madrid: Debate, 2006.

Ramos, Marcos A. *Protestantism and Revolution in Cuba*. Miami: North-South Center of the University of Miami, 1989.

Randall, Margaret. *Cuban Women Now*. Toronto: Women's Press, 1974.

Ratliff, William. "Cuban Military Policy in Sub-Saharan Africa." In *Cuban Internationalism in Sub-Saharan Africa*, ed. Sergio Díaz-Briquets, 29–47. Pittsburgh: Duquesne University Press, 1989.

Redruello, Laura. "Algunas reflexiones en torno a la película *Alicia en el pueblo de Maravillas*." *Cuban Studies* 38 (2007): 82–99.

Republic of Cuba, Ejército de Alfabetizadores Brigadas Conrado Benítez. *Cumpliremos!* Havana: Imprenta Nacional, 1961.

Republic of Cuba, Gobierno Revolucionario, Ministerio de Educación, Comisión Nacional de Alfabetización. *Alfabeticemos*. Havana: Imprenta Nacional, 1961.

———. *¡Venceremos!* Havana: Imprenta Nacional, 1961.

Republic of Cuba, Instituto Nacional de la Vivienda. *40 años de la vivienda en Cuba*. Havana: Instituto Nacional de la Vivienda, 1999.

Republic of Cuba, Oficina Nacional de Estadísticas. *Anuario estadístico de Cuba (2006)*. Havana: ONE, 2007.

————. *Anuario estadístico de Cuba (2009)*. Havana: ONE, 2010.

————. *Anuario estadístico de Cuba (2010)*.Havana: ONE, 2011.

————. *Anuario estadístico de Cuba (2011)*. Havana: ONE, 2012.

————. *Panorama social y económico de Cuba (2010)*. Havana: ONE, 2011.

Ritter, Archibald R. M. "Canadian-Cuban Economic Relations: Past, Present, and Prospective." In *Our Place in the Sun: Canada and Cuba during the Castro Era*, ed. Robert Wright and Lana Wylie, 246–81. Toronto: University of Toronto Press, 2009.

————. *The Economic Development of Revolutionary Cuba*. New York: Praeger, 1974.

————. "Survival Strategies and Economic Illegalities in Cuba." *Cuba in Transition* 15 (2005): 342–59.

Rivero Caro, Adolfo. "Antecedentes del movimiento de derechos humanos." Siglo XXI, Cuban Committee for Human Rights. http://www.sigloxxi.org/Anexos-libro/anex-00.htm.

Rivero García, José, ed. *Crónicas de la isla*. San Juan: Carta de Cuba, 2003.

Roca, Sergio. *Cuban Economic Policy and Ideology: The Ten Million Ton Harvest*. Beverly Hills, Calif.: Sage, 1976.

————. "State Enterprises in Cuba under the New System of Planning and Management." *Cuban Studies* 16 (1986): 153–79.

Rodríguez Beruff, Jorge, ed. *Cuba en crisis: perspectivas económicas y políticas*. San Juan: Editorial de la Universidad de Puerto Rico, 1995.

Rodríguez Loeches, Enrique. "El crimen de Humboldt 7." In *La sierra y el llano*, ed. Edmundo Desnoes, 139–55. Havana: Casa de las Américas, 1961.

Roman, Peter. *People's Power: Cuba's Experiment with Representative Government*. Boulder, Colo.: Westview Press, 1999.

Romero, Carlos A. "South-South Cooperation between Venezuela and Cuba." In *The Reality of Aid, South-South Development Cooperation: A Challenge to the Aid System?* Quezon City, Philippines: IBON Books, 2010. http://www.realityofaid.org/wp-content/uploads/2013/02/ROA-SSDC-Special-ReportEnglish.pdf.

Rosenthal, Mona. *Inside the Revolution: Everyday Life in Socialist Cuba*. Ithaca, N.Y.: Cornell University Press, 1997.

Rudolph, James D. *Cuba: A Country Study*. 3rd ed. Washington, D.C.: Foreign Area Studies, American University, 1985.

Ruiz, Ramón Eduardo. *Cuba: The Making of a Revolution*. New York: Norton, 1970.

Ryan, Henry Butterfield. *The Fall of Che Guevara: A Story of Soldiers, Spies, and Diplomats*. New York: Oxford University Press, 1998.

Safa, Helen I. "Women and Household Change in the Special Period." In *Cuba: contrapuntos de cultura, historia y sociedad*, ed. Francisco A. Scarano and Margarita Zamora, 207–27. San Juan: Ediciones Callejón, 2007.

Sánchez, Juan Tomás. "Cuba: An Unreliable Producer of Sugar." *Cuba in Transition* 6 (1996): 260–61.

————. "Cuba y el etanol: proyecciones para una economía privada." *Cuba in Transition* 17 (2007): 199–205.

Sánchez, Yoani. *Havana Real: One Woman Fights to Tell the Truth about Cuba Today*. Brooklyn, N.Y.: Melville House, 2009.

Santana, Sarah M. "The Cuban Health Care System: Responsiveness to Changing Needs and Demands." In *Cuba's Socialist Economy toward the 1990s*, ed. Andrew Zimbalist, 115–27. Boulder, Colo.: Lynne Rienner, 1987.

Sartre, Jean-Paul. *Sartre on Cuba*. New York: Ballantine Books, 1961.

Scarpaci, Joseph L. "Emerging Food and *Paladar* Market in Havana." *Cuba in Transition* 5 (1995): 74–84.

Scarpaci, Joseph L., Roberto Segre, and Mario Coyula. *Havana: Two Faces of the Antillean Metropolis*. Foreword by Andrés Duany. Rev. ed. Chapel Hill: University of North Carolina Press, 2002.

Schlesinger, Arthur M. *A Thousand Days: John F. Kennedy in the White House*. Boston: Houghton Mifflin, 1965.

Schoultz, Lars. *That Little Infernal Republic: The United States and the Cuban Revolution*. Chapel Hill: University of North Carolina Press, 2009.

Scott, James C. *Weapons of the Weak: Everyday Forms of Peasant Resistance*. New Haven, Conn.: Yale University Press, 1985.

Segal, Aaron. "Dance and Diplomacy: The Cuban National Ballet." *Caribbean Review* 9, no. 1 (1980): 30–32.

Segre, Roberto. *Lectura crítica del entorno cubano*. Havana: Editorial Letras Cubanas, 1990.

Shayne, Julie D. *The Revolution Question: Feminisms in El Salvador, Chile, and Cuba*. New Brunswick, N.J.: Rutgers University Press, 2004.

Shearman, Peter. "Gorbachev and the Restructuring of Soviet-Cuban Relations." In *Cuba after Thirty Years: Rectification and Revolution*, ed. Richard Gillespie, 63–83. London: Frank Cass, 1990.

Sims, Harold D. "Cuban Labor and the Communist Party, 1937–1958: An Interpretation." *Cuban Studies* 15, no. 1 (1985): 123–47.

Sinclair, Minor, and Martha Thompson. "Going against the Grain: Agricultural Crisis and Transformation." In *A Contemporary Cuba Reader: Reinventing Revolution*, ed. Philip Brenner, Marguerite Rose Jiménez, John M. Kirk, and William LeoGrande, 156–67. Lanham, Md.: Rowman and Littlefield, 2008.

Skaine, Rosemarie. *The Cuban Family: Custom and Change in an Era of Hardship*. Jefferson, N.C.: McFarland & Company, 2004.

Skoug, Kenneth N., Jr. *Cuba as a Model and a Challenge: July 25, 1984*. Current Policy no. 600. Washington, D.C.: U.S. Department of State, 1984.

Smith, Earl E. T. *The Fourth Floor: An Account of the Castro Communist Revolution*. Washington, D.C.: Selous Foundation Press, 1987.

Smith, Lois M., and Alfred Padula. *Sex and Revolution: Women in Revolutionary Cuba*. New York: Oxford University Press, 1996.

Smith, Robert, ed. *What Happened in Cuba: A Documentary History*. New York: Tawyne, 1963.

Smith, Wayne S. "Our Dysfunctional Cuban Embargo." *Orbis* 42, no. 4 (1998): 533–44.

———. *The Closest of Enemies*. New York: W. W. Norton, 1987.

Stermer, Dugald. *The Art of Revolution: Castro's Cuba: 1959–1970*. Introduction by Susan Sontag. New York: McGraw-Hill, 1970.

Stubbs, Jean. *Cuba: The Test of Time*. London: Latin American Bureau, 1989.

———. "Revolutionizing Women, Family, and Power." In *Women and Politics Worldwide*, ed. Barbara J. Nelson and Najma Chowdhury, 190–207. New Haven, Conn.: Yale University Press, 1994.

Suárez, Andrés. *Cuba: Castroism and Communism, 1959–1966*. Cambridge, Mass.: MIT Press, 1967.

———. "The Cuban Revolution: The Road to Power." *Latin American Research Review* 7, no. 3 (1972): 5–29.

———. "Leadership, Ideology, and Political Party." In *Revolutionary Change in Cuba*, ed. Carmelo Mesa-Lago, 3–21. Pittsburgh: University of Pittsburgh Press, 1971.

Suárez, Virgil. *Going Under*. Houston: Arte Público Press, 1996.

Suchlicki, Jaime. *Cuba: From Columbus to Castro and Beyond*. 4th ed. Washington, D.C.: Brasseys's, 1997.

———. "El desafío de Cuba y Venezuela a la seguridad del hemisferio: implicaciones para Estados Unidos." *Documentos CADAL* 8, no. 110 (2010): 1–8.

Sullivan, Mark P. "Cuba: U.S. Restrictions on Travel and Remittances." Congressional Research Service Report, October 16, 2009. http://www.fas.org/sgp/crs/row/RL31139.pdf.

———."Cuba: Issues for the 112th Congress." Congressional Research Service Report, November 6, 2012. http://www.fas.org/sgp/crs/row/R41617.pdf.

Sweig, Julia E. *Inside the Cuban Revolution: Fidel Castro and the Urban Underground*. Cambridge, Mass.: Harvard University Press, 2002.

Symmes, Patrick. *The Boys from Dolores: Fidel Castro's Schoolmates from Revolution to Exile*. New York: Pantheon Books, 2007.

Sznajder, Mario, and Luis Roniger. "Política, ethos social e identidad en la Cuba contemporánea." *América Latina Hoy* 29 (2001): 155–78.

Szulc, Tad. *Fidel: A Critical Portrait*. New York: William Morrow, 1986.

Thomas, Hugh. *The Cuban Revolution*. New York: Harper and Row, 1977.

Togores González, Viviana. "Ingresos monetarios de la población, cambios en la distribución y efectos sobre el nivel de vida." In *Cambios en la sociedad cubana desde los noventa*, ed. Joseph S. Tulchin, Lilian Bobea, Marya P. Espina Prieto, and Rafael Hernández, 187–216. Washington, D.C.: Woodrow Wilson International Center for Scholars, 2005.

Torres, María de los Ángeles. *In the Land of Mirrors: Cuban Exile Politics in the United States*. Ann Arbor: University of Michigan Press, 1999.

Tozian, Gregory. *Fidel's Cuba: A Revolution in Pictures*. Photographs by Osvaldo Salas and Roberto Salas. Ed. Doug Smith and Ted Anderson. Hillsboro, Ore.: Beyond Words Publishing/New York: Thunder's Mouth Press, 1998.

Trento, Angelo. *Castro and Cuba: From the Revolution to the Present*. New York: Interlink Books, 2000.

Triay, Víctor Andrés. *Fleeing Castro: Operation Pedro Pan and the Cuban Children's Program*. Gainesville: University Press of Florida, 1998.

Turits, Richard. "Trade, Debt, and the Cuban Economy." In *Cuba's Socialist Economy toward the 1990s*, ed. Andrew Zimbalist, 165–82. Boulder, Colo.: Lynne Rienner, 1987.

Tzivelis, Vassiliki. "The European Union's Foreign Policy towards Cuba: It Is Time to Tie the Knot." Jean Monnet/Robert Schuman Paper Series, vol. 6, no. 7, Miami European Union Center, University of Miami, March 2006. http://www6.miami.edu/eucenter/Tzivelisfinal.pdf.

Ubell, Robert N. "High-Tech Medicine in the Caribbean: 25 Years of Cuban Health Care." *New England Journal of Medicine* 309 (1983): 1468–72.

United Nations Development Project. *Human Development Report, 1998: Consumption for Human Development*. New York: Oxford University Press.

Unzueta, Silvia M. "The Mariel Exodus: A Year in Retrospect." Metropolitan Dade County Government, Miami, 1981. Available at Cuban Information Archives Web site, http://www.cuban-exile.com/doc_026-050/doc0033.html.

United States Central Intelligence Agency. *World Factbook 1985*. Washington, D.C.: CIA, 1985.

U.S. Department of Commerce, Bureau of the Census. *Current Population Survey: Annual Demographic File, 1985*. Washington, D.C.: Bureau of the Census, 1985.

———. *1977 Survey of Minority-Owned Business Enterprises: Spanish Origin*. Washington, D.C.: Government Printing Office, 1980.

U.S. Department of State, Bureau of Public Affairs. "Cuban Support for Terrorism and Insurgency in the Western Hemisphere." (March 12, 1982).

———. "Human Rights in Cuba: An Update." *US Department of State Bulletin* (April 1989).

U.S. Information Agency. *Cuba Annual Report (1987)*. New Brunswick, N.J.: Transaction Books, 1991.

———. *Cuba Annual Report (1988)*. New Brunswick, N.J.: Transaction Books, 1991.

———. *Cuba Annual Report (1989)*. New Brunswick, N.J.: Transaction Books, 1991.

Utset, Xavier. "Creating Citizens: The Birth and Growth of the Cuban Internal Pro-Democracy Movement." Paper presented at the 22nd annual meeting of the Middle Atlantic Conference on Latin American Studies (MACLAS), March 31, 2001. http://www.sigloxxi.org/Archivo/creatingcitizens.htm.

Valdés, Nelson P. "La Cachita y el Che: Patron Saints of Revolutionary Cuba." As told to Nan Elsasser. *Encounters* 1 (1989): 30–34.

———. "The Radical Transformation of Cuban Education." In *Cuba in Revolution*, ed. Rolando E. Bonachea and Nelson P. Valdés, 422–55. New York: Anchor, 1972.

———. "Revolution and Institutionalization in Cuba." *Cuban Studies* 6, nos. 1 and 2 (1976): 1–38.

Valenta, Jiri. "Comment: The Soviet-Cuban Alliance in Africa and Future Prospects in the Third World." *Cuban Studies* 10, no. 2 (July 1980): 36–43.

Valladares, Armando. *Against All Hope*. New York: Knopf, 1986.

Vega, Jesús. *El cartel cubano de cine*. Havana: Editorial de Letras Cubanas, 1996.

Veintiséis. Havana: Editorial de Ciencias Sociales, 1970.

Villapol, Nitza. *Comida al minuto*. Santiago: Editorial Oriente, 1980.

Viva Kuba! Vizit Fidelja Kastro Rus v Sovestkiř Soyus. Moscow, 1963.

Waldron, Lamar. *Watergate: The Hidden History: Nixon, the Mafia, and the CIA*. Berkeley: Counterpoint, 2012.

Walters, Barbara, and Fidel Castro. "An Interview with Fidel Castro." *Foreign Policy* 28 (1977): 22–51.

Wasem, Ruth Ellen. "Cuban Migration to the United States: Policy and Trends." Congressional Research Service Report, June 2, 2009. https://www.fas.org/sgp/crs/row/R40566.pdf.

Welch, Richard E. *Response to Revolution: The United States and the Cuban Revolution, 1959–1961*. Chapel Hill: University of North Carolina Press, 1985.

Williams, Eric. *From Columbus to Castro: A History of the Caribbean, 1492–1969*. New York: Vintage Books, 1984.

Wyden, Peter. *Bay of Pigs: The Untold Story*. New York: Simon and Schuster, 1979.

Yafee, Helen. *Che Guevara: The Economics of Revolution*. London: Palgrave MacMillan, 2009.

Zimbalist, Andrew. "Incentives and Planning in Cuba." *Latin American Research Review* 24, no. 1 (1989): 65–94.

———. "Whither the Cuban Economy?" In *Cuba: The Contours of Change*, ed. Susan Kaufman Purcell and David Rothkopf, 13–29. Boulder, Colo.: Lynne Rienner, 2000.

Zimbalist, Andrew, and Claes Brundenius. *The Cuban Economy: Measurement and Analysis of Socialist Performance*. Baltimore, Md.: Johns Hopkins University Press, 1989.

Zimbalist, Andrew, and Susan Eckstein. "Patterns of Cuban Development: The First Twenty-Five Years." In *Cuba's Socialist Economy toward the 1990s*, ed. Andrew Zimbalist, 7–24. Boulder, Colo.: Lynne Rienner, 1987.

Index

Page numbers in italics indicate illustrations.

Africa, sub-Saharan, 95, 144–47, *145*, 150

Age, leadership, 229, 248–49, 272

Agrarian Reform Law of May 1959, 52–53

Agriculture and agrarian reform: diversification of, 64, 88, 90; food production and, 83–84, 185–86, 259–60; forced labor and, 115–16; land, 52–53, 64, 259–60; in new millennium, 242–44; revolutionary government and, 52–53, 64, 113–21, 185–86, 259–60, 313n22; structural, 190, *191*, 192; ten-million-ton harvest in, 113–21. *See also* Food production, distribution, and rationing; Sugar agroindustrial complex

Alarcón, Ricardo, 264–65, 277, 284, 285–86

ALBA. *See* Alianza Bolivariana para los Pueblos de Nuestra América

Aldana, Carlos, 189

Algeria, 94

Alianza Bolivariana para los Pueblos de Nuestra América (Bolivarian Alliance for the Peoples of Our America, ALBA), 231

Alliance for Progress, 96

Almeida Bosque, Juan, 24, 36–37, 140, 229, 249

Alonso, Alicia, 66–67, 109–10, *110*

Alonso, Nancy, 228, 247

Alphabetization campaign, 65, 301n61

ANAP. *See* Asociación Nacional de Agricultores Pequeños

Arenas, Reinaldo, 108, 120, 160

Armed groups: Batista opposed by, 21–22, 27–29, 30–42; class and race of, 21; counterrevolutionary, 75–76; M-26-7 within, 27, 28–29, 30, 32–33

Arrufat, Antón, 45

Art. *See* Literature, film, and art

Artists and intellectuals: Batista opposed by, 20–21; as exiles, 66, 108, 160; in history, 7; homosexual, 67–68; punishment of, 141, 142–43; revolutionary government and, 67–68, 107–8, 141–43; UNEAC, 67, 108–9

"The Art of Triangulation," triangulation, 10, 59, 68, 85, 93, 157, 263, 281

Asociación Nacional de Agricultores Pequeños (National Association of Small Farmers, ANAP), 62

Auténticos, 18, 26, 27, 28

Authoritarianism, 223, 226

Balsero cohort, 9; division involving, 221–22; exile or refugee, 182, 198–99, 215–18, 221–22, 247–48; poverty of, 221; trauma of, 215–17

Barquín, Colonel Ramón, 28, 41, 47

Batista, Fulgencio: armed groups opposing, 21–22, 27–29, 30–42; corruption of, 20; economy under, 20, 35; escape of, 41–42; intellectuals and students opposing, 20–21; military career of, 19; as "plantation overseer," 19–22; planter support for, 20; political history of, 18, 19–22; political violence from, 35; politicians and political groups opposing, 26, 27, 30–36; power after Moncada, 26; Prío coup from, 15–16, *17*, 19; prison and punishment for regime of, 48–49, 50, 54, 297n8; race of, 19; rebellion against, 16, 20–22, 23–42; revolutionary government and regime of, 48–49, 50, 54, 292n5, 297n8; U.S. on, 35–36, 40–41, 42; wealth of, 42

Luis Martínez-Fernández is professor of history at the University of Central Florida. He served as senior editor of the two-volume *Encyclopedia of Cuba: People, History, Culture* and is the author of *Fighting Slavery in the Caribbean.*